D1395034

(

The Forest, Park and Palace of Clarendon, *c*.1200-*c*.1650

Reconstructing an actual, conceptual and documented Wiltshire landscape

Amanda Richardson

BAR British Series 387
2005

This title published by

Archaeopress
Publishers of British Archaeological Reports
Gordon House
276 Banbury Road
Oxford OX2 7ED
England
bar@archaeopress.com
www.archaeopress.com

BAR 387

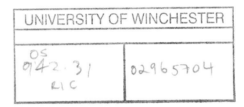

The Forest, Park and Palace of Clarendon, c.1200-c.1650: Reconstructing an actual, conceptual and documented Wiltshire landscape

ISBN 1 84171 825 4

Printed in England by The Basingstoke Press

All BAR titles are available from:

Hadrian Books Ltd
122 Banbury Road
Oxford
OX2 7BP
England
bar@hadrianbooks.co.uk

The current BAR catalogue with details of all titles in print, prices and means of payment is available free from Hadrian Books or may be downloaded from www.archaeopress.com

Contents

List of Figures

List of Tables

Preface

The main argument of this work is that the landscape and locality of Clarendon Forest and Park were strongly influenced by the presence (or, later, absence) of Clarendon Palace, which fell into decay in the late fifteenth century. This contention is addressed by taking the landscape as the unit for study, rather than focusing on the palace and extrapolating 'outwards'. A primary aim is to restore the wider conceptual landscape by considering the forest alongside the relict landscape of the park, and it is argued throughout that, because medieval forests are archaeologically elusive, the best way to achieve this is through an intensive documentary methodology. Attention is drawn throughout to the capacity of documents to illustrate how estates were managed over time. This is demonstrated particularly in Chapters Two and Three, the main findings of which (including observations of a significant change in attitude and landscape use in the early- to mid- fourteenth century) are drawn together in the conclusions of those chapters.

This publication represents an unprecedented systematic study of manuscript sources for Clarendon Park and Forest held at central and regional record offices, and is supported by references to printed primary sources. It has resulted in the compilation of a main computer database listing over 800 relevant documents held at the Public Record Office alone, from which those that might prove most useful were selected and transcribed.

The written sources themselves have informed the structure of the project. Their worth in a study such as this is explored in Chapter One, following a brief background history of Clarendon and an elucidation of the study's academic and historiographical context. Chapter Two then addresses ecology and economy, while the park's 'built environment' is considered in Chapter Three in order to provide new insights. Settlement is explored in Chapter Four, which reveals Clarendon Forest to have been a landscape of control in which assarting, in particular, was restricted. Chapter Five expands on this point by addressing 'closure' and conflict in the landscape. It examines also Clarendon's 'social topology', partly by employing gender as a tool to elucidate the nature of social closure, and ends by considering the palace as a scene of social negotiation. The Conclusion, Chapter Six, expands on the management of the forest and park and the phasing of the latter's use based largely on materials in Chapters Two and Three. It concludes that the hypothesis is supported; this unique landscape and locality was indeed profoundly influenced by the existence of a royal park and palace at its centre. Nevertheless, what has emerged strongly in the course of the study are the myriad ways in which the forest, in turn, shaped the 'lifecycle' of the palace.

Acknowledgements

This study is substantially the AHRB- and IHR- funded doctoral thesis which was completed in 2003. Thus my thanks must go to my supervisors, Professor Tom James and Dr Chris Gerrard, for their endless fund of knowledge concerning Clarendon Palace and Park. Thanks also to Professor Colin Platt and Dr Eleanor Scott, whose advice was invaluable, especially in the project's early stages. Research meetings with them all were a pleasure, and continually renewed my interest. My gratitude should also be extended to my examiners, Professors Grenville Astill and Barbara Yorke.

Others who have helped are almost too numerous to mention. First, thanks to Dr Andrew Reynolds for his astuteness at reading the landscape. Thanks also to James Bond, who walked Clarendon Park with me and reciprocated by taking me to Woodstock Park; to John Charlton, veteran of Clarendon's 1930s excavations, for his interest and support and for my first (and probably last!) glimpse of the inside of a gentlemen's club; to Dr Brian Dicks for generously offering to read Chapter Four; and to Mike Small for his experience in managing park deer and his patient consideration of my many questions. My gratitude goes also to Jeremy Ashbee and Dr Edward Impey of English Heritage for their continual support and humour; to local historians Michael Parsons, whose intimate knowledge of the Clarendon Forest area was indispensable, and Margaret Baskerville of the Bentley Wood History Society. I am indebted also to the British Deer Society, particularly Michael Baxter-Brown and course leaders Alan MacCormack and Nigel Pickering, as well as to my fellow students on the advanced stalkers' deer-management course (especially Boo, Paul and Sutty) for making the week so immensely informative and enjoyable.

Among others who have freely given advice are David Clements, Paul Everson, Alex Langlands, Stephen Mileson, John Phibbs, Simon Roffey, David Stocker, Christopher Taylor, Alex Turner and Dries Tys; Drs Oliver Creighton, David Crook, Bill Higham, Ryan Lavelle, Carenza Lewis, Rob Liddiard, Jacqui Mulville and Alecks Pluskowski, and Professors David Austin, Michael Hicks, Tony King and Roger Richardson. The staff of the Public Record Office should be thanked for their infinite cheerfulness, as should my fellow research students who supported me whenever I was down. I am indebted also to the AHRB and the IHR, without whose funding this study would not have been possible, and last but not least to my partner Ken, for his understanding throughout.

Abbreviations

BAR	British Archaeological Reports
BDS	British Deer Society
BL	British Library
CCR	*Calendar of Close Rolls*
CFR	*Calendar of Fine Rolls*
CHR	*Calendar of Charter Rolls*
CIM	*Calendar of Inquisitions Miscellaneous*
CIPM	*Calendar of Inquisitions Post Mortem*
CLR	*Calendar of Liberate Rolls*
CPR	*Calendar of Patent Rolls*
CSPD	*Calendar of State Papers, Domestic Series*
DOE	Department of the Environment
EHR	*English Historical Review*
IMC	International Medieval Congress
KAC	King Alfred's College, Winchester
KACC	King Alfred's College Consultancy
KACC I	King Alfred's College Consultancy, *Clarendon Park, Salisbury, Wiltshire: Archaeology, History and Ecology– English Heritage Survey Grant for Presentation, I,* English Heritage Project Number 1750 (Winchester, 1996)
KACC II	King Alfred's College Consultancy, *Clarendon Park, Salisbury, Wiltshire: Archaeology, History and Ecology– English Heritage Survey Grant for Presentation, II,* English Heritage Project Number 1750 (Winchester, 1996)
LPFD	*Letters and Papers Foreign and Domestic*
OUDCE	Oxford University Department for Continuing Education
PRO	Public Record Office, Kew, Surrey
PRS	Pipe Roll Society
RCHME	Royal Commission on the Historic Monuments of England
Rot. Litt. Claus	*Rotuli Litteram Clausarum in Turri Londinensi Asservati (Close Rolls)*
VCH Wilts	*Victoria County History for Wiltshire*
WAM	*Wiltshire Archaeological Magazine*
WRL	Wiltshire Reference Library, Trowbridge, Wiltshire
WRO	Wiltshire Record Office, Trowbridge, Wiltshire

viii

Chapter One: Introduction and Project Rationale

Clarendon Palace, a major medieval royal residence, has escaped total destruction, substantial later rebuilding and redevelopment of its landscape setting. There exists a considerable corpus of documentary research relating to the palace itself, but its landscape context has hitherto received little attention. This publication redresses the balance through systematic study of medieval and early modern documentary sources from *c.*1200–*c.*1650, extending previous studies due to the depth of its analysis and its wide chronological limits. In so doing it complements and extends published archaeological findings, most notably the Society of Antiquaries Report, *Clarendon Palace* (1988) and KACC's 1996 *English Heritage Survey Grant for Presentation*, the latter of which considered the palace's wider archaeological, environmental and historical context for the first time.[1]

The study expands on the works mentioned above in two major ways. First, it is envisaged as a landscape study in which *interrelationships* are examined, so that the palace is an issue rather than the primary focus. Second, original sources for Clarendon Forest in particular have hitherto been neglected. Even the KACC report was confined — for good archaeological and practical reasons — to study of the relict landscape of the park. Yet it seems impossible to examine Clarendon, at least in the medieval period, without considering the forest which was responsible for the palace's siting and was an integral part of the administrative, symbolic and physical landscape.[2] This study focuses on precisely that issue, its main argument being that the landscape and locality of Clarendon Forest were strongly influenced by the presence (or, later, absence) of the palace. A primary aim is to restore the wider conceptual landscape by considering the forest alongside the relict landscape of Clarendon Park, and it is argued throughout that, because medieval forests are archaeologically elusive, the best way to achieve this is through an intensive documentary methodology.

This introductory chapter sets out the current understanding of the history and physical background of Clarendon Forest, Park and Palace, including a brief introduction to Clarendon Forest and the medieval forest system. It also elucidates the academic context to this study, together with a brief summary of the most recent work in the park and at the palace site. There follows a critique of the main classes of written sources which form the basis of this, the first in-depth study of Clarendon Forest, Park and Palace. The question of how far the documentary record can shed light on past landscapes in general, and on that of Clarendon in particular, will be addressed, and what documents *can* tell us about past landscapes will be emphasised as well as what they cannot.

BACKGROUND HISTORY

A Brief History of Clarendon Palace and its Park

The remains of Clarendon Palace, the most westerly major royal palace in late medieval England, lie 5.63 km (3½ miles) east of Salisbury (est. 1220). The palace occupied an elevated position overlooking an inner park (see below, pp. 63-68), its surrounding deerpark, woodlands and major roads, and was set inside the royal forest of Clarendon (see Figures 1 and 8). Even as a ruin the site is extremely extensive (see Figure 32),[3] mirroring the equally large scale of the Forest of Clarendon whose bounds, in the form studied here, measured 35.40 km (22 miles) around, and of the deerpark, which at *c.*4500 acres (*c.*1821 ha) was the largest in medieval England (see below, Figure 73 and pp. 113-122).

The first sure evidence of a royal residence at Clarendon dates from the reign of Henry I (1100-35), who issued charters there from *c.*1116. However William I (1066-87) had visited sometime around 1072 (although whether buildings then existed is unknown) and a hunting lodge may have occupied the site in the Late Saxon period, perhaps associated with Edward the Confessor (1042-66), who held estates nearby (see below, pp. 7-11).

Henry II (1054-89) was fond of Clarendon, decorating the palace with bright colours and marble columns (see below, p. 59), and it was here that the council which produced the Constitutions of Clarendon (1164) sat, attended by fourteen bishops and many lay magnates.[4] Indeed it was Henry who changed the status of the residence from a hunting lodge to a 'palace' capable of housing the court as well as the king and his hunting parties. However the palace's zenith came in the reign of Henry III (1216-72), who, from very early in his reign, enlarged and embellished it to a state only marginally less magnificent than that of the Palace of Westminster.[5] It is essentially Henry's palace that was excavated from 1933-

---

[1] T.B. James and A.M. Robinson, *Clarendon Palace: The History and Archaeology of a Medieval Palace and Hunting Lodge near Salisbury, Wiltshire*, Society of Antiquaries Research Report 45 (London: Society of Antiquaries of London, 1988); KACC, *Clarendon Park, Salisbury, Wiltshire: Archaeology, History and Ecology–English Heritage Survey Grant for Presentation, I*, English Heritage Project Number 1750 (Winchester, 1996), p.60.

[2] It is likely that the palace stood on the site of an earlier, Anglo-Saxon royal hunting-lodge before a 'forest' was instituted (see below, pp. 7-11). However its continued use through the twelfth and thirteenth centuries and beyond, like many medieval palaces, owed a great deal to the forest's proximity.

[3] In 1994 a gridded fieldwalking exercise over the palace precinct covered 8250 square metres and recovered over 27,000 fragments of medieval roof tile, weighing 700 kilos, together with floor tile, brick, mortar and plaster, stone, faunal remains and some pottery (James and Gerrard, *Clarendon: A Royal Landscape*, forthcoming).

[4] James and Robinson, *Clarendon Palace*, p.4.

[5] James and Robinson, *Clarendon Palace*, pp.4-7, 8.

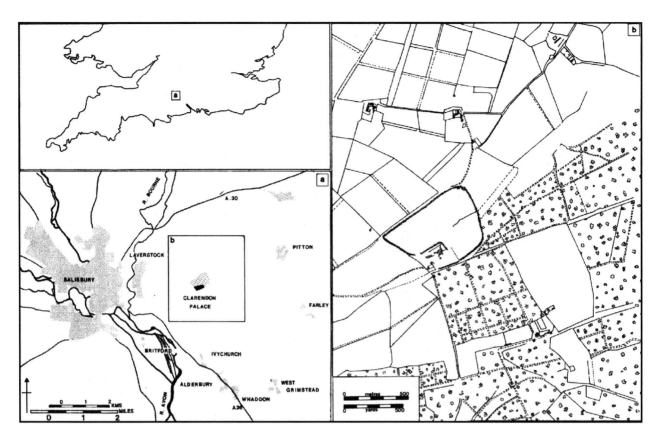

Figure 1. Location map showing the site of Clarendon Palace within the inner park. Reproduced from T. B. James and A. M. Robinson, *Clarendon Palace: The History and Archaeology of a Medieval Palace and Hunting Lodge near Salisbury, Wiltshire*, Society of Antiquaries Research Report 45 (London: Society of Antiquaries of London, 1988), fig. 1.

9 under Tancred Borenius.[6] On the accession of Edward I (1272-1307), many of the buildings were ruinous, partly due to a lack of royal visits occasioned by the Barons' Wars (1264-8), and few major additions were made through the remainder of the palace's history.

Buildings, however, can be repaired, and Clarendon was to remain a major royal residence for a further two hundred years. Through most of the fourteenth century, it continued to rank among the most popular and regularly-visited royal palaces, although the focus of building projects had by now shifted to its landscape surroundings. The deerpark was enlarged *c.*1317 by Edward II (1307-27) and Edward III (1327-77) began in earnest to build sometimes elaborate lodges within it (see below, Chapter Three, and Figures 34 and 73).

Richard II (1377-99) seems to have shown little interest in the palace, although he is supposed to have built a dancing chamber there, and the earliest Lancastrian kings seem never to have visited. Henry VI (1423-61, 1470-1) enjoyed only three stays, two of which were very brief. However while at Clarendon in 1453, he suffered his first major bout of insanity, leading to a rather longer royal visit than was usual (months rather than weeks). After

this, there is no record of any monarch setting foot in the palace. However major repairs were ongoing even into the late 1490s, so that although the palace had fallen out of use by the first decade of the sixteenth century, a definite decision to allow it to fall into decay does not seem to have been taken much before that time. But even after the palace's demise royal visits continued. Henry VIII (1509-47) stayed 'at Clarendon', perhaps in one of the lodges, in 1535.[7] Elizabeth I (1558-1603) came to the park in 1574, when she coursed deer with greyhounds, James I (1603-25) visited in the year of his accession, also in order to hunt, and Charles I (1625-49) in his turn paid for the upkeep of the park pale.[8] As far as is known Charles never went to Clarendon, although the court often stayed at nearby Wilton House, the seat of its then wardens, the earls of Pembroke. Royal visits may at least have been considered imminent, since the park's deer course (the 'Pady Course'; see below, pp. 80-82) was either constructed or comprehensively repaired *c.*1630.[9]

After the palace had fallen out of use, its place as the residential focus of the locality was taken for a time by Ivychurch House, used by the earls of Pembroke and their family in the later sixteenth century as a hunting-base

---

[6] For the excavations, see James and Robinson, *Clarendon Palace*, *passim*.

[7] *LPFD Henry VIII*, vol.9, p.467.
[8] WRO 549/8, *f.*23; PRO E 178/4728; *CSPD 1625-6*, p.550.
[9] *CSPD 1631-3*, p.114.

Figure 2. Stukeley's view of Clarendon Palace (1723), looking north. Reproduced from T. B. James and A. M. Robinson, *Clarendon Palace: The History and Archaeology of a Medieval Palace and Hunting Lodge near Salisbury, Wiltshire*, Society of Antiquaries Research Report 45 (London: Society of Antiquaries of London, 1988), pl. 1a.

(see below, p. 110). It seems to have fallen out of favour by the 1610s, although it still stood during Civil War. The house had been built after the Reformation on the site of Ivychurch Priory (*Monasterium Ederosum*) (see Figure 9), whose Augustinian canons had served the many chapels at the palace as well as others in the forest villages. The Priory lay on the Clarendon Park boundary adjacent to Alderbury (see Figure 5), and is believed to have been founded by King Stephen (1135-54). However its hilltop site, unusual for an Augustinian house, may betray Saxon religious occupation at the site — a view strengthened by a reference to it as a *monasterium* in 1109-10.[10] Ivychurch remained closely associated with the palace throughout the latter's history. As one of the most important institutions in the forest, it held much land in the locality along with many rights and perquisites, and its erstwhile prominence is commemorated in the landscape by the names Canon's Path and Canon Copse (see Figure 73) in the south of the modern park. Its priors were vociferous guardians of their rights, and its canons enthusiastic poachers (see below, p. 126), so that it will be encountered often in this study.

Clarendon finally passed out of royal hands in 1664 after having been granted to Edward Hyde on the occasion of Charles II's coronation, along with the title earl of Clarendon.[11] Although little is known of Hyde's tenure he was obviously fond of the park given the tirade with which he greeted Samuel Pepys after the navy had felled

some of his favourite trees there.[12] It is possible that Hyde's grandson, the third earl, built the first mansion house in the south of the park. Even in its present form, it bears many similarities to the first earl's Clarendon House in Piccadilly, built early in the 1660s. Moreover a structure considerably predating the first representation of the mansion on a map, dated to *c*.1713-48, has recently been discovered at its core.[13]

The estate has changed hands several times since the early eighteenth century, and the associated changes in landscape use and design have been set out by KACC.[14] However the palace was not restored to public consciousness until the 1930s excavations led by Tancred Borenius and backed by Mortimer Wheeler.[15]

With the demise of the palace and the concomitant relaxation of royal interest, Clarendon was, in a sense, 'opened up' to a wider audience. The early antiquarians who visited were forcibly impressed by Clarendon Park, and ignored the palace ruins almost completely, although Camden did note that the park was 'once beautified with a royal palace'. Leland, in his *Itinerary*, called the park 'a very large thing', and to Aubrey it was 'the best of England'. There may even have been excavations at or near the palace site, since Aubrey refers to Roman coins

---

[10] James and Gerrard, *Clarendon: A Royal Landscape*, forthcoming.
[11] KACC I, p.68.

[12] R. Latham and W. Matthews, *The Diary of Samuel Pepys*, vol. 5 (London: Bell and Hyman, 1971), p.203.
[13] T.B. James, pers. comm., KACC I, p.68.
[14] In addition, the landscape of the park from AD 1000 to the present day is currently being addressed in detail by Tom James and Christopher Gerrard (James and Gerrard, *Clarendon: A Royal Landscape* [forthcoming]).
[15] For the excavations see James and Robinson, *Clarendon Palace*, *passim*.

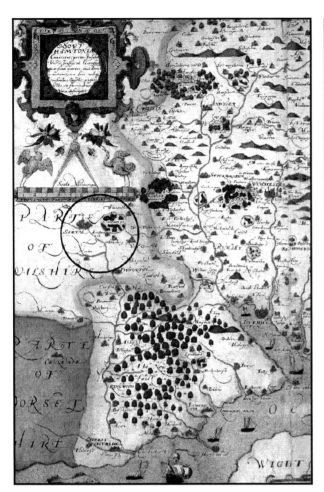

Figures 3 and 4 (L and R). Details of Hampshire and Wiltshire from Saxton's *c.*1590 *Atlas*, showing contradistinct interpretations of Clarendon Park. Elements of both the physical and cultural landscape are depicted in that parks are a dominant feature, reflecting the concerns of county society. In Fig.4, note 'Groveley Wood', west of Wilton; Buckholt Forest, to the east of the park, and Savernake Forest to its north. Reproduced from Chatsworth Library, *Christopher Saxton's 16th Century Maps: The Counties of England and Wales* (Shrewsbury: Chatsworth Library, 1992).

found *c.*1682. Visits were also made apparently by Defoe *c.*1685-90 and certainly by William Stukeley, who sketched the palace ruins in their landscape setting in 1723 (Figure 2).[16]

By the close of the eighteenth century the palace, rather than the park, had become the focus of interest, no doubt aided by its Ozymandian qualities at the dawn of the Romantic Movement (although Colt Hoare, in his *History of Modern Wiltshire* [1837], paid attention to the development of Clarendon's landscape, and even to the forest and its customs).[17] But why had the landscape been the focus of comment for sixteenth- and seventeenth-century antiquarians? First, we will see in Chapter Four that the park was an important element in the social networks of county and local 'gentry' society in the late sixteenth and early seventeenth centuries (see Figures 3 and 4). Second, early antiquarian travellers were passionate not about the past, but about things new and functioning (although they were also interested in

curiosities, so that some, like Camden, might occasionally mention the palace as such).[18] Thus we have Camden before 1590 pronouncing Clarendon Park 'very commodious for keeping and breeding Deer', and Aubrey in his 1680s notes expressing wonder at its 'twenty coppices, and every one a mile round'.[19]

Noteworthy parallels exist between the great era of antiquarianism and today. Landscape and environment are again uppermost, although for very different reasons given what has been called our 'exaggerated fixation' with things historical.[20] In addition, 'more [amateur historians] are interested and active in research than ever before'.[21] This has consequences for medieval and later history and archaeology. Although the prehistoric past remains popular, at times of rapid social change such as this, people tend to look to more recent times for

[16] KACC I, p.22, 23. James and Robinson, *Clarendon Palace*, p.47.
[17] KACC I, pp.22, 23, 25.

[18] R. Strong, *Lost Treasures of Britain: Five Centuries of Creation and Destruction* (London: Guild Publishing, 1990), p.7.
[19] KACC I, pp.22, 23.
[20] Strong, *Lost Treasures of Britain*, p.3.
[21] C. Lewis, *Particular Places: An Introduction to English Local History* (London: The British Library, 1989), p.4.

reassurance.[22] Taking an example close to Clarendon itself, the introduction to *Whiteparish: 100 Years of an English Village*, published by the village's Historical and Environmental Association, remarks that 'the last one hundred years of [the past] millennium contains much that we can relate to', and that readers will 'be able to read a…complete picture of the life that spawned them'.[23] Most pertinently, its first chapter reviews the natural history of the village, so that landscape and environment are prioritised in the communal identity.

The key point about writing landscape history is that it functions, in a sense, to appropriate history 'for the people' — those who lived in the past and those alive today. This has ramifications for ancient monuments, which have become 'fixed points in personal landscapes...visitable and touchable things...that give people a sense of belonging to a place'.[24] When trees around Prudhoe Castle (Northumberland) were removed, English Heritage met with vociferous local opposition. This had nothing to do with its place in fourteenth-century history as a Percy stronghold, nor in architectural history as the site of 'the earliest oriel window in any castle in northern England.[25] As Fowler explains, 'people *liked* [Prudhoe's] trees; they were their trees, part of their view, part of their scenery when they took the dog for a walk'.[26] Similarly, in elucidating recent English Heritage–based endeavour at the palace ruins, including their clearance and consolidation, James and Gerrard point out that for some 'the site [retains] a secluded, romantic atmosphere which no-one [wishes] to see lost'.[27] Mike Parker Pearson, too, prioritises the concept of place in developing public interest in local history and archaeology, a notion that has been made yet more concrete with the instigation of the Countryside Stewardship Scheme, which seeks to combine landscape, wildlife, historic and access interest [28] and which Clarendon Park gained in November 1999 (see below pp. 15-16).

There is, therefore, a growing emphasis on historic monuments as foci of communal ownership. They are no longer isolated 'relics',[29] and the premise of this project is timely. Writing the landscape history of a high-status

monument reappropriates its landscape for everybody. The storyboards that will be erected at the palace site, which will also point out visible features of the relict landscape, will ensure that the Clarendon we will see at the end of the English Heritage-funded five-year management plan (below, pp. 15-16) will not only be that which was the property of the medieval monarchy. It will be the Clarendon that belonged to all those who lived around it, and, moreover, to those who live around it and visit it today.

Anglo-Saxon and Other Antecedents
Knowledge of the period 600-1086 at Clarendon is hazy, although it has been suggested that the area had retained limited relict high-status or administrative functions centred on erstwhile Roman occupation in the park.[30] However Edward the Confessor's estate at Broughton (Hants) may provide a clue as to why part of Buckholt Forest in Hampshire was traditionally administered with those of Clarendon and Melchet (see below, p. 7 and Figure 7). Certainly East Dean— immediately east of the border between Clarendon and Buckholt and closely allied to West Dean, the base of the Walerand hereditary wardens (see Figures 8 and 12) — was described in 1086 as attached to the manor of Broughton.[31] Unfortunately nothing is known about the frequency of royal visits, but the estate seems to have rendered the 'farm of one night' (*firma unius noctis*), originally a render in kind believed to have originated to provide for the royal family when on circuit.[32] Nevertheless The Confessor may frequently have visited the area, since there was another important royal estate nearby at Wilton. Moreover he and his brother Tostig received news of the 1065 Northumbrian rebellion at St Peter's Church, Britford (on Clarendon Forest's western border until the late fourteenth century) and there is no reason to think this was an isolated visit.[33]

Alderbury was also significant in the late Anglo-Saxon landscape, having almost certainly been a Minster — a community of priests established to minister to the parochial needs of local people — from around the seventh century. Evidence includes the settlement's 'relatively substantial' entry in Domesday Book, the fact that the Hundred bears its name (see below, Figure 6), and that it retained dependent chapels at Farley and Pitton (Figure 5).[34] If so, it probably had judicial as well as religious functions, especially if the name derives from

[22] Lewis, *Particular Places*, p.4.

[23] E. Chase *et al.*, eds, *Whiteparish: 100 Years of an English Village* (Salisbury: Whiteparish Historical and Environmental Association, 2000), p.1.

[24] P. Fowler, 'Archaeology in a Matrix', in *Archaeological Resource Management in the UK: An Introduction* (Stroud: Sutton Publishing, 1993), eds John Hunter and Ian Ralston, pp.1-10 (p.7).

[25] P.S. Fry, *Castles of Britain and Ireland* (London; BCA, 1996), p.173.

[26] Fowler, 'Archaeology in a Matrix', p.3.

[27] James and Gerrard, *Clarendon: A Royal Landscape*, forthcoming.

[28] M. Parker Pearson, 'Visitors Welcome', in *Archaeological Resource Management in the UK: An Introduction* (Stroud: Sutton Publishing, 1993), eds John Hunter and Ian Ralston (1993), pp.225-31 (p.229); Lesley Macinnes, 'Archaeology as Land Use', in in *Archaeological Resource Management in the UK: An Introduction* (Stroud: Sutton Publishing, 1993), eds John Hunter and Ian Ralston, pp.243-55 (p.252).

[29] G.D. Keevill, *Medieval Palaces: An Archaeology* (Stroud: Tempus Publishing, 2000), p.163.

[30] KACC I, p.46.

[31] R. Lavelle, 'Royal Estates in Anglo-Saxon Wessex' (unpub. doctoral thesis, King Alfred's College, Winchester, 2001), p.114.

[32] For farms of one night, see Lavelle, 'Royal Estates in Anglo-Saxon Wessex', p.11. Amesbury was also a farm of one night (*ibid.*, p.66).

[33] M. Parsons, *The Saxon Inheritance* (New Milton: Leonard Michael Parsons, 1990), pp.37-8. It has been argued, due to the richness of embellishment of the church, that royal ownership of Britford probably stretched back to c.800 (J. Pitt, 'Wiltshire Minster *Parochiae* and West Saxon Ecclesiastical Organisation' [unpub. doctoral thesis, King Alfred's College, Winchester, 1999], p.41).

[34] Pitt, 'Wiltshire Minster *Parochiae*', pp.26-8; James and Gerrard, *Clarendon: A Royal Landscape*, forthcoming.

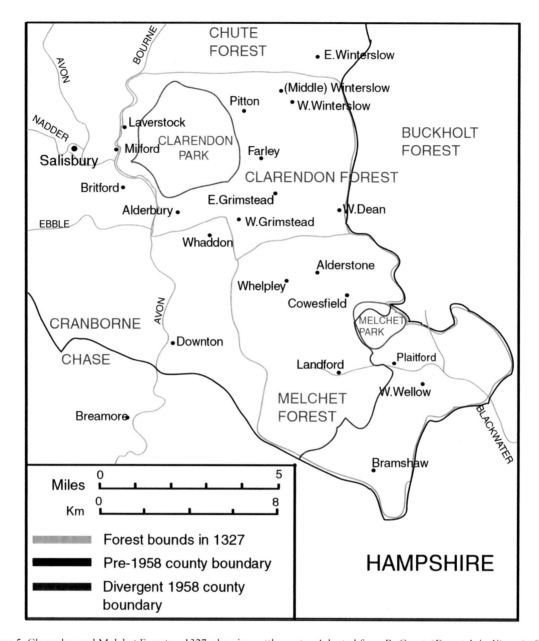

Figure 5. Clarendon and Melchet Forests c.1327, showing settlements. Adapted from R. Grant, 'Forests', in *Victoria County History Wiltshire IV* (Oxford: Oxford University Press, 1959), ed. E. Crittall, pp. 391-457 (p. 454).

'the old/former borough' (cf. Aldwych in London), as has been argued.[35]

Alderbury lies on a well-worn footpath running between yet another nearby royal estate, Amesbury, and another, Lyndhurst (Hampshire), each of which also rendered the farm of one night.[36] A close connection has been demonstrated between night's farm central manors and post-Conquest forests. Many, like Broughton, were close to forest bounds (see below, Figure 7), so that the origins

of post-Conquest forests may lie in the presence of earlier royal hunting spaces.[37] In addition, Domesday refers to forest land between Broughton and Breamore (see Figure 5), on the Avon south of the forest in the form studied here, which may equate to 'what had once been part of a substantial royal estate' (and may also reveal the pre-thirteenth-century bounds of the forest).[38]

Domesday records also that the woodland in Britford was in the king's hands, and that lands in the manor of Downton, and in Winterbourne Earls, Laverstock and

---

[35] James and Gerrard, *Clarendon: A Royal Landscape*, forthcoming. Other interpretations include 'a burh or strong point belonging to a lady called Aethelwaru', and that the 'd' is a later insertion inspired by the presence in 1087 of a priest called Alward (*Parsons, The Saxon Inheritance*, p.47).
[36] Parsons, *The Saxon Inheritance*, p.47.

[37] Lavelle, 'Royal Estates in Anglo-Saxon Wessex', p.173. Broughton lies on what was the northern limit of Buckholt Forest.
[38] Lavelle, 'Royal Estates in Anglo-Saxon Wessex', pp.114-5.

Milford were in the king's forest.[39] Thus, as KACC have said, 'we can infer a royal forest at Clarendon in the eleventh century, and perhaps before, though it would be assuming too much to conclude that the bounds were those of the later perambulations'.[40]

The manors from which most settlements in Clarendon Forest sprang are also recorded in 1086 (see Figure 5). West Winterslow had belonged to the Abbess of Amesbury and the Saxon Earl Harding under The Confessor, and was in the hand of Earl Morton by 1086. East Winterslow was in the hand of Earl Alberic, and Middle Winterslow was possessed by Ulward and Uluric, the king's thegns.[41] Similarly, West Grimstead was held by the Saxons Cola and Edmund, who had also held their manors before the Conquest, and East Grimstead by the Norman Waleran, huntsman, tenant-in-chief and warden of the New Forest (which then included the Forest of Clarendon),[42] who held also both West and East Dean.

Of other settlements at Clarendon mentioned in Domesday, Farley was held by the king's thegn, Aluric, and Pitton by Uluric the huntsman, by service of warding the Forest of Clarendon.[43] Alderbury was held in chief in 1086 by both Waleran (again), and 'Edward', almost certainly an ancestor of the Heyras family who held by service of keeping the king's harrier packs at least from the twelfth century (see below, pp. 136, 140).[44] Milford, too, was held in chief by Humfrey de Lisle and Ulvret the thegn, as king's huntsman.[45]

This concentration of hunting staff in the manors nearest to what would become Clarendon Park is noteworthy. Together with other evidence outlined above it suggests that the park formed the core of a larger delineated hunting space before the Norman Conquest. Indeed what we think of as Clarendon Park probably has much earlier origins than either the forest or the palace. James and Gerrard have recently surmised that it 'may have been reserved for hunting as just one part of the wider...forest as early as the late seventh century, and so remained free of settlement'.[46] It must have been in place before parishes were formed, since Figure 6, showing parish boundaries, reveals that the adjacent parishes of

Alderbury Hundred abut onto it. In addition, most of the fifteen Bronze Age barrows in the park are on or near the line of the park pale (see Glossary), and two Middle Saxon cemeteries at Petersfinger on its south western periphery suggest that that part of the boundary at least existed in the fifth- to sixth-centuries, already cleared of woodland. Although the enlargement of the medieval deerpark to what was probably its present size will be demonstrated below (see below, p. 116), it was evidently defined by boundaries visible in prehistory.[47] Thus the park, which still exists as a private estate is perhaps unique as a contiguously-used physically delineated landscape, at least in Wiltshire.

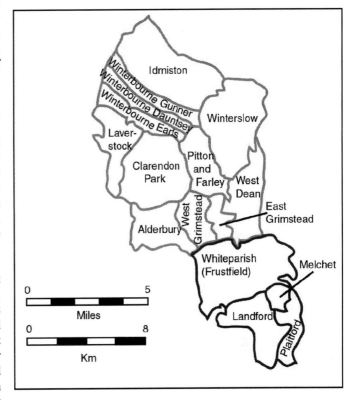

Figure 6. The parishes of Alderbury and Frustfield Hundreds.
Adapted from an original by Alex Langlands.

Clarendon Forest and the Forest System
Clarendon Forest, whose 1327 perambulation (see Figure 8) forms the core study area of this study, was disafforested over a century after the palace had fallen into ruin, sometime before 1610, (although the park remained as the last vestige of royal forest in Wiltshire before its disparkment in 1664). But through most of the period studied it was central to the management of a network of mostly Wiltshire forests.[48] These comprised Melchet immediately to the south, part of Buckholt directly to the east and, from 1236, the Forest of Groveley (although see p. 11, below) several

[39] R. Grant, 'Forests', in *The Victoria County History for Wiltshire, IV* (Oxford: Oxford University Press, 1959), ed. E. Crittall, pp.391-457 (p.427); J. Bond, 'Forests, Chases, Warrens and Parks in Medieval Wessex', in *The Medieval Landscape of Wessex*, Oxbow Monograph 46 9 (Oxford: Oxbow Books, 1994), eds M.Aston and C.Lewis, pp.115-58 (p.122).
[40] KACC I, p.46.
[41] W.H. Jones, *Domesday for Wiltshire* (London: Longman, Roberts and Green, 1865), p.243; Parsons, *The Saxon Inheritance*, p.68.
[42] Jones, *Domesday for Wiltshire*, p.218.
[43] Jones, *Domesday for Wiltshire*, pp.216, 229
[44] R.F. Atkinson, *The Manors and Hundred of Alderbury: Lords, Lands, and Livery* (Alderbury: Richard F. Atkinson, 1995), pp.40-1.
[45] Jones, *Domesday for Wiltshire*, p.224; R. Colt Hoare and J.G. Nichols, *The Modern History of South Wiltshire: Vol.5 Part 1, Containing the Hundred of Alderbury* (London: John Bowyer Nichols and Son, 1837), p.222.
[46] James and Gerrard, *Clarendon: A Royal Landscape*, forthcoming.

[47] James and Gerrard, *Clarendon: A Royal Landscape*, forthcoming. Burials of this date were often placed on pre-existing territorial boundaries, probably in order to reinforce territorial claims (Andrew Reynolds, pers. comm).
[48] Buckholt was in Hampshire.

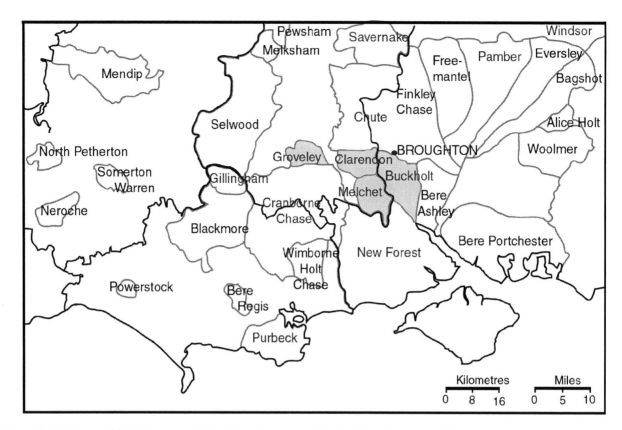

Figure 7. The forests of the Wessex area in the thirteenth century, with the Clarendon group of forests highlighted (county boundaries are in black). Note Broughton, the site of Edward the Confessor's estate on the border of Buckholt Forest. Adapted from J. Bond, 'Forests, Chases, Warrens and Parks in Medieval Wessex', in *The Medieval Landscape of Wessex,* Oxbow Monograph 46 (Oxford: Oxbow Books, 1994), eds M. Aston and C. Lewis, pp.115-58, fig. 6.1.

kilometres to the west.[49] Together these were, on occasion, known as'Clarendon Forest' (with obvious pitfalls for the historian). And apart from the period 1259-69, when the Wardens of Clarendon were installed at Salisbury Castle, the palace was the hub of their administration.

Medieval forests were areas delineated by defined boundaries (perambulations) and their primary role was as hunting spaces reserved exclusively to the crown.[50] Far from our modern conception of the term, they were not necessarily heavily — or even predominantly — wooded, although many, like Clarendon, had royal

demesne woods at their core.[51] Instead forests might encompass a variety of natural topography, and are thus almost impossible to identify archaeologically. Indeed, because many had crown estates as nuclei (again, like Clarendon) the presence of royal hunting lodges and manors are a surer guide to their provenance.

Figure 8 shows mappable perambulations of Clarendon Forest; that of 1327, in grey, being the core study area of this project. The 1327 perambulation has been claimed as the earliest possible to trace on the ground,[52] and it certainly represents the widest extent of Clarendon Forest known to exist. Yet collaboration with locals who are familiar with the landscape ensures a greater degree of success.[53] In some forests, where the countryside has changed very little, it is possible to walk with certainty

---

[49] Melchet was disafforested in stages from 1577-1614, Buckholt was disafforested with Clarendon Forest, and Groveley was granted to the earl of Pembroke sometime in the sixteenth century (R. Grant, *The Royal Forests of England* [Stroud: Alan Sutton Publishing, 1991], pp.226, 223, 224).

[50] Very occasionally forests were reserved for mighty subjects, most notably the bishop of Durham (see C.M. Fraser, 'Prerogative and the Bishops of Durham, 1267-1376', *EHR* 74 (1959), pp.467-76 (pp.470-2), who exercised the right to make forest law within them. However this was exceptionally rare. Where open hunting spaces were granted to subjects they were usually chases – for example Cranborne Chase in Dorset and Wiltshire - unenclosed but delimited areas which remained under the remit of common law rather than forest law (Bond, 'Forests, Chases, Warrens and Parks', p.115).

[51] That at Clarendon was the wood of 'Penchet', and that the name was frequently used to refer to the forest itself suggests a strong link between demesne woods and the forests established around them.

[52] Hence its use in Grant, *VCH Wilts* (p.454).

[53] I am indebted here to Margaret Baskerville, who lives on the site of 'Shirmel' (see Figure 8) for walking part of the 1327 perambulation with me, and, especially, to the local historian Michael Parsons, who has verified my interpretation of the perambulations deconstructed by him in *The Royal Forest of Pancet* (New Milton: Leonard Michael Parsons, 1995).

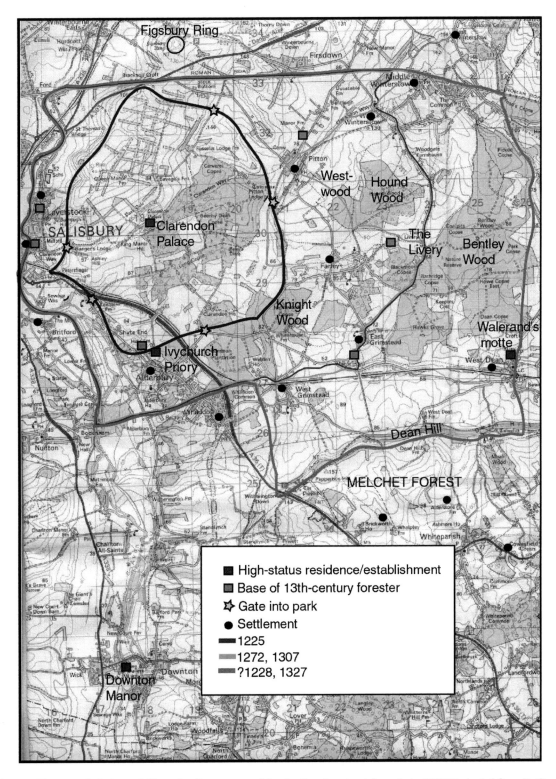

Figure 8. The perambulations of Clarendon Forest mapped for the first time apart from that of 1327 (adapted from R. Grant, 'Forests', in *VCH Wilts. IV* [Oxford: Oxford University Press, 1959], ed. E. Crittall, pp.391-457 [p.454]).
OS Map reproduced with kind permission of the Controller of Her Majesty's Stationary Office,
© Crown copyright NC/05/100041476.

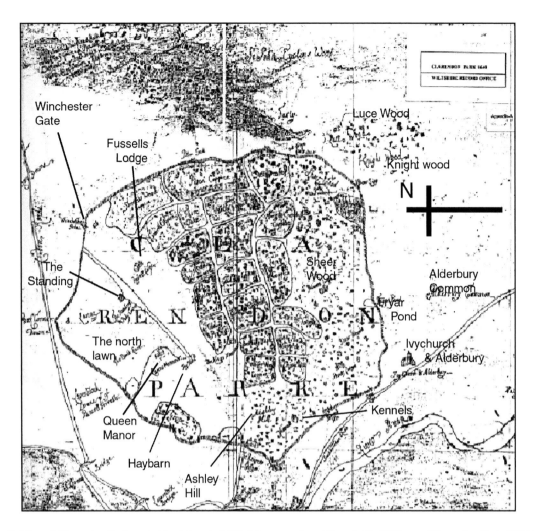

Figure 9. Map of Clarendon Park probably dating to 1640. Map reproduced from J. McWilliams, 'Clarendon Park 1600-1750: From Medieval Deer Park to Post-Medieval Estate' (unpub. BA dissertation, King Alfred's University College, Winchester, 1996), Appendix A. Note the deer course running south-west to north-east.

the same bounds perambulated by the medieval surveyors. However Clarendon is not generally one of them, not so much because the landscape itself has changed, rather the nomenclature of many of the features and areas described. Only those with detailed and longstanding local knowledge will be aware, for example, of the nicknames of fields and paths — perhaps remembered from childhood — which may be significant in interpretation.[54] Without the help of such people, Figure 8 could not have been produced, since, apart from details in maps by Saxton (*c*.1576) and Speed (*c*.1610), no maps of the forest or park exist predating that of *c*.1640 (Figure 9).[55] Thus the maps here — and all graphs — have been created for the study from information in the documents listed in the bibliography (unless otherwise stated), overlain on maps redrawn or reproduced from secondary sources.

Clarendon's perambulations will be discussed in greater detail in Chapter Five. However it should be pointed out here that, being conceptual rather than physical boundaries they are not ideal for ascertaining the extent of a forest at any given time. Rackham has said that their greatest value is as descriptions of contemporary countryside.[56] Apart from this, and the local significance of the types of boundary markers used to form such conceptual boundaries, their analysis over time is of limited value in a study such as this. What their fluctuations reflect *in primis* are the shifts in power — national rather than local in scale — that lay behind the forest system as a political issue in the thirteenth and early fourteenth centuries, and this issue will be discussed in Chapter Five.

'The forest system' is a term employed to describe the way forests were run from 1066.[57] The date is not

---

[54] See, for example, chapter one of Parsons's' *The Royal Forest of Pancet.*

[55] Although see below, p. 63.

[56] O. Rackham, *The Last Forest: The Story of Hatfield Forest*, 2nd edn (London: Dent, 1993), p.65.

[57] Although the forest system was at its height in the thirteenth century, and went into terminal decline from 1327, it survived in places into the

coincidental since it is generally accepted that forests were imported by the Normans, although the word itself, whose precise meaning is unknown, is first recorded in seventh-century Merovingian royal charters.[58] This is not to say that Anglo-Saxon kings did not possess delineated hunting grounds. In fact work currently in progress suggests continuity (rather than *contiguity*) between many late- Anglo-Saxon deer reserves and later medieval deerparks.[59] However, the present consensus is that 'pre-Conquest kings…do not seem to have enjoyed hunting rights beyond those enjoyed by any other landowner in his own demesne', and that forest law, and its post-Conquest administration, was initiated under William I.[60] As Ryan Lavelle has put it, 'hunting could…be said to have become institutionalised for at least the later Anglo-Saxon kings, [but] hunting grounds were not'.[61]

Medieval forests operated not under common law, but forest law, which in individual forests was administered by a hierarchy of officials headed by the forest warden.[62] The office of warden was often linked with the keepership of royal castles,[63] but at Clarendon it was associated with that of the palace. This was not always the case, however. In the thirteenth century, when both forest system and palace were at their zenith, Henry de Dun (warden 1236–*c*.1239), Adam Cook (1239–*c*.1247) and Robert Walerand (1259–*c*.1266) were appointed as keepers of the king's forest and houses;[64] Robert of Glastonbury (1266–*c*.1269), Stephen de Eddeworth (1269–*c*.1273), and Robert de Stopham (1249–*c*.1259), of the forest and *manor*.[65] The distinction between the manor and the 'king's houses' seems to have been a real one, since under Robert de Stopham the bailiwick was split; a steward (David Carpenter) being responsible for the king's houses, and a warden for the forest and manor.[66] The arrangement would have made sense, since the eponymous Carpenter worked at Clarendon throughout the 1250s, probably overseeing many of the artistic works commissioned at the palace.[67]

It is generally held that Groveley Forest was added to the Clarendon bailiwick from 1236. However this stems, apparently, from the wording of Walter de Langford's appointment to the wardenship in that year, in which he was explicitly given seisin of both forests.[68] Yet it is impossible to rule out Groveley as coming under the bailiwick of Clarendon before this merely because it previously went unmentioned. There may have been an early link between the two in any case, since most of the Wiltshire lands of Waleran the huntsman, Clarendon's first warden, were concentrated both in what would become Clarendon Forest and around Groveley.[69] Groveley may have been incorporated in 1228, the year of Henry III's majority, when he removed Clarendon from the New Forest bailiwick under which it had previously been administered, effectively reorienting its landscape westwards towards the newly-created city of Salisbury (see below, p. 88). If so, this was a politically astute move, since it would have left the bishop's new city effectively sandwiched between Clarendon, Melchet and Groveley Forests — nothing if not a manifestation of royal power and authority in the wider landscape.

The current study supports the contention that Groveley came under the purview of the warden of Clarendon Forest before 1236.[70] Both John of Monmouth (warden 1223–*c*.1232) and Peter des Rivaux (1232–*c*.1236) received royal mandates concerning Groveley, and verderers for Clarendon and Groveley are mentioned together in a 1234 mandate.[71] In addition, Henry *filio* Nicholas, apparently Rivaux's deputy at Clarendon, was organising gifts of wood and deer from Groveley in 1234 and 1235.[72] Moreover it was Henry *filio* Nicholas who was commanded, in 1236, to hand over the king's houses at Clarendon 'with the aforesaid *forests*' to Walter de Langford.[73] Whoever Henry was, someone responsible for the houses at Clarendon had charge also of Groveley and Clarendon Forests before 1236.[74] By studying *all* calendared (and many other) references to Clarendon Forest, rather than only the key document classes and those calendared letters patent addressed to appointed wardens (as did Grant in his *VCH* contribution), this study has not only added the names of deputy wardens to lists of the forest's officers, but has also shed light on aspects of its history.

---

nineteenth century and there were intermittent attempts to revive its effectiveness, most notably under Henry VII and Charles I (Grant, *The Royal Forests of England, passim*; C.R. Young, *The Royal Forests of Medieval England* [Leicester: Leicester University Press, 1979], *passim*).

[58] Rackham, *The Last Forest*, p.38.

[59] Rob Liddiard, pers. comm.

[60] Grant, *VCH Wilts*, p.392. For the constitutions of Cnut, which have been proved to be a later forgery, see D.J. Stagg, ed., *New Forest Documents A.D. 1244-A.D. 1334*, Hampshire Record Series 3 (Winchester: Hampshire County Council, 1979), p.5.

[61] Lavelle, 'Royal Estates in Anglo-Saxon Wessex', p.173.

[62] See Glossary for further information on the forest officers and courts described here.

[63] Bond, 'Forests, Chases, Warrens and Parks', p.124.

[64] *CCR 1234-37*, p.259; *CPR 1232-47*, p.142; *CLR 1226-1240*, p.465; *CPR 1258-66*, p.28.

[65] *CPR 1266-72*, p.69; p.336.

[66] That Stopham had charge of the manor and forest is evident from the terms of his appointment. See *CPR 1247-58*, p.40; *CLR 1247251*, p.228.

[67] James and Robinson, *Clarendon Palace*, p.29.

---

[68] *CPR 1232-47*, p.142.

[69] Grant, *VCH Wilts*, p.393.

[70] See also N.A. Richardson, 'Clarendon: The Palace in the Forest - The Establishment, Operation and Control of Jurisdiction in the Reign of Henry III' (unpub. MA Dissertation, University of Southampton, 1999), pp.40-1.

[71] *CCR 1231-4*, pp.45 (1232), 99 (1232), 266 (1233), 517. No other forest is mentioned.

[72] For example *CCR 1234-7*, pp.30, 36, 127, 128.

[73] *Dominus rex commisit eidem Waltero [de Langford] domos suas de Clarendon', cum forestis Clarendon et Graveling' custodiendas quamdiu ei placuerit. Et mandatum est Henrico filio Nicholai quod domos illas cum predictis forestis ei liberet (CCR 1234-7, p. 259)*.

[74] It is possible that Henry was an under sheriff, Ela, Countess of Salisbury being sheriff of Wiltshire at the time. However, he had received mandates concerning Groveley during the tenure of the previous sheriffs also.

Several of Clarendon's forest wardens were notable political players, including William Longespée (warden 1216-17), Robert Walerand (1256-c.1266), John Mautravers (app. 1330) and Roger Mortimer, Earl of March (app. 1354). By the time of the latter's appointment, most wardenships (and forestships) were sinecures, and that Clarendon followed this general trajectory is evident in its fifteenth-century wardens, who included John Beaufort, Earl of Somerset (app. 1405) and Humphrey of Lancaster (app. 1410). However, the fact that its wardens were often great courtiers from a much earlier date indicates that this was a particularly prestigious appointment,[75] no doubt largely due to the presence of the palace. Indeed Henry III made the wardenship an appointive office in 1228,[76] presumably in order to use it as an instrument of patronage and to safeguard royal interests. Prior to this the Walerand family had exercised their office on a hereditary basis, rendering annually a farm of £22.10s. for The New Forest (including Clarendon Forest) plus a 50s. tithe to the canons of Salisbury.[77] Similarly, that the wardenship ran on a semi-hereditary basis from the mid-sixteenth century is illustrative of the relaxation of royal interest in the forest and in Clarendon as a whole after the palace's demise. In 1553 the earl of Pembroke and his son were granted the wardenship in survivorship, and the office was held by the family until the Commonwealth.

Under the wardens were teams of foresters, who either farmed their bailiwicks (see Glossary), or held them on a hereditary basis. The latter, known as foresters of fee, had charge of Clarendon Forest. At the height of the forest system, they were the de Milfords, de Pittons and de Laverstocks, whose surnames derived from vills in the forest (see Figure 5). Thus, three foresters of fee were responsible for Clarendon. The Loveraz family were foresters for Buckholt, although the de Pittons had duties there also.[78] For Melchet Park (implying that the Clarendon foresters were responsible for Melchet Forest) there were the de Grimsteads, who appear to have been the most prosperous of the foresters of fee.[79] They held the manor of that name in Clarendon Forest with the patronage of the church of West Grimstead, a plethora of tenants and much land. Their responsibilities were 'keeping [Melchet Park], taking all the issues, saving to the king vert and venison, and pannage exceeding 6s.8d.' and they held the bailiwick 'of the king by service of 40s.

fee farm yearly to be rendered by the hands of the [warden] of Clarendon'.[80]

After the foresters of fee, at least in the thirteenth century, came underforesters, classified either as riding or walking foresters. Their duty was the routine one of protecting the forest and dealing with violators of forest law.[81] Thus their responsibilities were similar to those of the foresters of fee, who might appoint them, and there were considerable overlaps. For example, James de Pitton (d.1255) was forester of fee for Clarendon and riding forester for both Clarendon and Buckholt. For Clarendon he might appoint another horseman to carry out his duties, but he was to keep the bailiwick of Buckholt himself on horseback. Under him were to serve two foot serjeants for Clarendon, and one for Buckholt.[82] Thus riding and walking foresters each patrolled defined wards, although, naturally, the former were responsible for wider areas.[83]

The lesser forest officers were all unpaid. First there were the verderers, who were intended to be a check on remunerated forest officers and so were directly responsible to the crown rather than to the forest warden. Thus they were often men with considerable clout, and they were always knights. Cox has it that the average number of verderers for a forest was four, and two for smaller forests. This was the case at Clarendon, although two verderers were appointed for Melchet Forest also.[84]

Next in the forest hierarchy come the regarders, of whom there were always twelve — although judging by their prominence in later documentary sources (see below, pp. 51-52) they had replaced verderers in terms both of status and of practical effectiveness by the sixteenth century. The regarders' main duties were to make the triennial regard (see Glossary), to attend forest courts and to make various inquiries in the forest.[85] Finally, the agisters, who were usually regarders, were responsible for overseeing agistment (see Glossary) in the king's demesne woods.

Apart from the verderers, all the above officers came under the purview of the justice of the forest (of whom, from 1236, one was appointed for the north, the other for the south of the River Trent), and each was bound to attend the circuit court known as the forest eyre (see Glossary). This was the highest forest court, concerned mainly with pleas of the vert (damage to, and theft of, wood) and of the venison (poaching of deer), and ostensibly took place every seven years. However the intervals between eyres were in fact much longer, and from c.1287 onwards, they were supplemented and gradually replaced by other procedures such as

---

[75] Compare the somewhat less well-known wardens of most other Wiltshire forests (Grant, *VCH Wilts*, pp.434-57).

[76] *CCR 1227-31*, p.79.

[77] Grant, *VCH Wilts*, p.429.

[78] 'James de Putton, *alias* de Puton:...La Bokolt forest, one virgate of land held of the king in chief by service of keeping the bailiwick of la Bokolt by himself on horseback, and one foot serjeant at his own cost, and twenty shillings to the king's [warden] of Clarendon' (*CIPM I: Henry III*, p.88).

[79] See C.A.F. Meekings, ed., *Crown Pleas of the Wiltshire Eyre, 1249* (Devizes: Wiltshire Archaeological and Natural History Society Records Branch, 1961), pp.132-6 for more of their properties and connections.

[80] *CIPM Vol. II: Edward I*, p.416.

[81] Grant, *Royal Forests*, p.116.

[82] *CIPM Vol. I: Henry III*, p.88.

[83] Grant, *Royal Forests*, p.116.

[84] J.C. Cox, *The Royal Forests of England* (London: Methuen, 1905), p. 18 (in Sherwood there were six); Grant, *VCH Wilts*, p.430.

[85] Grant, *Royal Forests*, p.128.

commissions of inquiry into 'the state of the forest' (see below, p. 24).[86]

Since eyres were organised on a countywide basis, their occurrence (as far as we know) represents the principal time when forest officers from various forests came together. But there is little evidence that they had overarching functions independent from the lesser, more local, forest courts run by the verderers and regarders and presided over by the wardens of individual forests or their deputies.[87] Nevertheless, the officers of discrete forests must have collaborated from time to time, and many had interests outside their own bailiwicks. For example the Esturmy wardens of Savernake Forest in north east Wiltshire (see Figure 7) held in chief Cowesfield Esturmy in Melchet (see below pp. 98, 100, 106).[88]

Like all medieval English mechanisms for administering justice, forest courts developed on a pragmatic, *ad hoc* basis. They evolved primarily from the forest's separateness as an area reserved exclusively for royal use, and its importance as a source of crown revenue.[89] Thus forest courts, arguably to a greater extent than common law courts, were first and foremost a means of raising cash. Indeed this is substantiated in various eyre rolls where the scribe had kept a running total of amounts collected.[90] What was once considered by historians to be a harsh and brutal system was in fact nothing of the sort. As long ago as 1905, Cox pointed out that by the thirteenth century, even if 'a man was determined to poach venison, he met with a far lighter punishment if the offence was committed in a royal forest than if he was dealt with by the common or manorial law'.[91] While permissible activities were clearly defined, in practice most offences, especially those of the vert, were tacitly condoned in return for the payment of fines. Thus Judith Bennett has found that the inhabitants of Brigstock Manor in the Forest of Rockingham could expand their tillage by converting wasteland into arable with something like impunity.[92] This, however, was far from the case at Clarendon, as will be shown in Chapter Four.

PHYSICAL BACKGROUND

Geology and Land Use

Clarendon Forest does not fit neatly into the geological 'chalk and cheese' pattern ascribed to Wiltshire.[93] The area is clearly defined, recognisable at a glance in maps of the county as a whole, and accords more with the geology stretching southwards into Hampshire, and the New Forest of which it was originally a part.

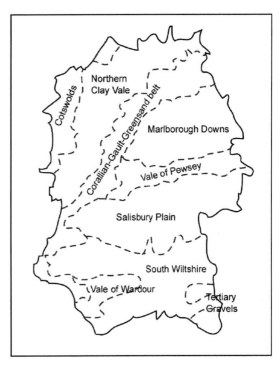

Figure 10. Wiltshire, showing major topographical divisions. The areas occupied by Clarendon and Melchet Forests are clearly visible under 'tertiary gravels'. Adapted from C. Lewis, 'Patterns and Processes in the Medieval Settlement of Wiltshire', in *The Medieval Landscape of Wessex*, Oxbow Monograph 46 (Oxford: Oxbow Books, 1994), eds M. Aston and C. Lewis, pp.171-93, fig. 8.3.

However, Clarendon does correspond with the geological underpinnings of the 'royal settlement pattern' of south east Wiltshire (Figure 11), consisting of areas of chalk with occasional clay capping which dominates also around Ludgershall and Marlborough.[94] But on close inspection, it is debatable how significant the clay-with-flints deposits actually were to Clarendon's establishment as a royal hunting-ground. Only areas which remain wooded, such as Hound Wood and around a third of the core of the park's coppices, share this geology, and Bentley Wood is comprised mainly of chalk in its northern half and clay in its southern. In fact the forest's

[86] Bond, 'Forests, Chases, Warrens and Parks', p.123; Grant, *VCH Wilts*, p.395. For a discussion on forest courts and the interrelationships between them, see Young, *The Forests of Medieval England*, pp.74-113.
[87] Young, *The Royal Forests of Medieval England*, p.91.
[88] The Esturmys, or Sturmys, held the hereditary wardenship of Savernake from 1086 to the fifteenth century (see Grant, *VCH Wilts*, p.420).
[89] C. Smith, 'The New Forest in the Fourteenth Century: A Jurisdictional Vacuum?' (unpub. paper given at *Recent Research in Fifteenth-Century History*, University of Southampton conference, September 1999), p.1.
[90] Young, *The Royal Forests of Medieval England*, pp.90-1.
[91] Cox, *The Royal Forests of England* p.11.
[92] J.M. Bennett, *Women in the Medieval English Countryside: Gender and Household in Brigstock Before the Plague* (Oxford: Oxford University Press, 1989), p.11.

[93] C. Lewis, 'Patterns and Processes in the Medieval Settlement of Wiltshire', in *The Medieval Landscape of Wessex* (Oxford: Oxbow Books, 1994), eds M. Aston and C. Lewis, pp.171-93 (p.172).
[94] J.N. Hare, 'Agriculture and Rural Settlement in the Chalklands of Wiltshire and Hampshire from *c*.1200-*c*.1500', in *The Medieval Landscape of Wessex*, Oxbow Monograph 46 (Oxford: Oxbow Books, 1994), eds M. Aston and C. Lewis, pp.159-69 (p.160).

geology is complex (Figure 12), the northern park and forest being mainly Upper Chalk (soft, with flints), the dominant rock-type of the Salisbury area.[95]

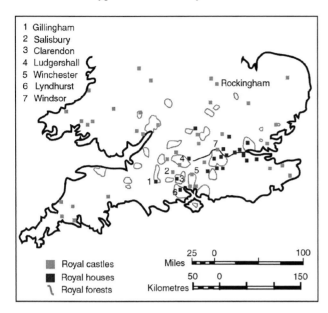

1 Gillingham
2 Salisbury
3 Clarendon
4 Ludgershall
5 Winchester
6 Lyndhurst
7 Windsor

Rockingham

■ Royal castles
■ Royal houses
〳 Royal forests

Miles   25 0   100
Kilometres 50 0   150

Figure 11. Royal castles in the reign of Henry VI, and royal houses and forests in that of Edward III. Adapted from H. M. Colvin, *The History of the King's Works: Volume I – The Middle Ages* (London: HMSO, 1963), figs 26 and 27.

The greater part of Clarendon Park, therefore, could in no way be described as 'marginal'. Indeed the launds, set aside for the deer, occupied land of moderately high potential.[96] Thus in the medieval period they were a signifier of status and ostentation which may stem from a deliberate disregard for economic potential intrinsic to the medieval noble mindset.[97] This was a landscape deliberately set up to distance itself from economic management while it was, paradoxically, almost entirely bound up with deer-management, as will be shown in Chapter Two.

Another major soil-zone in the forest is centred on Alderbury and the Grimsteads, and bounded on the west by the Avon, its southern edge effectively dividing Clarendon and Melchet Forests. It is comprised in the main of London Clay (sandy loam) bordered by a strip of Reading Beds (mottled clay) with an internal core of Bagshot Beds (sand) and some Plateau Gravel. This area can be more securely defined as marginal (albeit a subjective term based on the prominence given to arable

farming by historians), although Alderbury parish was, in many ways, the most exploited part of Clarendon Forest. Its clay and sand supported a tile industry that dominated rooftile production in Wiltshire from at least the early fourteenth century,[98] and sand was often dug from Ivychurch, from within the park and from Alderbury for building works at the palace.[99] Indeed it cannot be entirely coincidental that Alderbury was historically the forest's most significant vill (see above, pp. 7-8).

BACKGROUND CONTEXT

Clarendon Palace, a Listed Grade II building and Scheduled Ancient Monument (Wiltshire 318) now reaching the end of a five-year English Heritage-Funded consolidation and presentation plan, has played a key role in the historiography and archaeology of medieval palaces. The 1933-9 excavations represent the first organised archaeological examination of a late medieval English royal palace site,[100] and the 1988 Society of Antiquaries Report, whose publication testifies to the importance of this unique site and its relict landscape, arguably kick-started the resurgence of the field as an academic endeavour, since it led ultimately to the first modern synthesis of medieval palaces.[101] Moreover archaeological work carried out in the park by King Alfred's College and others for the best part of twenty years represents a unique opportunity to discover a medieval royal landscape which has remained largely undisturbed (compared to the surroundings of Windsor Castle, for example).

In fulfilling their brief to publish the 1930s excavations, the authors of the 1988 report revealed opportunities for future reinterpretation of the evidence. However, the nature of the work meant that analysis of primary sources referring to anything but the palace itself was impossible. The report was the culmination of eleven years trawling through dusty excavation records, and by the time of publication the effect of landscape studies was beginning to be felt in medieval archaeology. To some it did not go far enough, and the resulting 'lost opportunity' to clarify the 'relationship of Clarendon Palace to its medieval hinterland' — in particular to Salisbury — was remarked upon, as was the lack of discussion of the use of Clarendon's forest resources at the palace and elsewhere.[102] This study will address precisely those

---

[95] The north of Melchet Forest shares this upper chalk geology, which must have made the assarting there, noted by Taylor, so attractive (C.C. Taylor, 'Whiteparish: A Study of the Development of a Forest-Edge Parish', *WAM* 62 [1967], pp.79-102, *passim*).

[96] In 1802 Fussells Lodge was valued highest, in terms of tithes, of the Clarendon farms at £71.13s, and at Savage's Farm 'all was arable' except for some pasture around the yard and garden (WRO CHAPTER/96, 'Survey and Valuation of the Tithes of the Manor of Clarendon in the County of Wilts: The Property of the Dean and Chapter of Sarum', 1802, *ff*.13, 5).

[97] M. Johnson, Behind the Castle Gate: from Medieval to Renaissance (London: Routledge, 2002), pp.42-3.

[98] J.N. Hare, 'The Growth of the Roof-tile Industry in Later Medieval Wessex', *Medieval Archaeology* 35 (1991), pp.86-103 (p.89).

[99] E.g. PRO E 101/459/27; PRO E 101/459/29. Sand is also described as coming from Milford in 1363 (PRO E 101/460/2), although this is more likely to have been loam or valley gravel.

[100] For the excavations, see James and Robinson, *Clarendon Palace, passim*.

[101] T.B. James, *The Palaces of Medieval England c.1050-1550: Royalty, Nobility, the Episcopate and their Residences from Edward the Confessor to Henry VIII* (London: Seaby, 1990). For the excavations, see James and Robinson, *Clarendon Palace, passim*.

[102] P. Saunders, Review of James and Robinson, *Clarendon Palace, WAM* 84 (1991), pp.155-7 (p.156).

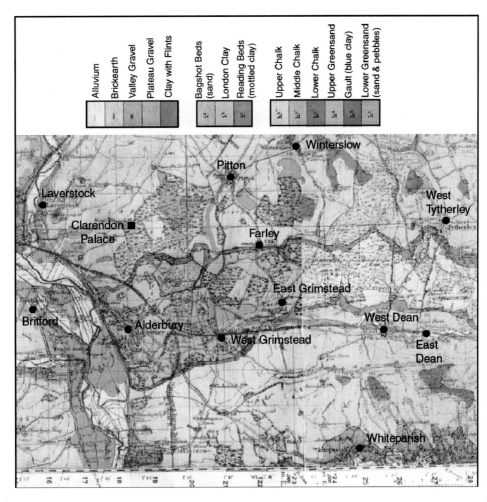

Figure 12. The geology of the Clarendon Forest area. Taken from two separate maps with settlement names overlaid for greater clarity. Original maps taken from geological surveys on the six-inch scale by W. Whitaker, C.E. Hawkins, Clement Reid, F.J. Bennet and A.J. Jukes, 1896 (no. 298, Salisbury, and no. 299, Winchester, repr. 1950).

issues by observing periods of over-exploitation and conservation of wood resources in tandem with records of building works at the palace (below, pp. 54, 83-84), and by considering relations between Clarendon and the city of Salisbury in depth for the first time (below, pp. 85-90).

Nevertheless, in stating that 'only Clarendon still provides an opportunity to study a prime medieval royal palace in its landscape context',[103] the 1988 report did highlight the possibility of future work on the palace's immediate surroundings. This opportunity was taken up in the 1996 *English Heritage Survey Grant for Presentation* (KACC I and II). The report, commissioned by English Heritage, ran to 253 pages and included a gazetteer of 400 sites and monuments in the park. Its brief was to investigate all sites and monuments of all periods within the study area, 'from... Neolithic long-barrows...through Bronze Age, Iron Age and Roman sites to a Second World War night-decoy airfield, searchlight station and modern farm buildings'.[104] However, no further original archive work was

undertaken, and the report identified future historical research as 'essential in order to reinterpret the palace and the archaeology and history of its wider landscape'.[105] Thus the pressing need for a study such as this, the first to analyse systematically even calendared references to the park and forest, has long been acknowledged.

Following the 1996 report, a historic landscape management plan was drafted (1998),[106] which included a ranking of all sites in the park and a draft plan for their future management. This led, in its turn, to a successful application for a ten-year Countryside Stewardship scheme (1999), and the five-year consolidation of the palace site, costed as a joint endeavour between the Clarendon estate and English Heritage, began in 1998. Finally, James and Gerrard's forthcoming work, based, like this study, on the 1996 report, will include some archival analysis and the results of archaeological fieldwork undertaken up to the end of 2003.[107]

---

[103] James and Robinson, *Clarendon Palace*, pp. 270-71.
[104] James and Gerrard, *Clarendon: A Royal Landscape*, forthcoming.

[105] KACC I, p.60.
[106] KACC, *Clarendon Park, Salisbury Wiltshire: Historic Landscape Management Plan* (Winchester, 1998).
[107] James and Gerrard, *Clarendon: A Royal Landscape*, forthcoming.

The principal difference between the studies mentioned above and this study is their geographical parameters. This is the first Clarendon-based work to address the forest alongside the park, and to give it equal — and sometimes preferential — prominence in the discussion. This said, the 1988 report did mention Clarendon Forest, albeit very briefly, and the KACC 1996 report (whose study area comprised the park in any case) deliberately began its post-Conquest chapter with a two-page section on the forest '[due to the] previous neglect of the topic',[108] again, an implicit plea for a study such as this. However given its extremely wide chronological span, and the lack of original archive work, the surface was barely scratched.

Evidence concerning Clarendon Forest has, however, been widely employed in general works on forests, particularly Cox's *The Royal Forests of England* (1905), Young's *The Royal Forests of Medieval England* (1979) and Grant's *The Royal Forests of England* (1991). Due to their extremely wide briefs, such works necessarily 'avoid individual variation and eccentricity...[and concentrate] on...features...that were typical'. [109] Moreover each was concerned primarily with elucidating forest administration. This was an aspect of Clarendon Forest covered in this writer's MA dissertation.[110] Thus it will thus not be addressed in this study, at least in isolation. Evidence from Clarendon Forest was also set out, in a section of its own, in Grant's *VCH* contribution 'Forests' (1959) and, most recently of all, in Bond's 'Forests, Chases, Warrens and Parks in Medieval Wessex' (1994), whose narrower geographical parameters allowed for rather wider, and certainly more detailed, discussions.

This latter point highlights the key argument for the necessity of this project. Grant's *VCH* contribution and Bond's 1994 paper are sound regional studies — although since Bond is a landscape archaeologist/ historian writing in the 1990s, his work is inevitably more wide-ranging than was Grant's, who was primarily interested in describing the administration of individual forests rather than their cultural or physical dimension. Each work is valuable to a study such as this, not least for comparative purposes (as, indeed, are the other general works cited), and each involved limited original documentary research. But neither encompassed the breadth of documents analysed here. As Colvin remarked when reviewing the Society of Antiquaries report, historians of particular buildings, for whom even a cursory mention may be significant, will use even calendared materials in a vastly different way from writers of syntheses.[111] The same is true of historians of particular landscapes and localities. Young said as much in 1979 when he recognised that ideally his work 'would

have been preceded by detailed studies of individual forests written by scholars with local knowledge'.[112]

This study will play a role in advancing the subject of royal forests in general through detailed analysis of one forest in particular. It will answer Young's call, being as detailed a study of Clarendon Forest from *c*.1200–*c*.1650 as documents allow. Whereas the works discussed above provide general overviews on either local or national scales, this study broadens and deepens the study of medieval forests, finding, for example, that groups of forests such as Clarendon, Melchet and Groveley may purposely have been managed for the variety of resources they could provide (see Chapter Two). Its findings will also be relevant to medieval studies as a whole. As Giovanni Levy has said, 'only a paradoxical...distortion of perspective would suggest that the...life of one village [or, indeed, locality] is of no interest beyond its meaning on a local scale'.[113]

Palaces, Documents and Landscape
The recent re-emergence of medieval palaces as a field of study is a further academic context for this study. The subject's trajectory, and a clue for its recent prominence, is discernible in the output of John Steane. Palaces were a very small part of his 1984 survey of medieval England, published almost exactly mid-way between Platt's *Medieval England* (1978), and Hinton's *Archaeology, Economy and Society* (1990),[114] and each can be seen as elements in the coming of age of medieval archaeology as a whole. Subsequently, *The Archaeology of the Medieval Monarchy* appeared alongside the first modern syntheses of medieval palaces,[115] at a time when it was beginning to be felt that 'the activities and preoccupations of kings, their families and courtiers, had been given inadequate treatment by medieval archaeologists'.[116]

Steane's latest work considers palaces as part of the archaeology of power.[117] Herein lies the main reason for the recent acceptance of palaces as a worthy academic subject. As Moreland suggests, if we are to understand fully the historical past, and the world in which non-élites lived, we cannot afford to ignore explicit material expressions of power and status. 'Mansions and castles

[108] KACC I, p.48.
[109] Young, *The Royal Forests of Medieval England*, p.viii.
[110] See Richardson, 'Clarendon: The Palace in the Forest', *passim*.
[111] H.M. Colvin, Review of T.B. James and A.M. Robinson, *Clarendon Palace*, *Medieval Archaeology* 34 (1990), pp.276-7 (p.277).
[112] Young, *The Royal Forests of Medieval England*, p.viii.
[113] G. Levy, 'On Microhistory', in *New Perspectives on Historical Writing* (Cambridge: Polity Press, 1991), ed. P. Burke, pp.93-113 (p.96).
[114] J.M. Steane, *The Archaeology of Medieval England and Wales* (London: Guild Publishing, 1984); C. Platt, *Medieval England: A Social History and Archaeology from the Conquest to 1600 AD* (London: Routledge and Regan Paul, 1978); D.A. Hinton, *Archaeology, Economy and Society: England from the Fifth to the Fifteenth Century* (London: Seaby, 1990).
[115] James, *The Palaces of Medieval England*; S. Thurley, *The Royal Palaces of Tudor England: Architecture and Court Life 1460-1547* (Yale University Press: London, 1993).
[116] J.M. Steane, *The Archaeology of The Medieval English Monarchy* (London: Batsford, 1993), p.10.
[117] J.M. Steane, *The Archaeology of Power: England and Northern Europe AD 800-1600* (Stroud: Tempus Publishing, 2001).

are as much material remains from the past as are the middens, wells, and house foundations of the poor'.[118]

Conversely, palaces have been rendered to an extent apolitical. At the very least, postprocessualism's acknowledgement of a plurality of pasts permits even socialists to study them unashamedly. The élite life that might be uncovered does not negate the lot of the commoners who lived within spitting distance. As even Roy Strong acknowledges, 'heritage' is apart from party politics in that it '[provides] myths upon which both the left and right draw', and it is no coincidence that current academic interest in royal palaces stems from the 1980s, when the heritage industry itself came into being.[119]

Important contributions have been made to the subject on the European stage. Well-attended international conferences were held at the OUDCE in 1994, 1997, and 2003, at the latter of which a paper based on the findings of this study was presented, adding a valuable (and still novel) landscape dimension. The French contribution has been particularly strong, witnessed by the publication of Annie Renoux's *Palais médiévaux* (1994) and *Palais royaux et princiers au Moyen Age* (1996).[120] Increased international co-operation may owe something to the fact that the EC is becoming an increasingly important source of funding. As Gerrard has pointed out, this is likely to stimulate debate about common European phenomena, leading to a concentration on 'widespread and visible monument classes' such as castles and monasteries (and, indeed, palaces).[121] This is the context into which this project will fit.

In England, institutionalisation, with the founding of Historic Royal Palaces in 1989, has been significant in the subject's historiography. So too was the Windsor fire of 1992, which provided opportunities for 'rescue' archaeology at the castle, leading to increased interest from archaeologists and the publication of key archaeological texts and interpretations.[122] Indeed, a sure sign of a sea-change is that the latest general work on palaces has been written not by a historian but an archaeologist.[123] This is not to say that archaeology did not feature in earlier syntheses, notably James's *Palaces*

of Medieval England (1990), but doubtless there was a reluctance on the part of late- twentieth-century archaeologists (the century 'of the common man'[124]) to tackle such supreme and symbolic 'material expressions of power and status'.[125] The furore that ensued after the Windsor fire soon became a debate about the place and purpose of the monarchy itself, largely because the castle *was*, indisputably, emblematic of monarchy.

In Keevill's work, although the import of the documentary record in 'the way archaeologists study palaces' is recognised,[126] the discussion of written sources is fairly limited. His paragraph on palatial landscapes, too, seems marginalised — no doubt a reflection of the subject's immaturity. Keevill acknowledges that 'the impact of palace building on landscapes has been under-appreciated in the past',[127] but no place is given to the document as part of the armoury of evidence of the archaeologist of those landscapes. Such marginalisation of written evidence is supported by many archaeological theorists, who advocate combining archaeological and historical evidence only at the point of synthesis so that each discipline becomes a source to be cross checked.[128]

Perhaps a more fruitful integration of written and material sources is that of John Dunbar in *Scottish Royal Palaces* (1999). Although his stated focus is domestic and residential function, and he has 'not attempted to deal with the many other aspects of the subject' (including, presumably, the landscape context),[129] Dunbar's study demonstrates how documentary references to the use of a building's surroundings can shed light on phasing and evolution. For example, he uses records of the purchasing of 35 roods of ground in 1427-8 at Linlithgow to illuminate the repositioning of the main entrance for better visual effect. Dunbar suggests also that references to the grazing of horses employed on construction work in the early 1480s on Linlithgow's meadows are evidence for a previously unrecognised major building campaign, and there is a willingness to consider the documentary evidence itself 'in the light of changes in the financial administration of...royal works', rather than merely to read into gaps in the documentary record a corresponding absence of construction works.[130] In this way, written sources become more than repositories of raw data. Moreover, the landscape and documentary references to it

[118] J. Moreland, *Archaeology and Text* (London: Duckworth, 2001), p.103.
[119] Strong, *Lost Treasures of Britain*, p.220. The National Heritage Act was passed in 1980 and English Heritage set up in 1984.
[120] A. Renoux, ed., *Palais médiévaux (France-Belgique): 25 ans d'archéologie* (Maine: Université du Maine, 1994); *Palais royaux et princiers au Moyen Age* (Maine: Université du Maine 1996). The latter, in particular, discusses not only the monuments themselves, but the landscapes in which they were set.
[121] C. Gerrard, *Medieval Archaeology: Understanding Traditions and Contemporary Approaches* (London: Routledge, 2003), pp.207-8.
[122] For example S. Brindle and B. Kerr, *Windsor Revealed: New Light on the History of the Castle* (London: English Heritage, 1997); C. Wilson, 'The Royal Lodgings of Edward III at Windsor Castle: Form, Function, Representation', in *Windsor: Medieval Archaeology, Art and Architecture of the Thames Valley*, BAA Conference Transactions 25, (Leeds: Maney Publishing, 2002), eds L. Keen and E. Scarff, pp.15-94.
[123] Keevill, *Medieval Palaces: An Archaeology*.

[124] J.M. Steane, *Medieval English Monarchy*, p.10.
[125] James, *The Palaces of Medieval England*; Moreland, *Archaeology and Text*, p.103.
[126] Keevill, *Medieval Palaces: An Archaeology*, p.55.
[127] Keevill, *Medieval Palaces: An Archaeology*, p.162.
[128] E.g. R. Gilchrist, *Gender and Material Culture: The Archaeology of Religious Women*, (London: Routledge, 1994), p.10; S. Tabaczynski, 'The Relationship Between History and Archaeology: Elements of the Present Debate', *Medieval Archaeology* 37 (1993), pp.1-14 (p.11).
[129] J.G. Dunbar, *Scottish Royal Palaces: The Architecture of the Royal Residences During the Late Medieval and Early Modern Periods* (East Linton: Tuckwell Press, 1999), p.3.
[130] Dunbar, *Scottish Royal Palaces*, pp.6, 11.

are part of the overall narrative instead of being sidelined into a paragraph in the conclusion.

But on the whole, works on medieval palaces have escaped the general trend to view monuments in their landscape contexts apparent, for example, in Muir's discussion of castles and defensive features in *The New Reading the Landscape* (2000).[131] Indeed, the impetus for such ideas as applied to the medieval period comes from recent work on castles, which are increasingly seen as more than discrete monuments. Rather they have become foci of administrative networks, centres of lordship, and even part of the settlement pattern.[132] In contrast, general works on palaces, although always in the forefront of ideas about the 'inner landscapes' of gardens, appear to take rather less account of wider surroundings apart from the odd mention of deer parks.[133] This may be because — in contrast to the 'hinterlands' of castles — so few of their surroundings survive. Again, thisproject is timely. It moves the study of Clarendon forward from the core buildings of the palace and the park out into the wider landscape, for example in considering forest settlement (Chapter Four).

The situation is beginning to change, however. Today Steane discusses deerparks in rather more detail.[134] Yet there is no explicit analysis of the ways in which the landscape itself functioned to reflect and reinforce the very power which is the subject of his study. Again, Johnson's recent work on castles, focusing on just such issues, provides a direct contrast.[135] Most pertinently here, we are a long way from any analysis of the interrelationships between royal forests, parks and palaces as addressed by Creighton concerning (again) castles.[136] Astill's recent paper on Windsor, one of the most popular royal residences throughout the Middle Ages, may be considered an exception and his aim, to 'look beyond the walls [and] maintain a sense of perspective…by attempting to set the castle in the context of its surroundings' is echoed strongly here.[137]

To conclude, the clarification of the 'relationship of Clarendon Palace to its hinterland' has been called for since the early 1990s (see above, p. 22).[138] Thus this study aims to reconstruct as far as is possible the medieval and early modern landscape by considering the place of Clarendon Forest alongside the park, the interrelationships between each of them, the palace and the wider locality. And it will do so using a documentary methodology.

PROJECT RATIONALE

Problematical Spaces? Documents and the Landscape
David Austin, has called the landscape 'a…problematical space, partly because we are raiding the data of the documentary historian'.[139] Thus in some ways little seems to have changed since 1969, when Platt drew attention to the 'barrier…[separating] the excavator from the searcher of archives'.[140] In British medieval studies, at least, Orser and Fagan's comment that 'historical archaeologists must be as adroit at archival research and documentary interpretation as they are at…artefactual analysis' seems ingenuous,[141] perhaps because of the longevity of medieval history as a discipline and the sheer weight of documentary evidence. However, a new attitude to written evidence is beginning to emerge. As early as 1996, Johnson talked of the 'arbitrariness of disciplinary boundaries'. More recently, Moreland has opined that the argument that written sources produced by and for the élite can tell us nothing about the 'lower orders' is as nonsensical as the parallel notion that archaeological evidence is somehow more 'democratic'.[142]

Although *lacunae* in the documentary record continue, rightly, to be highlighted by archaeologists — for example Gerrard,[143] who points out that little can be gleaned from the written record about animals in everyday rural life unless they were bought or sold — others are beginning to suggest that the prejudices of archaeologists themselves have limited its use. Moreland, for example, points out that although written sources have been treated as if confined to ideological and political structures, they were in fact crucial elements in élite power, and thus 'very frequently concerned with ensuring control over production and distribution'.[144] As the highest landholder in England, the Crown was more concerned with most with control over its lands and resources. Thus the information provided by the central and administrative documents studied here is invaluable in its scope, despite the fact that those who transcribed

[131] R. Muir, *The New Reading the Landscape: Fieldwork in Landscape History* (Exeter: University of Exeter Press, 2000), pp.223-44.
[132] See particularly Oliver Creighton's *Castles and Landscapes* (London: Continuum, 2002).
[133] Contrast 'deerparks' (1 reference) and 'gardens' (10 references, three of more than one page) in the index of James, *The Palaces of Medieval England*. See also Steane, *Medieval English Monarchy*, pp.117-22.
[134] Four pages on parks, hunting and lodges as opposed to a paragraph on gardens (Steane, *Archaeology of Power*, pp.272-5, 107).
[135] Johnson, *Behind the Castle Gate, passim*.
[136] Creighton, *Castles and Landscapes,* particularly pp.185-93.
[137] G. Astill, 'Windsor in the Context of Medieval Berkshire', in *Windsor: Medieval Archaeology, Art and Architecture of the Thames Valley*, BAA Conference Transactions 25, eds L. Keen and E. Scarff (Leeds: Maney Publishing, 2002), pp.1-14 (quote at p.1).
[138] P. Saunders, Review of James and Robinson, *Clarendon Palace, WAM* 84 (1991), pp.155-7 (p.156).

[139] D. Austin, 'The Case Study: Okehampton Park', in *From the Baltic to the Black Sea: Studies in Medieval Archaeology,* One World Archaeology 18, eds D. Austin and L. Alcock (London: Routledge, 1997), pp.54-77 (p.69).
[140] C. Platt, *Medieval Archaeology in England: A Guide to the Historical Sources*, Pinhorns Handbooks 5 (Isle of Wight: Pinhorns, 1969), p.1.
[141] C.E Orser and B.M. Fagan, *Historical Archaeology* (New York: HarperCollins College Publishers, 1995), p.16.
[142] M. Johnson, *An Archaeology of Capitalism* (Oxford: Blackwell Publishers, 1996), pp.3, 97; Moreland, *Archaeology and Text*, pp.17-19.
[143] Gerrard, *Medieval Archaeology*, p.203.
[144] Moreland, *Archaeology and Text*, p.30.

and processed it may not have been familiar with Clarendon's landscape itself.

Historians, who have 'traditionally [exhibited little] interest in...material culture',[145] have also taken on board the same broadly anthropological definitions of culture current in archaeology, which stimulate the idea that buildings and landscapes (and indeed documents) should be read in new ways. Emergent theoretical and methodological parallels are striking. Overarching models like gender and closure theory have been adopted by both archaeological and historical thinkers, providing opportunities for more meaningful discourse between the disciplines.[146] Resulting methodologies have prompted many medieval archaeologists to search for wider social meaning when considering the built and landscape environment instead of 'worrying endlessly about...crucks or types of roofing materials'. [147] Similarly, historians have forsworn the quantitative methodologies of the 1970s which effectively reduced complex documentary information into what was perceived to be raw empirical data.[148] Most now accept Foucault's parallel of the document as monument, giving prominence to 'the underlying structures...and the discourses that created it'.[149]

This recent convergence belies the fact that documents, and documentary historians, have always made important contributions to landscape studies. Desk-based projects continue to make full use of the *VCH* and Colt Hoare — and a glance at the bibliography here will show that this study is no exception. Moreover W. G. Hoskins, who famously recommended that historians should pull on their boots and 'get [their] feet wet' was himself an economic historian.[150] The real question, posed by C. C. Taylor in 1974, is whether landscape studies can best be done by one person (the polymath) or whether co-operative enterprises yield better results.[151] The former

has been criticised, as 'a huge Heath Robinson apparatus'.[152] However it is the contention here that 'total landscape archaeology' cannot be carried out successfully by one person alongside an effective 'total documentary landscape history', at least for a landscape for which as much written evidence survives as that for Clarendon Forest and Park. Indeed, Taylor himself had acknowledged by 2000 that landscape history had, in the intervening 26 years, gone from a 'relatively simple narrative' to an explosive complexity which precluded its writing in ways he had once envisaged.[153]

Clearly, though, confining oneself to one form of evidence cannot reveal more than a fragment of the total picture, and Astill's 'sense of perspective' will be unachievable.[154] Some degree of total landscape history should at least be attempted. Nevertheless, even the most successful integrated archaeological/historical studies of landscape seem inevitably weighted towards one or other discipline. John Hunt, in his study of the Honour of Dudley, sought to 'integrate the use of both archaeological and documentary sources',[155] which he achieved with some aplomb. But Carenza Lewis, reviewing Hunt's work, commented that the 'study of the landscape is used essentially to help illuminate the nature of lordship, rather than vice versa'.[156] It is likely that this study would prompt a similar response. As Austin has said, total histories, employing many sources, are a theoretical possibility. The problems lie in the practicalities.[157]

Given archaeological and other work in progress at Clarendon (see below, pp. 21-22), the role of this study can be compared to that of John Hare in the 1959-98 landscape study of Fyfield and Overton, Wiltshire.[158] Hare's 'Agriculture and Land Use on the Manor of Overton 1248-1539' was a specially commissioned, rounded piece of research in itself,[159] and was used to underpin discussions of the archaeological and environmental evidence, supplementing rather than leading the archaeological programme. Fowler lists the uses to which the documents were put including 'peopling' the landscape and villages, locating 'new'

[145] P.A. Stamper, 'Landscapes of the Middle Ages: Rural Settlements and Manors', in *The Archaeology of Britain: An Introduction from the Upper Palaeolithic to the Industrial Revolution*, eds J. Hunter and I. Ralston (London: Routledge, 1999), pp.247-63 (p.250).

[146] For closure theory, see D.A. Hinton, '"Closing" and the Later Middle Ages', *Medieval Archaeology* 43 (1999), pp.172-82, *passim*; Johnson, *Archaeology of Capitalism*, pp.77-96; S.H. Rigby, *English Society in the Later Middle Ages: Class, Status and Gender* (London: Macmillan Press, 1995), *passim*.

[147] D. Austin, 'The "Proper Study" of Medieval Archaeology', in *From the Baltic to the Black Sea: Studies in Medieval Archaeology*, One World Archaeology 18 (London: Routledge, 1997 (1997), eds D. Austin and L. Alcock, pp.9-42 (p.24). The value of such 'obsessions' in providing the groundwork for more recent social archaeologies should not be negated, however.

[148] For a full discussion of the merits and drawbacks of such works, see E. Powell, 'Social Research and the Use of Medieval Criminal Records', *Michigan Law Review* 79 (1981), pp.967-78, *passim*.

[149] Johnson, *Archaeology of Capitalism*, p.4.

[150] W.G. Hoskins, *Local History in England*, 3rd edn (London: Longman, 1984), p.3; Kate Tiller, *English Local History: An Introduction* (Stroud: Alan Sutton Publishing, 1992), p.20.

[151] C.C. Taylor, 'Total Archaeology or Studies in the History of the Landscape', in *Landscapes and Documents*, eds A. Rogers and T. Rowley (London: National Council of Social Service Publications, 1974), pp.15-26 (p.15).

[152] S. Stoddart, 'Early Studies of Landscapes: Editorial Introduction', in *Landscapes from Antiquity*, Antiquity Papers 1, ed. S. Stoddart (Cambridge: Antiquity Publications, 2000), pp.7-10 (p.7).

[153] C.C. Taylor, 'The Plus Fours in the Wardrobe: A Personal View of Landscape History' in D. Hooke, ed., *Landscape: the Richest Historical Record*, Society for Landscape Studies Supplementary Series 1 (London: The Society for Landscape Studies, 2000), pp.157-62 (p.157).

[154] Astill, 'Windsor', p.1.

[155] J. Hunt, *Lordship and the Landscape: A Documentary and Archaeological Study of the Honour of Dudley c.1066-1322*, BAR British Series 264 (Oxford: John and Erica Hedges and Archaeopress, 1997), p.11.

[156] C. Lewis, Review of Hunt, *Lordship and the Landscape*, *Medieval Archaeology* 43 (1999), pp.320-2 (p.322).

[157] Austin, 'Okehampton Park', p.76.

[158] P. Fowler, *Landscape Plotted and Pieced: Landscape History and Local Archaeology in Fyfield and Overton, Wiltshire* (London: Society of Antiquaries, 2000).

[159] Fyfod Working Papers 43 (see Fowler, *Landscape Plotted and Pieced*, p.39).

features and suggesting areas of future research.[160] Nothing more can be hoped for this study and its role within the Clarendon Project as a whole.

One of the main strengths of documentary study in the long series is the ability to provide evidence for change. In addition, transformations in the layout, form and content of the documents themselves can illuminate shifts in mentality through time, as Johnson, Perry Marvin and especially Michael Clanchy have shown.[161] Clearly, what was important to the central authorities who compiled the records of thirteenth and fourteenth-century forest eyres — deer, then rents from assarts, then trees — was not the same as those who set in train the surveys and inquisitions of the early seventeenth — trees, restriction of assarting, then deer (closely followed by rabbits and any other means of economic exploitation). Here is the documentary evidence for 'how lords managed lands' on a grand scale.[162] In this way, interrelationships between Clarendon Palace, its landscape and locality will be assessed — the primary purpose of this project.

At its most basic, the theoretical and methodological base of this study is clearly, in archaeological parlance, that of the 'monument in context', where emphasis is given to the deliberate positioning and situation of monuments — seen as centres of activity rather than as isolated entities — in order to understand those monuments through their settings.[163] Clarendon Palace was nothing if not a centre of activity, as indeed was Clarendon Park, as demonstrated in a discussion of its lodges and ancillary buildings in Chapter Three. Moreover, a documentary methodology facilitates the 'widening out' of the landscape context from the physical constraints of the park.

On one level, then, this study exists as an element in a long-term venture, giving context to a unique historic monument currently at the end of a five-year consolidation and conservation plan. Yet it aspires to more than the collection of data, endeavouring also to reconstruct landscapes familiar to those who lived and worked at Clarendon in the medieval and early modern periods. This may be easier to strive for than to achieve — although Johnson contends that 'the difficulty in piecing together non-literate attitudes and actions...lies not in the evidence, but in the restrictive ideas and attitudes that we...bring to that evidence', employing the concept of 'resistance' in order to understand the actions of non-élite social strata.[164] The approach here is similar. Resistance at Clarendon, in the form of parkbreak and

poaching, are addressed in Chapter Five, which focuses on the landscape as a matrix for conflict and negotiation.

Recent studies have attempted to recover conceptual medieval landscapes, often by eschewing historical geography approaches prioritising economic and functional needs as prime motivators in landscape evolution. Instead, many are consciously initiatory.[165] Corcos, for example, consciously '[asks] questions that may not necessarily yet have answers'.[166] Yet as Duffy points out, 'attempts to reconstruct the configuration of...landscapes are less prone to misinterpretation when using empirically-grounded descriptive data'.[167] Tys, too, speaks of the necessity of employing 'empirical reconstruction [in order to]...deduce, hypothetically, which decisions and choices were made concerning the development of the landscape', while Corcos asserts that empirical evidence and databases are 'fundamental' in forming meaningful perspectives and interpretations concerning the psychological/cognitive contexts of settlement and land use.[168]

This study attempts, like those above, to view landscape as a form of material culture and to 'enter the mindsets' of its occupants. Certainly Clarendon is ideal for examining how the landscape was created by élites and how it was sustained by the officers of the forest and park and others, as James and Gerrard's forthcoming work on Clarendon Park will demonstrate.[169] However, it is not always easy to reconstruct other perspectives using the documents concerned, concepts like 'resistance' notwithstanding. Accordingly, much of the methodology used here will also have an empirical flavour, particularly in Chapter Two, where the economy of the forest and park are the focus. In addition, like Corcos, who 'leans heavily on secondary material' while attempting to 'inject an element of the more abstract...approach',[170] this study makes good use of secondary sources, especially in Chapter Four where previous work on Wiltshire settlement is employed extensively alongside fresh readings of taxation records.

In the end the theoretical base here, like that of most current landscape studies, is eclectic. However it is as well to reiterate that one role of this study is to sample

[160] Fowler, *Landscape Plotted and Pieced*, p.41.

[161] Clanchy, *From Memory to Written Record*, *passim*.

[162] C. Dyer, 'Documentary Evidence: Problems and Enquiries', in *The Countryside of Medieval England*, eds G. Astill and A. Grant (Oxford: Blackwell Publishers, 1988), pp.12-35 (p.16).

[163] T. Darvill, C. Gerrard and B. Startin, 'Archaeology in the Landscape: A Review', (unpub. draft typescript for *Landscape History*), p.4; C. Tilley, *A Phenomenology of Landscape: Places, Paths and Monuments* (Oxford: Berg Publishers, 1994), p.14.

[164] Johnson, *Behind the Castle Gate*, p.162.

[165] E.g. N. Corcos, *The Affinities and Antecedents of Medieval Settlement: Topographical Perspectives from Three of the Somerset Hundreds*, BAR British Series 337 (Oxford: John and Erica Hedges and Archaeopress, 2002); P.J. Duffy, 'Social and Spatial Order in the MacMahon Lordship of Airghialla in the Late Sixteenth Century', in *Gaelic Ireland c.1250-c.1650: Land, Lordship and Settlement*, eds P.J. Duffy, D. Edwards and E. FitzPatrick (Dublin: Four Courts Press, 2001), pp.115-37; D. Tys, 'Development of the Medieval Settlement Pattern and Landscape on the Coast of Flanders (900-1500): Integrated Historical Research and Archaeological Survey', unpub. paper given at Leeds IMC, 2000.

[166] Corcos, *Affinities and Antecedents*, pp.1-2.

[167] Duffy, 'Social and Spatial Order' p.116.

[168] Corcos, *Affinities and Antecedents*, p.194. Tys's pages are unnumbered.

[169] James and Gerrard, *Clarendon: A Royal Landscape* (forthcoming).

[170] Corcos, *Affinities and Antecedents*, p.2.

documents previously neglected by historians, in tandem with ongoing archaeology. Although the intention is to take into account fresh ways of looking at the landscape, it would be foolish to make over-ambitious claims for this project as a groundbreaking work of landscape theory. Nevertheless, its base is interdisciplinary, linking fieldwork and historical documentation for one of the most significant English medieval forests, a surprising number of elements of which survive today.

Methodology: The Practicalities
The very survival of original documents poses its own problems. They are 'a continuous stream of the past's self-knowledge whose contents both inform and constrain'.[171] Indeed, Clarendon is exceptionally well documented from the thirteenth to the seventeenth century, and one could probably spend a lifetime on transcriptions alone. Hence it has been decided to study in depth those original sources that will shed most light on landscape and settlement. These are the Exchequer and Chancery forest records (PRO E 32, DL 39, C 47), the Exchequer Pipe Rolls (PRO E 372), taxation documents (PRO E 179) and records of building works found in various classes. Alongside the published calendars of rolls, these documents will form the backbone of this study as far as the medieval period is concerned.

It is common to speak of the landscape as a palimpsest, but it is rarely acknowledged that 'it is a palimpsest dominated by post-medieval features'.[172] Here, Clarendon is somewhat of an exception, since the medieval landscape in the form of the deerpark and its coppices, still dominates. However the buildings of the estate are all post-medieval, and even our knowledge of the layout of the medieval deerpark derives largely from a map of c.1640 (Figure 7). Original documentary sources are extremely informative for the early modern period. Of particular note are the Regarders' Certificates in Exchequer Accounts Various (PRO E 101) and the various early modern inquisitions, special commissions and interrogatories (e.g. PRO E 123, E 134, E 178). It has not been considered fruitful to trawl through unindexed classes of documents for references. However, the Exchequer Declared Accounts (PRO E 351), whose format facilitates ease of reference, were an exception. They might have filled gaps in our knowledge as to building programmes in the park in the sixteenth and early seventeenth centuries, a period at Clarendon which has received little attention from scholars.[173] A focus on the early modern period generally will elucidate processes operating in the landscape once the palace was

removed as the hub of the administrative and material landscape around it.

After copious reading and preparation, this project began with perusal of the lists and indexes in the PRO, resulting in a database of over 700 Clarendon documents, each with a *précis* of its contents. During the second extended visit to Kew, unpublished 12th-century Exchequer Pipe Rolls (E 372) were transcribed, and others checked against duplicates (E 352) which hold additional information. Records of 16th- and 17th-century royal building works (E 351) were also examined, and other 17th-century documents sampled. Thus by June 2000 the 12th and 17th centuries had largely been dealt with, so that further research at Kew could proceed along more thematic lines.

In addition, by summer 2000, every indexed reference in the calendars of Close, Patent and Fine Rolls had also been transcribed fully and entered into a further database, representing a significant resource for future studies. Data from it have been sorted by subject (deer, building works, forest officers, land-use, etc.) as well as arranged diachronically in order to observe trends, and these have been checked when necessary against the databases containing the manuscript sources. During a third extended visit in August 2000, all relevant references in the Lay Subsidy class (E 179) were transcribed with a view to settlement pattern analysis, and work on the Clarendon Forest documents was begun. Transcription of these was completed over further extended visits, in December 2000 and January 2001. Late sixteenth- and early seventeenth-century primary forest sources have proved especially informative. Unlike earlier documents, many were compiled by those familiar with the landscape (such as the forest's regarders), so that a different perspective may be realised. A final three-week visit to Kew took place in October 2001, in order to collate records of building works, and this was followed by a week at the Wiltshire Record Office in summer 2002 where further accounts and other documents were transcribed and added to the data bases.

Rather than limit the study at the outset by period, the sources have dictated which chronological foci to pinpoint. The result is a very clear juxtaposition of the late 13th/14th and late 16th/early 17th centuries as far as evidence for the exploitation of forest resources is concerned. Yet key documents from other periods within the study's remit have also been employed — for example rabbits are a key issue in the fifteenth century, and feature strongly in Chapter Two. Such apparent shifts in the faunal economy of deer parks, to what Tom Williamson has called 'intermediate forms of exploitation', can illuminate changing attitudes to nature in early modern England, and thus new perspectives on the natural world.[174]

[171] Austin, 'The "Proper Study"' p.11.
[172] I. Whyte, 'The Historical Geography of Britain from AD 1500: Landscape and Townscape', in *The Archaeology of Britain: An Introduction from the Upper Palaeolithic to the Industrial Revolution* (London: Routledge, 1999), eds J. Hunter and I. Ralston, pp.264-79 (p.264).
[173] KACC I, p.62.
[174] P.A. Stamper, Review of *Making English Landscapes: Changing Perspectives*, Bournemouth University School of Conservation Sciences

Yet we must be clear about what the documentary evidence *will* allow us to know and what it will not. Our view of the countryside is conditioned by the kind of evidence that has survived, and the compilers of the (largely administrative) documents analysed in this study were probably unfamiliar with Clarendon 'on the ground'. Yet the pasts we uncover 'may...involve what was actually happening but was either not perceived as significant or not perceived at all',[175] and we must not exchange the feeling that the documents will tell us all we want to know for an impression that they can tell us nothing. Indeed, much has been achieved as far as locating and transcribing documentary evidence is concerned, and there is ample scope to analyse economy and productivity for Clarendon Forest in a similar way that Stamper has done for Pamber Forest, Hampshire, or Bond for Woodstock Park.[176] While this is hardly the cutting edge of current landscape theory, it is essential because Clarendon Forest has never been approached from such an angle in its own right. Nevertheless, when reconstructing landscapes through written sources, the resulting picture can (to an extent) only be that which the documents allow us to see.

Clarendon in the period studied here is primarily an administrative landscape in two respects. First because it patently *was*, at least on one level. Royal forests had no physical markers, or at least no fences erected around them (unlike parks, which are consequently easier to discuss in archaeological terms — see Glossary). Instead they were spaces defined primarily by what Paul Bordieu has called a 'social topology', in the form of forest officers authorised to police them.[177] Second, as an area of Royal Forest, royal demesne, and a major royal residence, most of the evidence for Clarendon's 'natural' and built environment comes from centralised administrative sources. Although the landscape was as multi-faceted and subjective to contemporaries as any other, depending on whom was experiencing it and how, to the documentary historian it is *first and foremost* administrative.

THE DOCUMENTS

Medieval Documents

Exchequer Pipe Rolls

Certain classes of document are worthy of detailed treatment here. One such is the Exchequer Pipe Rolls (E 372), if only because it commences before any other class studied. The purpose of the pipe rolls was, of course, to record the sums that bailiffs and other officials paid into the Exchequer. Or rather what they should pay ....or at least what those who had gone before them had once paid. And there is the rub. Names might appear on a particular roll belonging to those who had been dead for centuries, their recorded payments no longer relevant. For example in the roll for 1458-9 we find that the sheriff must render 16½.d. for Andrew de Grimstead's 5½ acres of waste in Clarendon Forest. The unwary might assume an aged Andrew was still arrenting the same amount of waste for the same sum in 1536-7.[178] Yet Ralph Perot, the last heir of the Grimsteads, had surrendered his interest in their extensive property in Melchet Forest (including their 20 acres of woodland) in 1406.[179] In this sense, the value of the Exchequer Pipe Rolls in a study such as this is restricted, although not to have checked them would have been unthinkable. Where they are most useful is for early references to the palace, although these are rare and difficult to locate. For example lead and dyes dispatched to Clarendon in 1179-80 appear under Surrey, from where they were sent.[180]

Topographical information is also limited. The exchequer was interested in financial return rather than detail, and all the rolls tell us in this instance is the acreage of waste an Andrew de Grimstead had once arrented. Where the waste *was* is up to us to find out elsewhere.[181] What is more problematic generally is whether such areas of waste remained static — and we are certainly not going to find out from this class of documents alone. Here the Forest Eyre rolls (E 32) and related classes are much more valuable.

Twelfth-century pipe rolls do contain information on forest matters from a time before extant forest eyre rolls.[182] But the fact that the sheriff rendered a certain sum for pleas, wastes and purprestures for the whole of Wiltshire in a given year is of little help in a study of a particular forest or the exploitation of an individual landscape. Perhaps more than any other category of

---

Occasional Paper 3; Oxbow Monograph 93 (Oxford: Oxbow Books, 1998), *Medieval Archaeology* 42 (1998), pp.216-7 (p.217).

[175] Fowler, *Landscape Plotted and Pieced*, p.202.

[176] P.A. Stamper, 'The Medieval Forest of Pamber, Hampshire', *Landscape History* 5 (1983), pp.41-52; J. Bond 'Woodstock Park in the Middle Ages', in J. Bond and K. Tiller, eds, *Blenheim: Landscape for a Palace* (Stroud: Sutton Publishing Ltd, 1997), pp.22-54.

[177] The '"social topology" of a given institutional field [in which] various positions emerge relative to the kinds of capital circulating in it and to the transitive trajectories of its defining practice, namely the hunt' (W. Perry Marvin, 'Slaughter and Romance: Hunting Reserves in Late Medieval England', in *Medieval Crime and Social Control*, eds B.A. Hanawalt and D. Wallace [Minneapolis: University of Minnesota Press, 1998], pp.224-52 [p.233]).

---

[178] PRO E 372/304; PRO E 372/382.

[179] M. Parsons, *Sharps and Pollards* (New Milton: Michael Parsons, 1993), pp.22-3.

[180] *Et p(ro) plumbo (et) coloribus missis Clarend' (et) Wudest(ock) .vj. li. (et) .vj. s....*

[181] The present Hawksgrove is probably the 'wood of Odo de Grimstead' mentioned in a 1225 perambulation (M. Parsons, *The Royal Forest of Pancet* [New Milton: Michael Parsons, 1995], pp.7, 9); BM Stowe MS.798 for the perambulation.

[182] See D. Crook, 'The Records of Forest Eyres in the Public Record Office, 1179 to 1670', *Journal of the Society of Archivists* 17 (1996), 183-93, *passim*.

medieval documents, the pipe rolls typify Harvey's observation that 'whatever the purpose of any record or relic of the past, it was not to tell us today what the landscape of the past looked like',[183] and they are best employed in conjunction with other sources.

Forest Eyre Rolls and Related Documents

To begin with the PRO E 32 class (Justice of the Forest: Records Formerly in Receipt of Exchequer), this is where the records of forest eyres are held, along with some of the documentation forest officers, such as local foresters, verderers and regarders, prepared for those eyres. There are also inquisitions *de statu foreste*, from the mid fourteenth century after forest eyres went into decline.

Some eyre rolls commence with a list of forest officers, delineated by their office, and others give the names of those that we can guess are forest officers. This can only be useful since in the chancery rolls only wardens are generally named, or verderers when they needed to be replaced. Forest Eyre rolls, therefore, add to our knowledge of Clarendon's 'social topology' (see above, p. 16). Among the most useful information in these first sections of the eyre rolls is that which sets out the townships expected to attend, as the range of vills named indicates which were considered to be in the legal bounds of the forest at any one time.[184]

The forest eyre rolls can demonstrate the complexity of social interrelationships evident in the forest, and there is ample scope for wider study of the subject through the pledges listed alone. In addition, they also contain much information on poaching, although numbers of deer indicated should not be taken as an accurate figure, since few poachers were caught, and when they were they might not have been prosecuted. 'The humble individual killing a deer rarely came before the courts, and when he did he was pardoned'.[185] However, it is possible to analyse comparative numbers taken from the Clarendon forests (Buckholt, Clarendon, Groveley and Melchet) and from different areas inside Clarendon Forest itself, as well as to evaluate which species were most prominent. From the early fourteenth century especially, familiarity and the high level of dependence on animals had manifested itself in a 'vocabulary...particularly rich in descriptive terms'.[186] Thus references to *fecones* (fawns), prickets and sorrells (see Glossary) and the like, as well as the usual *dama* and *damus* (does and bucks) in the case of fallow alone allows a measure of sexing and ageing of cervine populations which is unachievable even when observing live herds from the fourteenth century onwards, shedding light on medieval management techniques.

More quantitatively useful are the arrents of wastes found in the forest proceedings. Here, too, there are more topographical references. For example PRO E 36/75 (1299-1305), now in the Exchequer: Treasury of Receipt Miscellaneous class sets out waste arrented to the Priory of Ivychurch in 1301-2, as 112 acres next to the priory.[187] This is one of many such examples, each set out with entry fines and value per acre. There are similar figures for assarts, often with a pedigree for each, which are of prime importance for study of settlement and land-use. Information on agistment is also found in the forest eyre rolls. For example the huge roll for the 1330 eyre alone (PRO E 32/207) contains agistment figures for Groveley from 1280-1332; for Melchet from 1300-33 (albeit with several breaks), and for Clarendon from 1280-1332.

In general, the eyres of the reign of Edward III (1327-77), which are the most detailed, represented harsh royal policy which 'met with widespread opposition from...subjects, who took advantage of [the king's] absences from England to make wholesale depredations upon the deer in his forests and parks'.[188] Thus comparing the eyre of 1330 with that of 1355 may indicate how far this was the case at Clarendon. This is a crucial question, as it will indicate whether or not the presence of the palace meant the area was exceptionally well policed. On the other hand, the palace, as headquarters of the forest administration, may have represented rather a challenge which rendered parkbreak all the more symbolic.

Other forest documents are less useful. The class C 47 (Chancery Miscellanea [Forests]) perambulations have been extensively published elsewhere, although they have been mapped here for the first time in order better to understand shifts in the administrative landscape (Figure 83). DL 39 (Duchy of Lancaster and Justice of the Forest South of Trent: Forest Records) represent a revival of 'true' forest eyres, although they are less informative than earlier examples.

Later Forest Documents

The later forest documents (to be more precise, those sixteenth- and seventeenth-century sources concerned with the running of the park) are detailed as far as economy is concerned. They also give a more intimate perspective than do the earlier forest eyre rolls. Whereas the latter are administrative documents written up in court years after offences took place by those who probably did not know the landscape concerned, many of the early modern documents are penned (sometimes literally) by the regarders, men of means who knew the landscape intimately. Other classes, particularly the interrogatories,

---

[183] P.D.A. Harvey, 'The Documents of Landscape History: Snares and Delusions', *Landscape History*, 13 (1991), pp.47-52 (p.47).

[184] Stamper, 'Pamber', p.43.

[185] Rackham, *The Last Forest*, p.61.

[186] G. Astill and A. Grant, 'The Medieval Countryside: Approaches and Perceptions', in *The Countryside of Medieval England* (Oxford: Blackwell Publishers, 1988), eds G. Astill and S. Grant, pp.1-11 (p.10).

[187] *Joh(an)nes de Crokesle...arrentavit...priori & convent(u)m monast(er)ij ederosi .Cxij. acr' de solo R'. iux(ta) monast(eriu)m ederosum in eadem foresta.*

[188] Grant, *The Royal Forests of England*, p.167.

contain eyewitness information and reading them has something of the flavour of oral history.

Regarders' Certificates and Related Documents

The scope for study of Clarendon's economy in the early modern period is evident in the Certificates of Regarders, which are spread across many classes. For example, amounts of browsewood taken for fodder for the deer are often recorded in detail. Set out too might be the use of dead trees and fees (estovers) which went to the ranger, warden and foresters, as well as lists of trespasses noted by the regarders.[189] Moneys gained from coppice-sales were ploughed back into the coppices themselves for making hedges and the like, so that wood-management techniques, too often the preserve of medieval scholars, can be explored.

In addition more general documents, such as regarders' articles, for example PRO E 178/2446 (Special Commissions, which commences c.1558) provide an overview of the concerns of the Crown at the close of the sixteenth century in detail.

Inquisitions into the State of the Forest, Interrogatories and Special Depositions

These documents provide much eyewitness information, as well as illustrating further the concerns of the Crown, in particular the overriding preoccupation with control over timber stocks. Indeed, when compared to the Inquisitions *de statu foreste* of the later fourteenth century, which are concerned equally with deer, a shift in attitude concerning forests is particularly clear. This changed emphasis produced the many articles for spoil of woods in Wiltshire, which in turn resulted in court cases which it is possible to trace across several document series.

The Special Depositions (e.g. E 134/18 & 19Eliz/Mich I, 1575-77) are particularly interesting for the views of ordinary people, as well as insight into management techniques. Some interrogatories cover aspects of the economy other than trees, including E 178/4728 (1612), which illustrates the importance of the rabbit warrens (to the Earl of Pembroke, if not to the king!), as well as holding extensive information on the park's coppices and their management.

Taxation Documents

Every relevant taxation document from 1281-2 (PRO E 179/196/12) to 1642-3 (PRO E 179/259/25) has been transcribed in order to shed light on settlement in Clarendon Forest, including the deserted and shrunken villages just over the 'border' in Melchet Forest

(Alderstone, Cowsfield Esturmy, Whelpley and More).[190] Even from a cursory glance at lay subsidy information, it is obvious that these throve well into the sixteenth century. In addition, fifteenth-century taxes in particular provide some of the only information available concerning the income and wealth of the most affluent members of local society,[191] useful supporting evidence for understanding of the families who managed the forest and park, at least.

Clearly there are problems. Generally only the wealthy paid taxes, so that the full demographic picture is unobtainable. Here the poll taxes of 1377 (PRO E 179/196) are an exception, since the intention was to tax every man, woman and child over the age of fourteen.[192] In addition, the tax's novelty meant evasion was less easy. Of course, the poll taxes cover only a very limited timespan, so that we are left with a snapshot of the situation in 1377. A surprise — which some might think incidental — was the number of relatively well preserved seals on some of the poll tax documents (although unfortunately few for the Clarendon vills), which might reflect forest office in the contemporary mindset. For example in E 179/196/37/1 (1377), there are several representations of stags or bucks (one with an apparently erect penis).

As for the records of fifteenths and tenths, there is a trap hidden in them akin to that of the pipe rolls. After 1334 through to the seventeenth century, all (with a very few exceptions) are copies of the tax of 1332.[193] Thus only the pre-1334 subsidies are anywhere near an accurate reflection of the situation at the time. It is as well to be familiar with every document class before research is embarked on, and it is only unfortunate that every document class is not yet accompanied by a PRO handbook!

Taxation records that include names, or at least a count of assessed members of the community, are clearly of more value to this study than those that provide only a sum for each vill. However, even the latter facilitate comparison. In each case, information (for example total numbers of taxpayers) has been noted. Carenza Lewis has demonstrated the potential for the use of taxation records in comparative settlement studies, albeit on a countywide scale,[194] and it is hoped that their use in the study of a more limited area may add to such data.

---

[189] E.g. PRO E 101/140/14, m.3.

[190] See C.C. Taylor, 'Three Deserted Medieval Settlements in Whiteparish', *WAM* 63 (1968), pp.39-53 and 'Whiteparish: A Study'.
[191] M. Jurkowski *et al.*, *Lay Taxes in England and Wales 1188-1688*, Public Record Office Handbook 31 (Richmond: PRO Publications, 1998), p.xxxviii.
[192] Jurkowski *et al.*, *Lay Taxes*, p.56.
[193] Jurkowski *et al.*, *Lay Taxes*, pp.xxxi, xxxiv.
[194] C. Lewis, 'Patterns and Processes' p.178.

Accounts and descriptions of officers

There are several types of account relating to Clarendon, of varying value to this study, and since they are scattered through document classes they are difficult to locate. Exceptions are the early fifteenth-century 'rabbit accounts' in SC6/1050 (Ministers' and Receivers' Accounts). This class also contains a series of ledgers of Clarendon underwood sellers running from 1341-60, and then again for the early 1420s (SC 6/1050/21 and 22). Another exception are the deer expenses found in E 101/593 and E 101/595 running from 1368-1618.

The rabbit accounts run from 1414-15, 1418-20, 1419-21, 1420-2, 1421-2 (duplicated in E 364/57, Exchequer Pipe Office: Foreign Accounts), and 1423-4 — rather brief snapshot of this element of the economy, but it nonetheless facilitates comparison of value and numbers taken. The documents tell us the names of those who compiled the accounts and of their supervisors (rather charmingly 'the supervisors of the king's rabbits'), who caught the coneys and when they were taken.

As to the deer expenses in Exchequer Accounts Various: Sheriffs Accounts (E 101/593-5), these are of little or no value. Each piece usually contains an indentured order from the Monarch (in French), commanding the sheriff to provide sustenance for the deer in Clarendon Park; occasionally an indenture between the warden of Clarendon and the sheriff; and the sheriff's account for expenditure on the deer. The amount spent is always £10 or less, which invariably amounts to 30 cartloads of hay, which the sheriff is often commanded to deposit in the grange. Anyone looking for detailed information will be sorely disappointed.

Exchequer: Pipe Office: Declared Accounts (E 351)

At the outset it was hoped, since this document class commences in 1500, that it might contain information on royal building works in Clarendon Park at the latter end of the timescale for this project. Unfortunately this did not turn out to be the case, although expenditure on Queen Manor, Rangers Lodge and the park pale is recorded for 1614 and 1617.[195] As usual in exchequer documents compiled by central government there is little topographical detail. However there is ample scope for comparison with other royal buildings, which may highlight reasons why Clarendon's development as an early modern park was arrested. There is much information, also, for 'deer houses' and lodges elsewhere, which can provide some context for developments at Clarendon. For example at Theobalds in 1625-6, deer houses were repaired by 'putting up proppes and mending the tyleing of them', and two lodges had 'outhouses and guardens'.[196] In 1623-4, Greenwich Park lodge also had

a garden and contained a gallery, the ceiling of which was being embellished.[197]

The other focus of interest in this class of documents is that royal progresses are set out in detail. In 1603-4, James I and the court came from Nonsuch through Basing and Farnham to stay at Winterslow, then Salisbury, then at Wilton House with the earl of Pembroke.[198] This must have been the occasion when James I hunted in Clarendon Park and ordered that the earl destroy the coney warrens.[199] The E 351s show also that in 1605-6 the court stayed at Farley and at Ivychurch, and that it visited Salisbury on 9 further occasions up until summer 1634-5.[200]

The Calendars of Rolls

It is appropriate to end this brief discussion with the calendars of rolls, whose value to a study such as this is almost unquantifiable - and certainly too wide-ranging to which to do justice to in one paragraph. The chancery rolls in particular (charter, close and patent) 'provide minutely detailed information about the countryside and people of England as viewed by the king's government'.[201] Yet the same could be said of many of the documents used in this study. Written sources have always been crucial to landscape studies. They are especially valuable regarding the organisation of estates and the ways in which their management changed over time,[202] the focus of the following chapter.

---

[195] PRO E 351/3385 *ff.*2, 7d.
[196] PRO E 351/3243.

[197] PRO E 351/3257.
[198] PRO E 351/3239.
[199] PRO E 178/ 4728.
[200] PRO E 351/3241.
[201] M.T. Clanchy, *From Memory to Written Record: England 1066-1307* (London: Edward Arnold, 1979), pp.49-50.
[202] Astill and Grant, 'The Medieval Countryside', pp.1-2.

Chapter Two: Economy and Environment

Recent landscape studies have concentrated on the place of human agency rather than the physical environment.[1] However, economy can reveal much about the place of a given forest in the forest system as a whole, as both Rackham and Stamper have shown.[2] As such it must be the first port of call for any scholar attempting analysis of a forest for the first time, and no apology is made for its centrality in this study. Paul Stamper's work on the thirteenth- and fourteenth-century exploitation of Pamber Forest, Hampshire is particularly useful. In examining numbers of deer and trees ordered by the Crown, Stamper revealed shifts in royal policy from conservation to active exploitation of resources from the mid-thirteenth century,[3] and part of the purpose of this chapter will be to observe similar processes at Clarendon.

DEER

In view of Clarendon's exceptionally large medieval deer park, every aspect of cervine management deserves detailed discussion. But there was also a forest. Where archaeology comes into its own in the relict landscape of the park, documents are the key to understanding the forest, restoring more fully the wider medieval landscape. Interrelationships between Clarendon, Groveley and Melchet Forests (with part of Buckholt, Hampshire), which were administered together, can also shed light on medieval and later deer management.

The function of Clarendon Palace, too, is highlighted by taking the deer into account. Certainly fence month (*mensis vetitis*), from 20 June to 20 July, when deer were traditionally in fawn, was avoided even by that most frequent royal visitor, Henry III (1216-72). The significance of the seasonality of royal visits is discussed in greater detail in Chapter Three, but clearly the change from the late thirteenth century to summer rather than winter visits is noteworthy (see p. 27), probably equating with transformations in hunting practice.

The Palace in the Forest
The precise dates of deer seasons were influenced by local factors until comparatively recently. An inscription of 1713 in Rushmore Lodge, Cranborne Chase, stipulates that 'noe Buck be killed after Hollyrood-day [14 September] and noe doe after Candlemas [2 February] in each season'. However, later in the century bucks might be taken until 25 September, a date chosen in order to coincide with Shroton Fair and the first day of fox hunting.[4] Today the open season for stalking fallow bucks and red stags (the terms are species specific:

hereafter bucks and stags) is 1 August to 30 April, while that for hinds and all does (red and fallow/roe female deer) runs from 1 November to 29 February.[5]

Little is known of twelfth- and thirteenth-century hunting seasons, although a formal agreement of 1247 concerning the hunting of bucks in the Forest of Charnwood, Leicestershire, again terminated on 14 September (Holyrood Day), having commenced on 1 August. Holyrood Day is also generally given as the terminal date in the fourteenth century (that for roebucks ran between 1 August and 29 September). Bucks are in their best condition in August and September, just before the rut, and this was known as the season of fat (*tempus pinguedinis*), which the early fifteenth-century *Boke of St Albans* has as between 24 June and 14 September.[6]

Both Henry II (1154-89) and Henry III seem to have avoided high summer at Clarendon, their sojourns invariably taking place during the doe season (*fermison*) in winter. Six of Henry II's eight visits that can be dated with certainty fell between November and March, the remaining two in April and June, suggesting that if hunting took place it was in the form of a cull — an aid to deer-management.[7] As today, male deer in the Middle Ages were probably over-hunted, and more likely to suffer higher mortality due to their habits and wider range. They will also emigrate (at least in the open forest), so that 'culling somewhat fewer males than females is a good rule to follow'.[8]

The season for wild boar coincided with that of the doe. Classic French hunting treatises place it from the Feast of the Holy Cross or from Michaelmas (14/29 September) to 30 November, which the *Boke of St Albans* extends to Candlemas (2 February).[9] Wild pigs were brought to Clarendon under Henry III (below, p. 27). However they were almost certainly present earlier, and the winter visits may have occurred in order to take advantage of this, although from what we know of Henry III it is difficult to imagine him hunting boar — to Gaston Phoebus the most dangerous animal in the world.[10] Moreover, as with most medieval kings there is no record of Henry actually hunting in person and the many orders to forest wardens

---

[1] See Gerrard, *Medieval Archaeology*, p.228.
[2] Rackham, *The Last Forest*; Stamper, 'Pamber'.
[3] Stamper, 'Pamber', p.51.
[4] T.W. Wake Smart, *A Chronicle of Cranborne and the Cranborne Chase*, 2nd edn (Wimborne: The Dovecote Press, 1983), pp.132, 141.

[5] J. Clifton-Bligh and D. Griffith, *Lowland Deer Management: A Handbook for Land Managers* (Fordingbridge: British Deer Society, 2000). p.61. Male roe deer are also bucks, although they are clearly delineated from fallow in medieval documents (*damus* and *capriolus*). The term 'roebucks' is used here.
[6] D. and N. Chapman, *Fallow Deer* (Machynlleth: Coch-y-bonddu Books, 1997), pp.48-9; J. Cummins, *The Hound and the Hawk: The Art of Medieval Hunting* (London: Weidenfeld and Nicholson, 1988), p.33.
[7] For Henry II see R.W. Eyton, *Court, Household & Itinerary of King Henry II Instancing Also the Chief Agents and Adversaries of the King in his Government, Diplomacy, and Strategy* (London: Taylor and Co., 1878).
[8] Clifton-Bligh and Griffith, *Lowland Deer Management*, pp.46-7.
[9] Cummins, *The Hound and the Hawk*, p.97.
[10] Cummins, *The Hound and the Hawk*, p.96.

in the thirteenth-century Liberate and Close Rolls requiring them to admit to their bailiwicks the King's huntsmen attest that most hunting was done by professionals. [11] Nevertheless, doe-culls would have provided a sense of occasion and supplied the resident court with a ready source of venison, even if they were chiefly a spectator sport.

Over the course of his reign, Edward I (1272-1307) spent 26 days at Clarendon in January and February, but a full 40 between early August and September 10 — the buck season. This is by no means decisive evidence that Edward was any more a hands-on hunter than his predecessors, as his winter visits attest. But in the summer he stayed longer, and Trivet claimed that stag-hunting was the king's favourite sport and that he hunted in person, preferring to use a sword rather than a spear. [12] The new trend might explain some of the features in the park and forest dating from this time, including the trenches (*trenchia*) made in Clarendon Park and elsewhere from the beginning of the reign. [13] Those at Clarendon, dug *c*.1276, predate the Statute of 1284 which prescribed that strips of open land be made alongside tracks in order to give travellers a sense of security, [14] and they may result at least in part from altered hunting preferences and the need to manage deer alongside woodland resources. The advantages of open spaces in woods in which deer can be seen and controlled is slowly becoming acknowledged today, and wide rides are increasingly encouraged. [15] The trenches would have allowed hunters to get behind deer and drive them at speed towards the launds in the case of bow and stable hunting (below), they would also have lent themselves to hunting *par force de chiens*, which involved seeking in woodland the finest specimens available, chiefly of stags but sometimes of bucks, by sight and with specialized dogs. [16] Either way, the trenches represent increased use of the wider landscape as far as deer hunting and management were concerned. Certainly hunting fallow on horseback became popular through the fourteenth century, [17] and this would have necessitated a larger hunting area. Clarendon Park had now become more definitely a hunting landscape.

It is significant that the change, from the late thirteenth century, to predominantly summer visits went in tandem with increased manipulation of the landscape. Even in bow and stable hunting, used for both bucks and does and more suited to deer parks, the landscape was best well marked out. Kill-sites were planned beforehand, and the terrain governed the position of the many archers (the

stand), the 'stable' (beaters) and veuterers (dog-handlers). This form of hunting, a clear signifier of status in view of the sheer numbers of hunt servants involved, developed into the deer coursing of the sixteenth and seventeenth centuries, when both stable and stand became permanent, physical structures.

A similar development can be seen in the documents sent out to wardens authorising the entry into their forests by the king's huntsmen. Under Henry III and Edward I, little detail is given apart from the number of deer the huntsmen are expected to take, and (occasionally) instructions for subsequent treatment of the venison and where it should be sent. For example in November 1255, the warden of Clarendon was ordered to admit Philip and Richard de Candover to take 30 hinds from Groveley Forest, after which the venison should be received by the sheriff, salted down and kept in safe custody. [18] In the last quarter of the thirteenth century, orders become slightly more informative concerning 'the formal pageantry of the chase'. [19] In December 1275, the warden was to admit Henry de Candover to Clarendon Forest to take 20 does and to 'aid and counsel him in so doing, as the king has sent with him certain of the king's yeomen to take the said does'. [20] But suddenly, for a short time between *c*.1312 and *c*.1316, there is a sudden explosion in detail which parallels the concern with etiquette in hunting procedure displayed in fourteenth-century hunting-manuals. For example:

To the sheriff of Wilts. Order to pay to the king's yeoman John Lovel, whom the king is sending with two berners, *four* veutrers, *24 running* daemericii *dogs, a* bercelet *and 16 greyhounds to take fat venison in the forest of Claryndon ,his wages during his stay in his bailiwick, to wit 12d. daily and 1½d. daily for each of the* berners, *2d. daily for each of the* veutrers, *and ½d. daily for each of the dogs, greyhounds, and the* bercelet, *delivering to him salt for the venison and carriage for the same to Westminster.* [21]

Suddenly, the number of deer to be caught is less of an issue than the hierarchy of dogs and staff involved. This runs in tandem with increased delineation of hunting landscapes, particularly the enlargement of parks under

[11] Rackham, *The Last Forest*, pp.51-52.

[12] M. Prestwich, *Edward I*, 2nd edn. (London: Yale University Press, 1997), pp.6-7, 115.

[13] *CCR 1272-79*, pp.318, 334, 363.

[14] *CCR 1272-9*, p.318; Rackham, *The Last Forest*, p.92.

[15] R. Prior, *Trees and Deer: How to Cope with Deer in Forest, Field and Garden* (Shrewsbury: Swan Hill Press, 1994), p.54.

[16] See Cummins, *The Hound and the Hawk*, pp.33-5.

[17] Chapman, *Fallow Deer*, p.184.

[18] *...Et mandatum est vicecomiti Wiltes' quod illas bissas ab eis recipiat et eas saliri et salvo custodiri faciat donec rex aliud inde preceperit. Et custum salicionis illius, cum rex illud sciverit, faciet ei allocari...*(CCR 1254-6, p.236).

[19] Rackham, *The Last Forest*, p.53.

[20] *CCR 1272-9*, p.261.

[21] *CCR 1313 – 18*, p.5 (1313). *Daemericii* are buckhounds (*dami* – fallow deer), a bercelet was probably something like a beagle, a berner was probably the man or boy charged with feeding the dogs, and the *veutrer* (fewterer) was originally in charge of the *veltre* – a breed of dog which hunted bear and boar, a greyhound or greyhound cross (Rackham, *The Last Forest*, p.54; Cummins, *The Hound and the Hawk*, p.12; A. Rooney, *Hunting in Middle English Literature* [Cambridge: D.S. Brewer, 1993], p.168, M. Parsons, *The King's Sergeants* [New Milton: Leonard Michael Parsons, 1993], p.71).

Figure 13. Deer ordered from Clarendon Forest & Park (from Calendars of Rolls)

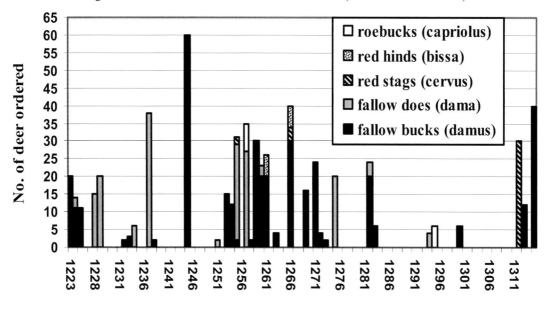

Edward II (1307-27), which will be referred to below.[22] For Clarendon at least such orders were invariably issued between March and July, in contrast to thirteenth-century examples, so that they may echo a shift from workaday doe-culling to more formalised buck-hunting in which members of the court could partake.[23]

But exactly how hunting worked in Clarendon and elsewhere in the Middle Ages is unclear. It has recently been claimed that deer hunting, at least on horseback, would have been impossible even in a park the size of Clarendon, stag hunts in particular requiring a straight 10 or 20 mile run.[24] But red deer do not seem to have been kept in Clarendon Park (below, p. 29), and there is no reason why fallow could not have been hunted there even on horseback.[25] For this the sloping terrain in the Launds would have been eminently suitable. The stable, stationed along the edges of woods or the ridges of valleys, guided the deer along a predetermined route, using the lie of the land.[26] A vivid description is given in the fourteenth-century *Sir Gawain and the Green Knight*, illustrating the merging of deer-management (here doe-culling), with bow and stable hunting. The deer, driven down a valley, attempt escape, but are turned back by the stable, lined up along the ridge:

Deer ran through the dale, distracted by fear,
Hastened up the high slopes, but hotly were met
By the stout cries of the stable, staying their flight.

They let through the antlered harts, with their
handsome heads,
And the brave bucks too, with their branching palms,
For this fine lord had forbidden, in fermisoun time
That any man should molest the male of the deer
The hinds were held in the valley with hey! and ware!
The does driven with din to the depths of the dale
Then the shimmering arrows slipped from the
bowstring...[27]

Park managers today continue to use sloping terrain to give advantage in live catch-ups,[28] although admittedly culling itself occurs in a much less spectacular fashion.

Under Edward III, a sudden change in seasonality of visits after 1333 from winter to summer may be explained by the need to restock and repair Clarendon Park before the court could enjoy buck-hunting. Orders were given as early as March 1327 for repairs, 'as the king understands that the hedges and palings are broken down in many places, so that his deer can issue from the park'.[29] Then in November 1328, immediately after a royal visit to the Salisbury area, an order was issued to fell timber in Chute Forest to enclose the launds at Clarendon 'because the enclosure about them is so broken down that [the king's] deer can get out...', followed by a similar mandate in February 1331. Nonetheless, the park was evidently well-stocked by this time, because in August 60 bucks were to be taken from

---

[22] Astill, 'Windsor', p.11.
[23] *CCR 1307–13*, pp.465, 494 (July, November); *CCR 1313–18*, pp.5, 157, 239, 355 (July, March, July, July).
[24] J. Phibbs, pers. comm.
[25] M. Small, pers. comm.
[26] Cummins, *The Hound and the Hawk,* pp.48, 55.

[27] Quoted in Cummins, *The Hound and the Hawk,* p.54. This type of hunt was, significantly, called 'king's hunt' in the *Master of Game*, written between 1406-13 (Rooney, *Hunting in Middle English Literature*, p.166), perhaps because of its ubiquity in royal parks.
[28] M. Small, pers. comm.
[29] *CCR 1327-30*, pp.269, 18.

Figure 14. Deer ordered from Groveley Forest (from calendars)

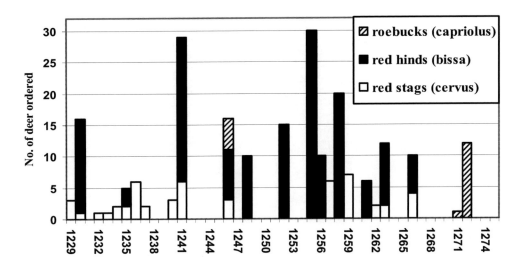

'the park and laund'.[30] Presuming that some kind of management plan was followed rather than an indiscriminate kill, and providing that the aim was the maintenance of herd numbers, a cull of 60 bucks produces a roughly-estimated spring population of at least 750 fallow, prior to births (which might be expected to add a further 150 animals to the total).[31] This was a time of remodelling as well as of repair, including a new pond dug by 1335, perhaps a necessity given the numbers of deer indicated.[32] This said, fallow are not attracted to water in the same way as are red deer. Nor do they depend on its supply to the same extent, getting most of the moisture they need from dew and feeding.[33]

Deer Species at Clarendon
There is little doubt that from at least the early thirteenth century Clarendon Park and forest were stocked exclusively with fallow, so that there are good grounds for thinking that the deer population in the forest came originally from the park. Figure 13 shows orders from the calendars of rolls for deer to be taken in Clarendon Forest and Park. Almost all are fallow, the 30 red stags ordered in 1312 from 'the Forest of Clarendon' being a notable exception. A few red deer *are* mentioned in Clarendon Forest in the Middle Ages, invariably in its woods. A stag was killed in Bentley Wood in 1249 and another in 1327; two hinds were taken in 1304 and *c*.1370 in Houndwood and Westwood respectively, and the forest eyre roll of 1488 mentions one hart among

warrants for 121 does and 21 bucks in the period from 1470-88.[34] However the 1312 figure is so anomalous that it is likely that the red deer in question actually came from Groveley as part of the 'Forest of Clarendon'. Groveley, heavily wooded and devoid of settlement, would have suited red deer, and indeed Figure 14, showing deer ordered from Groveley recorded in the calendars, reveals that that species predominated.

Figure 15, a graph of information concerning deer species from both the calendars and forest-related sources (*i.e.* illegally as well as legitimately taken), reinforces these conclusions. Peaks caused by the forest eyres of 1256-7, 1262-3, 1330 and 1355 are evident, and actual numbers poached are likely to have been far higher than indicated. Nevertheless, the comparative data are illuminating, and it is hard to argue that Clarendon possessed anything less than a preponderance of fallow.

It is noteworthy that recorded figures for roe deer, although miniscule, peak in the mid-thirteenth century and around 1300. A universal late medieval disdain for the species has probably been overplayed due to its removal from the protection of forest law in 1338. Roe were classed as rascal by stag and buck hunters, chiefly because they hide in covert as long as possible, unlike red and fallow, which run well.[35] However they probably appealed more than other species to those hunting as individuals, as they do to today's stalkers. Indeed in medieval literature they are 'described with a greater approximation to affection than any other beast'.[36] Nevertheless, it is significant that orders for roe rise at Clarendon only when fallow were apparently scarce, for

[30] *CCR 1327–30*, pp.332, 329, 341; *CCR 1330–33*, p.185; *CPR 1330-34*, p.161.
[31] Based on *Cull Planning Maintenance Model: Fallow Deer*, designed by D. Griffiths and produced by the British Deer Society on the BDS Advanced Stalker Course, 18-23 November 2001, Bisley. The figures produced are as accurate as modern stalkers can achieve, but it must be stressed that they can function only as a rough guide.
[32] *CCR 1333-7*, pp.425-6. The pond is probably that which still exists outside Savage's Farm Cottage, on the basis of its location in the former launds, among other things (C. Gerrard, pers. comm.).
[33] Chapman, *Fallow Deer*, pp.109, 179; M. Baxter-Brown, *Richmond Park: the History of a Royal Deer Park* (London: Robert Hale, 1985), p.22.

[34] PRO E 32/198, m.17*d*; PRO E 32/207, mm.2, 3*d*.; PRO E 32/318, m.14; PRO DL 39/2/20, m.2. Interestingly, Margaret Baskerville (Bentley Wood History Society) has reported sighting red deer there in recent years.
[35] R. Almond, 'Medieval Deer Hunting', *Deer* 9, no. 5 (1994), pp.315-18 (p.316).
[36] Cummins, *The Hound and the Hawk*, p.88.

Figure 15. Clarendon: Deer Species 1220-1380

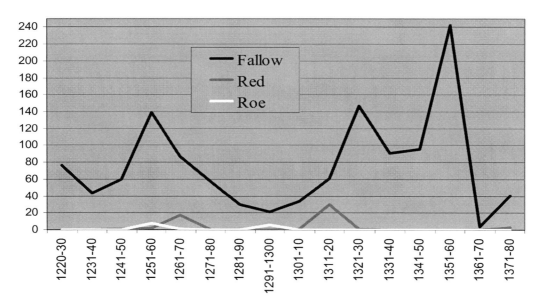

example six roebucks for the bishop of Salisbury in December 1295,[37] and that few were given as gifts in the thirteenth century even from Groveley, compared to the higher-status red.

Roe numbers appear anyway to have been low at Clarendon from the early thirteenth century. Tellingly, they are never mentioned as having been poached there, apart from one doe in 1262.[38] Bond has put the spread of coppicing forward as a reason for the species' apparent extinction in southern England by the fifteenth century, hazel in particular being an important part of its diet.[39] And coppicing was certainly going on at a major scale in Clarendon Park from at least the early fourteenth century and probably earlier. Clearly the roe's habits, especially its colonisation of hedgerows and other small areas of woodland, would have made it unwelcome in a compartmentalised park. In contrast 51 roe are recorded as having been poached and given as gifts from Groveley between 1246 and 1355. Indeed, in 1273 the king's surveyors declared 'there are many roe [in Groveley Forest] but other kinds of deer are scarce', and in 1331 there seems to have been an effort to stock the forest with fallow from Clarendon Park.[40]

As timber increasingly became the focus of forest management in the early modern period, a species of relatively uncontrolled deer would have been increasingly unwelcome. But roe could not have been entirely shunned by huntsmen, since an illustration from an early seventeenth century copy of *The Master of Game* depicts

them alongside the other species.[41] And if 'rascal' deer are taken to be roe rather than young or inferior deer,[42] they appear to have been widespread at sixteenth-century Clarendon. From November 1572 to April 1573, 237 'rascall' deer were reported dead in the park, including 62 in the laund.[43] This number would be high even today when roe have colonised Clarendon Park to the exclusion of all other species. Nevertheless the parliamentary surveyors of 1650 estimated that there were 3,000 deer 'of severall sorts' in the park (953 'of several sorts' were noted in Windsor Great Park), and that eighteenth-century writers spoke of roe as 'formerly abundant' suggests relatively recent memory.[44] But it is probable that bucks, does, fawns, prickets and sorrels etc. were the 'sorts' in question, rather than deer species *per se*. Although fallow, red and roe deer bones were identified in the 1961 excavations at the palace, Aubrey (1626-97) states that two of the quarter-keepers, Hunt and Palmer, could remember a time when there were 7,000 deer in the park, all fallow.[45] Their preponderance is corroborated by an offer made in 1637 by Thomas, Lord Arundel, to sell Wardour to Charles I (1625-49) because:

His majesty has about Salisbury great command of fallow deer in Clarington Park, in Cranbourne Chase, and in Groveley, yet he has no park of red-deer, nor

[37] *CCR 1288-96*, p.466.
[38] PRO E 32/199, m.10.
[39] J. Bond, 'Forests, Chases, Warrens and Parks', p.125.
[40] *Et multi sunt ibi capreol(i) set pauce alie bestie* (PRO C 143/31/B); *…facez p[re]ndre en n(ot)re dit Park duzz…deynis & dayines visz & les facez mettre en n(ot)re foreste de Gravele* (PRO E 32/214).

[41] J. Roberts, *Royal Landscape: The Gardens and Parks of Windsor* (London: Yale University Press, 1997), p.117, fig.116.
[42] D.J. Stagg, ed., *A Calendar of New Forest Documents: The Fifteenth to Seventeenth Centuries*, Hampshire Records Series 5 (Winchester: HRO, 1983), p.291.
[43] WRO 549/8, f.16.
[44] J. McWilliams, 'Clarendon Park 1600-1750: From Medieval Deer Park to Post-Medieval Estate' (unpub. BA dissertation, King Alfred's University College, Winchester, 1996), Appendix E, p.84; Roberts, *Royal Landscape*, p.118; R. Prior, *Deer Watch: Watching Wild Deer in Britain* (Shrewsbury: Swan Hill Press, 1993), p.99.
[45] McWilliams, 'Clarendon Park 1600-1750', p.39.

Figure 16. 1930s view from the north kitchen across the kitchen courtyard to the salsary. One of the factors identifying the building is the so-called 'blood and guts drain' visible at left of its southern wall. Venison was probably brought here from all the Clarendon Forests to be salted down. Reproduced from T. B.James and A. M. Robinson, *Clarendon Palace: The History and Archaeology of a Medieval Palace and Hunting Lodge near Salisbury, Wiltshire*, Society of Antiquaries Research Report 45 (London: Society of Antiquaries of London, 1988), pl. 22a.

any house of his own fit to entertain his majesty or the Queen.[46]

As is often the case, the very decisive evidence in the documents concerning the preponderance of fallow is not corroborated by the archaeology, which (until recently) revealed a bias in favour of red deer remains at the palace site.[47] These may well have come from outside Clarendon Forest proper, perhaps from Groveley, and been brought to the salsary, built *c.*1235-6 (see Figure 16), before being salted down and sent on to wherever the king wanted them delivered. Indeed the palace seems to have functioned almost as a venison factory at least for the Clarendon Forests and sometimes for a wider area, as an order in the Liberate rolls of 1241 to the bailiff of Marlborough to send all the venison in his keeping to Clarendon shows.[48] Other interpretations might be that

red deer were reserved for the royal table, or that what remains visible at the palace site is a late phase of archaeology, when red deer were more common. Here both the paucity of documentary evidence for much of the fifteenth century and the damage to contexts during the 1930s excavations is to be lamented.

Function of the Park

Many questions arise concerning Clarendon Park. Why construct such an enormous deer park and continue to order the bulk of the deer from the forest, apparently the case through the thirteenth and fourteenth centuries? The answer probably lies in terminology. Although the wording of many orders suggests that deer were taken from the surrounding forest (or forests), it is again likely that they came from the park. Figures 17 and 18 show deer taken from Clarendon's constituent forests 1223-1331 as recorded in the calendars and in forest-related documents, and it reveals significant deer-management at Clarendon. Hardly any animals were ordered from the Forest of Melchet, the main supplier of timber trees (below), and perhaps surprisingly, few were ordered from Buckholt.

Curiously, aside from the twelve male and female fallow sent to Groveley Forest in 1331, there are few records of live deer being sent elsewhere from Clarendon. In 1228, soon after the park was enclosed by Henry III, 'S. de

[46] *CSPD 1637-8*, p.55. This extract has erroneously been interpreted by recent writers as a 'project...to turn Clarendon into a royal "park of red deer"' (KACC I, p.62), probably due to the wording used by Grant (R. Grant, 'Forests', in *VCH Wilts, IV* [Oxford: Oxford University Press, 1959], ed. E. Crittall, pp. 391-457 [p.431]): 'a project was considered...to provide a "royal park of red deer", since Clarendon Park...contained fallow deer only'). This only shows the value of returning to the original sources, as Rackham advocates, so as not to write the 'pseudo history' of landscapes (O. Rackham, *The Illustrated History of the Countryside* [London: BCA, 1994], p.15).
[47] J. Mulville, pers. comm.
[48] *CLR 1240-5*, p.91. In 1259-60, a total of 50 Clarendon fallow bucks were ordered to be salted down and sent to the king at Westminster (*CLR 1251-60*, p.474; *CCR 1259-61*, p.91).

Malo Leone' was to have 15 live does from 'the new forest of Clarendon';

Figure 17. Deer ordered from the Clarendon Forests, 1223-1331

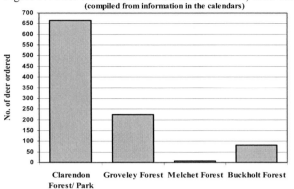

William Marshall, Earl of Pembroke, was to receive another 20 for his park at Hampstead Marshall in 1229, and in 1282 and 1294, William de la Cornere and Nicholas Morel were each sent four 'good does', suggesting they were to be used for breeding.[49] The next mention is in 1481-2, when 60 live deer were taken by the earl of Arundel, probably from the park, followed in the next year by a further 'six loads'.[50] Presumably at this time, after the demise of the palace, little hunting was taking place at Clarendon, and the deer were not needed there. Thus, despite its size, the park seems not to have functioned primarily as a breeding-ground, at least while the palace was in use.

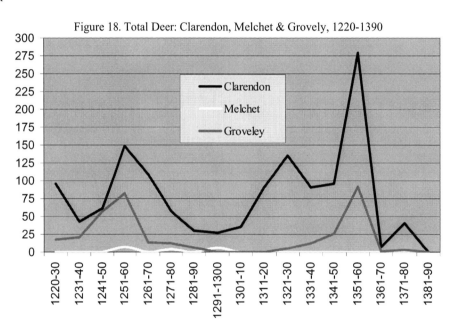

Figure 18. Total Deer: Clarendon, Melchet & Grovely, 1220-1390

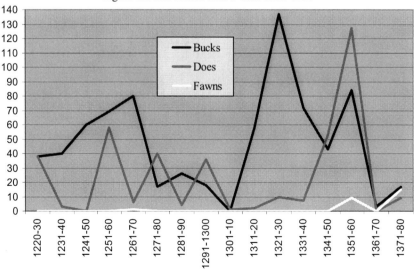

Figure 19. Clarendon: fallow deer 1220-1380

---

[49] *CCR 1227-31*, pp.25, 151; *CCR 1279-88*, p.171; *CCR 1288-96*, p.367.
[50] PRO DL 39/2/20, m.2.

Figure 20: Deer taken from Clarendon Forest, 1205-1375

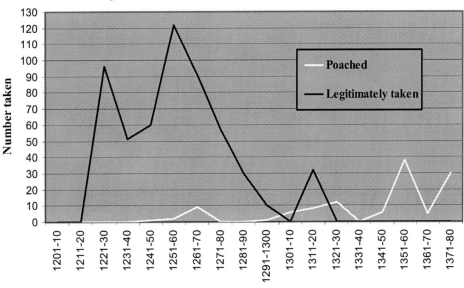

Figure 21: Deer taken from Clarendon Park, 1205-1375

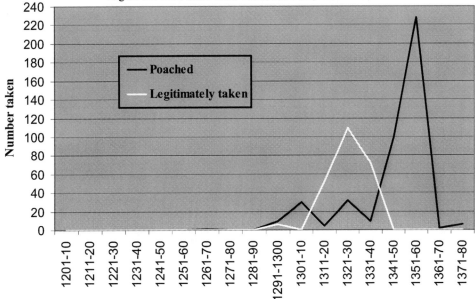

A breakdown by sex and age of fallow ordered and poached from Clarendon is illuminating (Figure 19). There is a significant rise in numbers of male deer taken in the early fourteenth century, confirming the emphasis on buck hunting indicated by the seasonality of royal visits. Indeed the peak of 138 bucks around 1325 is significant compared with the previous high point of 81 bucks *c*.1265, just over half of which were sent to Henry III as provisions during the Barons' Wars (1264-8).[51] Numbers then drop considerably *c*.1270–*c*.1310. Indeed the survey of 1273 states that the park was badly enclosed and that no game existed in Clarendon Forest except very old bucks, 'although it is reasonably well stocked with

[?does] and...fawns'.[52]

Deer Population: Trends Over Time
Figure 15 shows a sharp fall in numbers of deer ordered from Clarendon *c*.1265-*c*.1305. Alongside an unusually eager request for 12 roes from Groveley to be 'sent to the king with all speed and without fail' there are a few rare orders for deer from Melchet and for others from the 'foreign wood of Clarendon', *i.e.* outside the park pale, 'from wherever least damage may be caused'.[53] There is a noticeable and sudden rise also in bucks ordered from the park and forest of Gillingham from 1292-5,

[51] *CLR 1260-7*, p.231; *CLR 1267-72*, p. 90.

[52] *...de venacione dicunt non sunt ibi multi vet(er)es dami set rac(i)o(n)abiliter b(e)n(e) repleta est de damis & juventib(us) best(iis)* (PRO C 143/31/B).
[53] *CLR 1267-72*, p.202; *CCR 1268-72*, pp.491, 518,

suggesting that normal routes of supply were depleted.[54] Most significantly, although the king was at Clarendon in 1289, he was ordering that does be taken and salted down elsewhere before being sent on to Westminster.[55]

Clarendon, and the park in particular, may have been overhunted from the mid-thirteenth century, just as excessive harvesting of timber trees led to a lack of fodder (below, pp. 40-41) — a classic example of breakdown of a localised environmental chain. Deer-stocks may also have suffered badly during the Barons' Wars when the forest administration decamped to Salisbury Castle (see Chapter Five). Certainly gangs of poachers entered the park 'by day and by night' in order to hunt the king's beasts.[56] There were also legislative reasons for the shortfall. In 1270 a royal mandate was issued stating that any writ concerning vert or venison was to go straight to the Justice of the Forest rather than his subordinates (*i.e.* individual forest wardens), ratifying a general prohibition of the late 1260s on 'taking vert or venison from...[the king's] forests or woods within a certain period of time'.[57] But although the evidence reviewed here is in part the result of the prohibition, the legislation itself, born of a new concern to conserve forests as an asset, was a reaction to existing conditions.

Figures 20 and 21, showing numbers of deer taken legitimately and poached from the forest and the park, reveal the fall in deer numbers around the turn of the fourteenth century. The reduction of deer poached in particular suggests their numbers were genuinely low. In 1300, orders for bucks from Clarendon Forest continued to specify that they should come from 'outside the king's laund', suggesting that stocks in the park itself were to be conserved. But by 1313 there seems to have been some recovery, since bucks were to be taken both within and without the launds, and in 1315 a full 40 were to come from the same, more than any other forest or park listed.[58]

The figures bear out an increased emphasis on conservation in the late thirteenth and early fourteenth centuries. Orders dropped sharply from the turn of the century to *c*.1315 in particular, around ten years before peak exploitation of bucks, representing, presumably, the progeny of those cohorts. Numbers of does taken remained low until the rise in the 1350s representing the arrival of the eyre, and it certainly seems they were being left alone as a matter of policy. A similar pattern can be seen *c*.1235-45, on the face of it causing buck numbers to rise. But more does than bucks were taken through the 1270s-90s, causing an attendant fall in numbers of adult male deer.

After the Palace

In the 1488 eyre, fewer than ten deer are reported to have been taken without warrant at Clarendon, in stark contrast to that of 1355. This low figure is hard to credit, especially after the preceding long period of unrest and civil war, and the reason must be that for one reason or another trespasses of the venison were not adequately recorded; evidence, perhaps, of a nascent shift in perception as to the primary function of forests — or at least this particular forest. Yet Stagg notes that most of the proceedings in the 1488 New Forest eyre continued to concern deer, '[confirming that] the primary importance of the forest was still as a game reserve'.[59] Stagg observes also the many references to tree-felling in the New Forest, and surprisingly there is little emphasis on this at Clarendon either. Instead the majority of proceedings concern claims of rights in the forest and park. The impression is already one of a fossilised administrative landscape, and of claims being pressed concerning a locality that had effectively passed out of royal memory.

Another reason for the paucity of poaching in the 1488 eyre may be the disease prevalent around that date. 2438 fallow are reported to have died of murrain at Clarendon in 1471-3, so that the original head count must have been phenomenal.[60] Nevertheless, in 1484-5 'Lovell' (probably the royal huntsman of that name) and his men killed 100 bucks and 200 does, prickets and fawns, so that there must have been relatively quick recovery.[61]

Clarendon Park today contains 1,737 hectares, and an ideal number of fallow deer for a park of that size is 868 (one deer per two hectares). However, if the animals were allowed to breed without effective culling programmes or frequent hunting, which seems to have been the case especially after the palace went out of use, murrain would have been rife. Diseases such as TB and Anthrax do affect deer. However, it is likely that overstocking was responsible for the repeated incidences of murrain reported over the course of the late-fifteenth and sixteenth centuries. When deer populations are out of balance with the environment, body weight in particular is affected, and this can result in 'winter death syndrome', provoked by a mixture of cold and poor nutrition.[62] This is why deer-houses were erected in parks, whose launds might contain little vegetation able to provide shelter.

That there were considerable numbers of deer at Clarendon is attested by the attention given to the collecting of browsewood through the sixteenth and seventeenth centuries. Fallow eat mostly grass, and in

[54] E.g. *CCR 1288–96*, pp.232, 233, 236, 239.
[55] *CCR 1288-96*, p.15.
[56] E.g. *CCR 1261-4*, p.47.
[57] Young, *The Royal Forests of Medieval England*, p.76; *CCR 1268-72*, pp.5-6.
[58] *CCR 1296-1302*, p.353; *CCR 1313–18*, pp.5-6, 239.

[59] Stagg, *New Forest Documents: Fifteenth to Seventeenth Centuries*, p.ix.
[60] PRO DL 39/2/20, mm.2, 15.
[61] PRO DL 39/2/20, m.13.
[62] J. Birrell, 'Deer and Deer Farming in Medieval England', *Agricultural History Review* 40 (1992), pp.112-26 (p.117).

ideal conditions browse very little,[63] so that the collection of large amounts of browsewood yearly suggests either that it was considerably cheaper than hay (although this was supplied for winter up to at least 1617-18), or that there were too many deer for the launds — and the hay — to support. As Camden commented c.1590, 'the extensive park of Clarendon is well calculated for breeding and feeding deer',[64] and it seems likely that this was the park's main function in the early modern period in view of the considerable investment of the foresters' time represented by the annual cutting of browsewood.

Deer populations as a whole probably increased through the fifteenth and sixteenth centuries due to reduced pressure on woodland and the increased uptake of pastoral economies.[65] And what little evidence there is from 1500-1650 suggests that Clarendon Park carried a high deer population throughout. From November 1573 to November 1575, 852 were hunted and killed, including 340 on the day of Elizabeth I's (1558-1603) visit in 1574, while 75 died of murrain, and there were reckoned to be 7,000 sometime in the early seventeenth century. By 1650 3,000 fallow deer remained, by 1651 only 500, and by 1661 none at all.[66] Thus the terminal date of this study coincides, rather fittingly, with the last of the medieval deer.

RABBITS

The earliest mentions of rabbits at Clarendon, in the 1355 eyre, are made in conjunction with hares.[67] Hares still proliferate on the estate, and it is possible that a hare warren existed there long before the arrival of conies. Certainly a c.5km hare warren existed in the fifteenth century on land which had once been part of the adjacent Forest of Chute.[68] It has even been recently suggested that where warrens are mentioned in medieval documents, or where 'warren' appears in a field- or place-name, hares are referred to, since the term 'coneyger' was commonly used for rabbits.[69] At any rate, hares were probably common in the diet at Clarendon Palace, as they were at noble tables in general, and at least one bone probably from a brown hare (Lepus capensis) was found in the 1930s excavations.[70]

Although rabbits are not referred to in connection with Clarendon until c.1355, they were evidently at Groveley long before, since the 1330 eyre roll cites several cases of

rabbit poaching there going back, in one case, to 1289.[71] This is quite early as the first certain mention of mainland rabbits in England (in the royal park of Guildford) comes in 1237.[72] Although no pillow mounds have been noted in the Groveley area, a purpose-built warren is likely, especially since the forester of fee William Quentin and his underforesters were among the 'common malefactors and destroyers of...coneys' in question.[73] By 1330 the Quentin bailiwick comprised the east of Groveley Wood. In this area, the circular ditch and bank earthworks associated with a lodge can still be seen (SU 33 07), and perhaps the warrens were nearby. No details are mentioned in the 1330 eyre, although in 1354 Henry de Harnham was fined 20s. for taking rabbits with snares and ferrets, which suggests they were not kept in above-ground breeding hutches, or clappers.[74]

Location

The places from which rabbits were taken are more easily interpretable from the sources for Clarendon than for Groveley. Roger de Kyngeton, archdeacon of Salisbury, caught rabbits with his greyhounds in 'le Schapegore de Milford' c.1355, clearly near Sharpegore (later Shergall) gate south of Milford. It was reported in 1372 that John Cusyn of Salisbury had come 'into the field of Milford above Ashley's Bailey (asshlesball')...and placed there a snare called a hay in order to take the king's rabbits', while John Weston and William Parker also caught conies in the field of Milford (see Figure 22).[75]

Pillow mounds have not so far been identified inside Clarendon Park. But although 'the field of Milford' suggests common land, the fact that John Cusyn broke the king's paling to get to the rabbits indicates that they were kept inside it. Ashley Hill, inside the park to the west of Petersfinger, has been known by that name since at least the early post-medieval period,[76] and both coneygers and hare warrens were often situated on hills. Indeed attention has been drawn to this siting as a signifier of very high status (as were rabbits themselves, especially before the Black Death), enhancing the visibility of warrens in the landscape and thereby

[63] N. Pickering, 'Habitat Monitoring and Protection Techniques', BDS Advanced Stalker Course, November 2001, Bisley.
[64] McWilliams, 'Clarendon Park 1600-1750', p.26.
[65] Birrell, 'Deer and Deer Farming', p.124.
[66] WRO 549/8, ff.7-23d; KACC I, p.62; McWilliams, 'Clarendon Park 1600-1750', pp.39-40.
[67] PRO E 32/267, mm. 6d., 13.
[68] Bond, 'Forests, Chases, Warrens and Parks', p.145.
[69] J. Phibbs, pers. comm.
[70] James and Robinson, Clarendon Palace, pp.31, 263.

[71] PRO E 32/207, mm.4d., 4. In the latter case, 17 Edward I. Many pleas in this eyre go back to the time of 'Edward son of King Henry'.
[72] B. Short 'Forests and Wood-Pasture in Lowland England' in The English Rural Landscape (Oxford and New York: Oxford University Press, 2000), ed. J. Thirsk, pp.122-49 (p.137).
[73] PRO E 32/207, m.4d.; PRO E 32/215, m.1d.
[74] PRO E 32/267, m.13; For the clappers, see Short, 'Forests and Wood-Pasture', p.138.
[75] PRO E 32/267, m.6d; PRO E 32/271, m.6. The earliest mention of an 'Ashley' at Clarendon is in 1532, when Richard Ashley was deputy to Richard Lister the deputy warden (E 101/595/21/2 no.5). Interestingly, Lister was custodian of the rabbits in 1539-40 (E 372/385 [Wiltes, m.1d.]).
[76] KACC, Clarendon Park, Salisbury, Wiltshire, Archaeology, History and Ecology-English Heritage Survey Grant for Presentation, II (Winchester, 1996), fig. 9.1.

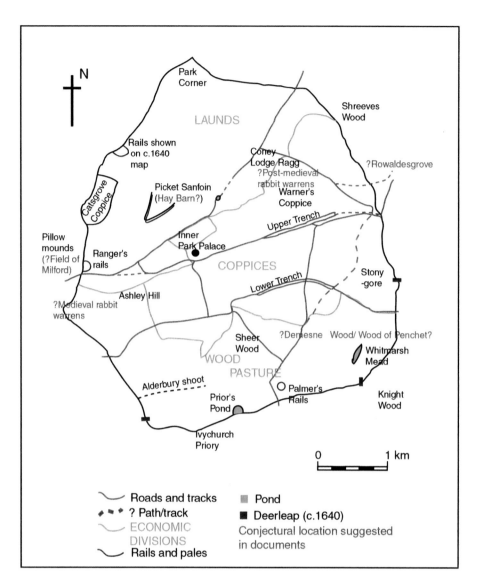

Figure 22. Clarendon Park showing aspects of economy and locations mentioned in text.
Adapted from KACC, *Clarendon Park, Salisbury, Wiltshire: Archaeology,*
History and Ecology–English Heritage Survey Grant for Presentation II,
English Heritage Project Number 1750 (Winchester, 1996), figs 8.1, 9.1.

'demonstrating their owner's "ownership" of the territory in which they sit'.[77] Thus it may be no coincidence that Ashley Hill, on the same prominent scarp on which the palace sits (see Figs 22 and 23), is close to the main entrance to the park from Salisbury.

Today's Ashley Hill Field, directly south of Ashley Hill itself, is adjacent to the site of the old Shergallgate. Alternatively, pillow mounds survive just outside the park at Burroughs Hill (SU 29 16) opposite Milford, so that this may have been the field in question, the rabbits paled in within it. Coneygers were sometimes enclosed, primarily to prevent escapes, and when the abbot of Keynesham received the right to construct a rabbit warren

in Filwood Chase his first act was to construct the stone wall that would surround it.[78] Either way, it appears that the south-western area of the park was associated with rabbits in the mid-to late-fourteenth century. This may account for the relative ease with which Thomas, canon of the priory of Ivychurch — also in the south-west of the park — was able to '[hunt] the king's conies within and without the bounds of the forest' (including, presumably, the park) *c*.1370.[79]

The first reference to an officer connected with rabbits comes with the appointment of Nicholas Ricoun as launderer in 1396, by which time they appear to have been firmly within the park pale. Ricoun was given

---

[77] D. and M. Stocker, 'Sacred Profanity: the Theology of Rabbit Breeding and the Symbolic Landscape of the Warren', *World Archaeology* 28 (1996), pp.265-72 (p.268).

[78] Bond, 'Forests, Chases, Warrens and Parks', p.146.
[79] *CPR 1367-70*, p.458.

Figure 23. Aerial view of Clarendon Palace in the 1930s looking south-west along the scarp in the direction of Ashley Hill. Reproduced from T. B .James and A. M. Robinson, *Clarendon Palace: The History and Archaeology of a Medieval Palace and Hunting Lodge near Salisbury, Wiltshire*, Society of Antiquaries Research Report 45 (London: Society of Antiquaries of London, 1988), pl. 8a.

there may have been more than one rabbit warren. There may have been one on the site of the present Warner's Copse, again sited on a scarp, and recorded as 'Warnerscopice' in 1477 and as Warner's Coppice or Warne Wood in 1640.[84] As KACC has pointed out, the 1650 field name 'Coney Lodge Ragg' (now 'Pumphouse') may also be significant. This is especially so in the light of James I's order of 1603 to destroy the 'game of conies' because the burrows were 'daungerous for his ma[tie] to ride after his delight and sporte',[85] since at this time hunting seems to have centred on the area adjacent to Coney Lodge Ragg, occupied by the Pady Course.

Clearly by the late sixteenth and early seventeenth centuries rabbits were not kept in entirely controlled conditions, as evidenced by a 1604 Warrant to Stay Process for Clarendon Woodspoils, in which it was stated that:

> There happened in Claringdon about viij or nine yeres past [c.1596] so extreme a drougth that the verie grounde being burnte the Conies most p(ar)te died, some fled the p(ar)ke, some gatt into the younge Coppice & did hurt, w[c]h never chanced before nor after that Sumer.[86]

A document of 1594 outlining the selling of a plot of thorns, significantly called 'the ragges', verifies this:

> There is much hurte and spoyle done this yere in her ma[ties] Coppice by reason of the greate number of Connyes remayninge in the saide Coppice and the Coppic(es) are like to falle in further decaye, if order be not shortlie taken for redresse.[87]

It appears, then, that Clarendon's early modern rabbits were kept in a designated area or areas in burrows, and that their numbers had increased enough to cause problems by the 1590s. The arrangements were probably similar to those noted by parliamentary surveyors in 1650 at Windsor Great Park, where the keepers had stocked 'a game of conies, the burroughs whereof extend themselves scatteringly over a great parte of the [Manor Walk]'.[88]

Procedure

A Bohemian traveller had reported seeing 'rabbits and hares without number' in Clarendon Park in 1465,[89] and the explosion in Clarendon's rabbit population may be linked with the demise of the palace. It may be postulated that the paucity, then cessation, of royal visits and the resulting drop in frequency of formal hunting

custody of the 'deer and coneys of the laund' as were all subsequent appointees to the post, and this may owe a great deal to the game law of 1390, which stigmatised further poaching by essentially privatising the animals themselves as well as the enclosures in which they were kept.[80]

Ricoun's appointment reveals that rabbits in the 1390s possessed a status equal to that of the deer. However by 1419 they are included as saleable commodities alongside trees and underwood in an inquiry.[81] The appointments of previous launderers, for example the earliest, that of Griffin Vaughan in 1324,[82] make no mention of rabbits (although neither do they mention deer, so that the existence of warrens at Clarendon earlier in the fourteenth century remains a possibility). The laund at this time stretched south at least as far as the present Rangers Lodge, so that possibly the same area of the park, around Milford, is in question.

The rabbit accounts for Clarendon, which run from 1414-24, also imply that there were warrens inside the park. For example in 1418-20 'Paid to William Hostaler of Salisbury...for taking of the king's rabbits *within* the park of Clarendon...22s.7d.', although later accounts, for example that of 1421-2, specify rabbits taken in Clarendon Park and its surrounds.[83] On the other hand

[80] *CPR 1391-6*, p.683; Perry Marvin, 'Slaughter and Romance', pp.247, 228-9.
[81] *CPR 1416-22*, p.270.
[82] *CPR 1324-7*, p.27.
[83] *Idem computan' in denar' solut Will(elm)o Hostaler de Sar(um) p(ro)...capc(i)o(n)e cunic(u)lor(um) Regis infra p(ar)cu(m)*

p(re)d(i)c(t)u(m)...xxij.s.vij.d. (PRO SC 6/1050/17). ...*infra p(ar)cum & p(re)cinctu(m) predict'* (PRO E 364/57, m.3).
[84] KACC I, p.56; PRO E 178/4728/I.
[85] PRO E 178/4728/A.
[86] PRO E 146/3/1, *f*.1.
[87] PRO E 101/140/14, m.1.
[88] Roberts, *Royal Landscape*, p.253.
[89] KACC I, p.56.

meant that the park was regarded more and more as a larder for game from the third quarter of the fifteenth century.

Yet the evidence for exploitation of rabbits at Clarendon from the mid-fourteenth century, and particularly Groveley from the late thirteenth, implies that this had been an ongoing process. It highlights a functional difference between the two forests, and represents a discernible shift in the purpose of Clarendon Park from exclusively a hunting reserve to a money-making concern. Rabbits were regarded as a pest by hunters, whose dogs might easily be distracted by them from the chase, and those who hunted them (primarily peasants according to medieval illustrations) were regarded with scorn. As Edward of York declaimed in the *Master of Game*, 'of conynges speke I not, for no man hunteth for hem but yit be *bisshunters* [fur-hunters], and thei hunte hem with ferettis and with long smale haies'.[90]

The early fifteenth-century rabbit accounts contain much information about the practice of catching conies. In 1418-20, Thomas Randolf of Salisbury, who served as rabbiter throughout the accounts until 1423, and John of Alderbury were employed for their capture, while William Hostaler of Sarum provided four hays (large nets) amounting to 180 fathoms. In this case 5s.4d. was paid to John Mason for four ferrets, the average number in the few documents available, the lowest being three and the highest nine. The ferrets were invariably provided with milk and sustenance by Alice Cornemonger — the 'Alice Hunt' mentioned in 1421-2 is almost certainly the same person.[91]

The procedure seems to have involved the employment of men to re-excavate the heads of burrows and lay nets, before the ferrets did their work.[92] Those paid to capture the rabbits were assisted by a launderer,[93] who would have had daily charge of the warrens and known where the most rabbits could be got, and the whole operation was overseen by two forest officers, probably verderers.[94] Once caught, the conies were skinned and gutted in various lodges, for which task candles were always purchased, presumably to provide light throughout the

night.[95] Indeed the job may have been a twenty-four hour one throughout, since ferrets and hays were seldom used together. Whereas ferreting was a daytime sport, taking rabbits with hays (known today as long-netting) occurred at night when the rabbits were feeding, involving 'only men and perhaps a dog or two'.[96]

Profits

Consumption of rabbits was a signifier of high status before the Black Death (1349). Once they began to turn feral, and with rising individual prosperity after the plague, they became fare for a wider public and were exploited also for their pelts.[97] By the early fifteenth century, the market had expanded and the records of ports such as Poole, Dorset, indicate significant exports of furs and skins.[98] The money made from the Clarendon warrens in this period is impressive (although wages and provisions invariably ate away most of the profits) as are numbers of rabbits involved (see Table 1). Indeed, that the revenue from the farm of conies amounted to £100 in 1495 suggests that very large numbers were involved — by 1455 the Dean and Chapter of Salisbury alone had received a tithe of four dozen couples (96 rabbits) annually.[99] At least, it is a sizeable amount compared with £3.6s.9d. for the warrens at Waltham in 1547,[100] even allowing for the progressive decrease in value of rabbits from the early fourteenth century.

Such profits as there were no doubt account for the farming out of the keeping of the king's rabbits from the later fifteenth century. In 1466, for example, the Earl of Arundel was granted for life 'all the rabbits within the forest and park of Claryngdon, alias Paunset...with license for him and his servants...to enter the forest and park and set engines to take the rabbits', for which he rendered 100s. yearly, although the launderer had to be supplied with wages and his winter and summer robes from the profits.[101] When William, Earl of Pembroke's appointment as forest warden, launderer and 'lieutenant of the conies within the said park' was ratified in 1553, the warrens realised £200 a year. He was entitled to take them with 'dogs, nets and other engines', rendering £6 p.a., as much as Edward Baynton, knight (launderer, 1537-8) used to render.[102] By 1609-10, John Stockman, a regarder in 1603-7, was being asked to pay the £6.10s he owed for the office, 10s. being the yearly entry fine. There must have been fierce competition, for if anyone

---

[90] Cummins, *The Hound and the Hawk*, p.236.

[91] PRO SC 6/1050/17; PRO E 364/57, m.3.

[92] *p(ro) foussur' Warenna Regi ib(ide)m...de misis c[r]isoribus* (PRO E 364/57, m.3).

[93] E.g. *Et sol' Joh(ann)i launder conducto ad advinand' & auxiliand' vendito [&] de...laboranti circa capc(i)o(n)em Cunic(u)lor(um)...* (PRO SC 6/1050/18). Richard Etton's grant for life as launderer 'and keeper of the deer and conies of the laund' was confirmed in 1417 and appears to have run until 1433 (*CCR 1413-19*, p.338; *CPR 1429-36*, p.263), so that John was probably among his staff.

[94] Thomas Ringwood, named as rabbit supervisor in 1419-21 was relieved of his office as verderer in 1436 due to illness and old age, and Walter Shirley, mentioned in the same account, was pronounced 'not fit' to continue in the office in 1424 (PRO SC 6/1050/8; *CCR 1435-41*, p.74; *CCR 1422-9*, p.91).

[95] E.g. *Solut' p(ro) xij li candel(orum) empt' & expendit p(er) div(ersi)s noctes tam tempore ext(ra)ct(i)o(n)is visc(er)um cunic(u)lor(um) infra logeas p(ar)ci p(re)d(i)c(t)i* (SC 6/1050/19).

[96] Cummins, *The Hound and the Hawk*, p.237.

[97] James and Gerrard, *Clarendon: A Royal Landscape*, forthcoming.

[98] Bond, 'Forests, Chases, Warrens and Parks', p.145.

[99] KACC I, p.56; Parsons, *Pancet*, p.65.

[100] *CPR 1547-8*, p.245.

[101] *CPR 1461-7*, p.512; See *CPR 1476-85*, p.327; *CCR 1476-85*, p.262, concerning John Shorter's appointment as launderer, 1482.

[102] *CPR 1547-53*, p.276; PRO E 372/385 (*Wiltes*, m.1d.).

	Received	Wages etc.	Profit	No. recorded	Individual rabbits
1418-20	£24.16s.	£16.21s.½d.	£8.14s.2½d.	82 dozen, 4 brace	992 rabbits
1419-21	£27	[14]s.2½d.	£24.5s.9d.	90 dozen, brace	2160 rabbits
1420-2	£19.19s.6d.	£17.3s.6d.	£2.16s.	74 dozen, 5 brace	898 rabbits
1421-2	£18.6s.	£17.8s.4d.	17s.8d.	61 dozen, brace	732 rabbits
1423-4	£11.2s.	?	?£11.2s.	37 dozen, brace (includes Groveley)	888 rabbits

Table 1: Summary of Rabbit Accounts for Clarendon Park and surrounds.[*]

[*] From PRO SC 6/1050/17, 18, 19, 20, 22, m.1, E 364/57. The 1414-15 account (PRO SC 6/1050/14) is illegible.

bid more, John was to put up an equal amount if he wished to retain the franchise.[103]

Decline

Stockman was farmer of the conies from 1596, and along with Henry, late Earl of Pembroke (d.1601) was the subject of an interrogatory *c.*1612 which aimed to ascertain the nature and extent of the losses occasioned by the destruction of the Clarendon warrens *c.*1603.[104] The coneygers may have been regenerating by this time, as the pipe roll of 1609-10 optimistically mentions 'all and singular rabbits then being or thereafter present by breeding or appearing within the park'.[105] The questions in the *c.*1612 interrogatory concerned the leasing of the custody of the warren to either Stockman or the earl of Pembroke; whether the warrens were destroyed; whether they were destroyed by James I's command and if not by whose; and what yearly loss the earl had suffered due to their destruction. The four respondents, each of whom had known the park since their youth, included John Fussell, quarter-keeper, and William Phillipps, mayor of Wilton. Most had heard of the lease — according to the mayor 'a lease [by Elizabeth I] to John Stockman to the use of the earl of Pembroke' — and agreed that the warren was destroyed at the king's command because the burrows were 'daungerous for [him] to ride after his delight and sport' and for the 'increase and preservation of the deer'. Although none could provide a figure, they all agreed that the earl had 'suffered great loss'.[106] In fairness to James I, the above-mentioned references to damage to wood-crops in the 1590s indicates that the rabbit population had got out of control — even allowing for the foresters' concern to avoid blame.

PIGS

In the mid-thirteenth century, Clarendon Forest appears to have been well-stocked with pigs. The first mention is in September 1244, when a full 300 of the bishop of Winchester's swine were sent to be fattened there to be 'kept by sure keepers' before ending up in the royal larders at Westminster in time for Christmas.[107] But a 1248 order to the forest warden to agist all pigs and prevent them from routing (*ne foyneare possint*) by fitting them with nose-rings need not mean that numbers were out of control, since in the following year, 6 boars and 8 sows were commanded to be sent to Clarendon from the Forest of Dean. The male to female specification suggests re-stocking rather than fattening for the table, however, and these were probably wild pigs brought in for the hunt, by this time largely confined to the Forests of Pickering (Yorkshire) and Dean.[108]

Although Rackham has it that by the mid-thirteenth century wild pigs were almost extinct in England, Bond cites references to a wild boar taken at Bishopstoke (Hampshire) in 1355-6, four more in Iwerne Wood, Cranborne Chase, in 1456, and to their presence in Savernake Forest as late as 1539-43.[109] However, wild swine were kept in parks into the early modern period,[110] and it is possible that these were escapees. Bond has stated also that wild pigs were still present into the fourteenth century in Clarendon Forest — presumably the descendants of Henry III's imported boars and sows. But again, it is never easy to tell whether fourteenth-century documents refer to the forest or the park, and it is possible that they were kept in the latter, where the traditional connotations of bravery associated with boar-hunting noted by Rooney would have imbued their observers with an aura of martial chivalry.[111] If so, however, the exercise appears to have been short-lived. The only other reference to any kind of pig (as opposed to pannage) at Clarendon in the calendars — a fact interesting in itself — refer to those of the prior of

[103] PRO E 101/542/21;...*si aliquis al(ius) plus denarii voluer p(er) intro p(er) annu(m) ffraud vel malo ingenio q(uo)d tuc idem Joh(an)nes tale p(er) eadem soluer teneat si custodi sive ffirma tener volent sup(ra)dict(a)...*(PRO E 372/455 [*Item Wiltes*]).

[104] PRO E 372/455 (*Item Wiltes*); PRO E 101/595/41/5 and 6; PRO E 178/4728/B.

[105] *Johannes Stockman gen. deb(et) vj. li. x. s. p(er) annum de custodi sive ffir(a) omn(ium)(et) singulor(um) cunic(u)lor(um)...modo existen' sive impost(ero) [p]res[t]en' renovitu' sive emergen' infra p(ar)cu(m) de Claringdon* (PRO E 372/455 [*Item Wiltes*]).

[106] PRO E 178/4728/A.

[107] *CLR 1240-5*, p.266; James and Robinson, *Clarendon Palace*, p.30.

[108] *CCR 1247-51*, pp.88, 265; Rackham, *Illustrated History*, p.19.

[109] Bond, 'Forests, Chases, Warrens and Parks', p.126.

[110] Rackham, *The Last Forest*, p.45.

[111] See Rooney, *Hunting in Middle English Literature*, pp.78-85. Certainly a place called 'La Borheytes' was recorded as within the park in 1320-1 (PRO E 32/207. m.3*d*).

Ivychurch in 1249 and 1252.[112] Further mentions are limited to forest eyre rolls and related documents, and it must be concluded that Clarendon pigs were never 'a local specialty' based on the forest, as Rackham has found for Hatfield.[113]

The forest documents show that, once again, there appears to have been more scope to operate against the tenor of the Forest Charter in Groveley than at Clarendon, at least in terms of hiding the sometimes obvious physical evidence. In the eyres of 1330 and 1355, the parson of Great Wishford, Robert Cole and Henry de Haversham were indicted for raising pigsties large enough to keep 42, 20, and 12 swine respectively.[114] Apart from that of the Prior of Ivychurch, the one example of a pig-house in Clarendon was relatively well-camouflaged, being built c.1355 by William Randolf, forester of fee, 'inside a great oak' large enough to shelter 12 pigs.[115]

This is not to say, however, that Clarendon was devoid of pigs in the fourteenth century. In 1355 it was alleged that both Giles de Beauchamp, forest warden, and Thomas de Bitterley, his deputy, kept 20 pigs each in the park at pannage time, to the detriment of the pasture of the king's deer, and John de Tudworth, William de Pitton, and John le Porter were accused of keeping a further 60 between them there in the same eyre.[116] Undoubtedly 100 illegal pigs in the forest is a great number, but the accusations should be viewed with caution, since Beauchamp and Bitterley had been disgraced and were accused of myriad forest offences.

For the fifteenth century, little evidence survives. However in 1423, the prior of Ivychurch released to the king his right to keep, among other animals, '20 swine and the issue of those swine' in a pasture.[117] Nothing more is heard until 1488, when William Barry was presented for having 4 swine in the park, John Wilson of Winterslow for 8, and the prior of Ivychurch for 6,[118] a situation which had probably proceeded unchecked since the demise of regular forest courts very early in the century, exacerbated by the palace having effectively gone out of use.

Pannage
Pannage figures for Clarendon are hard to come by before the 1360s, again probably due to the lack of mast in the forest and park. However pannage exits in a Wiltshire inquisition of 1371-5 (see Table 2) afford comparison

with other forests. The exits at Clarendon for 1373 amounted to 12s.2.½d., lower than any forest recorded except Morpeth, at 5s.2d, and Alice Holt, whose exits run over two years. The highest was the forest of Windsor, at 63s.7d., again over two years, as was Buckholt, also quite high, at 41s. Therefore of the Clarendon Forests listed, Melchet was the highest in terms of pannage exits at 27s.5d., followed by Buckholt (averaged out over two years at roughly 20s. p.a.) with Clarendon the lowest, signifying perhaps that domestic pigs were not welcome in a hunting forest. For the thirteenth century, agistment and pannage figures are much higher, suggesting that pigs and other animals had once been more significant in the economy (Table 3). This may equate with the greater use of the forest and particularly the park, for buck-hunting from the late thirteenth century, as much as from timber (and mast) depletion.

1374 and 1375	PRO E 32/285	Windsor	63s.6d.
1374 and 1375	PRO E 32/285	Alice Holt	25s.
1374 and 1375	PRO E 32/285	Buckholt	41s.
1373	PRO E 32/285	Clarendon	12s.2.1½d.
1373	PRO E 32/285	Morpeth	5s.2d.
1373	PRO E 32/285	Rutland	25s.2d.
1373	PRO E 32/285	Cleeve	62s.6d.
1373	PRO E 32/285	Rockingham	13s.4d.
1373	PRO E 32/285	Whittlewood	15s.9d. 20 marks (for 80 pigs in the forest)
1371	PRO E 32/271	Melchet	27s.5d.

Table 2: Pannage Exits taken from Forest Inquisitions

Agistment
The reason for the paucity of references to pigs at Clarendon through the remainder of the thirteenth and into the fourteenth century may be found in the agistment figures, running from 1246-67 and 1279-1333.[119] For Clarendon, the only years up to 1333 for which collections were made were 1246-7, 1248-52, 1253-4, 1256-7,1257-8, 1259-61, 1262-3, 1282-3, 1286-7, 1289-90 and 1294-5. For those when no agistment took place, the reason given is 'deficient mast' (*nichil pro defectu' pesson*').[120] This verifies findings concerning depleted stocks of mature trees, particularly oaks (below, p. 49), especially as agistment figures for Melchet follow a very similar pattern. In 1330 it was explained that there was no mast at Clarendon from 1298-9 to 1327 because:

---

[112] *CLR 1247-51*, p.269; *CCR 1251-3*, p.278.

[113] Rackham, *The Last Forest*, pp.85-6.

[114] PRO E 32/207, m.6; PRO E 32/267, m.13. A Robert Cole was acting-verderer for Groveley in 1338 and de Haversham was a Clarendon (and/or Groveley?) verderer and underwood-vendor c.1361-77 (PRO E 32/261; PRO E 32/318).

[115] *William Randolf fecit sibi unam porc(ariam) in uno gross(o) querc(o) in Claryndon a qua exi[er]unt doudeci(m) porci[s]'* (PRO E 32/267, m.13). Presumably most were piglets.

[116] PRO E 32/267, mm.7, 13.

[117] PRO E 32/279; *CCR 1422-9*, pp.75, 106.

[118] PRO DL 39/2/20, mm.16, 16d.

[119] PRO E 32/198, m.8; PRO E 32/199, m.4; PRO E 32/200, m.5; PRO E 32/207, m.12.

[120] PRO E 32/207, m.12.

1222-3	PRO E 352/33	Clarendon & Groveley	pannage & other exits (3 years)	£60
1223-4	PRO E 372/68	Buckholt	pannage	33s.
1249	*CLR 1247-51*, p.269	Clarendon	pannage	62s.
1252	*CCR 1251-3*, p.293	Buckholt	pannage	100s.
1252	*CCR 1251-3*, p.294	Groveley	pannage	35s.5d.
1255	*CCR 1254-6*, p.25	Clarendon Forest (wood of Panchet)	pannage	£9.8s.5d.
1255	*CCR 1254-6*, p.251	Melchet		29s.7d.
1263-4	PRO E 32/200	Clarendon Forest	pannage	£6.13s.9d.
1264-5	PRO E 32/200	Clarendon Forest	pannage	14s.4d.
1265-6	PRO E 32/200	Clarendon Forest	pannage	14s.9d.
1266-7	PRO E 32/200	Clarendon Forest	pannage	19s.4d.
1273-4	PRO E 159/48	Clarendon Forest	pannage	£12

Table 3: Pannage Figures, 1223-74

In the 27th year of Edward son of King Henry [1297-8], the lord king caused all oaks in the...bailiwick to be felled and sold so that there was no agistment in the aforesaid bailiwick throughout the aforesaid time.[121]

Similarly, there was no mast from the first year of Edward III to the sixth, so that 'the king ordered that no agistment should take place in that time'.[122] In contrast, not a single year's agistment was missed for Groveley in the same period from the last quarter of the thirteenth century, suggesting that the paucity of timber orders from that forest in the late thirteenth and early fourteenth centuries (see below, p. 49) was a matter of policy rather than necessity.[123]

Poor agistment figures were probably compounded by the enclosure of the park *c.*1317, followed by further prohibitions. In a document of 1330-1 delineating the extent of herbage for which compensation should be made to Giles de Beauchamp, warden, the Clarendon regarders stated that the herbage of Clarendon Park was worth nothing because 'subsequent to the enclosure of the...park, only deer are to be found there, and agistment of other animals has been prohibited'.[124] Similarly, *c.*1330 the jurors of a forest inquisition found that while pasture in Melchet was worth around 20s. per year to the Crown and that in Groveley was common pasture, in

Clarendon Park 'the king can take no herbage beyond the sustenance of his deer'.[125]

By 1330, the loss of agistment revenues had caused a knock-on effect throughout the landscape. In particular, an annual payment of 100s (£5) towards the lighting of Ivychurch Priory, customarily paid from the issues of the manor, had been owed 'for some time', during which the prior had evidently petitioned repeatedly to recover his losses. According to the forest officers, the situation had arisen because the king, in a parliament at Salisbury, had prohibited agistment in the park 'in order to have more ample pasture for his deer'. Giles de Beauchamp replied that there were no issues from which he could make the payment except £4 of rent of assize and the agistments of cattle that used to be made, 'extended...in the king's presence to £10 yearly', and that this sum had customarily gone to the keepers. Besides, he went on, the king had promised the £10 to him as recompense for the loss of agistment returns, so that he could put it annually towards repairs to the park pale. Eventually John Mautravers, justice of the forest south of Trent, was ordered to pay the arrears to the prior, and to find the 100s. henceforward from sale of underwood 'in the forest now or to be made for this cause'.[126] The episode marks a change in land use in Clarendon Park from a mixed, wood-pasture economy to one devoted to deer and trees which may have amounted to wholesale enclosure.

---

[121] '*D'ann' eiusd(e)m R'. xxvij & ab illo anno usq(ue) annu(m) rr. E t(er)cij post co(n)questu(m) p'm'u n(ullo) p(ro) def(ec)tu' pesson' eo q(uo)d p(re)d(i)c(t)u anno xxvij° Reg' E' fil' R' Henr' [20 Nov 1298-99] d(omin)us Rex p(ro)s't[?ni] & vendidi fecit om(n)es querc' de eadem balli'a ita q(uo)d n(u)ll(u)m agistamen[to] in ead(e)m balli'a toto temp(or)e p(re)d(i)c(t)u' (PRO E 32/207, m.12).*
[122] PRO E 32/207, m.12.
[123] In 1328, the king ordered that no agistment should take place in Clarendon Park either, but that areas should instead be given over to coppicing (*CCR 1327–30*, p.341), although elsewhere it was claimed that this was done for the preservation of the deer. Either way, agistment at Clarendon is never again referred to in the calendars.
[124] PRO C 47/11/8/10.

[125] *Dicunt q(uo)d in p(ar)co de Clarendone nichil potest Rex cap(er)e ultra sustentac(i)o(ne)m ferar(um) d'm' R. q' nu(n)c su(n)t Dicunt eadem q(uo)d pastura in melchet vale[n]t p(ro) annu(m) xx.s. p(er) estimac(i)o(ne)m pastura de Grovele est co'i's & nullius valoris ad p(re)s'iom d'm' Regis ut credunt (PRO E 32/215, m.2d.).*
[126] *CCR 1330-3*, p.7.

OTHER HUSBANDRY

Meadowland

Deer-expenses for Clarendon Park run from at least the 1360s to 1617-18, and although these show that 30 cartloads of hay were bought annually for £10 or less, it is never stated from whence the hay came. However it is probable that much of it came from Clarendon Forest, for — not surprisingly in a wood pasture economy — most allusions to land use involve meadow. These references may be misleading because the general distinction between 'meadow' as land principally mown for hay and 'pasture' as directly grazed by livestock is rarely clear cut, [127] but clearly meadowland was important in the economy.

The meadows at Clarendon seem to have operated by custom. In an assize of novel disseisin of 1249, William le Butler was accused of depriving Henry de Dun of common pasture after the hay had been lifted from William's meadow in Clarendon Forest. [128] Exactly where the meadow was is not stated. However, there were commons at Alderbury, Farley, Whaddon and Winterslow, as well as the 'king's meadow' in the parish of St Martin, somewhere near Milford, [129] and an area of common meadow and pasture, which seems to have centred on the king's demesne wood, at Whitmarsh. The eyre roll of 1355 states that from 1340-50, Giles de Beauchamp had enclosed 5 acres in the park at ?Whitmarsh ('Wynt[ur]usnissch'), and had grown hay there, and in 1355 the earl of March claimed the profit of 'a meadow in Clarendon Park, called Whitemerssh'. [130] This was almost certainly part of the land imparked by Edward II, which had included waste in Whitmarsh, and indicates possible confusion over its status after *c*.1317. As with most meadowland, this was on a floodplain, offering ideal conditions for the production of hay. [131]

Meadowland was an important element in the landholdings of Clarendon's forest officers, their acreage rising over time, particularly through the fourteenth century, before seemingly falling off again. For example Richard de Heyras held 3a. of meadow in Alderbury and John de Grimstead 4a in East Grimstead at their deaths in 1257 and 1288 respectively. [132] In 1322, Robert de Micheldever's holdings as forester of fee, then under dispute, included 16½ acres of meadow in Laverstock, and in 1348 John de Turbeville, as guardian of the seven year old John de Grimstead, took delivery of 20a of meadow in Alderbury. [133] It can have been no accident

that the foresters held much of their evidently profitable lands around Milford and Laverstock, at least in the thirteenth century. An assessment for the fifteenth and tenth of 1591-2 records that the 553½ acres of pasture appertaining to the tithing of Milford was 'muche better' than that of Bishopstone (to the north-west) and that its meadows too were of very high quality. [134]

In general, the evidence presented here corroborates the noted trend for increased meadowland through the medieval period, although the relatively small plots involved suggest that the wide range of herbs, shrubs and browse in the wooded economy provided a longer grazing season in any case. [135] Thus in 1501, Robert Pippard held of the king in chief not only 20a. of pasture and 16 of meadow, but also 10a. of woodland and 20 of furze and heath, in Alderbury 'by fealty and a rent of 2s. annually for all services'. [136]

Agriculture

Records of crops grown in Clarendon Park are virtually non-existent. However Ivychurch had arrented 112 acres of waste in the forest near the priory by 1314, which they might enclose with a ditch and hedge and bring into cultivation, and in the 1355 eyre we hear that of the original 112 acres, 108 had been 'enclosed within the ditch of the aforesaid park'. [137] Whether they continued to cultivate the land is unclear, although in 1330 all 214 acres of old assarts taken into the park *c*.1317 lay fallow (*iacent frisc'*). [138] Nevertheless, crops were evidently still grown around the priory into the 1360s. When Thomas Grote, forester, came to attach a dog of John Staunton, servant of the prior of Ivychurch, John 'came within the prior's close with the said dog on a lead guarding his master's crops'. [139]

As for Clarendon Forest, most of the few medieval references to crops come in the form of land grants and customary perquisites. For example in 1255 Ivychurch Priory held an acre of land granted them by the forester James de Pitton in 'Apsfurlang', Pitton, on which crops were grown (*inbladacione*). [140] But the priory's manor of Whaddon seems to have supplied its corn in the following century. In 1361 the prior granted to the rector of East Grimstead, in addition to a sum of money, 'a bushel, well-measured, of good wheat, dry, clean and well winnowed, and of the best sort of their cultivation to be taken week by week out of their manor of

Archaeological and Natural History Society, 1939), p.109; *CCR 1346-9*, p.435.
[134] PRO E 178/2348.
[135] Williamson, *Shaping Medieval Landscapes,* p.165.
[136] *CFR 1485-1509*, p.323.
[137] *CFR 1307-19*, p.206; *It(e)m clam' h(ab)ere cent(u)m a duodeci(m) acr' de vasto foreste p(re)d'c'e ab antiquo s' & successoribus suis arrentat[is] quar(um) centu(m) & octo acr' infr(a) fossatu(m) foreste p(re)d'c'e inclus*. This is changed to 'within the ditch of the aforesaid park' later on the same membrane (PRO E 32/267, m.18*d.*).
[138] PRO E 32/208, m.1.
[139] *CPR 1367-70*, p.458.
[140] *CPR 1247-58*, p.455.

[127] T. Williamson, *Shaping Medieval Landscapes: Settlement, Society, Environment* (Macclesfield: Windgather Press, 2003), p.163.
[128] M.T. Clanchy, ed., *Civil Pleas of the Wiltshire Eyre, 1249* (Devizes: Wiltshire Record Society, 1971), p.41.
[129] *CCR 1247-1251*, p.313.
[130] PRO E 32/267, m.11; *CPR 1354-8*, p.198.
[131] Williamson, *Shaping Medieval Landscapes*, p.164.
[132] *CIPM* Edward I, II, pp.101, 416.
[133] R.B. Pugh, ed., *Abstracts of Feet of Fines Relating to Wiltshire for the Reigns of Edward I and Edward II* (Devizes: Wiltshire

Whaddon'.[141] By 1419, Ivychurch held fishery rights at Alderbury, rent from Mummeworth Mill, 5 acres of meadow in Milford and Laverstock, and one acre of several pasture at Sharpegore 'in Milford and Laverstock...between the prior's meadows called Sharpegoremede and Canonmede'.[142]

The forest eyre rolls show that much land in the forest was cultivated. For example in 1262-3, it was presented by the regarders that 9½ acres of old assart in Pitton were cultivated, and that the prior of Ivychurch's 7 acres of old assarts in Clarendon Forest were sown with grain and oats by warrant of the king.[143] By 1330 40½ acres of old assart were cultivated in Farley, 31 acres and 1 rod were sown in Pitton, 7 in Alderbury and 4½ in Winterslow. The plots in Pitton were small, with 10 people holding 1 acre or less, while only two men held comparably-sized plots in Farley.[144]

Cultivated purprestures were almost without exception located in Melchet rather than Clarendon Forest.[145] None at all were listed for the latter in the 1355 eyre, whereas in 1256 at least 5, amounting to 12 acres, had been cited. Three of these were in Farley, one (of six acres) in Dean, and the other in Pitton.[146] One must conclude that in Clarendon Forest, arable cultivation became less viable than elsewhere because the attitude of its royal owners compounded demographic decline.

The *Nonarum Inquisitiones* of 1340-1, recording the tax on corn, wool and sheep also contain useful information concerning agriculture at Clarendon. For the parish of Alderbury, it was estimated that the church possessed in demesne two virgates of arable land worth 10s. and that it received tithes of hay worth 60s. per year.[147] West Grimstead parish was assessed at £4.10s. and the parson held 17 acres of land in demesne worth 3s.6d. a year. The church also had pasture (*partum*) there, a tithe on hay worth 20s. per year, and tithes worth 6s.8d. on linen, hemp, ?dairy produce (*albivitulorum*) and chickens,[148] suggesting Grimstead's agriculture was more varied than Alderbury's. Nevertheless, neither entry mentions pasture of oxen, pigs, sheep and lambs, valued at 6s.8d. for the neighbouring parish of Figheldene, outside the forest.[149] Indeed, sometime after 1330 an inquisition into the state of the forest stated that although the foresters had pastured their animals in the demesne of Clarendon

to the detriment of the king's deer, no other horses or cattle existed in Clarendon Forest, no doubt because of the restrictions on agistment mentioned below (**p. 76**).[150] Each is a sure sign that Clarendon was reserved as a hunting forest, due in turn to the court's regular visits to the palace. As Lord Admiral Howard explained to Elizabeth I of hunting reserves generally in 1592:

Heretofore the herbage and pannage...have been reserved for the increase of the game, and the keepers are stinted to a certain number of cattle, because the grounds shall not be overlaid, and the feed be kept sweet, without which the deer cannot prosper.[151]

Animal Husbandry

The prominence of wool in the local economy was no doubt responsible for the highly irregular measure of admitting sheep to Clarendon Forest in the 1250s, precisely when their rearing was expanding rapidly in England.[152] Before this, even the de Milford foresters of fee could pasture all beasts except sheep and goats.[153] There are good reasons for this. Both fallow and roe are wary of sheep. As the duke of Wellington put it, 'the smell is ...one which they not only dislike, but which makes them feel insecure [because it]...lessens their ability to wind danger'.[154] Yet in 1258, Reginald de Drumar was allowed pasture of sheep for a term at Clarendon. It was stipulated, however, that they were to graze only where 'least damage' would be caused,[155] suggesting they were kept well away from deer, and probably also from wooded areas. It is unlikely that they would have been allowed into the park, and they were probably kept around Milford and Laverstock, especially as Drumar was to pasture them 'saving the right of Jordan of Laverstock', a forester of fee. No other Wiltshire forest seems to have admitted sheep at such an early date, despite the centrality of wool to the county's economy, and Clarendon's proximity to Salisbury may have been responsible for the concession.

---

[141] *CPR 1361-4*, p.163.
[142] *CIPM 1399-1422*, p.351.
[143] *et fu(er)u(n)t inblad' se[n]il de frum' & sem[t]* (PRO E 32/199, m.6).
[144] PRO E 32/207, m.7.
[145] For example the two acres of '*t(er)re arrabil' claus' ffoss' & basa haya quas Thom' Arnold... modo ten' & arrent'* in Landford (PRO E 32/267, m.15).
[146] PRO E 32/215. The six-acre purpresture in Dean and one of two acres in Farley are again reported as old purprestures in the 1330 and 1269-70 eyre respectively (PRO E 32/207; PRO E 32/200).
[147] *Nonarum Inquisitiones in Curia Scaccarii: Temp Edwardi III* (London: Record Commission, 1807), p.167. See also Jurkowski *et al.*, *Lay Taxes*, pp.43-6.
[148] *Nonarum Inquisitiones*, p.168.
[149] *Nonarum Inquisitiones*, p.172.

[150] PRO E 32/215, m.1.
[151] *CSPD 1591-4*, p.289. Howard was objecting (at length) to 'the demands of A.B.' for a lease to himself of the herbage and pannage of all forests, parks, warrens and chases (*ibid.*, pp.288-9).
[152] For example, the bishop of Winchester's flock had increased from 15,000 sheep in 1208 to 30,000 in 1259 (R.F. Treharne, *Essays on Thirteenth-Century England* [London: Historical Association, 1971]; Cox, *The Royal Forests of England*, pp.24, 44.
[153] Grant, *VCH Wilts*, p.430.
[154] C. Coles, *Gardens and Deer: a Guide to Damage Limitation* (Shrewsbury: Swan Hill Press, 1997), pp.67-8.
[155] *CCR 1256-9*, p.227; *Pro Reginaldo de Drumar'.- Rex concessit Reginaldo de Drumar' quod a festo Sancti Johannis Baptiste Proximo futuro usque ad finem duorum proximo sequentium habeat de gracia regis pasturam ad ducentas oves in foresta de Clarendon ubi ad minus dampnum regis eas habere poterit, salvo jure Jordani de Laverstok' et aliorum forestariorum regis ejusdem foreste. Et mandatum est Roberto de Stopham', ballivo regis de Clarendon', quod ipsum Reginaldum dictas oves in predicta foresta, ubi ad minus dampnum regis et minus detrimentum ejusdem foreste providerit, usque ad finem dicti termini habere permittat sicut predictum est* [Marlborough, 2 June 1258].

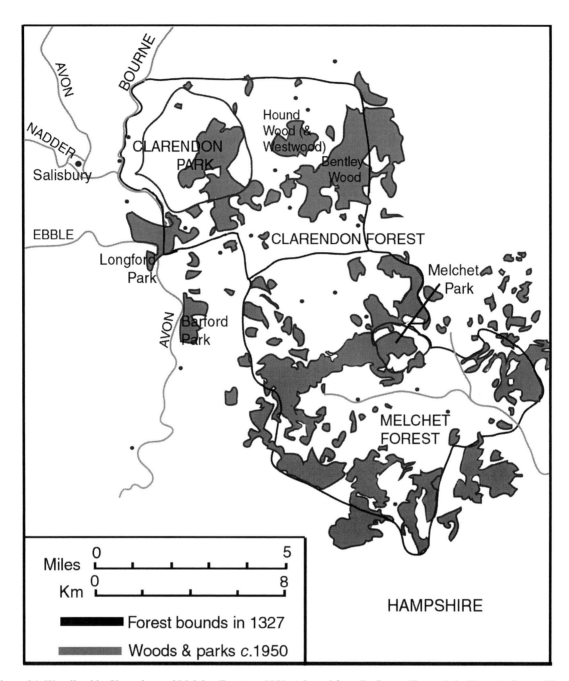

Figure 24. Woodland in Clarendon and Melchet Forests *c*.1950. Adapted from R. Grant, 'Forests', in *Victoria County History, Wiltshire IV* (Oxford: Oxford University Press, 1959), ed. E. Crittall, pp.391-457 (p.454).

By the fourteenth century, it seems to have been increasingly difficult to keep sheep out of the forest. Giles de Beauchamp was even accused, in the 1355 eyre, of pasturing sheep in the park (along with horses, heifers, 20 chickens, 20 pigs, six oxen and six calves), his animals having grazed in the coppices as well as the launds, to the detriment of the forest.[156] In 1325, William of Wykeham (as prebendary of Woodford), had the right to keep 168 sheep in the forest alongside six horses, two mares, six oxen and two cows, probably near Pitton.[157] However sheep seem to have been especially prominent in the manor of Winterslow, particularly in Houndwood and Westwood (see Figure 24). In the same eyre, Anne Despencer claimed the right to pasture all animals except goats in the woods, which pertained to her manor of Winterslow, for herself, her men and tenants, as long as sheep remained outside the covert.[158] The rector of the church of West Winterslow claimed the same right as did John Hugges of Winterslow.[159] That the claims were made suggests that sheep had been common around Winterslow for some time.

---

[156] PRO E 32/267, m.11.
[157] Parsons, *Pancet*, p.26.

[158] PRO E 146/3/11.
[159] PRO E 32/267, m.17.

A variety of other animals were pastured at Clarendon. The prior of Ivychurch had held the right to keep 40 oxen and cows (*boves & vaccas*) in the park since 1322-3, and 20 ringed pigs in the forest quit of pannage from before 1251, according to charters he proffered in the 1355 eyre.[160] It is probable that the charter concerning the cattle amounted to special permission to keep them in the park. As mentioned elsewhere, the park seems to have been both enlarged and enclosed in 1317, no doubt necessitating written evidence of pre-existing rights, and indeed this was the year in which they were first granted the pasture according to the calendars.[161] Also in 1317, Stephen de Pulton was made parker 'with pasture in the park for 6 cows, 3 mares and 3 colts' as long as he should remain in office, and John de Tudworth, William Randolf and William de Pitton, foresters of fee, are recorded in the 1355 forest eyre roll as having the right by serjeanty to pasture their animals in the king's demesne wood, worth, it was estimated, 6s.8d. each.[162]

The various forms of husbandry associated with Clarendon made the wardenship very lucrative by the mid-fourteenth century. In a 1355 *inspeximus*, Roger Mortimer (1328-59) claimed profits of attachments in all the Clarendon forests, both of persons and animals not agisted, all old coppice-hedges, the croppings of trees, housebote, cablish, loppings after every regard, afterpannage, and all impounded strays remaining a year and a day. In addition there were the profits of Whitmarsh Mead in Clarendon Park and those of 'a meadow without the park called Kyngesmeade, for the sustenance of his horses and other animals'. This suggests that both Whitmarsh Mead and King's Mead were common land, and that the latter in particular was used to graze the cattle and horses of the forest officers and others. Indeed, after the death of every forester of fee, Mortimer claimed the right to his best riding horse as heriot, with saddle and bridle (as well as his cloak, cap, sword, leggings, spurs, horn, bow, barbed arrows, and his 'dog called a bercelet').[163]

Mortimer claimed also all nuts and honey from each of the Clarendon forests. Whether or not an apiary existed at Clarendon is unclear, but evidently much honey could be found in the park, and was collected for the warden and foresters. The inquisition *c.*1330 states that the warden had had honey from Clarendon Park since the date of the previous forest eyre, although as far as the jurors knew none had been found in either Melchet or Groveley.[164] By the time of the 1355 eyre, this right (claimed by Mortimer as warden the very same year), had

become an offence, Giles de Beauchamp being accused of taking 'all honey found in the park throughout the time that he was warden', to the value of £24.[165] As described below (**p. 205**), nuts were also gathered in Clarendon Forest, and it seems from extents recorded in the 1355 eyre that each forester of fee had three men to gather them.[166]

Fishponds

Pryor's Pond (see Figure 9), in the south-west corner of 'Dairy Field', pertaining to Ivychurch, was described as 'a large fishpond' in 1652.[167] It was evidently in operation *c.*1330, when the prior took wood 'for his kitchen and fishpond' to the destruction of the forest.[168] However, no further archaeological or documentary evidence of fish management at Clarendon has been found, and in view of the 22 bream sent to the palace from Marlborough *c.*1255, it is possible that fish were not farmed there for the royal table.[169] Here, Clarendon's location must be borne in mind, situated close to many rivers. There may have been no need to dig fishponds when the Avon was alive with 'trout, pike, chubb, roach, grayling and eels', indeed before the introduction of weirs and canals from the mid eighteenth century it was common to see Salmon swimming upstream to spawn above Salisbury.[170] This is entirely plausible since in 1419 the priory of Ivychurch, despite possessing its own fishpond, held rights at 'a fishery' at Alderbury in the River Avon worth 40s.[171]

In 1355, Elizabeth de St Omer, Lady of Britford, successfully claimed the right to fish her half of the Avon, precisely where it bounded the south-west corner of Clarendon Park, 'without interference from the...ministers of the forest',[172] suggesting that fishing here was tantamount to poaching, and that the fish pertained to the king. Similarly, 133 years later Thomas Milborne was careful to claim evidently lucrative fishing rights pertaining to the Manor of Laverstock along the River Bourne between Mumworth Mill and the 'mill called braunemylle', as well as the right to raise amercements from transgressors there.[173] In addition, it must be remembered that through Groveley Forest there was access also to the Nadder and Wylie, and fish may have been brought from there to the palace much as Groveley's deer probably were. Indeed, fishermen occasionally appear in the forest documents, and at least one, John le Fissche(r) of Salisbury, was familiar enough

---

[160] PRO E 32/267, mm.17, 18*d*. By 1423, the right to pasture 20 pigs *and their piglets* had been added (*CPR 1422-9*, pp.75, 106).
[161] *CPR 1313-17*, p.628.
[162] *CPR 1313-17*, p.645; PRO E 32/267, m.15.
[163] *CPR 1354-8*, p.198.
[164] *Dicunt q(uo)d Ball'i de Clarendon qui p(ro) temp(or)e fuerunt post ultima Pl(ac)ita foreste h(ab)uerunt mel [in]ventu(m) in p(ar)co de Clarendon. et fforestar' de feodo in Melchet. et in Grovele nullu' mel [in]venit(ur) ut credunt* (PRO E 32/215, m.2).
[165] *CPR 1354-8*, p.198.
[166] PRO E 32/267, m.15
[167] KACC I, p.56; McWilliams, 'Clarendon Park 1600-1750', Appendix G, p.106.
[168] PRO E 32/215, m.1.
[169] KACC I, p.56.
[170] T.J. Woodall, 'Britford Church and Parish: Notes on Their History' (WRL [acquired 1943], reprinted from the *Wiltshire County Mirror and Express*, undated), p.4.
[171] *CIM 1399-1422*, p.350.
[172] PRO C 260/86/16/B.
[173] PRO DL 39/2/20, m.17.

with the landscape to get caught digging from the king's marlpit in the park *c.*1355.[174]

Trends Over Time

There are signs that the economy at Clarendon underwent major changes in the first half of the fifteenth century. As well as the increased concentration on rabbits discussed above, Ivychurch Priory, now in decline, evidently had little need for pasture in the park, relinquishing its claim in favour of a grant in frank almoin of the Priory of Uphaven and the Chapel of Charlton (Wiltshire).[175] The increasing tendency (again) to over-exploitation is evident in a 1455 decree of Richard Duke of York as justice of the forest, in which the Dean and Chapter of Salisbury were informed that, if necessary due to lack of forest resources, their tithe on coppice or any wood trimmed from felled timber might be rendered as cash on an acreage basis.[176] In the wider landscape too things were changing, Groveley Forest having been rented to Lord Stourton in 1448 for 3s.4d. 'saving to the king the free chase for the king's...deer therein and pasture and herbage therefor and the king's lodge therein and the high wood by the lodge containing 30 acres, which has never been coppiced'.[177] By the final quarter of the century, the value to the Crown of some revenues at Clarendon had declined to the extent that it was more profitable to surrender them. In 1483 Margaret Basset was granted 'the herbage and pannage of the king's park of Claredon [sic] and a tenement within the town of Clarendon of the yearly value of 13s.4d. which she had of the gift of the king's kinsman the late Earl of Warwick'.[178] The forest system had collapsed, and the palace appears to have been regarded now as a series of tenements comprising a 'town', probably a symptom of its disuse by the court since the late 1450s.

By the first half of the sixteenth century horses may have been routinely pastured in the park in a way that they had not been previously. In the reign of Henry VIII (1509-47), the warden, Robert Throckmorton, was allowed to pasture 12 cows, a bull and 9 geldings there. He was also allocated £4 herbage per year for 'goynge of the king's horses in the saide park betwene the two hollerode [Holy Rood] dayes'. This is likely to have been between 3 May (*Inventio Sancte Crucis*) and 14 September (*Exaltatio Sancte Crucis*), especially as Throckmorton had all the 'wynt(er) grasse remaynynge to hymsealfe aft(er) the removynge of the kynges hyghenes' horses'.[179] Obviously meadowland was still an important aspect of the economy. Incidentally, the presence of 'the king's horses' may betray a building campaign for which no other evidence survives, perhaps of the standing and deer

course (see below, p. 80), whose construction is traditionally placed in Henry VIII's reign.[180]

This is not to say that horses were prohibited from the park in earlier times, but references proliferate from the late fifteenth century after the palace went out of use. A building-works account of 1482-97 records repairs to 'La Horsery' near the Warden's Lodge, and includes many references to the purchase of goods relating to 'the kings horses', including a 'horselock' for the king's cart, a horse collar and halters (*capistris*). Horses themselves were also bought, including a grey horse costing 8s. in 1484-5, and in 1485-6 a ?yellow (*gusij*) horse for 8s.4d., a white horse for 15s.3d., and a brown horse from John Batter for 9s., while 6s. was spent on shoeing the king's horses for three years.[181] This information may also be a consequence of the extensive building works carried out at this time.

Regulations concerning pasturing generally become more definitely laid down in the sixteenth century, and there is the overriding impression that the principal concern was to conserve the vert. For example in 1566-7, the articles of instructions for regarders, in this case for Melchet Forest, instructed keepers not to put 'horses beastes shepe Coltes calves Swyne or other cattell' into coppices until the 'springe(s) of the sayd coppices' were eight years old.[182] This was in any case the end of the coppice-cycle, since underwood was cropped on four-eight yearly cycles.[183] If any animal was found in the coppices, the regarders were to impound it, for which they would be rewarded 2d., or 1d. if the foresters had sanctioned its pasturing.[184] No such transgressions are recorded in the regarders' certificates for Clarendon in the 1560s and 70s, although an interrogatory of 1575-7 concerning woods and trees 'supposed to be heretofore fallen in the forest of Pauncett', asked whether young growth in the coppices had been 'bitten hindered spoiled and wasted' by horses and other beasts.[185] One respondent stated that the warden and keepers had had pannage in the park, and another replied that although the coppices had been reasonably kept, the keepers had been 'torninge in of theire horses'. Cattle had also broken in, largely because of breaks in the coppice-hedges caused by the stickers of Salisbury (below, p. 52), many of which can still be traced on the ground,[186] and similar reports carry thorough the first quarter of the seventeenth century.[187]

[174] PRO E 32/267, m.13*d.*
[175] *CCR 1422-9*, pp.75, 106.
[176] Parsons, *Pancet*, p.56.
[177] *CPR 1446-52*, p.160.
[178] *CPR 1476-85*, p.365.
[179] PRO E 101/519/22.

[180] T.B. James, pers. comm. Typically, PRO E 101/519/22 is undated.
[181] PRO E 101/460/16.
[182] PRO E 178/2400, article 7.
[183] James and Gerrard, *Clarendon: A Royal Landscape*, forthcoming.
[184] PRO E 178/2400, article 12.
[185] PRO E 134/18&19Eliz/Mich I. Again, in 1596-7, a special commission for the spoil of woods in Wiltshire asked whether the 'younge spring(es) of her Ma^(t(es)) Coppices in the said Countie [were] kept & preserved from the hurt and destruction of Cattell or Connyes as they ought to be by the Lawes and Statut(es) of this Realme' (PRO E 178/2446).
[186] PRO E 134/18&19Eliz/Mich I, no.1; C. Gerrard, pers. comm.
[187] E.g. PRO E 178/4728/D, m.2.

Increased pasturing of cattle in the wider park must have caused problems for the deer, for in 1603 it was recommended that rails should be made so that they could be fed 'by them selves from other cattell by the...hayhouse'.[188] The paddock course and its parrocks suggest that deer at this time were kept in more controlled conditions than had once been the case, and penned deer in particular will shy away from all farm animals, kicking and butting any that get too close.[189] Both roe and fallow are as wary of cows as of sheep, which may further explain late thirteenth- and early fourteenth-century restrictions on agistment at Clarendon, when deer stocks seem to have been low.

It is possible that the early seventeenth century saw the first agriculture, perhaps even surreptitious assarting, in the park. In 1605-6, some of the freeholders of Laverstock were indicted for having broken up and sowed a parcel of 'layne [?laund] ground', for dividing it by lot among themselves, and for planning 'this Somer to breake upp more...wch in the memory of man hath not bene broken upp'.[190] Certainly by 1661 much of the park had been ploughed up, including the launds, since a lease of 1692 pertaining to Queen Manor Farm cites also 250a. of arable land.[191] But in 1605-6, although the palace had long gone and royal visits were so irregular as to be hardly worth a mention, the Crown continued to jealously guard its prerogatives until the park was sold off by Charles II in 1664.

WOOD MANAGEMENT

By analysing numbers of deer and trees ordered by the Crown from Pamber Forest, Paul Stamper identified a shift in royal policy from conservation to active exploitation of woodland resources in the mid thirteenth century.[192] It has been shown that this was the case concerning deer at Clarendon (above, pp. 33-34), and indeed deer populations probably decreased generally in this period due to the considerable reduction of their habitat.[193] A major focus of this section will be to analyse evidence for exploitation of lumber at Clarendon in order to ascertain whether such conclusions apply equally to its wood-crops.

The park today comprises large areas of managed woodland (see Figure 25), and has done for hundreds of years. Unlike Woodstock Park, for example, always an almost exclusively wood-pasture landscape,[194] it was compartmentalised from at least the early fourteenth century and probably contained defined coppices much earlier. Groveley Forest had included coppices as early

as the 1252,[195] and letters close throughout the 1220s are full of references to 'our cablish vendors of Clarendon', although 'cablish' may indicate windfallen wood and therefore opportunistic profit-making rather than coppice-management *per se*. What is clear is that a wealth of documentary evidence exists for woodland management at Clarendon throughout the period studied and beyond.

Figure 25. Great Netley Copse, Spring 2002.

There is ecological and archaeological evidence also. Of surviving coppices, Home Copse, Great Gilbert's Copse and Pitton Copse have been classified as ancient woodland. Many, however, were replanted in the nineteenth century so that their earlier makeup is irrecoverable. Nevertheless, some coppice-stools in Hendon Copse, which contains a great Beech c.8.25 metres in girth, are 'very ancient', and the edges of many are marked with pollarded beeches of the type often used to mark boundaries in coppiced woodlands.[196]

Function of the Clarendon Forests
The park most frequently mentioned in the thirteenth-century calendars in connection with the Clarendon Forests is not Clarendon, but Melchet Park, under the purview of the de Grimstead foresters of fee until the mid-fourteenth century, and thereafter of their successors. This 'park' appears to have been a hay — an enclosed space which functioned chiefly to provide lumber. Figure 26 shows quantifiable orders for trees from Melchet Forest recorded in the calendars. Almost all are oaks (*quercus*), or *robora*, usually translated as oak trunks or stumps, and generally given as gifts for fuel. In contrast, Buckholt was exploited chiefly for its beech, and the lists of transgressions in the 1355 forest eyre roll show that it

[188] PRO E 101/542/21, f.1.
[189] Coles, *Gardens and Deer*, p.68.
[190] PRO E 123/29, f.92.
[191] McWilliams, 'Clarendon Park 1600-1750', p.50.
[192] Stamper, 'Pamber', *passim*.
[193] Birrell, 'Deer and Deer Farming', p.124.
[194] Bond, 'Woodstock Park in the Middle Ages', p.41.

[195] 'Order is given to...enclose, at the king's command, all open spaces in the King's wood of Groveley from which [underwood has been sold], so that the king should suffer no loss...and that the men of Barford and Wichford should not be inconvenienced by the emparking of their animals in those closes...and the king wishes that when the aforesaid underwood has regrown, the said men shall have their common rights there as has been the custom' (*CCR 1251-3*, p.122).
[196] KACC I, pp.54-5; Clarendon Park Ecology Archive, courtesy of D. Clements, Hendon Copse/Canon Copse, Wilts 15, Pitton Copse, Woodland Record Sheet map no.184, compiled by G.Lewis.

Figure 26. Wood ordered from Melchet Forest/Park (compiled from information in the Calendars of Rolls)

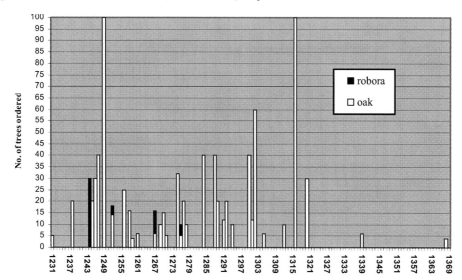

Figure 27. Wood ordered from Clarendon Forest (compiled from information in the Calendars of Rolls)

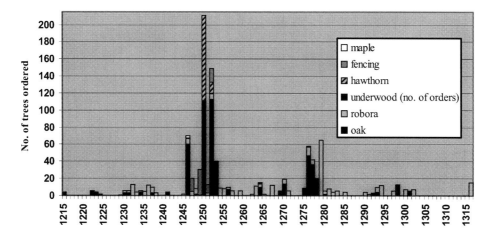

remained almost exclusively a beech wood in the mid-fourteenth century.[197]

Figure 27, charting orders for wood from Clarendon Forest in the calendars from 1215 to 1316, exhibits more diversity. There are the usual grants of *robora*, chiefly gifts to noblemen and women for their hearths; some beech and two maples, which in this case went to make wooden pots for the king's almonry at the palace.[198] Again, oak predominates, and of the large amounts requested in 1250 and 1252, most went on repairs to the palace and park pale. Finally, Figure 28, representing orders for timber from all the Clarendon forests reveals that, of each of them, Clarendon was the greatest provider of timber in the period 1215-1339, just as it was for deer (see above, p. 32).

Figure 28. Number of standard trees ordered, 1215-1339 (compiled from information in the Calendars of Rolls)

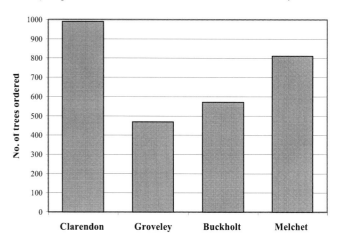

[197] PRO E 32/267, mm.12, 12*d*.
[198] *CCR 1242*-7, p.488.

Much of its lumber was, of course, used to maintain the park and palace, and the peak years of exploitation of wood stocks through the thirteenth century coincide with major building programmes there. However, a sizeable amount also went to Salisbury Castle at Old Sarum and to the cathedral, as well as to other local interests. In times of war or extensive building works, timber might be sent further, as in 1223 when Clarendon oaks were sent to Winchester for works at the castle and 1339, when six oaks went from Melchet for use in the fortifications at Southampton.[199]

Conservation and Exploitation: Trends over Time

Figures 21 and 22 reveal that peaks and troughs in the exploitation of timber are similar for Clarendon and Melchet Forests. There was over-exploitation in the 1240s, and also between 1250 and 1260, as Stamper has found. This is true for Groveley Forest also. Stocks there seem to have been particularly depleted so that grants for wood tail off completely after the 1270s, and those in Clarendon Forest were low by the late 1250s. In May 1257, a year of famine, the felling of oaks there was forbidden due to previous diminution.[200] By 1268, amid increased complaints that oaks promised by the king had not yet been received, Robert Walerand apparently had to make do with second-hand lumber, felled beforehand for use at the palace, instead of the usual gifts of timber oaks.[201] However attention was given to the problem. In December 1268 a prohibition on taking vert and venison from all royal forests and demesne woods was issued for an interval of three years, and the charts show that in this period there was indeed a fall in orders.

Clarendon's wood stocks seem still to have been depleted at the turn of the fourteenth century. In 1301 an order to sell wood to the value of £100 was amended because 'it appears that to sell £100 worth of wood in Clarendon Forest…would be to the destruction of that Forest'.[202] One must conclude that the late thirteenth and early fourteenth centuries were times of extensive exploitation followed by backsliding at crisis point. From this time, Groveley and Clarendon, especially the park, began to be exploited chiefly for their underwood. Melchet continued to be the main provider of timber, and the lodge built in Melchet Park in 1357 is symptomatic of the need to preserve and guard it.[203]

Edward I's policy of making the forests profitable led to more pronounced demarcation of woodland on the ground, for example the trenches made sometime before 1276 in Clarendon Forest, probably the Upper and Lower trenches running through the park (see above, Figure 22).

There has been much discussion of the purpose of such *trenchia*. Although they would have 'opened up' the landscape for buck-hunting, they were also a source of lumber, as evidenced by the regarders' comment in 1330 that Walter Gacelyn, warden, and others had 'wasted [the wood between Pitton Gate and Whitmarsh] by making a trench from Blakehegg to the Poleteresclos, and taking underwood from it in order to enclose [Clarendon Park]'.[204]

Such demarcation continued through the first half of the fourteenth century. Coppice-wood was ordered to be made in the park 'in suitable places' in 1328 to make up for the shortfall caused by the lack of agistment (see above, p. 41), in 1334 John de Harnham was appointed to make new coppices in the park, and his successor, William Randolf, was to enclose them in 1336 with a low hay, or hedge. Thus, most of the surviving coppices may date from this time. Later, in 1354, John Everard and John de Harnham were commanded to enclose coppices in the forest and park with hedges, but they were not ordered to make new coppices.[205]

Yet as early as 1318-24, Clarendon's coppices were already delineated by name, including Cowgrove (*Cougrove*) and Stoneygore, from which most of the underwood in this period seems to have come.[206] More underwood was taken from 'a place called Candelstikkewie' near Ivychurch Priory, and from below 'le Witeshute', presumably Alderbury Shoot or Whitmarsh, and a 1330 roll of regards describes underwood called 'le Shete' outside the gate of Clarendon Manor as having been wasted before 1324 by order of Edward II.[207]

The palace could be a drain on woodland resources, as evidenced by Edward II's December 1316 order for 100 oaks from the Forest of Clarendon, to be used for repairs to 'houses and wells within the manor…as the king intends coming thither within a month'. The timescale was somewhat optimistic, and Clarendon Forest proper obviously still could not supply so much timber, as in May 1317 the mandate was amended so that the oaks should come from Melchet.[208] Then in 1328 timber for repairing the park pale was to be taken from Chute Forest, so that lumber appears still to have been in short supply.[209]

Stamper suggests that the widespread fall in timber grants between 1310 and 1320 may be due either to a fall in demand — unlikely in this case — or in the ability of

[199] *Rot Litt Claus* I, p.541; *CCR 1339-41*, p.158.
[200] *CCR 1256-9*, pp.131.
[201] E.g. *CCR 1268-72*, pp.56-7; *The warden of the manor of Clarendon is ordered to cause Robert Walerand to have that old timber in his custody which the king lately had felled for a certain room by the gate* (*Ibid.*, p.11).
[202] *CPR 1292–1301*, p.593.
[203] *CCR 1354–60*, p.356.

[204] PRO E 32/208. m.1.
[205] *CCR 1327-30*, p.341; *CCR 1333-7*, pp.268-9; *CFR 1327-37*, p.475; *CFR 1347- 56*, p.417.
[206] PRO SC 6/1050/5, mm.4, 1, 3.
[207] PRO SC 6/1050/5, mm.1, 3; PRO E 32/208, m.1. Probably today's Alderbury Shoot.
[208] *CCR 1313–18*, pp.384, 389.
[209] *CCR 1327-30*, p.341.

royal demesne woods to supply it.[210] At Clarendon the balance of supply and demand must have been thrown out of kilter since Henry III enlarged the palace in the 1230s, and the rise of Salisbury and wholesale assarting in Melchet Forest in particular (see Chapter Four) must also have placed a huge burden on woodland resources. From the first quarter of the fourteenth century, repairs were funded with money gained from selling underwood rather than random (and sometimes unrealistic) royal orders for timber trees. Compartmental coppicing of the kind seen in Clarendon Park and Groveley Forest indicates strong lordship,[211] and delineation of royal and private woodland on the ground in the late thirteenth and early fourteenth centuries can be seen as symptomatic of control over a forest system now arguably on the wane. This was a nationwide phenomenon, but at Clarendon, conservation was a contingency measure prompted by a localised, exceptional thirteenth-century boom. It now became increasingly a self-sufficient landscape with the park as its hub, intensive coppicing no doubt the only way to cope with the constant repairs to such an extensive pale.

Most trespasses of the vert in the 1330 eyre concern underwood, suggesting that timber trees remained scarce (although 30 'great oaks' were taken illegally from somewhere in the forest), and in 1334, timber for repairs to the keep of Salisbury Castle and 'the king's mills there' came from Melchet and Chute Forests, Clarendon Forest providing only underwood for the mill's hurdles and sluices.[212] However, by the mid-fourteenth century some recovery is evident. A post-1330 inquiry into the state of the forest listed over 1000 oaks felled in Clarendon Park since the last eyre (1330) alongside 1300 from Melchet Park.[213] Many must have gone towards Edward III's building works — certainly much timber from Clarendon and Melchet was used on the new Lodge on the Laund in 1341-4.[214] The eyre of 1355 lists the theft of more trees than that of 1330, including 83 oaks, 19 *robora*, and four apple trees from Clarendon Park. In addition, Giles de Beauchamp was accused of felling 100 oaks and oak saplings worth 15s. in Clarendon Forest for work on his house, and 60 more were taken from the park by William de Pitton for repair of his houses in Pitton.[215] By 1368-72, Andrew de Dodmanstone, deputy warden, was able (allegedly) to purloin and sell 120 oaks, having claimed they would be used on the construction of 'lodges' for fence month.[216]

After the last true forest eyre in 1355, there is inevitably less information about medieval timber stocks. Letters close and patent also become less detailed, their focus on appointments rather than instructions. However, the significance of wood in forest economies is evidenced by

the wording of appointments made. The wardenship was worth 40 marks p.a. in the 1380s, and in 1381 both Alan de Buxhull and Baldwin de Bereford, retainers of Edward III and Richard II (1377-99) and outgoing and incoming wardens respectively, were granted profits of all browsewood, brushwood, and bark cut or fallen in Clarendon Park and Forest, and in Buckholt, Groveley and Melchet 'receivable by [them] for fencing the premises or otherwise'.[217] The precedent for such grants — and for most of the warden's perquisites — seems to be Roger Mortimer's schedule of 1355, in which he claimed:

> ...all old hays made round the king's coppices...when [they] are removed according to the assize of the forest;...all croppings of trees felled;...'housebote' sufficient for the houses assigned to the bailiwick;...wind-falls;...[and] loppings after every regard made... in the said forests...[218]

Such perquisites had probably long existed, but they appear not to have been set down in writing before 1355, after which rights to such profits from were outlined as a matter of course in wardens' appointments.

Other information concerning trees at fourteenth-century Clarendon concerns sales of underwood. The highest returns came after high winds, when windfallen wood was sold. Thus in 1364, windfalls from the park and Forest brought in £186.5s.2d. In 1365, £108.9s.6d. was raised, followed by £53.7s. in 1366, and £8.9s. the following year — a total of £356.10s.5d. over a four year period.[219] But high winds also affected buildings, and the moneys raised from underwood sales went towards their repair. £62 of the returns of 1365-7 went towards repairs at the 'king's new lodge' and at the palace, including the Knight's Hall and rooms in the king's and queen's apartments.[220]

Apart from underwood accounts, fifteenth-century records are largely silent concerning lumber. However, there are occasional details about the types of trees grown. In 1423-4, 300 Buckholt beeches were sold to 90 persons for £27.13s.8d., and 50 ash trees from Clarendon Park went to 16 persons, fetching £7.18s.2d.[221] But in 1441-2, while £56.19s. was raised for repairs at Clarendon from 400 beeches from Buckholt and 200 oaks from Melchet, no trees were sold from Clarendon.[222] Indeed in view of the wording of wardens' appointments noted above, the 1406 grant to Thomas Lynford and Richard Jewell to sell 150 beeches from Buckholt Forest for repairs at Clarendon 'as no profits pertain to [the manor, park and lodges] by which they can be repaired' indicates intermittent shortages of wood at Clarendon

[210] Stamper, 'Pamber', p.47.
[211] Rackham, *The Last Forest*, p.55.
[212] PRO E 32/215, m.1; PRO E 32/207, m.6d; *CCR 1333-7*, p.254.
[213] PRO E 32/215, m.1.
[214] PRO E 101/593/18, m.1; PRO E 101/593/20.
[215] PRO E 32/267, m.7; PRO C 260/89/32/B.
[216] PRO E 32/318, m.22.

[217] *CPR 1381-5*, pp.57, 48, 52.
[218] *CPR 1354-8*, p.198.
[219] E 101/140/4.
[220] PRO E 364/2, m.7d.; BM Add.Roll 26594, m.1.
[221] SC 6/1050/22, m.2.
[222] PRO E 101/140/10.

during the first half of the century.[223] The depletion appears to have been countrywide, and again the Crown moved to conserve its resources. In 1413 the keeper of the forest this side Trent was ordered to:

...command all foresters within his bailiwick until further order to execute no warrant for oaks, lopping of boughs or underwoods, which belong to the crown, and to suffer none to be executed, safe keeping any oaks cut down for timber, and not delivering them up until the king be otherwise advised.[224]

In addition, in 1419 a commission was set up to enquire into 'all sales of great trees and underwood...within the king's park of Claryngdon', suggesting it was the subject of particular concern. [225] However by the 1450s underwood stocks, at least, were thriving. The pipe roll of 1458-9 lists £22.3s.10d. received for building works from 30a. of underwood (and 50 beeches) from Culverhill coppice, £18.23d. from Beechy Maples coppice, 119s. in Wydmore coppice and £22.3s.8d. in Radenelles coppice, alongside a further 300 beeches from Buckholt worth £23.14s.4d.[226]

That the forest eyre of 1488 for Clarendon was chiefly concerned with claims of rights rather than transgressions of the vert or of the venison has already been discussed (above, p. 34), and it seems probable that it represents the perceived need to keep the forest system intact with respect to the rights of local gentry, rather than its revival 'from the top down'. But even claims to wood-perquisites, so vital in a forest economy, are few. Only the rector of Winterslow claimed housebote and heybote, in this case in Houndwood and Westwood.[227]

Sixteenth- and Early Seventeenth-Century Wood Management

A paucity of evidence in the early sixteenth century may indicate that woodland management went into decline after the palace's demise. But from the reign of Elizabeth I (1558-1603), documents survive concerning all aspects of the organisation of wood stocks following attempts to legislate woodland preservation in the middle of the century, prompted by 'the combined demands on the forests by Elizabethan society'.[228] The value of wood rose sharply, and the crown guarded more jealously than ever its timber stocks through harsh fines and stringent legislation, including interrogatories, which allow us to hear, for the first time, the voices of those who knew the landscape intimately.

Late sixteenth-century regarders (the 'preservators of the queen's woods') worked to detailed articles of instruction, at the head of which came the order that they must mark with an axe all trees to be removed, of whatever description. Nobody was to cut underwood 'under p(re)tence of newe makynge of laund(es) or Rydyng(es) or under p(re)tence of...makynge wyder ...launds or Rydyng(es)' without their having first been informed, and they must keep annual books listing offences of the vert, noting the names of the perpetrators and the value of the trespass. They were to be paid annually 4d. in every pound due the crown for wood sold over and above hedging expenses, and to receive firewood allowances of 5s. or less of maple, thorn, hazel, 'old stubbes of decayed okes asshes or beches or...the bletron or waterbowes of oak asshe or beche'.[229]

It was clearly in the regarders' interest to ensure that woods were well-managed that good records were kept, and the articles were followed in the Clarendon Forests as elsewhere. In 1567-73, the Buckholt regarders reported that they had had a sealing-axe made with 'a peculier marke, and a bagge to keepe the same', which would remain in the custody of one of them. The regarders of Clarendon Park went one step further. They had their own axe with an individual mark, its bag assigned to one of them and the 'seale' to another, the latter 'not occupied tyll we mete togyther'. In 1569-70 they reported five windfall oaks as having been taken, alongside 12 felled by Alexander Kercherd, ranger, 'as p(ar)cell of his Fee', and 40 'old dotard oaks' as part of the warden's fee 'appoynted by the county wch hath bene accustomed many yeres past longe oute of mans memory, and cut downe to the lorde warden...or his deputie'. William Travis felled 64 oaks which he delivered to the six keepers at nine seams (horse-loads) a week, keeping six seams a day for himself 'for his travail and paynes'. In addition, 104 oaks were felled to repair the lodges, and Sir George Penruddock, the deputy warden, sold off Fair Oak Coppice for £30.10s.2d. The coppice, 29½a. in area, had contained over 23a. of saleable underwood and three yards of waste ground. Its hedge, measuring five acres and six yards, was made anew with the money raised and furnished with 'a newe borde gatt' costing £5.2s.[230]

The regarders' certificates contain much information about the cutting of deer browse. At Woodstock, this was a duty of the tenants of surrounding manors, but at Clarendon, at least in the sixteenth century it fell to the foresters (the park's quarter keepers), who prepared 5400 faggots and 17 loads of 'talle wood' for the winter of 1570 alone. [231] The arrangement must have caused friction, for in 1571-2 the regarders complained that whereas elsewhere people were specially appointed for the task, at Clarendon 'ev(er)y keper doth cutt downe

---

[223] *CPR 1405-8*, p.179.
[224] *CCR 1413-19*, p.16. Interestingly, Queen Joan pressed for an exception in her Forest of Whittlewood, so that underwood sold prior to the order might be removed by its buyers (*Ibid.*, pp.32-3).
[225] *CPR 1416-22*, p.270.
[226] PRO E 372/304, *rot*.75, m.2.
[227] PRO DL 39/2/20, m.12.
[228] J. Perlin, *A Forest Journey: The Role of Wood in the Development of Civilisation* (London: W.W. Norton, 1989), pp. 171, 177, 182.

[229] PRO E 178/2400.
[230] PRO E 101/140/11, mm.1-4.
[231] Bond, 'Woodstock Park in the Middle Ages', p.41; PRO E 101/140/11, m.4.

what they lyst wthout any order, w^{c}h we do muche mislike'.[232]

The 1566-7 articles of instruction required browsers to make oath annually that browsewood would be used only to 'releve the deer in harde wether', and not for their own profit. Neither were they to use oak if alternatives were available, and even then the boughs should be small enough for a buck to turn with its antlers.[233] But in 1570-1, the regarders, apparently concerned for timber stocks, reported that 54 trees had been taken by the keepers:

all w^{ch}...they should burne in there lodg(es), but some of them Sellyth ev(er)y sticke and burneth of the quenes wood...and ffrome this tyme [Easter] *untyll the sprynge of the yere the...Semer doth loppe oke ffor the fuell and burnynge wood, w^{c}h is to Syxe kepers ev(er)y of them ix semes a weke and he hym selfe ev(er)y daye Syxe Semes w^{c}h we thinke will not long contynewe.*[234]

The following year, they complained that the keepers used oak for browse despite there being 'Suffycient...of thornes maple and hasell', and that some took browsewood and faggots out of the park before they had had a chance to inspect it.[235]

Undoubtedly the new legislation pitched regarders against foresters, an effect that can be seen in the Clarendon sources throughout the late sixteenth and early seventeenth century. However, it does seem that the foresters were guilty of many misdemeanours in the late sixteenth century, culminating in the processes of 1598 concerning 'greate wastes and spoyles' in Clarendon Park.[236] At this time there were concerns about wood stocks generally, as well as the erosion of ancient customs which had preserved the ecological balance. This is clear from a letter of 1592 from Lord Admiral Howard to Elizabeth I in which Clarendon Park is specifically mentioned. Howard expressed misgivings about plans to lease out the herbage and pannage of forests, parks and chases since 'experience has proved the utter destruction of woods, by warrants and grants for the sale of dotards, under colour of which the soundest trees have gone'. Although the overriding concern was the preservation of good timber for the navy, he pointed out that 'as A. B. has also a grant of dead blocks, roots, windfalls, etc., the deer cannot lie quiet, for the workmen and carriages must continually pass to and fro'.[237]

Others, too, had their eye on Clarendon's wood, namely the stickers, entitled to gather dry wood in the park. In the fourteenth and fifteenth centuries, launderers were entitled to two or three stickers and the prior of Ivychurch

one, and they seem to have originated as appointees who collected sticks in return for payment on the one hand, and aged paupers or mendicants exercising the right in exchange for two chickens annually on the other.[238] This latter tradition seems to have been revived in the sixteenth century. Sometime before 1570, the Buckholt regarders reported that 'whear in the Tenth article is...a consideration for the poor to have...Sticke(s), of that hereafter we will see unto accordinge', and by 1571 they had recorded the names of those in adjoining parishes allowed to collect sticks on appointed days.[239]

At Clarendon, 'adjoining parishes' included those in Salisbury, and the 'stickers of Salisbury' soon acquired a bad reputation. In 1572, Edward Greene told the regarders that he made up his deer-browse as soon as he had cut it, contrary to the articles, because otherwise the Stickers of Sarum would 'Carrye [it] awaye as fast as he doth browse the same', and in 1575 Robert Bundy blamed them for breaking hedges so that cattle had entered the coppices.[240] There were still problems in 1594, when Alexander Thistlethwaite and John Pilgrim reported, in an account of the sale of Catsgrove Coppice:

There is...greate hurte and spoile done in her ma^{ties} Coppic(es) by stickers that frequent the Parke daylie in breakinge and spoylinge the hedges and stemes of the said Coppice.[241]

Again in 1606, the young hedge of Beechy Maples Coppice, was described as 'muche [t]orne & spoyled w^{t}h sticker(es) & hunter(es)'. Such damage prompted defensive measures. In 1604 the regarders reported that a 'plott of thorns and bushes' was being grown around Pitton Coppice 'for keepinge out stickers from steling the coppice',[242] and in Beechy Maples Coppice in 1606:

Certaine stems of hasell & ashe [were] *lefte in the hedge ground taken by the fello[ns] y[et] keepeth & lokethe unto the coppice wood, for savinge the same from ffelinge.*[243]

which may amount to the same arrangement. There is no doubt that the abundance of firewood in the park was important to the stickers, who saw no reason why they should be excluded from its use, and the situation is reminiscent of attempts to keep 'poor people', customarily entitled to collect dead wood, out of Windsor

---

[232] PRO E 101/140/11, m.5.
[233] PRO E 178/2400.
[234] PRO E 101/140/11, m.5.
[235] PRO E 101/140/11, m.5.
[236] E 123/24, f.198.
[237] *CSPD 1591-4*, pp.288-9 (p.289).

[238] *CPR 1436-41*, p.495; *CPR 1391-6*, p.683; '*Memorandum* that on 8 July [1423]...the chancellor delivered to... the treasury a writing indented made by Walter prior of Ivychurch Priory...being a release of their claim in...the said park for 40 oxen and kine and 20 swine...and in a certain profit in the park, namely a man commonly called a 'stikker' daily entering the park to gather wood there to their use and fetch it thence to the priory' (*CCR 1422-9*, p.75); PRO E 32/318, m.22 (1372).
[239] PRO E 101/140/11, mm.1, 6.
[240] PRO E 101/140/11, m.10; PRO E 134/18&19Eliz/Mich I, no.1.
[241] PRO E 101/140/14, m.1.
[242] PRO E 101/140/14, mm.6, 4.
[243] PRO E 101/140/14, m.6.

Great Park in the eighteenth century.[244] At a time of 'great sickness' in Salisbury *c*.1627 Warner's Coppice was spoiled when 'the poore of Saru(m) came dayly to the said Parke and pulled upp the Coppice hedges in many places', and in 1635 it was recorded that Edward Gandy was paid:

> his Wages for repayringe and amendinge of the yonge copice hedges about divers of the same young copice in Claringdon p(ar)ke and for keepinge awaye of poore & disorderlye p(er)sons from spoylinge of the same copice as hath ben formerlye allowed.[245]

The stickers remained a problem until the close of the period studied, and no doubt beyond. In 1649, the council of state had heard that great spoil was being committed on timber 'fit for the use of shipping' in Clarendon Park 'which is an irreparable damage to the commonwealth', although a riot was feared should the justices of the peace proceed against the stickers, again identified with the poor of Salisbury. The justices were told to 'take order with the poor not to make those wastes and spoils, and find some means for their present employment, and if they shall proceed in such spoils, to proceed against and punish them'.[246] Doubtless Clarendon Park was compromised by its position adjacent to the city. Indeed, when transgressions were listed in 1615, the perpetrators were mostly Salisbury men, including John Blathat, innkeeper, and John Coppinger and Christopher Elliot, gents, who between them shredded over 30 oaks.[247]

Nevertheless, the park and its coppices continued to supply Clarendon, although this now applied more to the administrative landscape than its buildings. The foresters' fee wood has already been mentioned, and by 1600 they, along with the bowbearer, each received 5 marks worth annually.[248] Up to *c*.1572, whenever a coppice was sold one acre went to the warden or his deputy, and until the 1550s rangers had all windfalls and trees pulled up by the roots providing their worth was less than 40s. Sometimes the old forest relationships endured, for example the oaks given yearly to George Penruddock as deputy warden were 'appoynted by summe of the cuntrye adioyninge unto the said p(ar)ke'.[249] Another important payment from coppice sales might go to an auditor. At least, in 1634 an accountant was paid £25 for 'rydinge charges and dyett' for himself, his man and their horses, for 40 days 'spent in setting of the workmen to dytchinge and hedginge, and seeinge that the same workmen did make a sufficient dytch & hedge in all the

places of the fence', and 'for coming four score miles to pass the account'.[250]

The regarders' certificates also reveal vestiges of the old forest relationships. When coppices were sold, surrounding villages were listed first among the purchasers. Thus in 1590-1, Alderbury had one acre of Goodales coppice, Grimstead four, Laverstock five and Winterslow eight. Other vills represented included Gomeldon, Idmiston, Fisherton, Quidhampton, and Winterbourne. Together these were known as the nine townships.[251] Each was in Alderbury Hundred, but they may all have been in the forest during the twelfth century, thus having customary claims on its resources. In this case, each paid a nominal fee of 46s.8d., but amounts vary for different coppices, and it is likely that in the end the full market price was charged. Perlin has noted that this trend ran in tandem with the end of manorialisation — 'why should [lords] give away an item for which others would pay dearly?' — and that the resulting market economy made woodlands more vulnerable. Those who had previously received wood by custom were now more inclined to obtain it by cheating or theft, and when Gilbert's Coppice was sold in 1600, 'rotten dead trees wch beare noe green leafe' were sold to the queen's use 'wch woulde otherwise (as heretofore) have bene purloyned away and not benefitte come thereof'.[252]

Further acreage from Goodales Coppice *c*.1590 went to the ranger (seven), the verderers (nine), the earl of Pembroke (28), and three of the quarter-keepers (67). The whole coppice, sold over six or seven weeks, brought £59.4s.1d. From this, £20.13s.4d. was deducted, and ten acres was given as tithe to Salisbury Cathedral, as was the custom.[253] Such tithes were still taken as late as 1635. When Beechy Maples and Little Hindon coppices, totalling 75a 30 perches, were sold in that year 6a 81 perches went as tithe wood 'unto the Prebende of the Cathedrall Church of Sarum as hath ben auntyentlye used'.[254] Usually, an amount seems also to have gone for charitable purposes, as in 1594, when 120 lugs of Catsgrove Coppice went to 'Henry Pati[e], John Webbe, W^m [K]ydghill W^m Du[r]ante, Andrewe Bastard and other poore men',[255] perhaps official 'stickers'. Also deducted from the Goodales Coppice account was £13 to make a new fence, measuring about 10 furlongs, of which the nine townships made part. Indeed in 1635 they are described as owing 'Suyte & service...as of auntyent

---

[244] Roberts, *Royal Landscape*, p.123.
[245] PRO E 178/4728/I.
[246] *CSPD 1649-50*, pp.347-8.
[247] PRO E 178/4728/D.
[248] PRO E 101/140/14, m.3.
[249] PRO E 134/18&19Eliz/Mich I, no.1. After *c*.1550 all windfalls etc. went to George Penruddock (*ibid*).

[250] WRO 2478/2, *f*.5.
[251] PRO E 101/140/14, m.3.
[252] Perlin, *A Forest Journey*, p.188; PRO E 101/140/14, m.3.
[253] PRO E 101/140/12, m.1.
[254] WRO 2478/2, *f*.2. Indeed, the Dean and Chapter received tithes well into the nineteenth century, for example in 1693 an indenture between them and the earl of Clarendon specified that they should have tithes for the following 21 years, 'yielding and paying therefore yearly...unto the said Dean & Chapter...at the great West Door of the cathedral...the...rent of thirteen pounds six shillings and eight pence' (WRO Chapter/95/1). See also WRO Chapter/96 (1802).
[255] PRO E 101/140/12, m.1.

tyme used'.[256] This was probably also the case in the medieval period, although little evidence survives, and elsewhere it is recorded that the vills were customarily paid 2d. per perch, 'as Auncienlie used'.[257]

Significantly, the longest of the 1566-7 articles for regarders had been that concerning the preservation of underwood, particularly the making of coppice-hedges. These were to be made by the 'advice, consent and counsel' of the regarders, who would recommend especially methods of construction likely to be most beneficial in preserving young crops. Coppices were to be surrounded by ditches with hedges set atop their banks, and the foresters were to inform the regarders of the cost.[258] The hedge at Goodales in 1590-1 had a new gate with locks, and was composed of at least 11 loads of stakes, for which seven small trees had been felled.[259] Sometimes stakes were made from the 'topps' of trees, as at Catsgrove in 1594, which was hedged rather than fenced. Afterwards, someone was paid — in this case 6s.8d — to care for and mend the young hedge.[260] At Gilbert's Coppice in 1600, a Mr Moore made 263 lugs of hedge, and was paid 53s.4d. for its maintenance over two years, and for much of the first half of the seventeenth century the hedge keeper was Edward Gandy of Farley, (b. *c*.1580).[261]

Tree species grown in the coppices are rarely mentioned, but appear usually to have been oak, maple and ash. Indeed James I had advised, probably on his visit in 1603, that Catsgrove Coppice be sown with 'Acornes, Ashen keys, Hawthornes and such Like for ye [increase] of woode'.[262] Other information is more obscure. In 1600, Gilbert's Coppice was sold, including 36 lugs of hedge and 102 lugs of 'hedlond and Fether(es)', described as:

> *Certaine [p]latt(es) standinge s[c]atteringe by the hedge grounde w^c^h we call ffether(es), sould unto the coppice keeper [for 16s.8d.] that sheweth ev(er)ye may his woode.*[263]

It is possible that the 'feathers' were some kind of guard to protect the hedgerow's young shoots. Certainly they were in the province of the hedgekeeper. What is meant by the oak 'spine stacks for the copice hedge' mentioned in 1635 may be less obscure.[264] However it is noteworthy that contemporaries thought in terms like headlands, associated with earlier field systems. In 1606 that of Beechy Maples Coppice, measuring 98 lugs, was claimed by the deputy woodward as his fee, which suggests it

yielded a crop.[265] It is possible that the 'two parallel banks, possibly representing a former trackway alongside the coppice' archaeologically examined around Catsgrove Coppice in 1996 was such a headland, particularly as it was found to be associated with a belt of diverse scrub, suggesting an early date.[266] But more work needs to be done on early modern wood-management in order to elucidate such terms.

By 1640, there was a perception that the old ways of woodsmanship were lost. The regarder William Wimbleton complained that coppice-hedges were made too late in the year, so that the wood was green 'whereby the hedge cannot last soe longe by Twoe Yeares'. If they were made with stronger wood 'as auntientlie they have byn', the coppices might be better preserved. Henry Hayden of Salisbury, employed to sell coppice-wood, also said that the wood was not felled 'in due season, nor the ditches upon w^c^h the hedges are made, settle & stand soe firme as they would doe if they were made sooner in the Winter', and another deponent suggested that the hedges should be strong and high, 'as in former tymes'.[267] Many witnesses blamed bad practice on the fact that workmen were owed wages, and indeed in 1625 there were already complaints that John Essington the woodward was withholding the pay of the men employed to repair the park pale, and doubts that he 'properly accounts for the King's money received by him for the sale of coppices'.[268] Thus, although the Civil War and Interregnum are often cited as reasons for the 'waste and spoil' of Clarendon Park in the seventeenth century,[269] royal disinterest and the malpractice of the park's officers, rather less spectacularly, were also to blame.

CONCLUSIONS

Documentary sources provide much evidence for how Clarendon was administered over time. Most noteworthy, at least in terms of fauna, is the fact that both park and forest were managed almost exclusively for fallow deer through the entire period studied. This new finding, made possible through analysis of forest eyre documents and calendared sources, goes some way towards resolving questions concerning the landscape, for example the lack of provision of water in the park.

Yet red deer, although not prolific, did exist in Clarendon Forest, and the fact that both they and fallow were subject to the same peaks and troughs suggests that over-exploitation of their habitats was significant. The amount of reported thefts and orders for both species fell in all the Clarendon forests (see Figure 17) particularly from *c*.1260-70 until *c*.1310-20 when orders again rose — rapidly in the case of fallow — perhaps not surprisingly the period when the park was enlarged and refenced.

---

[256] WRO 2478/2, *f*.3.
[257] PRO E 101/140/14, mm.1, 6. For the pale, see PRO E 101/460/2, mm.1-2.
[258] PRO E 178/2400.
[259] PRO E 101/140/12, m.1.
[260] PRO E 101/140/14, m.1.
[261] PRO E 101/140/14, m.3; PRO E 178/4728/I; WRO 2478/2, *f*.4*d*.
[262] PRO E 178/4728/D.
[263] PRO E 101/140/14, m.3.
[264] WRO 2478/2, *f*.4.

[265] PRO E 101/140/14, m.6.
[266] KACC I, p.67.
[267] PRO E 178/4728/I.
[268] *CSPD 1625-49*, p.255.
[269] E.g. McWilliams, 'Clarendon Park 1600-1750', pp.43-4.

Orders of deer from Clarendon fell from a peak of 150 *c*.1258, to 26 animals *c*.1295. Such a decline at this time is not unusual, suggesting that it rested on more than a lack of royal interest in Clarendon (although a lack of quarry may have been a factor in the concurrent paucity of royal visits). Birrell, quoting Rackham, has pointed out that the 1240s and 50s were peak years for deer production generally. In the mid-thirteenth century the king was receiving (or ordering) an average of 607 deer a year from his forests and parks and by 1273-86 the number had fallen to *c*.181 annually.[270]

The rise and fall of deer populations is echoed by the data concerning trees. Lumber was over-exploited in the 1240s, and particularly from 1250-60, prompting the 1257 prohibition on felling at Clarendon and a few other forests. Although this phenomenon was soon recognised by the Crown to be very widespread, indicated by the 1268 nationwide mandate prohibiting the taking of vert and venison from any of the king's forests for three years (see above, p. 49), the extensive works at the palace in the 1250s must have had an effect on Clarendon's forest resources as a whole. The effect of frequent building works on park deer generally is evident in Lord Admiral Howard's remarks in 1592 that due to constant felling and on-site carpentry (a frequent occurrence at Clarendon, as will be seen in the following chapter) 'the deer cannot lie quiet, for...workmen and carriages must continually pass to and fro'.[271]

Conversely the deer, and the park in general, probably suffered due to neglect occasioned by the relatively few royal visits from the 1270s until *c*.1317. Indeed it seems not to have been until the third decade of the fourteenth century that timber stocks recovered fully in the forest in general, there being no mast at Clarendon from 1298-1327 on which pigs might forage. Although this might stem from a corresponding lack of timber trees due to the earlier over-exploitation, it seems to have rested on Edward I's 1296-7 order that all oaks in Clarendon Forest should be felled and sold.[272] In other words, this was a pro-active rather than reactive policy.

Titow has found that sales of wood were highest on the bishop of Winchester's estates during periods of active assarting, so that clearance was taken advantage of as a means of boosting manorial incomes. In such instances wastes were often deliberately freed up in order to be designated assarts (see Glossary) and thus bring in regular profits.[273] A similar process was set in train at Clarendon at the turn of the fourteenth century. Edward I's order to fell all oaks, coupled with the 1304 arrentations of (? the resulting) wastes, including the Priory of Ivychurch's 112 acres, are evidence of a new attitude regarding management for profit (see above, p.

42). Such a policy may also be linked to the corresponding paucity of royal visits, in that Clarendon at this time seems to have been managed for profit rather than pleasure. The introduction of compartmentalisation (see Glossary) may have taken place also. Certainly certain coppices were defined by name by at least 1318-24,[274] highlighting a move away from a purely wood-pasture economy, a shift further evidenced by the fact that there was little or nothing in the way of a pig economy at Clarendon after the thirteenth century.

The policy regarding management exclusively for profit was reversed by *c*.1317, when the park was enlarged and, presumably, restocked with deer, and through the rest of the century a balance between pleasure and profit (or at least practicality) seems to have prevailed. It had to. The sheer size of the park meant that on the one hand it could be fashioned into what was perhaps the prime example of an élite 'paradise on earth' (see below, p. 149).[275] On the other, repairs to its *c*.16 km pale may be equated with painting the Forth Bridge, so that its economics could never have been entirely profitable in a monetary sense. By the mid-fourteenth century, it was almost a self-perpetuating entity, no doubt aided by its system of coppices which were probably set out as seen today from 1334, or possibly as early as 1328 (see above, p. 49), and which raised £20-£35 per annum from 25-40 acres in 1330-3.[276]

In some ways Clarendon's medieval economy, and the way the estate was managed over time, was little different to anywhere else. However it is curious, in view of the sometimes very large cervine population, that it seems not to have supplied deer to other parks in a similar way as ('because of its comparatively large size') did Woodstock, and (particularly) Windsor.[277] On the other hand, unlike Woodstock, it seems in the period studied, always to have been intensively farmed for its underwood. These are merely contradistinct methods of managing a landscape meant for deer. One can either compartmentalise, *i.e.* fence underwood off from deer (as at Clarendon), or give it up completely and replace it with pollards and timber trees (as at Woodstock).[278] The former route is far less precarious and also offers the benefit of a reliable source of revenue and fencing materials. For example underwood sales from Clarendon Park and Forest from 1337-59 show an average annual

[270] Birrell, 'Deer and Deer Farming', p.125.
[271] *CSPD 1591-4*, pp.288-9 (p.289).
[272] PRO E 32/207, m.12.
[273] Titow, 'Land and Population on the Bishop of Winchester's Estates', p.64.
[274] PRO SC 6/1050/5, mm.4, 1, 3.
[275] A. Pluskowski (quoting A. Andrén), 'Power and Predation: Archaeological and Legal Evidence for Élite Hunting Space in Medieval Northern Europe' (unpub. paper given at *The International Medieval Congress*, University of Leeds, July 2003), p.8.
[276] Colt Hoare and Nichols, *The Modern History of South Wiltshire*, pp.173-4.
[277] See Bond, 'Woodstock Park in the Middle Ages', p.26; Roberts, *Royal Landscape*, p.115. Woodstock Park, of course, was considerable smaller than Clarendon. Even today, after considerable post-medieval enlargement, it is *c*.13km (*c*.8 miles) in circumference, compared to Clarendon's 16km.
[278] O. Rackham, *Trees and Woodland in the British Landscape*, revised edn (London: Pheonix Press, 1990), p.157.

income which fluctuated between £18 and a peak of £62 which it realised in 1357.[279] The decision to compartmentalise at Clarendon may owe a great deal to the loss of other incomes on the park's enlargement. The crown lost *c.*£1.15s.10d. annually with the moratorium on agistment (above, pp. 40-41), not to mention rents for the by now-enclosed wastes, whose entry fees in 1304 had amounted to £158.17d (see below, p. 93).[280]

Timber itself seems to have remained scarce until the mid-fourteenth century. In a survey of the palace and forest under Edward III, probably taken in 1327, it was stated that the king had heard of much 'waste and damage',[281] and before and during that decade lumber for works at the palace came primarily from Chute and Melchet Forests. Not until the Lodge on the Laund was built/repaired, in a document dated 1341–4, do we hear that significant amounts of timber were again coming from Clarendon (although much was still derived from Melchet and Chute).[282] By 1375-7, however, 1300 trees were felled in the park for works on the park pale, manor and lodges.[283]

After the reign of Edward III, royal visits to Clarendon were rare, and it is likely that the park was once more run more for profit than recreation. Evidence is sparse in the later fourteenth century, but the rabbit accounts of the first decades of the fifteenth show that the Clarendon warrens were extremely profitable (see Table 1). Again, Clarendon was not unusual in its exploitation of rabbits as a resource at this time, and it does seem that in periods when the court visited rarely, nationwide trends were followed and the principle of profit came to the fore. In the same period, a widespread shortage of timber trees is again evident, and the commission set up to enquire into sales of trees and underwood at Clarendon in 1419 suggest that the royal forest and park were a particular concern (see above p. 50). This may have been due to over-exploitation based largely on a profit principle, as has been suggested here for the very early fourteenth century — another time when the court rarely visited, if at all. Little had changed by the middle of the century, and in 1455 the Dean and Chapter of Salisbury were informed that their wood perquisites would probably instead have to be rendered as cash (see above, p. 46).[284]

Direct written evidence of deer populations is sparse, but in view of the reportedly large numbers in mid-century forests and parks elsewhere, and particularly of the vast numbers suggested at Clarendon in the last quarter of the fifteenth century (above, p. 34), it is reasonable to assume

that they thrived.[285] Indeed in the late fifteenth century, again probably due to a dearth of royal visits, Clarendon may have been used as a breeding-park in a way that it had not been previously. Hares (and presumably rabbits, which were, at least, being poached) also remained numerous.

The major concern at Clarendon in the sixteenth century, as elsewhere, was the preservation of trees and underwood. Despite the occasional misgivings voiced by the regarders, and the 1598 inquiries into wastes and spoils in Clarendon Park (see above pp. 51-52), timber stocks seem generally to have been maintained. Nevertheless, wood was systematically purloined by the people of Salisbury as well as some of the park's keepers, for which the loss of customary forest estovers and the almost complete withdrawal of royal interest may have been equally to blame.

By the seventeenth century there is evidence that Clarendon's coppices were not as well-maintained as they might be. Those familiar with the estate were quick to provide possible reasons and even James I advised on which seeds should be planted to best effect (p. 54). It will be remembered that he was also responsible for the destruction of the rabbit-warrens and the resulting loss of profit to the earl of Pembroke. Indeed, although Clarendon Forest and Park broadly followed wider trends as far as economy goes, it should never be forgotten that they were run at the whim of their royal owners - sometimes pursuing pleasure, sometimes profit. Behind most such decisions, however, was the need to preserve the venison for hunting, and here the great size of Clarendon Park made it exceptional. It still contained 3000 fallow deer in 1650, and 14,919 timber trees and saplings.[286] In 1664 enough remained to warrant the interest of the Navy, who had 'the trees in Clarendon-park marked and cut down'.[287] Thus, whatever the vicissitudes over the years, and although the forest had gone, the mainstays of Clarendon's economy thrived in the park to the end of the period studied and beyond.

---

[279] Young, *The Royal Forests of Medieval England*, p.126.
[280] Young, *The Royal Forests of Medieval England*, pp.128-9. Agistment figures for the large and profitable Forest of Sherwood amounted to an average income of £3.12s.6d. a year (*Ibid.*, p.129).
[281] PRO C 145/106/8/1.
[282] PRO E 101/593/18; PRO E 101/593/20.
[283] PRO E 364/10.
[284] *CCR 1413-19*, p.16; *CPR 1416-22*, p.270; Parsons, *Pancet*, p.56.

[285] See Birrell, 'Deer and Deer Farming', p.124; PRO DL 39/2/20.
[286] KACC I, p.62; Cox, *The Royal Forests of England*, p.322.
[287] R. Latham and Mathews, *The Diary of Samuel Pepys*, vol. 5, p.203.

Chapter Three: The Buildings of Clarendon Park

CLARENDON PALACE

Building accounts and surveys for Clarendon Palace held in the Public Record Office go back as far as the survey of 1273, commissioned at the accession of Edward I, and continue until 1496 in ever-increasing detail.[1] This is perhaps surprising considering that the last documented stay by a monarch, representing the end of the palace's life as a royal residence, took place in 1453.[2] Through the reigns of Edward IV (1461-83) and to a lesser extent Richard III (1483-85), who spent £25.7s.½d. on the property during his brief reign, attention was still given to great chambers and other buildings forming the royal residence proper, for example the king's chapel and old hall in 1464-71, and the King's Hall and the 'Duke of York's Chamber' in 1482-7.[3] Admittedly, where Henry VI (1422-61, 1470-1) had spent £181.14s.5½d. on Clarendon in the five-year period up to 1450, Henry VII (1485-1509) outlayed £138.3s.10d. up to 1496 over ten years.[4] Yet the latter sum is substantial, and there is little sign of conscious or decisive abandonment prior to the late 1490s, when decisions must have been made. Rather the period is reminiscent of the reign of Edward II, a king who visited rarely, yet spent prolifically, especially on improvements to the park.[5] Although we are aware that the palace had come to the end of its life, this does not mean that that was the intention in the last quarter of the fifteenth century.

Nevertheless, no record of any Yorkist or Early Tudor monarch having set foot in Clarendon Palace has been found. By the early 1490s, and increasingly through the intervening period, attention went to peripheral structures, ancillary buildings, the residents of officials and those most important or symbolic foci such as the king's chapel and the manor gates. In this way the palace continued to be read as a cipher for royal power — Winchester Gate had been battlemented from at least 1485-6, as was a 'new gate' in 1478 and another in 1486-7.[6] Indeed, although the palace itself was in no way jerry-built, there may have been an element of conspicuous display in its virtually continuous repair, especially under Henry VII and the Yorkists. Johnson has suggested that the deliberate and highly visible juxtaposition of old and new building campaigns in Ralph Cromwell's fifteenth-century Tattershall Castle — itself almost a pastiche of the maintenance process — was symbolic of the means to spend continually on one's

estates.[7] In addition, it must be remembered that even a high-status palace like Clarendon was never intended to house the court continually. Instead, it was partly symbolic, representative of its royal landlords when they were elsewhere (as they most often were). If the Yorkists and early Tudors could be seen to provide for its maintenance, far from their preferred retreats in the Thames Valley, so much the better.

There is clearly more to the story of Clarendon Forest, Palace and Park than royal visits, which were the exception at Clarendon as elsewhere. Even under Henry III, the most regular visitor, the average yearly stay between 1253 and 1269 was only eleven days (see Table 4). Although the decline of crown interest undoubtedly resulted in a parallel deterioration in the palace buildings, Clarendon Palace was a working environment for scores of people all year round, even at the height of its popularity. It was the hub of a network of local forests in the medieval period, and almost certainly venison was brought to it from each of them to be salted and dispatched elsewhere. In view of this, can anything be discerned by comparing the chronology of building campaigns with the visits of the forest eyre and other forest courts?

Building Campaigns and Forest Administration

Forest eyres were held at Wilton and Salisbury in the thirteenth and fourteenth centuries respectively. Hence they may be thought unlikely stimuli for extensive building campaigns. However the eyre of 1355, for one, was preceded by comprehensive roofing repairs and other works at the palace, costing over £187.[8] These included repairs to ancillary buildings, to the communal chapel and the Warden's Court, which may reveal the imminent arrival of forest dignitaries and staff. Indeed, buildings in and around the palace may have been routinely used for meetings of the regard and the lesser forest courts such as the court of attachment.

In the mid-fourteenth century, forest eyres were replaced by commissions of inquiry into the state of the forests, where justices of the forest or their deputies went on yearly circuits to hold inquests.[9] Most were held at Salisbury, but that of 1360, presided over by William of Wykeham as justice of the forest south of Trent and Clarendon's deputy warden Thomas Bradwell, was made 'at Clarendon', its jury comprising 73 persons. Given the numbers involved, and the high estate of some, sessions may have been held in the Great Hall, which underwent extensive repairs in the same period. Doubtless the Warden's Lodge played some role, and the construction

---

[1] PRO C 145/31 – PRO E 101/460/16. There is, of course, much information concerning thirteenth-century building works in the calendars, particularly the Liberate Rolls. However, it is without the remit of this study, whose primary focus is not the palace itself.
[2] James and Robinson, *Clarendon Palace*, pp.41-2.
[3] PRO E 101/460/16; PRO E 101/542/20; PRO E 101/460/16.
[4] See PRO E 101/460/10; PRO E 101/460/16.
[5] £81.3s.3d. from 1313-21, of which over £49 was spent on the park (PRO SC 6/1050/5).
[6] PRO E 101/460/16.

[7] Johnson, *Behind the Castle Gate*, pp.56-7.
[8] PRO E 101/459/29.
[9] Grant, *Royal Forests*, p.167.

at this time of a pale encircling the warden's court and the deputy's garden in the inner park (see below, p. 64) may even indicate the delineation of a purpose-built area set aside for forest administration.[10]

The forest inquest of 1373 was also held at Clarendon, and again it was preceded by works at the palace. These included, tellingly, repairs to the stables and ancillary buildings, the deputy's house, and the 'chamber called the Old Hall'.[11] The inquest of 1376, although held at Salisbury, followed repairs to the chapel in the manor, as had the forest eyre of 1355.[12] Doubtless the influx of forest officers and others at such times, connected with not only Clarendon but Buckholt, Groveley and Melchet Forests would have occasioned repairs and refurbishment.

Evidence for forest courts as a major impetus for building works is more clear-cut in the case of the lodges. Three forest inquests definitely held at Clarendon (1360, 1370 and 1373) were each preceded by major repairs.[13] That of 1360 followed work on 'la Lodge' and the Warden's Lodge, involving expenditure of up to £60 on the 'Keeper's Hall' from 1358-60. Work on the Warden's Lodge — referred to, perhaps not coincidentally, as 'the Warden's *Court*' — had run into the previous September, costing at least £29.17s., and had included the building of a new chamber complete with two garderobes. The 'King's New Lodge' underwent repairs and roofing just prior to the inquest of 1370, and 'La Lodge' and the king's chamber there were overhauled in 1371-3, before the inquest of 1373.[14]

Although expenditure on the Warden's 'Court' and the Keeper's Hall may indicate preparation for the arrival of forest officials, similar work took place prior to inquisitions held at Salisbury. Indeed one should question whether ongoing repairs, such as roofing, can produce anything but skewed results. In most cases, it may be more profitable to examine the scale of works carried out. The most striking example is the building of the Lodge on the Laund from 1341-44 before the 1346 Inquest into the State of the Forest, the first large-scale Forest Court to consider Clarendon Forest for sixteen years. Later, the 'King's New Lodge' was built (or repaired) from 1362-66 before a string of Inquests held at Salisbury in 1366, 1368 and 1369. No forest documents exist for fifteenth-century Clarendon apart from the eyre of 1488, held, as usual, at Salisbury, which took place during such a prolonged bout of works that it is difficult to draw any useful conclusions.

The evidence, then, for links between works at the palace and the arrival of the eyre is inconclusive, although a less tenuous connection may be suggested for the lodges.

However, with the demise of the more centralised forest eyre system and the rise of inquests of individual forests from the later fourteenth century,[15] Clarendon may have begun to serve a more prominent symbolic role in forest administration just as the palace entered the long period which witnessed its slow decline in terms of royal favour.

The Use of the Palace: Royal visits
Clarendon was a royal manor in the reign of William I (1066-87), and his is the first securely identified royal visit, in 1072. We do not know what buildings existed at this time, but Clarendon appears to have been at least a hunting-lodge.[16] Edward the Confessor (1042-66), for one, had probably come regularly to the area,[17] and it is tempting to believe that some folk-memory of his visits fostered Henry III's later affection for the place.

The 1130 Pipe Roll entry recording the visit of Henry I (1100-35) and his queen Adela of Louvain is the first evidence of a royal visit aside from the production of writs.[18] It indicates at least provision for storage at Clarendon, reading:

> ...47s. 5 1/2d. expended in the carriage of wine, corn, the king's and queen's robe from Woodstock to Clarendon: and for the allowance of Roger de Causton and for conducting him to [Woodstock] Park, and from Oxford to Winchester.[19]

The king's wine and cheeses were forwarded from Southampton in the same year.[20] A summer visit is indicated, since by 18 May Henry was at Arundel for Whitsuntide.

In Henry II's reign, work of a sumptuous nature was carried out at the palace, for in 1176-7 marble columns (*colu(m)pnis mamoreis*) were sent via Hampshire, probably from Purbeck. The palace must also have been decorative and brightly coloured, for the entry for Surrey in the Pipe Roll for 1179-80 records the carriage of lead and paints (*plumbo (et) coloribus*) to Clarendon.[21] That the king was personally fond of the place is evident from his comments during a dispute concerning Battle Abbey centring on a charter shown to the king at Clarendon;

> *If by a like charter and confirmation the monks could show this sort of right to this very Clarendon which I*

[10] PRO E 101/460/1.
[11] PRO E 32/272; PRO E 32/276, m.5*d.*; PRO E 101/542/12.
[12] PRO E 101/542/17.
[13] PRO E 32/279, 318 and 272; PRO E 101/460/1 and 2; PRO E 101/542/12.
[14] PRO E 101/460/1.
[15] See Cox *The Royal Forests of England*, Grant, *Royal Forests* and Young, *The Forests of Medieval England, passim.*
[16] James and Robinson, *Clarendon Palace*, p.2; KACC I, p.58.
[17] See above pp. 5-7.
[18] Adela was Henry's second wife. See A. Crawford, *Letters of the Queens of England 1100-1547* (Stroud, Alan Sutton Publishing, 1994), p.231.
[19] W. Farrel, *An Outline Itinerary of King Henry I* (repr. by permission of Messrs Longmans, Green and Co. from *English Historical Review* 24, 1919), p.131.
[20] J. Hunter, ed., *Magnus Rotulus Pipe 31 Henry I* (London: Record Commission, 1833), p.17.
[21] James and Robinson, *Clarendon Palace*, p.5.

YEAR	DATES	DAYS	YEAR	DATES	DAYS
1230	8 March 22-4 March	4	**1248**	12-25 June	14
1231	20-6 March 10-13 Nov 28-30 Dec	14	**1249**	28 Jan-26 Feb 27 Nov-22 Dec	56
1232	30 Mar-1 April	3	**1250**	18 June-28 July	41
1234	13-17 Dec	5	**1251**	7-23 June	17
1235	12-17 Dec	6	**1252**	29 June-15 July 16 Nov-2 Dec	34
1236	11-14 Feb 16-21 Dec 28-31 Dec	14	**1255**	15-25 May 16-22 Dec	11 7
1237	1-12 Jan 18-24 Dec	19	**1256**	3-10 July 1-14 Dec	8 14
1239	23 Sept-3 Oct 22 Nov-11 Dec	31	**1258**	23-30 May 30 Sep – 1 Oct	8 2
1241	8-11 July	4	**1260**	1-10 Sept	10
1244	8-14 Mar	7	**1267**	24 Nov-20 Dec	27
1245	12-18 Feb	7	**1268**	28 Nov-10 Dec	13
1246	25 Nov-21 Dec	27	**1269**	8-20 Dec	13
1247	6-19 July 12-23 Dec 28-9 Dec	28			

Table 4: Royal visits to Clarendon in the reign of Henry III.*
* Compiled from Anon., *Itinerary of Henry III: 1215-1272* (PRO).

dearly love, there would be no way justly for me to deny that it should be given up to them completely.[22]

But it was in the reign of Henry III that Clarendon became a major palace. Its development at this time has been amply discussed elsewhere, aided by the fortuitous juxtaposition of periods of intense embellishment with extant contemporary documentation, chiefly the liberate rolls. Moreover in the context of this study it is the *nature* of Henry's interest which is compelling, for at this period an explicit integration of the palace with its environs is evident.

Clarendon Palace had been undergoing refurbishment for at least a year when Henry's majority was declared in January 1227. In March, he ordered the sheriff of Wiltshire to enclose Clarendon Park without delay,[23] and by 1228, he was ordering the warden of his 'new forest of Clarendon' to capture fifteen does 'living in the...forest'.[24] The mention of a 'new' forest is interesting; particularly since an order thirteen years previously had already referred to 'our Forest of Clarendon'.[25] Cross referencing has shown that it is not an error of translation, and it is likely that the 'new' forest is an allusion to the forest's revised administration. That

is, the forest was now administratively distinct from the New Forest for the first time, precisely when the king was embellishing the palace and enclosing the park. At the same time, Salisbury, founded in 1220 and clearly visible from the palace precinct, was taking shape. One feels the locality was now viewed as a unit, the palace as its centrepiece and the landscape as a whole oriented westward towards Salisbury and Wiltshire rather than eastwards towards Hampshire and the New Forest.

Henry III's visits were relatively frequent from 1230 (when presumably work at the palace was relatively complete), and they must have made the court a visible presence in the local community (see Table 4). Nevertheless, his average stay was only eleven days a year and visits declined sharply from the early 1260s.[26] No sojourn at Clarendon is recorded between 10 September 1260 and 24 November 1267, coinciding with the civil wars, and royal visits after 1267 appear to have been limited to one a year. Of the 33 visits of the reign as a whole, 20 occurred in winter (chiefly in December, with 13 visits), six in spring (March and May), five in summer (one in June and four in July) and two in Autumn (September/October). Most winter sojourns took place *en route* to Winchester, where Henry spent eighteen Christmases during his long reign,[27] so that a visit to Clarendon in Advent appears to have been traditional.

[22] E. Searle, ed. and trans., *The Chronicle of Battle Abbey* (Oxford: Clarendon Press, 1980), p.217.
[23] James and Robinson, *Clarendon Palace*, p.8; *CLR 1226-1240*, p.23.
[24] *Mandatum est ballivis nove foreste de Clarendon' quod habere faciat S. de Malo Leone xv dammas vivas in predicta foresta de dono domini Regis* (*CCR 1227-1231*, p.25).
[25] *Rot. Litt. Claus* I, p.226.

[26] The longest stay was 56 days in 1249, the shortest three days in 1232.
[27] James, *The Palaces of Medieval England*, p.65.

If hunting was the purpose of these sojourns, does and/or hinds were probably the quarry, as discussed in Chapter Two, since winter seems to have been preferred. Seasonality in the visits of Edward I is less clear-cut in that, taking the reign as a whole, he seems to have stayed at Clarendon in every month except April and June. There are, however, marked deviations from the patterns set by his forbears in that only one visit took place in December (1305), and there is a preference for August and September.[28]

Edward II appears to have considerably enlarged the park *c*.1317, perhaps following his first recorded visit in February that year. His reign was not characterised by frequent visits, although from his movements we get a glimpse of how royal itinerancy operated in the early fourteenth century. The visit of 1317 was lengthy, from 2 February to 12 March, then 17 March to 13 April. Edward probably returned, in early September 1320, for the privy seal was at Clarendon from 5-13 September, as was the Wardrobe — which was invariably sent on ahead — from 4-12 September.[29] Work on the royal lodgings was carried out 'against the king's coming' from July 1321,[30] and the final recorded visit took place in August 1326, when the wardrobe was sent first to Grimstead. By 9 August it had arrived at Clarendon accompanied by the chamber, and from 11-27 August chamber, wardrobe king and privy seal were all at Clarendon.[31] The court would have arrived in the doe season in 1317, and the buck/stag seasons in 1320 and 1326.

An itinerary for Edward III has been compiled only up to 1334,[32] but information can also be gleaned from orders issued at Clarendon. Significantly, the palace is entered in the *Itinerary* as 'Clarendon Park', and indeed it is the park that seems to be uppermost in contemporary thought. References to the park and forest become difficult to disentangle since the terms are used interchangeably, while emphasis begins to be placed increasingly on the palace's environs through the construction of elaborate lodges in the park (below).

Like Henry III, Edward III appears not to have visited Clarendon until the year of his majority, in November 1330 when he was aged 18, although letters patent were sent from Salisbury in October and November 1328.[33] Indeed the *Itinerary* shows that November was the preferred month for visits in the early part of Edward's reign. At least, the privy seal was at Clarendon from 11-16 November 1330, then at Salisbury from the 18th to the 20th. Writs were issued at Clarendon in the King's name

in August of the following year,[34] and a further visit occurred in November, the privy seal being at Clarendon from 24 November to 2 December.[35] In 1332, both wardrobe and privy seal were at Clarendon from 7-12 July, probably connected to the birth of Princess Isabella (1332-79), since during his visit of 1331 the king had ordered the manor to be prepared for Queen Philippa's confinement the following year.[36] Wardrobe and privy seal returned from 10-15 November 1333, although the wardrobe arrived first and departed a day earlier, as in the previous reign. But from November 18-22 the privy seal was again at Clarendon, suggesting that the king stayed — or used the palace as a base — from 10-22 November.[37]

Through the remainder of Edward's reign, summer visits seem to have been preferred. In 1334, the court was at Clarendon at least from 22 August to 6 September,[38] and in 1343 a royal visit again occurred in July and August. If, as is believed to be the case, the king took the captured David II of Scotland hunting at Clarendon in 1347, a sojourn in the same season is probable, and in 1349 the administration was at Clarendon from at least 12 July to 12 August.[39] In this period, from 1341, the high-status Lodge on the Laund was built (see below, p. 56). Thus the park and its landscape were modified according to the needs of this king who enjoyed summer hunting at Clarendon from his early twenties into the last years of his reign. For example in 1370 he stayed from 26 July-15 August, a visit preceded by the roofing and cleaning of his chambers 'against the king's coming'.[40]

By Richard II's reign, government was more centralised and it is harder to determine where the court was at any given time. But although it has been said that Richard made little use of Clarendon,[41] he may have visited — or have been due to visit — as early as 1377, when a deerleap was constructed and repairs were made to the Lodge on the Laund and to various rooms at the palace 'against the coming of the king at hunting-time (*temp(or)e venac*')'.[42] In 1385, money spent on renovations at the palace, including a fireplace for 'the dancing-chamber', ran in tandem with extensive repairs to the park pale, which was 'partly in ruins'.[43]

This said, expenditure on Clarendon for the period 1384–8, at 63s.11d. for building works (at the palace only)

[28] E.W. Salford, ed., *Itinerary of Edward I*: Index (PRO, 1935).
[29] E.M. Hallam, *Itinerary of Edward II* (PRO, unpub.), pp. 146, 298, 260.
[30] PRO E 101/593/9.
[31] Hallam, *Itinerary of Edward II*, p.280.
[32] Anon., *Itinerary of Edward III and his Household: Regnal Years 1-7* (PRO 942.037). The pages of this volume are not numbered.
[33] *CPR 1327-30*, pp.332, 329.

[34] James and Robinson, *Clarendon Palace*, p.36.
[35] *Itinerary of Edward III*.
[36] *CCR 1330-3*, p.380.
[37] *Itinerary of Edward III*.
[38] *CPR 1334-8*, p.5.
[39] James and Robinson, *Clarendon Palace*, p.37.
[40] *CFR 1368-77*, p.90; *CPR 1367-70*, pp.458-9; PRO E 101/542/11.
[41] James and Robinson, *Clarendon Palace*, p.40.
[42] PRO E 101/499/1, m.3. Of course, the king in question may have been Edward III, who died that year.
[43] L.F. Salzman, *Building in England Down to 1540: A Documentary History*, special edn (Oxford: Clarendon Press, 1997), p.100; *CPR 1381-5*, pp.515, 519, 564, 567; *CPR 1381-5*, p.515.

compares badly with Richard II's other houses.[44] The next lowest was the manor of Berkhampstead, at £5.11½d., while the figures for Windsor (£172.18s.10½d.), Eltham (£192.16s.1½d.), Sheen (£208.16s.11d.), the Tower of London (£337.18s.4d.) and Westminster (£656.6s.8d.) show where the king's real affections lay. The only property mentioned which had less money spent on it than Clarendon was the lodge of Foliejohn, Windsor (7s.1d.). This and other lodges mentioned (Coldkennington, Guilford and Hathelburgh in the New Forest) may indicate the king's preferred venues for the chase. Perhaps significantly, Richard II was not a great hunter as were his three forbears. Nevertheless, writs sealed at Clarendon in 1389 were issued in early September,[45] at the close of the buck season.

The palace continued to be maintained until the end of the fifteenth century, but it remains difficult to make comments about the seasonality of sojourns if, indeed, many occurred. Henry IV (1399-1413) may have intended to visit, for in 1399-1400 stables were built both within and without the palace precinct, and the king's apartments and the park pale received attention, including the addition of a deerleap 68 ft long and 13 ft wide (20.73 x 3.96m).[46] Although Henry VI (1422-61, 1470-1) famously went mad at Clarendon in August 1453 (during the buck-hunting season!), his recorded visits are few — four throughout the reign — and were generally short. His first stay in August 1438 lasted only three days, after which he left for Salisbury. In July 1448 the court was in residence for four days, and a visit of 1450 occurred for reasons of state rather than for pleasure, coinciding with the trial of the murderers of Bishop Ayscough.[47] Henry's fourth visit, from early August to mid-December 1453, was that in which he suffered his bout of insanity. Thus the longest-ever royal visit to Clarendon (certainly the longest in the later medieval period), occurred because the king was unable to leave.

There is no record of any later monarch staying at the palace, and when Richard III visited the area in November 1483 he stayed in Salisbury,[48] even though the palace must have been habitable. He moved on from there to Winchester, but a long royal habit had been broken. Nonetheless, when Elizabeth I and later James I came to Clarendon, they came to enjoy the chase, as had their forebears, and did so during the summer months.

Examining the seasonality of royal visits to Clarendon has revealed something of the way the palace was used. But it has also shed light on its relationship with its immediate hinterland in the shape of the forest and

(especially) the park. In the reign of Henry III, the palace became an element in a unit with its environs. Visits invariably took place at Christmas and in early summer through the post-Conquest period, a clear indication that hunting was their purpose, does being in season in winter, bucks in summer. However until the reign of Edward I, so far as can be ascertained, the Court visited invariably in winter, probably in connection with the hunting of does, hinting at a yearly cull within an organised deer-management regime. Such management, of course, would have carried on with or without the presence of the court and through the later period discussed here, but it perhaps ceased to feature as a highlight in the royal calendar.

From the reign of Edward I, summer visits to Clarendon were the norm, in the buck season. The landscape was substantially modified to accommodate changes in hunting preferences, culminating in the fourteenth century with Edward III's definition of the launds, the digging of ponds, and the addition of at least one sizeable hunting lodge. This mirrors arrangements at Windsor, where each of the three Edwards preferred to reside in lodges rather than the castle. Edward II had extended the park as he had that at Clarendon — at Windsor involving the imparkment of over 1000 acres — while Edward III added a further 55 and constructed additional lodges.[49]

It has been said that the creation and extension of royal parks in the fourteenth and fifteenth centuries 'represented a major change in land-use and an extension of royal prerogative'.[50] This is undeniable (and will be further discussed in Chapter Six). Nevertheless few historians have addressed the impetus behind the process outside the personal preference of individual monarchs. As far as Clarendon is concerned, the change in seasonality of royal visits from the reign of Edward I indicates that here, transformations in hunting practices were a primary factor, and that such changes had an effect on the manipulation of the landscape.

THE GARDENS AND THE 'INNER PARK'

The gardens at Clarendon Palace await detailed archaeological study. Documentary evidence, too, is opaque, although the calendars provide many references to embellishment of the queen's garden, in particular, in the mid-thirteenth century. By 1252 it was 'remade and improved', including the erection of fences.[51] By the mid-to late fourteenth century, when Clarendon's landscape was generally more permanently delineated in the form of internal fences, pales, rides and trenches, its gardens appear more often to have been walled. In 1374-5 a stone wall was repaired, by four masons for twelve days, to the south of the queen's chapel 'between the

[44] PRO E 101/473/2, m.11.
[45] James and Robinson, *Clarendon Palace*, pp.40-1.
[46] James and Robinson *Clarendon Palace*, p.41; PRO E 101/502/15, m.10.
[47] James and Robinson, *Clarendon Palace*, pp.41-2.
[48] R. Edwards, ed., *The Itinerary of King Richard III 1483-1485* (London: Alan Sutton Publishing and the Richard III Society, 1983), pp.9-10.
[49] Astill, 'Windsor', p.11.
[50] Astill, 'Windsor', p.11.
[51] *CLR 1251-60*, pp.61, 90.

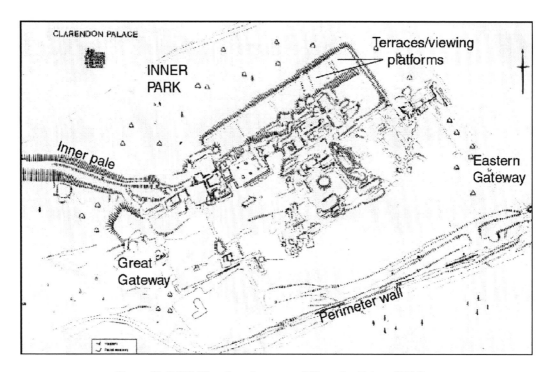

Figure 29. RCHME earthwork survey of Clarendon Palace (1994).

manor and the place called the Queen's Herber'.[52] Preparation for the arrival of the aged Edward III at hunting-time in 1377 included the purchase of 51½ quarts of lyme for repairs to the wall of the late queen's garden, which evidently screened it off from nearby kitchens.[53] In 1447-8, masons were at work mending the wall of the Prince's Herber, and 'amendyng of the wall in the kyngg(es) gardyn there'. There were fences also, since sixteen cartloads of pale were erected around the 'Princes Herber' and another fence was made in the king's garden.[54]

In 1447, Prince Edward (1453-71) was not yet born, and the Prince's Herber was evidently of some antiquity — a stone wall had been repaired 'between the manor and the place called the Prince's Herber' by four masons working for nine days in 1374-5. It is likely, given the likely scale of the walls mentioned, that it was within the complex known as 'Prince Edward's court', first recorded in 1250 and probably built for the young Edward I (b.1239).[55] The area has, unfortunately, not been subject to detailed archaeological evaluation, and the knowledge that it might have contained a garden is tantalising.[56]

Floral evidence is harder to come by than that of physical partitioning, although the continued presence of stinking hellebore (*helleborus foetidus*) and clematis at the palace site may give a clue to what was once cultivated in the royal gardens.[57] Green hellebore (*helleborus viridis*) was also noted in the 1930s, as was

Caper Spurge (*Euphorbia lathyris*). This native of the Mediterranean was recorded as 'very plentiful' in Clarendon Park in 1867 and 1937, when two to three acres of the species were noted in a 'newly coppiced part of Clarendon Wood'.[58] Less speculatively, it is possible that apple trees grew somewhere in the park, for in 1229 John of Monmouth was ordered to sell apple trees (*pomario*), among others, from his bailiwick.[59] That embellishment schemes incorporated attention to Clarendon's overall setting — including horticulture — is not in question, since a document of 1272-3 recording works set in train by the 1273 survey mentions 'the setting of plants in the king's garden at Clarendon'.[60]

The boundaries of knowledge concerning aesthetic medieval gardens are constantly being pushed back. It has been demonstrated that gardens were designed for their beauty from at least the eleventh century, and attention has been drawn to the number of medieval records for planting trees, including apple and pear, in

[52] *Pariet' petr(um) stant' ex p(ar)te Australi Capell' Regine int(er) maner(ium) & loc' vocat' queneherber'* (PRO E 101/542/14).
[53] PRO E 101/499/1, m.5.
[54] PRO E 101/460/10.
[55] *Pariet' petru(m) stant' int(er) maner(ium) & locu(m) vocat' Pryncesherber* (PRO E 101/542/14); James and Robinson, *Clarendon Palace*, pp.25-6, 118-22.
[56] Latham translates *herbarius* as 'arbour' or garden (R.E. Latham, *Revised Medieval Latin Word-List From British and Irish Sources* [London: Oxford University Press, 1965]).

[57] Clarendon Park Ecology Archive, Woodland Record Sheet map no. 184, compiled by G.Lewis.
[58] Mrs Campbell and B. Gullick, 'Notes on the Flora of the Salisbury District', *WAM* 46 (1934), pp.58-62 (p.58); B. Gullick, 'South Wilts Plant Notes, 1933 to 1937', *WAM* 48 (1939), pp.82-6 (p.83).
[59] *CPR 1225-32*, p.317.
[60] *Et in entis in gardino Rex de Clarendon' plantand'* (PRO E 159/47, m.13).

Figure 30. Tilting Field (the inner park) looking north, Spring 2002.

medieval parks. [61] It is into this framework that arrangements at Clarendon may fit, the royal apartments arranged along the scarp on the north of the palace complex with views over the park and the inner park. That views were taken into account is affirmed by the construction of a chamber 'towards the park', when the queen's gardens were improved in 1252.[62] At this time attention was given to the north east area of the palace generally, including the extension of the wine cellar which appears to have had a room above it (*ultra*) that would have provided views. Indeed, the importance of viewing platforms in the medieval mindset has been emphasized by the recent discovery of a purpose-built fourteenth-century 'garden mount', probably once topped by a gloriette, at Whittington Castle, Shropshire, while work at Ludgershall has also revealed the designed nature of thirteenth-century garden terraces overlooking the medieval landscape.[63] Similar viewing platforms are visible in Figure 29, although the gardens at Clarendon have not yet been systematically surveyed.

In view of the findings at Ludgershall, it is hard not to conclude that the inner park, visible from the royal apartments and from the palace as a whole, was meant for some kind of display. The field inside it is now called 'Tilting field', which may not be far wrong (Figure 30). In the thirteenth century it was known as 'the king's park', again suggesting that the inner park was designed as an adjunct to the royal apartments, affording views to activities therefrom.

Possible Buildings of the Inner Park

It is likely, then, that the inner park was designed at least in part as an aesthetic adjunct to the palace. However, by the early fourteenth century buildings may have existed within its boundary. A 1358 order for a new pale clearly places the Warden's Lodge somewhere outside the West Gate. From there to Derngate, the pale would enclose the king's stables, and in running to the East Gate of the manor it would encircle the warden's garden (Figure 31).[64]

This evidence is significant because in the 1930s Tancred Borenius claimed to have come across a 'medieval map' in Salisbury. The map allegedly revealed a demesne surrounding the palace and corresponding to the inner park, comprising 'a small park and gardens', with gates set into its boundary — the Great Gate, 'the Dering Gate' (Derngate), Pitton Gate, Slaygate and Winchester Gate. The Great Gate was almost certainly the western gatehouse of the palace, so that the map must have dated from after its construction in 1241.[65] Thus it is possible that the inner park was encroached on earlier than 1358. Is there any corroborative documentary evidence, especially in view of the fact that Borenius' map disappeared without trace almost immediately, and opinion is divided on whether it actually existed?[66] Major sources must be the survey of 1273 and records of its associated building works.

[61] J. Bond, *Somerset Parks and Gardens: A Landscape History* (Tiverton: Somerset Books, 1998), p.33.
[62] *CLR 1251-60*, p.90.
[63] S. Denison, 'News: Medieval Enclosed Garden Found at Welsh Border Castle', *British Archaeology* 65 (June 2002), p.6; P. Everson, G. Brown and D. Stocker, 'The Castle Earthworks and Landscape Context', in *Ludgershall Castle: A Report on the Excavations by Peter Addyman 1964-1972*, Wiltshire Archaeological and Natural History Society Monograph Series 2 (Devizes: Wiltshire Archaeological and Natural History Society, 2000), ed. P. Ellis, pp.97-119 (pp.101-2).

[64] PRO E 101/460/1.
[65] KACC I, p.57.
[66] T.B. James, pers.comm; C. Gerrard, pers.comm.

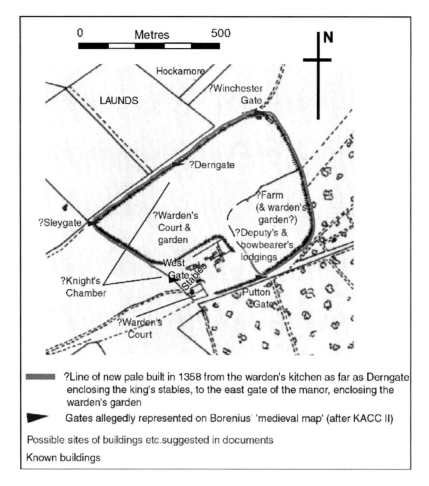

Figure 31. Possible buildings in and around the inner park (from information in documents referenced in the text).
Adapted from T.B. James and A.M. Robinson, *Clarendon Palace: The History and Archaeology of a
Medieval Palace and Hunting Lodge near Salisbury, Wiltshire,*
Society of Antiquaries Research Report 45 (London: Society of Antiquaries of London, 1988), fig. 1.

The Surveys

The 1273 survey of the palace appears not to be arranged topographically, but rather in a hierarchy of precedence. First, repairs necessary to the (king's) Hall and the king's apartments are listed, then the manor well, followed by the queen's apartments (see Figures 32 and 33). Rather more subsidiary structures are then set out, such as the pentices between the king's and queen's chambers, the house 'above' (*ultra*) the cellar, the stairs and pentice leading to the postern, and the queen's wardrobe, which appears to emphasise its separation from the rest of the queen's buildings.[67] The same may be true of the king's salsary, chandlery and wardrobe, necessary repairs to which are followed by structures perhaps located outside the palace proper. These include the almonry and its stable, the 'foreign chamber', John le Faukoner's

chamber and 'Barham's Chamber'.[68] The foreign chamber appears to have been the 'Knights' Chamber' mentioned elsewhere in documents (below), its very name placing it conceptually outside the palace.[69]

Conversely, these buildings may have been grouped together merely because they comprised ancillary buildings and staff accommodation (although these are usually topographically separate in medieval castles and palaces). Next come the king's and the warden's stables, which appear always to have been situated on the palace's west side, one of which may also have been outside the gates (below, p. 66).[70]

---

[67] It has been found that the wardrobes of thirteenth-and fourteenth-century queens were invariably the least permeable of their rooms, whereas those of kings were the easiest to access of their chambers (N.A. Richardson, 'A New Approach to the Study of Queens' Apartments in Medieval Palaces' [unpub. BA Dissertation, King Alfred's College, Winchester, 1998], pp.17, 27, 55).

[68] Le Faukoner and Barham cannot be identified from written sources, but they probably held office at the palace or in the forest at some time. Perhaps one was the deputy warden or constable and the other the porter or gatekeeper, since the deputy's house and the porter's lodgings are frequently mentioned in later documents, on the east and west sides of the palace respectively.
[69] Latham has *forinsecus* as 'foreign, external (to a district or community).
[70] PRO C 143/31/B.

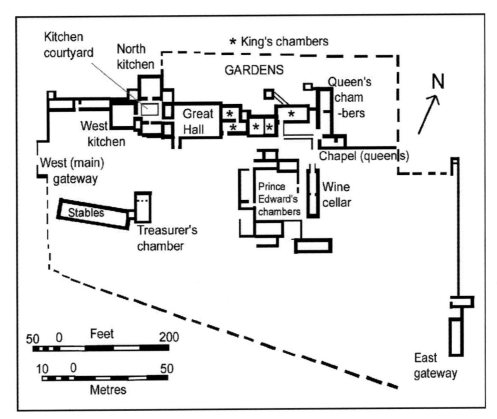

Figure 32. Composite plan of Clarendon Palace.
Adapted from J. M. Steane, *The Archaeology of the Medieval English Monarchy*
(London: Batsford, 1993), fig.62.

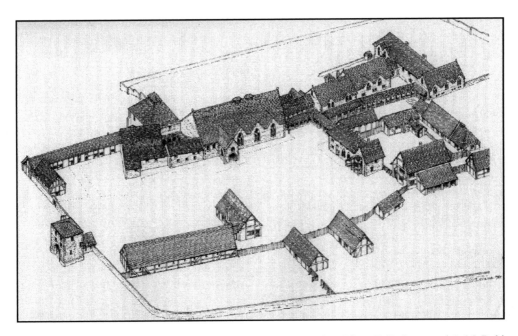

Figure 33. Reconstruction drawing *c.*1275, looking north east. Reproduced from T. B. James and A. M. Robinson,
Clarendon Palace: The History and Archaeology of a Medieval Palace & Hunting Lodge near Salisbury, Wiltshire,
Society of Antiquaries Research Report 45 London: Society of Antiquaries of London, 1988), fig.14.

The 1273 survey was followed by building works in the same year, and in the accounts ancillary buildings are mentioned first, contrasting with the survey's layout.[71] These include the long house by the great gate of the manor, which may be either the stable built in 1244, which is indeed very long at 38.1 x 8.23m (125 x 27 ft.) or the penthouse constructed in 1240 and described by James and Robinson, as the 'foreign chamber for the use of the knights'.[72]

A survey of 1276 begins, like the 1273 works account, with structures on the west of the site. The chamber over the Great Gate is mentioned first, then the foreign chamber (possibly the room south of the great gate outside the precinct wall) before repairs necessary to the 'chamber of the boys' are set out. This may refer to the king's children's' chambers, although the next structure mentioned is the prison, ordered to be made in 1268 probably by the West Gate with which it was certainly associated in the late fifteenth century,[73] and the 'boys' may have been pages or similar. From here, the surveyors listed the defects of the king's kitchen, then turned apparently to the south side of the courtyard to record those of the king's great stable, and the house of the almoner adjacent to the Prince's Chamber. The 'chapel in the outer court' (*capell' in curia extra*) is then mentioned, followed by the cellar, and then by what appears to have been the East Gate ('the gate opposite the wood'), which needed to be made anew. Thence, we return again to the king's apartments, the Great Hall ('the hall to the north') and Robert Walerand's Chamber. Finally, the king's kitchen and its pentice, the salsary, the queen's chamber, the alley between the king's and queen's chambers, the larder and the king's chamber and chapel were inspected.[74]

Although such groupings may hint at the association of structures on the ground, it is hard to draw firm topographical conclusions. For example, Robert Walerand's chamber seems to have been inside the palace proper somewhere in the area of the Great Hall and the kitchens, despite the fact that Walerand had been warden (1259-66) and that the warden's lodge or court appears elsewhere outside the precinct. However, Walerand was a great courtier, and would have been likely to have stayed in the most elevated accommodation. Moreover, later parallels suggest that keepers and other officials were generally provided with two lodgings; fairly substantial affairs in palaces themselves and others in parks or gardens nearby.[75] The firmest conclusion possible is that the foreign chamber, used by 'the knights'

was outside the West Gate, perhaps even in the inner park.

The Knights' Chamber
The suggestion that the Knights' Chamber was inside the inner pale dates from 1354, when it is described as 'by the Derngate'.[76] Clearly, this rests on the supposition that Derngate (OE 'deoren', animal; 'deor', deer; 'deorgeat', park, enclosure for animals) was one of the gates to the inner park.[77] Other evidence comes only by association. For example, the Knights' Chamber was repaired together with the warden's court and king's stable in 1366-7, and the warden's stable and the Great Gate in the west of the manor in 1374-5.[78] However, in 1241, a year after the Great Gate was moved to a more westerly position, Henry III had ordered Adam Cook, custodian of the manor, to build a privy chamber for the king's household wherever he saw fit, either within *or without* the court. The structure was to have four or five internal divisions, its interior strewn with straw, and evidently needed to be built with utmost haste, 'by day and by night this side of Friday', in time for the royal visit.[79]

By the mid-fifteenth century, the royal household is estimated to have numbered about 800, having risen from *c.*370-400 in the 1350s,[80] and all or most would have needed accommodation at the palace. The Knights' Chamber may thus have been the building mentioned *c.*1445-51 as the house where 'the household bene loogyd when thay come', and the 'house where the valets of the Crown customarily lie', tiled with 4000 tiles in 1467-8.[81] An 'outer chamber for the use of the king's esquires' is mentioned as having been built in 1268, again in conjunction with a long house adjacent to the Great Gateway, beside which a smaller gate was ordered to be built.[82] There is always the possibility that, rather than a gate in the north pale of the inner park, this was in fact Derngate, an alternative translation of which is the 'dark' or 'hidden' gate.[83] However, the very frequent association of the Knights' Chamber with the outside or external suggests that it was somewhere immediately outside the palace precinct.

The Warden's, Deputy's and Bowbearer's Lodgings
There is no doubt that the warden's complex was adjacent to Derngate and close to the Knights' Chamber. The 'court of the warden of Clarendon without Derngate' was unroofed, lathed and tiled in September 1354, so that it must already have been in that position. Two years later, it was tiled along with 'the stable without the manor gate' and mentioned alongside 'the manor gate towards

[71] PRO E 159/47, mm.12, 13.
[72] James and Robinson, *Clarendon Palace*, pp.81-2, 22, 24. The building identified archaeologically as the stable block may, however, be that built shortly after 1400 under Henry IV (*ibid.*, p.97).
[73] Salzman, *Building in England Down to 1540*, p.386; PRO E 101/460/10; PRO E 101/460/16.
[74] PRO C 47/3/48. Walerand was warden 1259-c.1266. Ironically, he seems to have spent much of his tenure in residence at Salisbury Castle (see Chapter Five).
[75] Thurley, *The Royal Palaces of Tudor England*, p.83.

[76] PRO E 101/459/29, m.3.
[77] A. Reynolds, pers. comm. (although see alternative, below); KACC I, p.57.
[78] BM Add. Ch. 26594; PRO E 101/542/14.
[79] James and Robinson, *Clarendon Palace*, p.24; *CCR 1237-42*, p.311.
[80] Astill, 'Windsor', p.7.
[81] PRO E 101/460/10, m.1; PRO E 101/542/20 (*log' domu' ubi valett' corone iacer' consuever'*).
[82] Salzman, *Building in England Down to 1540*, p.386.
[83] T.B. James, pers. comm.

Salisbury' (the West, or Great Gate). Moreover, the inner park pale was made 'from the warden's kitchen to Derngate to enclose the king's stables' in 1358-9.[84]

By 1363, the forest warden's complex boasted two halls (one old, one new), chambers, a kitchen and stable, all of which were being roofed. Once more, repairs to the Great Gate, the king's stables in the manor, the house over the manor gate, and the king's chapel were also attended to.[85] In 1366-7, the walls of the 'court of the warden of the park' were again repaired, this time against the coming of the king, as was the king's stable and the 'hall called Knyghtenehall'. Nevertheless, the chamber of Giles de Beauchamp (who actually *was* warden at the time) is mentioned alongside the king's chamber and buttery and various chambers in the queen's apartments, so that he may have resided in what were Robert Walerand's apartments in 1276 (above).[86]

Was the Warden's Lodge actually reserved for the deputy, who would have carried out most of his duties? It seems not, at least until the late fifteenth century. A house in the manor held by 'the deputy' was repaired in 1374-5, when three houses were also demolished to make way for a chamber for the foresters, a hay-store and a stable for the forest warden.[87] In addition, nails were bought in 1464-71 for the 'lodge of the Lord Warden and that of his deputy',[88] so that they were clearly different. It is possible, as has been suggested, that the warden's lodge was on the site of the present Ranger's Lodge, if the 'West Gate' signifies the western entrance to the park as a whole,[89] although it seems too often to be mentioned in conjunction with buildings on the west of the palace site, and one wonders if it occupied the site of the present King Manor (see Figure 31).

The warden's lodge apparently remained on the west of the manor in 1445-51, for it is listed alongside the Bolpit (the palace gaol in or by the West Gate), and the house where the household were lodged (see above, p. 66). It was tiled with 4000 tiles in 1447-8, which may be compared with the 2000 tiles used on the South Gate in 1445-6, and in 1461-72 its kitchen is again mentioned, so that it was still a sizeable establishment. Chimneys notwithstanding, its hall retained a central hearth, for which two cartloads of freestone were ordered.[90] Evidently by this time there was a porter's (gatekeeper's) lodging in the West Gate, for the porter's door is mentioned, verified by a reference to the door-keeper's chamber in 1477.[91] At this time the porter was George Middleton who held the post, along with that of the keeper of the manor, from 1461 to his death in 1479

when William Middleton, esquire of the household, inherited it and also became keeper in 1481.[92] Thus the gatekeeper or porter (actually the keeper of the manor) lived over the West Gate.

The deputy's lodgings may have been located at the East Gate. Indeed, the probable 'farm buildings' discovered at the south east of the palace precinct in the 1930s may have belonged to the complex.[93] At least, the lodgings were close to one of the manor gates. When they were renovated in 1399-1400, the walls of a stable were made by the gate near the deputy's house (*iux(ta) porta p(ro)pe do[mui] locumtenentes*).[94] The lodgings were of stone, for in 1371-4 a stone doorframe (*hostium pet'uu'*) was repaired, along with a chimney.[95] They also possessed kitchens, for a kitchen with a chimney was erected where the deputy's old kitchen had been.[96] However, by 1488-9, the deputy may have resided in what had been the Warden's Lodge, for two panes of glass were mended in 'the hall and chamber at the west gate of the manor where Master Milborne lies'.[97] Thomas Milborne was deputy warden to the Earl of Arundel, and if this hall and chamber were on the west side of the manor, then he, at least, may have 'lain' in the warden's lodge. Certainly the floor of a hall above (*supra*) the west gate was being repaired, and tiled with 1900 paving tiles at the same time.[98] But *supra*, like *ultra,* can mean 'beyond', and it is possible that the structure Milborne occupied was the warden's hall *beyond* the west gate, especially as the porter's lodgings, occupied by Middleton, were in the west gate itself (see above). George Middleton still held the keepership of the manor for life in 1491,[99] so that the deputy warden and the keeper of the manor remained distinct offices.

The lodgings beyond the East Gate were occupied in the late fifteenth century by the Bowbearer, an office that had originated as the service of carrying the king's bow when he hunted in the forest. They were either surrounded by or adjacent to an associated stone wall repaired in 1488-9.[100] The first record of the bowbearer's lodgings is in 1487, where tiling over the 'chamber of Walter Bowbearer' is mentioned.[101] Whether there was a bowbearer named Walter at this time, or he was an earlier incumbent, is unclear, and the nearest Walter chronologically is Walter Barowe (d. *c.*1470), verderer of the park and forest.[102] But since the office seems to have re-emerged just before the palace went out of use little more is heard. However, in 1575-7 the office was held

[84] PRO E 101/459/29, m.3d.; PRO E 101/459/30; PRO E 101/460/1.
[85] PRO E 101/460/2, m.2.
[86] BM Add. Ch. 26594, m.1; PRO C 47/3/48.
[87] PRO E 101/542/14; PRO E 101/473/2, m.11.
[88] PRO E 101/542/20.
[89] KACC I, p.52.
[90] PRO E 101/460/10; PRO E 101/542/20.
[91] PRO E 101/460/10; PRO E 101/460/14.
[92] *CPR 1461-7*, pp.96, 84; *CPR 1476-85*, pp.157, 242.
[93] James and Robinson, *Clarendon Palace*, pp.125-6.
[94] PRO E 101/502/15, m.9.
[95] PRO E 101/542/12.
[96] PRO E 101/502/15, m.9.
[97] *[Au]la & cam(er)a ad port' occidental man(er)ij* (PRO E 101/460/16).
[98] PRO E 101/460/16.
[99] *CCR 1485-1500*, p.149.
[100] PRO E 101/460/16.
[101] PRO E 101/460/16.
[102] *CCR 1468-76*, p.183.

by Thomas Hyle and, apparently, Alexander [Kertherd] (also ranger), and in 1635 by John Nicholas, whose job was to supervise trespasses of the vert and venison.[103]

The Gates
Fieldwork has revealed a number of locations in the inner pale where the gates of Borenius' 'medieval map' may have stood, indicated by a flattening of the pale and breaches in its outer ditch, and this has been taken as evidence that the map probably existed.[104] The existence of a demesne farm inside the inner pale is entirely plausible given its outer ditch, which would have kept deer out (see Figure 81). However it is possible that the map was at least bolstered by information in the document of 1358. In view of this it is useful to examine various documentary references to the gates Borenius cited.

Very few references to Derngate exist in original sources, and most have already been mentioned. All that can be established is that in 1354 the Knights' Chamber was adjacent to it and the Warden's Court, the king's stable and the king's forge 'outside' it, so that it may actually have been a gate into the palace precinct. Only the 1358 instructions for a pale running from the warden's lodge to Derngate, thence to the east gate of the manor (above, p. 63) locate it firmly in the inner pale.[105] However if Derngate was in the position suggested by KACC, interpreting Borenius' map (see Figure 31), it may be the enigmatic 'northgate of the manor' mentioned in 1476.[106] It is hard to see what other gate this might have been unless it was a door leading from the inner park into the royal gardens, or elsewhere into the north range.

Sleygate is first mentioned in 1356 when it was plastered along with the king's stable, the Warden's Lodge, the porch of the wine cellar and at least one chamber in 'Rosamonde'. The wording of the document is unclear, but Sleygate appears also to have contained a chamber at this time.[107] In 1371-4, it was associated with a stable and the deputy's lodge, and at this time a pale was built from it 'westwards to the corner called Park Corner by the high road near Salisbury that runs towards Winchester'.[108] If this is correct, Sleygate cannot be in the position postulated by KACC because the pale towards Park Corner would then run north-eastwards. But neither — for the same reason — could it have been the Sleygate at the site of the present Ranger's Lodge, and it may be that the north of Clarendon Park contained more internal divisions than we are yet aware of. In 1446-7, 74 perches of pale (*c.*372.2 m.) were made from the south of Sleygate towards Goodale's Pike ward.[109] This is almost certainly the Sleygate of the outer pale,

since Goodales Pike lay to its south at Petersfinger,[110] and all further references appear to relate to this gate. Nevertheless, Sleygate is mentioned with the warden's lodge, the deputy's lodge and the longhouse in 1461-72, which all appear to have been near the palace.

It has already been mentioned that the 'Great Gate (to Salisbury)' is the west gate of the palace. Winchester Gate is first alluded to in 1354, when hooks and straps were bought for 'a new gate called 'Wynchest(er)gate'.[111] However written sources seem always to refer to the Winchester Gate in the outer pale. The same may be said for Pitton Gate, first recorded in 1363,[112] and there is nothing in the documents to suggest that either Winchester Gate or Pitton Gate was ever located in the inner park pale.

This said, apart from the Great Gate all these gates — even Derngate, which can be most confidently placed on the palace periphery — are first mentioned in the mid-fourteenth century. Those in the outer pale may well have replaced earlier gates into the inner (original?) park, and shared the same names and orientation, thus Sleygate was at the west of an enlarged park, Pitton Gate to the east, and so on. If, as it seems, the park was enlarged to its fullest extent through the early fourteenth century, the raising of such gates to signify symbolic entry into a rarefied and increasingly exclusive royal hunting landscape would be a logical step.

THE LODGES IN THE WIDER PARK

Henry VII's building works of 1485-97 represent the culmination of a discernible drift from the palace proper toward an emphasis on the surrounding landscape. Most of the expenditure for 1493-5 went on the park pale and Queen Manor, while from 1492, Winchester Gate, Shergall Gate, Pitton Gate and Ivychurch Gate were refurbished. By the same token, probably all of Clarendon's active forest officials resided in or very near to the park by the mid- fourteenth century, so that shifts can be discerned in the landscape throughout the lifespan of the forest system. In what might be described as phase one, the focus of the administrative landscape was to the south and east. This was when William I instituted the forest system and the Walerand family, hereditary wardens until 1224, established their motte and bailey at East Dean. Since Clarendon and Melchet were then part of the New Forest, for which Walerand was warden, it is hardly surprising that the castle was inserted into

[103] E 134/18&19 Eliz/Mich I; WRO 2478/2, *ff.2d*, 5.
[104] KACC I, pp.57-8; C. Gerrard, pers. comm.
[105] PRO E 101/459/29; PRO E 101/460/1.
[106] PRO E 101/460/14.
[107] PRO E 101/459/30.
[108] PRO E 101/542/12.
[109] PRO E 101/460/11.

[110] KACC II, fig. 9.1.
[111] KACC I, p.57; PRO E 101/459/29, m.2*d*.
[112] PRO E 101/460/2, m.2.

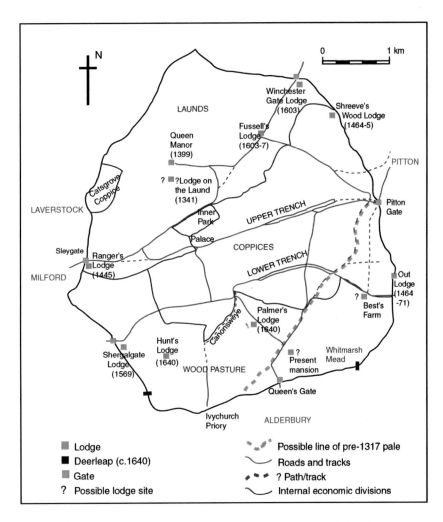

Figure 34. Clarendon Park showing medieval and early modern gates and lodges (with first documented mention of names).
Adapted from KACC, *Clarendon Park, Salisbury, Wiltshire: Archaeology, History and Ecology–*
English Heritage Survey Grant for Presentation II, English Heritage Project Number 1750 (Winchester, 1996), figs 8.1, 9.1.

the existing settlement pattern at their intersection. It is probable that at this time many of the lower forest offices remained in the Anglo-Saxon families that had performed them under the Late Saxon kings, and that they would have lived in the forest vills as before. Phase two, centring on the period when the forest system was at its height from the late twelfth to the late thirteenth century, saw wardens and deputies residing at the palace when (and if) they were in residence, with a few well-established and increasingly locally powerful families occupying serjeanties and living in the vills scattered through the forest. It is in the mid- to late fourteenth century that a contraction gains momentum, culminating in the clear prominence of the park over Clarendon Forest, and, in the end over even the palace. This process is most visible in the landscape in the proliferation, from the mid-fourteenth century, of lodges in Clarendon Park (See Figure 34. Cf. Figure 84).

The earliest firm reference to the enclosure of Clarendon Park, its hay — or hedge — to be 'made of our cablish' (see Glossary) comes in 1225.[113] There may not have

been any associated lodges until 1341, although a 'new chamber in the park', whitewashed in 1251, is a possible candidate.[114] Moreover, the 1341 order for a new lodge specifies 'repairs' involving the removal of rubble, which suggests site reuse, although its hall, for which foundations were dug, was certainly new.[115]

Rackham has commented that we cannot know what early lodges were, or even what they were for, since the archaeological evidence is scant and contemporary records 'assume that everyone knew'.[116] However we can glean much information from the written sources for Clarendon — enough to chart protracted building campaigns and in some cases to study particular structures. The documentary evidence for this new lodge, built from Spring 1341-4, is so detailed that it is almost constructed before one's eyes, and reveals it as an impressive undertaking. Constructed of flint finished

---

[113] *Rot. Litt. Claus* I, p.541.

[114] *CLR 1247-51*, p.362.
[115] PRO E 101/593/20, m.2; PRO E 101/593/18, m.2.
[116] O. Rackham, 'Lodges and Standings', in *Epping Forest through the Eyes of the Naturalist* (Romford: Essex Field Club, 1992), ed. M.W. Hanson, pp.8-17 (p.8).

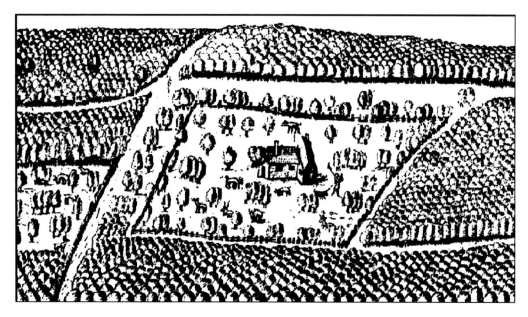

Figure 35. Groveley Lodge in 1598. Reproduced from O.G.S. Crawford, *Archaeology in the Field* (London: Phoenix House, 1960), fig.33. Note the deer both within and without the pale, and the cattle inside it.

with Tisbury stone, it comprised a hall, two chambers with chimneys and garderobes, a cellar with a pantry and buttery, its own kitchen, larder and stable and, by 1357, a well. The siting of this 'Lodge on the Laund' indicates that it was connected with deer-management and hunting, and the ditch and pale that surrounded it, topped with a hurdle fence, reveals it also as a classic park lodge (See Figures 35 and 43).[117]

Any speculation that the Lodge on the Laund was constructed purely for a forest official must be dispelled by the king's order, mentioned in 1343, for a new hall and other houses to be made there.[118] Although Edward III is not known to have hunted in person, his predilection for smaller, more private establishments in the grounds of his palaces is well-attested.[119] A visit to London made in 1354 by John de Hauydon to 'meet with the king's council concerning the well made at the Lodge and other negotiations touching works at the manor' also reveals strong royal interest,[120] and suggests that its purpose may have been close to the royal hunting lodges of popular imagination. Either way, the Lodge on the Laund was substantial, and references in 1354 to 'La Logge' suggest that it was still the only such building in the park.[121]

But lodges might be little more than storehouses for equipment or feeding-stations for deer in fence-months or during winter,[122] only marginally habitative in function. Indeed, lodges were built in Groveley Forest and Melchet

Park in 1357 expressly 'for the foresters there'.[123] These may have more definitely been 'working' lodges, a flavour of which can be gleaned from specifications for the park lodge at Greenwich in 1623-4, which included 'making rackes for the Deare breaking upp'.[124] Snapshots of such activities at Clarendon come in the early fifteenth century, when candles were provided for those gutting rabbits through the night in the park's lodges.[125]

The 1377 reference to the Lodge on the Laund is the last under that name. The next lodge recorded is Queen Lodge (hereafter Queen Manor), in 1399-1400, presuming *logea Regine* does not refer to the queen's lodgings at the palace. In addition, there are references to the king's 'new' lodge from 1362, although, the order speaks only of repairs, and walls are described as 'broken and decayed'.[126] Timber thrown down by the wind is mentioned, and since this was a year of 'tempest', the repairs were probably made to the (relatively) new Lodge on the Laund. Work at the 'new' lodge at this time included the erection of new walls, the replacing of louvres in the hall and the repairing of the pale 'behind the kitchen', while the stable, kitchen and chamber were roofed with 16000 Alderbury tiles, which may be compared with 15,700 rooftiles used on the palace's kitchens in 1336.[127]

[117] PRO E 101/593/20, m.4*d*.
[118] PRO E 101/593/20, m.3.
[119] Astill, 'Windsor', p.11.; C. Given-Wilson, *The Royal Household and the King's Affinity: Service, Politics and Finance in England 1360-1413* (London: Yale University Press, 1986), pp.33-34.
[120] PRO E 101/459/29, m.3*d*.
[121] PRO E 101/459/29, m.3*d*.
[122] Short, 'Forests and Wood-Pasture', p.128.

[123] *CCR 1354-60*, p.356. The earthworks of the enclosure surrounding that at Groveley are still visible (Rackham, 'Lodges', p.9).
[124] PRO E 351/3257.
[125] E.g. in 1420-22, *Solut' p(ro) xij l'l candel' empt' & expendit p(er) div(ersi)s noctes tam tempore ext(ra)ct(i)o(n)is visc[er]um cunic(u)lor(um) infra logeas p(ar)ci p'd'c'i q(ua)m tempore adq(ua)m [siosis] ffurettor(um) & fodic(i)o(n)is foram[inu]m Cunic(u)lor(um) p(ro) furettas...* (PRO SC6 /1050/19).
[126] *CPR 1361-4*, p.183; PRO E 101/460/2, m.2.
[127] PRO E 101/460/2, m.2.; PRO E 101/459/27, m.1.

In 1445-6 Queen Manor underwent considerable refurbishment. 1000 bricks were bought for its walls, and its well received attention. In 1449-50 it was paled, significantly along with the Haybarn (below, p. 79).[128] Repairs to Queen Manor and the Haybarn often occurred together, just as the 'grange on the laund' and the 'lodge on the laund' were roofed with thatch and tile respectively in 1377, and it is postulated here that Queen Manor was the same building under a new name.[129] The first reference to 'Queen Lodge' c.1399 referred only to the repair of gutters, so that the building could not have been entirely new. Most tellingly, a section of fourteenth-century roof reused in the present Queen Manor complex was constructed of trees felled c.1330,[130] around a decade before the first reference to (repairs at) the Lodge on the Laund, discussed above.

From 1493-5 there was another campaign of works at Queen Manor, and there is evidence that materials from the palace were reused — the tiles used cost nothing because they were carried from the king's storehouse at the palace.[131] The documents are then silent until c.1571, when 24 oaks were provided for laths. It is likely that these repairs were connected with the modernising of the park by the earl of Pembroke (below, p. 81). Certainly 37 oaks were felled for repair of the park pale in the same year.[132] This phase of repairs at the lodge may also be responsible for the traditional association of Queen Manor with Elizabeth I, who visited the park three years later in 1574.[133] She was lavishly received, but was forced by torrential rain to dine in a lodge while her retinue took shelter in the temporary 'banqueting house' that the earl had set up for the occasion, presumably nearby and overlooking the deer course, the start of which was situated somewhere on Hockamore Hill.[134]

In 1603 — again, significantly, the year of James I's visit (see above, p. 39) — eight 'tonnes' of timber were estimated for Queen Manor's repairs, which included tiling, carpentry and masonry. In 1607-8 and 1614-21, it was repaired again, the former campaign including 'wages for digging...stone at the King Manor' (i.e. the palace),[135] and the present Queen Manor, which has been dated typologically to the late seventeenth century, is partially faced with ashlar probably from the palace precinct. By 1640 all the lodges in Clarendon Park were described as ruinous in an interrogatory, Queen Manor singled out particularly as so dilapidated that 'Threescore

pound(es) will hardlie repaire it'.[136] In 1651, it was valued at £10 per annum. It had eight rooms, a cellar below stairs, seven chambers above stairs, a stable, two small paled garden plots, a 'comodious well', and was again associated with the Haybarn 'standing at the lower end of the Paddocke course'.[137]

Figure 36. Speed's 1610 map of Wiltshire (detail), showing 'Quene Lodge' in the north of the park, and King Manor. Reproduced from Genmaps, *Old Maps of Wiltshire* (http: //freepages.genealogy.rootsweb.com/~genmaps/genfiles/COU_ Pages/ENG_pages/wil.htm).

All the evidence indicates that this Queen Manor was the same structure as the earlier 'Lodge on the Laund'. Speed's map of the park in 1610 shows only King's Lodge (the gatehouse of the old palace) and Queen Manor (here Queen Lodge), as does Saxton (see Figures 36 and 4) although by that time many other lodges certainly existed, indicating that Queen Manor was then a notable structure. If 'Queen Lodge' was indeed a unit with the Haybarn, Pady Course and Standing, and located high in the present Hockamore Field (see Figure 37), a parallel may be drawn with the Lodge at Cranborne Manor, modernized in 1608, of which John Norden said in 1610 'at this lodge the whole park is discovered'.[138]

From the mid-fifteenth century, documentary references to lodges become more complex. Listed in 1445-6 are Ranger's Lodge, Queen Manor, Biston's Lodge, Ambrose Lodge, and Dale's Lodge.[139] The first two, at least were within the park. The ranger was a new forest official from the mid- fourteenth century, and the first at Clarendon was probably John Rangeour, mentioned in

---

[128] PRO E 101/460/10.

[129] PRO E 101/499/1, m.3.

[130] I. Tyers, *Tree-Ring Analysis of Three Buildings from the Clarendon Estate, Wiltshire*, ARCUS Dendrochronology Report, 429 (Sheffield: ARCUS, 1999), p.5. The present Queen Manor is on a 'new' site below the postulated elevated position of the Lodge on the Laund/earlier Queen Manor.

[131] PRO E 101/460/16.

[132] PRO E 101/140/11, m.5.

[133] KACC I, p.52, quoting Colvin, 1963; Nichols, 1823.

[134] James and Robinson, *Clarendon Palace*, p.45.

[135] PRO E 101/542/21, f.1; PRO E 101/542/22; PRO E 351/3385; PRO E 101/542/22.

[136] PRO E 178/4728/D.

[137] McWilliams, 'Clarendon Park 1600-1750', Appendix E, p.82.

[138] Wake Smart, *A Chronicle of Cranborne*, p.85.

[139] PRO E 101/460/10.

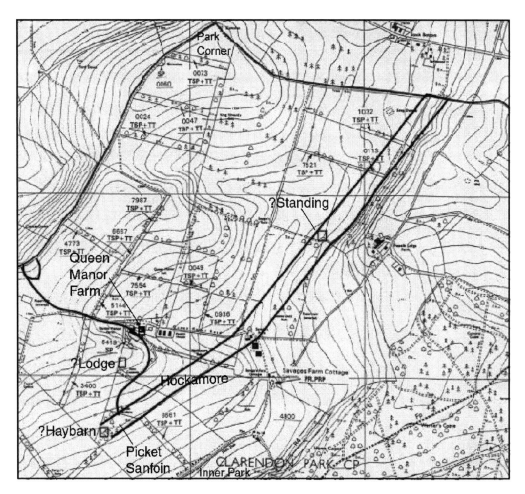

Figure 37. Clarendon's deer course (the Pady Course) and other features from the *c.*1640 map (above, Fig. 7).
The course is here plotted onto contours for the first time, so that its course varies slightly from that represented in KACC II (fig.9).

1353-4 when the de Tudworth family held their serjeanty by service of finding a ranger for Clarendon Park.[140]

The first extant mention of Ranger's Lodge occurs in 1445-6. The ranger may still have been Richard Nedham, servant of Humphrey, Duke of Gloucester, appointed in 1442,[141] although it is unlikely, given his status, that he actually occupied the lodge. Again, the roof was being tiled with 1000 tiles, but walls were being repaired rather than built anew. It had a well with a 'little house' over it incorporating a windlass,[142] probably the 'ffayre well house wth a great wheele & troffes for water wch is standing upon the playne and used by the kep(er)s for water for there necessarye use in ther lodges as also for the deere', mentioned in 1603 when the stable was 'much decayed', and tiling was recommended.[143] Although £331.16s.6d. was paid to John Essington, the woodward, in 1625 'to be employed in repairing the lodges and pales of Clarendon Park', and he received a similar warrant ten years later,[144] it seems the suggestion was not acted upon.

In 1640 Henry Howse, the ranger's servant, related that the stable 'lately fell downe and was like to have killed this deponent, his Master and others that were in the said stable'. Howse was clear that want of tiling — 'soe that ye rayne hath beaten into ye said howse these Three yeares last past to ye great decay of the tymber' — was to blame, and estimated that if this was not attended to, amendments would cost above £100.[145] The other lodges were described in similar terms, and given the date, on the eve of the Civil War, it is not surprising that the present lodges were all constructed after the Restoration.[146]

In the Parliamentary Survey of 1651, Ranger's Lodge, listed above Queen Manor, was valued at £15 per annum. By then the stable, which had two upper rooms was described as 'fayre'. The lodge contained a hall, a 'fayre wanscoted parlor', a buttery, kitchen, larder, washhouse and a mill house below stairs. The first storey comprised a dining room, 3 lodging chambers, a closet and two other rooms while the second storey consisted of a

---

[140] PRO E 32/267, m.16; *CPR 1327-30*, p.397.
[141] *CPR 1441-46*, p.84.
[142] PRO E 101/460/10.
[143] PRO E 101/542/21, *f.*1.
[144] *CSPD 1625-6*, p.550; *CSPD 1635*, p.550.

[145] PRO E 178/4728, 3*d.*
[146] The only exception is Dog Kennel Farm, which has been phased by the RCHME as 'late medieval', early seventeenth century, and 1700-50 (James and Gerrard, *Clarendon: A Royal Landscape*, forthcoming).

lodging and a garret. There was also a paled courtyard, a yard, a garden, two wells and a well-house below stairs.[147]

The Out Lodge is first referred to in 1464-5, as the new lodge in the Out Woods. At that date a chimney was being constructed with 2500 bricks and it was roofed with 8000 tiles. In 1492 it was 'The Out Lodge now called Stonyslogge', probably in connection with John Stone, a forester recorded on the pipe roll of 1519-20.[148] Its walls were being repaired, probably with masonry brought from the palace, where a labourer had spent three days collecting 'olde stuffe'. In 1570, 7 oaks were set aside for its repair, and in 1603, one ton of timber was recommended for repairs.[149] Subsequently little more is heard, although the survey of 1650 describes the lodge as having two ground-floor and three first-floor rooms, a barn, a small stable and 'two little garden plotts', the earthworks of which may still be seen.[150]

Henry VII appears to have lavished attention on the lodges of Clarendon's constituent forests soon after his accession, probably in connection with his attempt to revive the forest system and collect revenues. For example Groveley Lodge (see Figure 35) was provided with a new kitchen in 1487-8 on which 12,000 oak boards were used, and its stable fitted with planks, racks and a manger. It had a parlour, some of its 'houses' were roofed with thatch, and others with Alderbury tiles, and green wood was taken from Clarendon, presumably to be used as a building material.[151]

In 1476-8, another lodge appears to have been built at Clarendon. This was the 'new lodge at Sharpegoregate' (later Shergalgate), for which 23 oaks were supplied and 741 feet of timber used.[152] At the same time, references to Sleygate Lodge appear. This was almost certainly Ranger's Lodge, discussed above. Again, further lodges are mentioned, named for foresters. The site of the lodge of Richard Cole, a Clarendon Forester c.1479-80, is uncertain, although we are on firmer ground with Richard Mille's Lodge, Mille having been forester for the Whitmarsh bailiwick c.1484-8.[153] Possibilities are the site of Best's Farm and what would later become Palmer's Lodge, identified archaeologically to the north west of the present Clarendon Manor. Alternatively it may be the lodge traditionally believed to have been on the site of Clarendon Mansion itself, which occupies another ideal lodge-site with viewsheds particularly towards the Stoneygore area (see Figures 34 and 38).[154]

Clarendon House

Figure 38. Long view towards the late seventeenth-/early eighteenth-century mansion from Grimsditch field, Spring 2002, looking south west.

Mille's Lodge was roofed with Alderbury tiles, and a chimney was made with 400 bricks in 1488-9. In 1489-90 carpentry was carried out against the coming of the warden, Thomas, lord Arundel (1450-1524), and in 1492-3 its doors and windows were mended. John of Clarendon's Lodge also underwent roofing repairs. In addition, it was enclosed with 8½ perches of pale in 1490-1, the paling repaired again five years later.[155] This is hardly surprising, for a 'John Claryngdon' was one of the park's palicers in 1488 as well as being forester for Sharpegore Gate, and mentioned as a forester in 1519-2.[156] Therefore Mille's was probably Sharpegoregate/Shergalgate Lodge. This was in the wood-pasture area of the park, where temporary 'lodges' and booths were made annually (see below, p. 80), so that its occupation by a hedger/paler would have made sense.

Robert Nynge's Lodge, also mentioned in the 1490s, is the most securely identifiable of this group, Nynge being forester for Shreeve's Wood until at least 1499.[157] The site of his lodge has been identified archaeologically on the north eastern boundary of the park, where the remains of a small cottage, deep well and outgrown garden plantation remain visible.[158] In 1484-5, door furniture was being made for it, and in 1492-3 repairs included roofing with tiles carried from the palace. In 1495-6, its chimneys were mended with 'Tylesherdes', again from the palace, apparently in the mortar mix. Broken tiles are unlikely to have been held in the king's stores, and this is decisive evidence for the dismantling of at least some of the palace buildings.[159]

[147] McWilliams, 'Clarendon Park 1600-1750', Appendix E, p.82.
[148] PRO E 101/542/20; PRO E 372/365 (Item Wiltes).
[149] PRO E 101/460/16; PRO E 101/140/11. Repairs to Ranger's Lodge warranted 30 oaks, Queen Manor 24, Shergalgate Lodge 12, and Shreeves Wood and Whitmarsh Lodges 10.
[150] McWilliams, 'Clarendon Park 1600-1750', Appendix F, pp.97-8.
[151] PRO E 101/460/16.
[152] PRO E 101/460/14.
[153] PRO E 372/325 (Item Wiltes); PRO E 101/460/16; PRO DL 39/2/20.
[154] T.B. James, pers. comm.

[155] PRO E 101/460/16.
[156] PRO DL 39/2/20, m.3.; PRO E 372/365 (Item Wiltes).
[157] PRO E 372/345 (Item Wiltes).
[158] KACC I, p.52.
[159] PRO E 101/460/16. Even this evidence does not necessarily mean the palace was being consciously abandoned. As early as 1374-6, a boy was paid for collecting broken tiles (tegul' fract') during works at the palace (PRO E 101/542/12).

Sixteenth- and Seventeenth-Century Lodges

The early modern lodges are generally easier to identify. But some remain enigmatic, including 'The North Lodge next to the Laund', mentioned in 1575-7. This might be the present Queen Manor, whose oldest parts, suggested by brickwork and carpentry are 'perhaps early seventeenth century', Winchester Gate Lodge (later Pruett's Lodge) or Fussell's Lodge, which KACC tentatively suggested to have been built *c*.1600 because William Fussell occupied it in 1618.[160] The North lodge is associated in a deposition with (among others) George Batter, forester for Shreeve's Wood and keeper of the bailiwick of the launds,[161] so that on the face of it, Fussell's, with its view over the launds, would be the likely candidate. However, a distinction is made in written sources between the keeper of the *bailiwick* of the launds, and the keeper of the launds, i.e. the Launderer (Richard Booth), so that the North Lodge might nevertheless be Winchester Gate Lodge, nearer to Shreeve's Wood and perhaps occupied by Batter and others, while launderers resided at Fussell's. To cloud the issue even more, Fussell's Lodge is described as 'John Fussels Lodge called Wynchester gate Lodge' in 1603.[162]

The next campaign of repairs to the Clarendon lodges may have occurred in 1603-7, although the document in question is a survey and the works may never have taken place. Mentioned with John Fussell's Lodge are King Manor, Queen Manor, Ranger's Lodge, Shergalgate Lodge and the Out Lodge.[163] 45 tons of timber would have been used on these works, although the focus is on the parrocks and 'great rails' (probably the Pady Course and its appurtenances, see above), the haybarn and the well-house rather than the lodges alone. It seems feasible in the light of the visit of James I in Summer 1603,[164] and given his love of hunting, that there was a concerted effort at this time to fashion the landscape into a fully-functioning early modern hunting park.

In 1606, Queen Manor and Ranger's Lodge were singled out for repair, either because of their prominence or their relative decay. All the lodges were apparently dilapidated in 1640, although Palmer's Lodge was repaired at that time (with just one oak).[165] This wood, like that from the original Queen Manor/Lodge on the Laund, repaired in 1606, may have found its way into the present Mansion House since likely felling date ranges of some of its timbers fall between AD 1604-40, 1635-71 and 1638-67.[166]

THE LODGES: DISCUSSION

Siting

A great deal of thought went into the siting of lodges. In 1388, an inquisition was held before a lodge could be built in the Inglewood Forest, Cumbria, due to fears that the deer, disturbed by its inhabitants, might 'resort elsewhere to feed in open places where they would easily be taken by hunters and evildoers'. In addition, the lodge might disrupt the common pasture of forest-dwellers, since it would lie 'upon the common passage of...cattle to the river'.[167] There is no reason to believe that lodges were any less well-planned in Clarendon Forest, and in the biggest medieval deerpark in England the deer would certainly have been the first priority.

Yet it is difficult to locate securely many of Clarendon's lodges in the medieval period. That most listed in 1445-6 were named for foresters (Biston's Lodge, Ambrose Lodge, Doly's [?Dale's] Lodge) renders it difficult to ascertain which lodges are being referred to. However this does facilitate checking of the buildings against the foresters listed in the Pipe Rolls and elsewhere. Thus, John Biston was a Clarendon forester in 1429 for the park and also Buckholt Wood,[168] suggesting that 'Biston's Lodge' was somewhere in the east of the park. And Dale's Lodge may be named for the Doly (?Dely) family, foresters for Melchet at least from 1484-5.[169] If so it this may place Dale's Lodge in Melchet Forest.

The 'Lodge on the Laund' has been suggested by KACC to have been the precursor of Ranger's Lodge due to Colvin's assumption that it was built for Edward III's keeper.[170] But, as discussed above, it seems to have been a high-status building built for the king himself in the first instance. A description of how such lodges operated in the late seventeenth century is given by Celia Fiennes, *c*.1696:

> [At Lyndhurst] *is a house of the kings when he comes to hunt in the New Forrest and the Lord Warden of the Forrest is there when he comes to hunt and hawk, to whome comes all the Gentry of the County to waite on him; he dines at Night from 7 to 12 of the clock...[and] those that hunt with him...comes and dines or supps with him.*[171]

Almost certainly such a lodge would have been visible from the palace. There are substantial earthworks and the remains of a building in Hockamore Field, above the farm to its south west, associated with quantities of medieval pottery, thirteenth to fifteenth century rooftile and at least two sherds of inlaid Wessex floortile found

---

[160] James and Gerrard, *Clarendon: A Royal Landscape*, forthcoming; PRO E 134/18&19 Eliz/Mich 1 no.1; KACC I, p.63. However Queen Manor was rather 'in' than 'next to' the launds.
[161] PRO E 101/140/11, m.4.
[162] PRO E 101/542/21, *f*.1.
[163] PRO E 101/542/21.
[164] PRO E 178/4728.
[165] PRO E 178/4728, m.3*d*.
[166] Tyers, *Tree-Ring Analysis*, p.8.

[167] *CCR 1385-9*, pp.400-1.
[168] PRO E 372/275 (*Item Wiltes*).
[169] PRO E 101/460/16, D.
[170] KACC I, p.52.
[171] C. Morris, ed., *The Journeys of Celia Fiennes* (London: The Cresset Press, 1947), p.50.

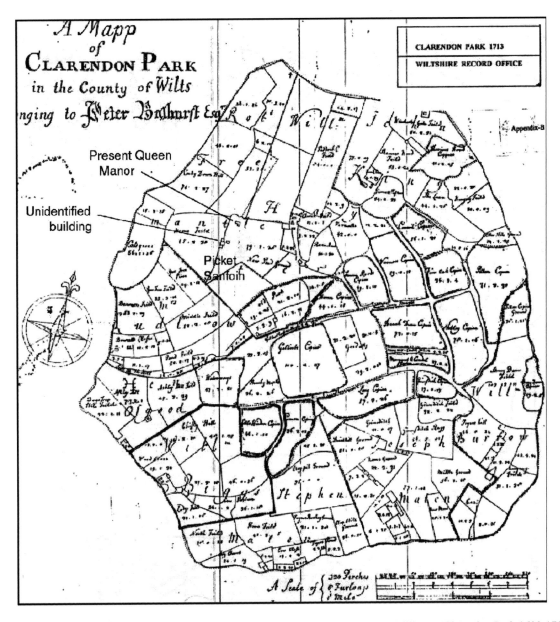

Figure 39. Map of Clarendon Park probably dating to 1713. Reproduced from J. McWilliams, 'Clarendon Park 1600-1750: From Medieval Deer Park to Post-Medieval Estate' (unpub. BA dissertation, King Alfred's University College, Winchester, 1996), Appendix B. This is near-contemporary with Stukeley's drawing (Figure 2, above), in which Picket Sanfoin is also shown with no north-eastern field boundary.

during fieldwalking in 2002 (some of which may have been brought from the palace during late- fifteenth-century repairs). In addition, an apparently wing-planned structure larger than the already existing Queen Manor Farm is shown on the boundary of the present fields Hockamore, Old Poultry and Picket Sanfoin (see Figure 39) on a map of 1713, its dimensions according well with the surviving lodge in Hatfield Forest, a timber-framed building of hall-house plan.[172] And although Stukeley's 1723 view does not represent any structure in this exact position, it does seem to reveal the roof of the present Queen Manor peeping over the brow of the hill, just as it does today, behind a substantial building above it, slightly to the right (see Figure 40). Fieldwalking has

established that this area, which immediately overlooks Queen Manor Farm, is associated with late medieval and post medieval finds that thin out towards the middle of the field, walking westwards.[173] In addition the remains of a wall are to be found in a clump of trees on the edge of the scarp, behind which the hillside looks to have been terraced.[174] There is another concentration of finds, again largely post medieval, about a third of the way down Hockamore, walking east, which may indicate the position of the 1713 structure, especially since ploughing has clearly dragged such debris down the hill in a southerly direction.[175]

---

[173] Finds from further south in Hockamore tend to be Roman (T. King, pers. comm).
[174] A. Reynolds, pers. comm.
[175] A. Turner, pers. comm.

---

[172] Rackham, 'Lodges', p.9.

Figure 40. Detail of Fig. 4, Stukeley's 1723 view across the palace site, showing possible building in Hockamore at centre. Reproduced from Reproduced from T. B. James and A. M. Robinson, *Clarendon Palace: The History and Archaeology of a Medieval Palace and Hunting Lodge near Salisbury, Wiltshire*, Society of Antiquaries Research Report 45 (London: Society of Antiquaries of London, 1988), pl. 1a.

Figure 41. View north west across palace site to Hockamore showing newly-cleared north wall of Great Hall, Spring 2002.

It is possible that either the Hockamore structure and/or that on the 1713 map was the Lodge on the Laund, later renamed Queen Lodge/Manor, before the present Queen Manor Farm was built nearby sometime in the seventeenth century. Indeed the presence in Queen Manor Farm of timbers felled between 1336 and 1372 give weight to this hypothesis.[176] Major works at the 'Lodge on the Laund', the 'lodge at Clarendon', 'the lodge', 'the king's new lodge', and/or 'the new lodge' were carried out from 1341-77, and since the 1341 reference is to 'repairs', a structure must already have existed.[177] Alternatively, the building on the 1713 map

---

[176] Tyers, *Tree-Ring Analysis*, p.5.

[177] See PRO E 101/593/18; PRO E 101/593/20; *CCR 1346-9*, p.464; PRO E 101/459/29; PRO E 101/459/30; PRO E 101/460/1; CPR 1361-4, p.183; PRO E 101/460/2; PRO E 364/2; BM Add. Ch. 26594; *CCR 1369-74*, p.39; *CPR 1367-70*, p.459; PRO E 101/542/12; PRO E 101/499/1.

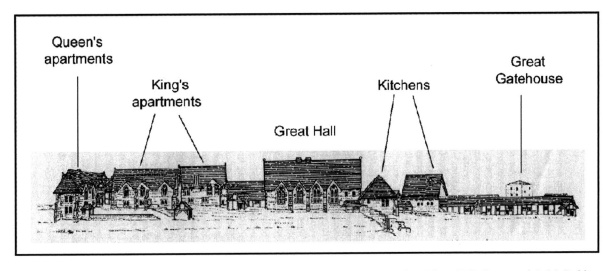

Figure 42. Reconstruction drawing of Clarendon Palace's north range, *c*.1275. Reproduced from T. B. James and A. M. Robinson, *Clarendon Palace: The History and Archaeology of a Medieval Palace and Hunting Lodge near Salisbury, Wiltshire*, Society of Antiquaries Research Report 45 (London: Society of Antiquaries of London, 1988), fig.15.

may be the Haybarn, which apparently still stood in 1692.[178]

In any event, Hockamore would be an ideal site for a royal lodge in view of its intervisbility with the main palace precinct (Figure 41). Moreover the inexplicable arrangement whereby no lodges overlooking the launds themselves may be explained by its disappearance. The lodge would indeed have been high on the launds with 360-degree viewsheds all around, so that it is not unfeasible that it was the residence of the launderer, an official first mentioned at Clarendon in 1324 when Griffin Vaughan was given custody of the launds.[179]

More generally, noteworthy concentrations of lodges in Clarendon Park existed, at least by the late fifteenth century and into the early modern period, including the triangle of Fussells, Winchester Gate and Shreeves Wood Lodges in the north east of the park. This 'bunching' can be partly explained by the varied duties of the keepers. The distinction between the 'Keeper of the Bailiwick of the Launds' and the launderer himself, both of whom would have required views over the launds, has already been discussed (above, p. 74). The incumbent of Shreeves Wood Lodge, of course, was responsible for Shreeves Wood, the remains of which are visible outside the estate boundary. But concentrations of lodges can be explained also through the principles of landscape demarcation according to sight-lines. Concerning this particular cluster of lodges, Shreeves Wood Lodge and its environs are hidden both from Winchester Gate/Prewetts and from Fussells due to the sharp drop in the terrain. Thus a lodge (and keeper) to police this part of the park was necessary.

Building Materials
The Lodge on the Laund seems to have been a high-status structure from its erection (or remodelling) in 1341. Plaster of Paris was brought from Lymington, Hampshire, and it was constructed largely from Tisbury stone, a fine to coarse grained oolitic limestone similar to Bath and Chilmark which the RCHME calls 'one of Britain's best building stones'.[180] Stonework recovered from the palace site, too, is almost all 'of the Chilmark type' (which includes Tisbury) so that the lodge may have been conceived in order to mirror those arrangements. Certainly some of the higher-status buildings in the palace's north range (Figure 42), facing the lodge's putative location in Hockamore, are known to have been executed in Chilmark stone from the thirteenth century, and the Great Hall was remodelled with stone quarried at Chilmark in 1358-9.[181]

The present Queen Manor Farm incorporates Chilmark-type ashlar in its exterior walls, although whether this came from the palace or another structure is likely to remain unclear, the 1607 reference to stone being dug at King's Manor for repairs to various lodges notwithstanding. Indeed, most lodges seem to have been built of stone throughout the period studied. However, the 'new lodge at Sharpegoregate', built *c*.1477, may have been timber-built, since no stone is mentioned in the relatively detailed building accounts. It may have been built of wattle and daub as branches were gathered at Sharpegore during its construction, and it may have been a temporary lodge or booth built for fence-month, since

[178] WRO 302/1, no.1.
[179] *CPR 1324-7*, p.27.

[180] RCHME, *Thesaurus* (http://www.rchme.gov.uk/thesaurus/bm_types/P/98123.htm).
[181] J. Ashurst and T.B. James, 'Stonework and Plasterwork', in T.B. James and A.M. Robinson, *Clarendon Palace: The History and Archaeology of a Medieval Palace and Hunting Lodge near Salisbury, Wiltshire*, Society of Antiquaries Research Report 45 (London: Society of Antiquaries of London, 1988), pp.234-58 (pp.234-5).

these seem to have been erected at Sharpegore annually (see below, p. 80).[182]

Shingles seem not to have been used on the lodges, even when the most prominent edifices at the palace were roofed with them, for example the king's chamber in 1356.[183] The Lodge on the Laund was tiled with Alderbury tiles in 1343, as were others including Groveley Lodge in 1357, 1478 and 1487, and Mille's Lodge in 1487.[184] There were probably more, but the origin of rooftiles is rarely mentioned. Other structures were thatched, including the Haybarn ('Grange on the Laund') in 1377, and outbuildings associated with Groveley Lodge in 1487.[185]

Bricks were used in royal palaces occasionally from *c*.1350,[186] and by the mid-fifteenth century most of Clarendon's lodges incorporated brickwork. 1000 were bought in 1445-6 for making walls at 'Queen's Lodge', a process which took 14 person-days.[187] This is noteworthy, not only because the present Queen Manor is the only structure on the Estate incorporating small (*c*.5cm thick), thus 'early' bricks, but also because at this time only chimneys and hearth-linings were made of brick, prior to its more general adoption in the following century.[188] If the lodge's walls were made largely of brick, its construction was innovative,[189] and it would have rated second in status to the earlier Lodge on the Laund (unless these were the same building). 2000 bricks were used in Dale's Lodge (probably in Melchet) in 1446-7, and 2500 in the 'new lodge in the Out Woods' in 1465.[190] Brick was also used in Mille's Lodge in 1487, but since only 400 were bought, almost certainly only its hearth or chimney were of brick construction.[191]

A noteworthy consideration is whether particular lodges were surrounded by ditches and pales, and where they were situated. In 1341-4, The Lodge on the Laund's pale measured 306.81m. in length (63 perches at 16ft per perch) and stood on a ditch 8ft (2.43m.) wide and 5ft (1.52m.) deep, commensurate with its status and its situation in the deer-managing areas of the laund. Queen Lodge's pale was mended alongside that of the Haybarn in 1449-50, taking together 15 loads of timber and 90 person-days to mend.[192] The Haybarn still possessed its pale, noted in 1486-7 as being of wattle and daub construction, in 1603 when it encompassed 15 acres (6.07 ha.).[193] Other lodges surrounded by pales were Groveley Lodge (see Figures 35 and 63), Dale's Lodge, whose pale measured 39½ perches (198.65m.) and Sharpegorgate Lodge, home of the palicer John of Clarendon *c*.1488-*c*.1520, for which 8½ perches (42.75m.) of pale were made in 1490-1.[194]

By 1650, Queen Manor seems not to have been paled, suggesting it had by then been rebuilt in its present position. Ranger's Lodge was, however, and the nearby 'Ranger's Rails' encompassed a substantial barn and 15 acres of land (6.07 ha), while at Hunt's Lodge there were two adjoining 'little yards paled in' measuring 2 rods (0.202 ha?) 22 perches (110.64m). A distinction may be made between these and 'the house called Dogg Kennell' near Shergalgate, whose garden, measuring 1 rod 26 perches, was fenced in not with a pale but a hedge. The adjacent dog kennel itself was set in a yard encircled by a brick wall.[195]

In the earlier period, though, the Lodge on the Laund possessed the most substantial known pale in the park and forest. The impact made by such palings in the landscape, usually termed 'rails' by the sixteenth century, is clear from the prominence given them in early modern maps (Figure 43). Thus pales around lodges served to highlight their status. But they also had a functional dimension, described by Celia Fiennes *c*.1696:

[The lodges in the New Forest] are disposed to Gentlemen that have under keepers...at these severall Lodges the Keepers gather [browse] and at certain tymes in the day by a call gathers all the Dear in within the railes which belongs to each Lodge and so they come up and feed upon this Brouce and are by that meanes very fatt and very tame so as to come quite to eate out of your hand; all the day besides they range about and if they meete any body, if it be their own keeper, without the pail of the Lodge they will run from him as wild as can be.[196]

Fiennes claimed that such 'Brouce Deare' were peculiar to the New Forest. This is unlikely especially in parks. Certainly there were domesticated deer at Clarendon in 1573, when 'Mr Rob(er)te Penruddocke(es) S(er)v(au)nte killed one of Bright's tame Deere'.[197]

[182] PRO E 101/460/14; PRO E 101/460/16; PRO E 32/267, m.7.

[183] PRO E 101/459/30.

[184] PRO E 101/499/1, m.3; PRO E 101/460/14; PRO E 101/460/16.

[185] PRO E 101/499/1, m.3; PRO E 101/460/16.

[186] James, *The Palaces of Medieval England*, p.112. Brick is present in the Clarendon floortile kiln, dated *c*.1250 (T.B. James, pers. comm.).

[187] PRO E 101/460/10.

[188] R. Turle, 'Clarendon Standing Buildings: An Evaluation of Standing Building Values and Management at Clarendon Park, Wiltshire' (unpub. master's thesis, Oxford Brookes University School of Planning and University of Oxford Department for Continuing Education, 1998), pp.44, 114; N.J. Moore, 'Brick', in *English Medieval Industries: Craftsmen, Techniques, Products*, eds John Blair and Nigel Ramsay (London: The Hambledon Press, 2001), pp.212-36 (p.212).

[189] Moore, 'Brick', p.212.

[190] PRO E 101/460/10; PRO E 101/542/20.

[191] PRO E 101/460/16.

[192] PRO E 101/460/10; PRO E 101/593/20 m.4*d*. I make no apology for the use of 'person-days' here. There is evidence in the Clarendon building records of at least one female carter (PRO E 101/460/16).

[193] PRO E 101/460/16; PRO E 101/542/21, *f*.1.

[194] PRO E 101/499/1, m.5; PRO E 101/460/16.

[195] McWilliams, 'Clarendon Park 1600-1750', Appendix E, pp.83-4.

[196] Morris, *The Journeys of Celia Fiennes*, p.50.

[197] WRO 549/8, *f*.12*d*. Robert Bright was forester for Shergalgate.

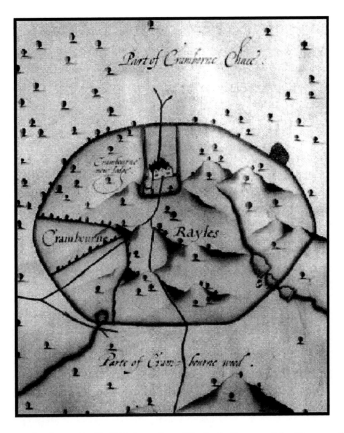

Figure 43. Cranbourne Lodge and rails, Windsor, from Norden's *Survey of the Honour of Windsor* (1607).
Reproduced from J. Roberts, *Royal Landscape: The Gardens and Parks of Windsor*
(London: Yale University Press, 1997), fig. 282.

Of lodges with pales in Clarendon Park, three, 'Queen Lodge' (with the Haybarn) the Lodge on the Laund and Ranger's Lodge were situated in or near the launds and were thus obviously connected with deer management. Neither is it surprising that Groveley and Melchet Lodges were encircled by pales, since these were probably the only purpose-built permanent utility buildings in those forests. Sharpegoregate (or Shergalgate) Lodge in the park was situated at the south west entrance to the park, well away from the laund areas. However, this was the wood pasture area of Sheer Wood, which seems to have been a deer-management area of some kind in view of the temporary lodges erected there (below, p. 80). At least, the pale reveals Sharpegoregate Lodge to have been more than a gatehouse.

OTHER STRUCTURES

In the royal landscape of Clarendon Park, lodges seem always to have been, or to have quickly become, relatively substantial affairs, and documentary evidence for more ephemeral, workaday structures is scant. The best documented ancillary building in the park was the grange or haybarn, first mentioned in 1372. A clue as to its origins may lie in the survey carried out early in Edward III's reign, which mentions a barn built 'by order of the late king [Edward II]' which would cost 40s. to

repair. However, Musty and Colvin believed this building to have occupied the south east corner of the palace site, where two structures were identified as barns in the 1930s.[198]

The Haybarn must have been sizeable enough to hold the 30 cartloads of hay provided for the deer each winter. It was thatched with five cartloads of straw in 1377, but by 1606 it was tiled. In 1486 it had a porch, and from at least 1450 it was surrounded by a pale.[199] In 1603 an estimate was made for the erection of a rail of 60 pooles (6.07 hectares) around it to prevent cattle from eating hay provided for the deer. The latter would, it was predicted, be greatly relieved.[200]

Whether or not this grange was associated with the new lodge of 1341, it was referred to in 1377 alongside references to the Lodge on the Laund.[201] In addition, a haybarn is represented on the map of *c*.1640 (Figure 9) close to Queen Manor at the western end of the Pady Course. Its siting may have allowed deer to be selected, when feeding, for corralling into the great rails before being driven up the Pady Course eastwards past the standing for the kill (below, pp. 80). But long before the

[198] James and Robinson, *Clarendon Palace*, pp.35-6.
[199] PRO E 101/460/16; PRO E 101/542/21, *f*.1; PRO E 101/460/10, m.1.
[200] PRO E 101/542/21, *f*.1.
[201] PRO E 101/499/1, m.3.

course was built the Haybarn would have attracted deer into full view of the palace so that they would have been an intrinsic part of views from it across the landscape.

There were also several wells at Clarendon, some of them substantial. The great well in the manor, first mentioned in 1273, needed cables 24 fathoms (43.9m.) long and possessed a large wheel in which three to four men ran in order to raise up water.[202] The purchase of iron furniture for it is a constant feature of fourteenth- and fifteenth-century building accounts, as is the retrieval of buckets from its depths.[203] The running-wheel was probably in place by 1317, when four men were paid to extract from the well water and rubbish (which had no doubt accumulated in the absence of royal visits), and candles were bought to light their work.[204] By 1356, there was a 'house over the well' with a tiled roof. In the same year, three men were paid to extract water from another well (or pool) in 'Roughden' against the coming of the king and queen, and by 1445-51, there were three wells, the king's well at the palace, the 'Quene Well' at Queen Manor and another at Ranger's Lodge, where a carpenter was 'settyng up right the lytyl hows ofer the Reng(er)ys welle'.[205] This must have been the 'ffayre well house wth a great wheele & troffes for water w[ch] is standing upon the playne' at Rangers Lodge in 1603.[206]

Of other structures associated with the park, a pinfold (pound) was made in 1479 at Shergalgate, probably used for impounding animals pastured illegally, and another had been constructed in Groveley Forest the year before.[207] There are also a few references to temporary booths or lodges erected there in fence-month. In 1358 Thomas de Bitterley, deputy warden, was accused of felling the king's wood in Clarendon over a period of six years to make lodges at Sharpegore in fence month, afterwards selling them for up to 50s. each.[208] In 1368-72, one of his successors, Andrew de Dodmanstone, sold for his own profit timber he claimed to have felled to make lodges for fence month, and in 1570 16 loads of maple and oak boughs were felled to make the ranger's booth at midsummer.[209] These may have been temporary hides, set up in preparation for the season when the deer were in fat (*tempus pinguedinis*), although fence-month is usually specified as the reason for their construction so that they were perhaps associated with caring for fawns

or ensuring that other animals were kept out of the wood pasture area.

Place-name evidence in Clarendon Forest suggests sites of structures associated with hunting. From an early medieval date, the village of Pitton may have been the site of mews (from 'Putta's tun' — the place of the falconer), and the hamlet called The Livery, once in the centre of Houndwood, implies the presence of wolfhound kennels (*luverettus* = wolfhound). Other packs may have been kennelled in Melchet Forest at Cowesfield Loveras and the village of Lover from an early date. If the kennels were Anglo-Saxon, then the ringing of Clarendon with such place-names suggests that the area of the present Estate was already a focus for royal hunting. Moreover their later continuity deep in the forest suggests the need for dogs to be kept well away from the park and its deer, although the *c.*1640 map shows a dog kennel in the park, to which Dog Kennel Farm in Alderbury today approximates. This was probably the site of the holding of the Heyras family, who held their serjeanty from the twelfth to the fourteenth century by keeping the king's harrier pack, and it may have been outside the deerpark at that time, the deer kept securely in the launds. Dog kennels were substantial and important buildings. Gaston Phoebus recommended that they should measure about 20 by 10 metres, and that at Clarendon in 1650 measured 15.2 x 4.5m. (50 x 15ft). At the rear would be a meadow, surrounded by paling, and there should be doors at the front and at the back, the latter of which would remain open.[210]

The Pady Course and Standing

The Pady Course and Standing are among the most archaeologically elusive of vanished structures in Clarendon Park. The route of the course can be reasonably accurately plotted using the map of *c.*1640 and the Parliamentary survey of 1651 together, since the latter describes the keepers' walks. However apart from a possible linear feature in the present Hockamore field above Queen Manor (Figure 39), no archaeological trace remains. The Standing, too, seems to have vanished entirely, although a recent geophysical survey has turned up what may be an L-shaped building oriented in the right direction.[211] In addition, the reuse of timbers in the present Queen Manor Farm may provide a clue as to its fate. A very large quarter-oak in the farm's fireplace was felled in spring/summer 1537, two years after Henry VIII's only known visit of 1535, which may be connected with the standing's construction.[212] A further two timbers have been dendrochronologically dated to 1525-61 and 1544 and cyma and ovolo mouldings, dated typologically

[202] E.g. *c.*1487, 'To Thomas Clark, Michael Water and John Hill, labourers, for running in the great wheel...throughout the vigil of St Lawrence' (PRO E 101/460/16).

[203] PRO C 143/31/B; PRO E 101/499/1. E.g. PRO E 101/459/29 (1354); PRO E 101/459/30 (1356); PRO E 101/460/2 (1362-3); PRO E 101/542/12 (1374-6); PRO E 101/460/7 (1420s). PRO E 101/460/10 (1445-51); PRO E 101/460/16 (1482-97).

[204] PRO E 101/459/27, m.1.

[205] E 101/459/30; E 101/460/10, m.1. 'Roughden' could be a misreading of rubbish ('Robeyse' in 1317).

[206] ; PRO E 101/542/21, *f.*1.

[207] PRO E 101/460/15; PRO E 101/460/14.

[208] PRO E 32/267, m.7.

[209] PRO E 32/318, m.22; PRO E 101/140/11, m.4.

[210] P. Henderson, 'Architecture in Parks', paper given at *Parks in the Landscape*, OUDCE conference, October 2000.

[211] Alex Turner, pers. comm.

[212] 'This day se'nnight the king will be at the Harry Grace Dieu at...Portchester, thence to Hampton, so to Salisbury and Claryngton...' (*LPFD Henry VIII*, vol.9, p.467).

Figure 44. Wide linear feature running south west-north east through Hockamore,
possibly the Pady Course, looking south (Photo: T. B. James, Spring 2002).

to the 1530s and 40s onwards and the 1550s to 80s respectively exist in both the farmhouse and its granary.[213]

There is a detailed description of the Clarendon standing in the 1651 survey. It had a turret, was 'built with timber and bricke and part covered with tyle', and was valued at £30.00. The deer course was evidently out of use, since 'old holes of the posts of the Paddock course' formed a bound of Theobald's Division,[214] but no decisive documentary evidence has been found for the construction of either. They may have been built sometime in the sixteenth century, since during Elizabeth I's visit to Clarendon Park in 1574 'many deer coursed with greyhounds were overturned'.[215] Indeed, one eyewitness reported that 340 bucks were killed that day — rather too many to have been hunted by more traditional means.[216] However there is a reference, in the answers to an interrogatory, to 500 oaks having been felled in Sheer Wood for 'making the Paddock Course and for other his Majesty's [services]' around 1630-3.[217] This tallies with a warrant of 1631 to pay £768.15s.4½d. to Philip, Earl of Pembroke 'for paling out a course in the park of Clarendon and repairing the Queen's Manor Lodge in the same park'.[218] Although both 'making' and 'paling out' may mean only repairs, the relatively late date is not beyond the realms of possibility. A similar course was constructed in Lodge Park, Gloucestershire, in the 1630s. This was described in 1634, by which time it

was fully operational, as having 'hansome contriv'd Pens and Places, where the Deere are kept, and turn'd out for the Course',[219] a function that may have been performed at Clarendon by the Haybarn and its associated structures. These may have included 'the parrocks in the lawne walk', mentioned alongside the 18-furlong (2.25m/ 3.62km) long 'great Rayles' (?the Pady Course) as in need of repair in 1603.[220] Rackham interprets the 'parockes' built in 1542-4 at Fairmead Park as enclosures for corralling deer, and in 1607-8, repairs included the setting of 14 gates into Clarendon's 'longe raile', suggesting intricate methods of penning and driving the animals.[221]

The spatial relationship between the Pady Course and the palace may betray earlier origins, however. Figure 40, Norden's map of Windsor Little Park shows that, like the Pady Course at Clarendon, it ran north-eastwards from the royal residence (cf. Figure 37). Each proceeded beneath steep scarps that would have provided views for spectators following the sport, and approximately half-way along both of them is a standing. Most significantly, Norden shows his deer being chased away from a sub-circular pen at the start of the course, from which they probably emerged. The spatial relationship of this pen with Windsor Castle almost exactly corresponds to that of the present 'Picket Sanfoin' field at Clarendon with the palace (see Figures 1, 37, 73) — and it is easy to imagine Windsor's pen later assuming the same sub-triangular

[213] James and Gerrard, *Clarendon: A Royal Landscape*, forthcoming.
[214] McWilliams, 'Clarendon Park 1600-1750', Appendix D, p.71.
[215] McWilliams, 'Clarendon Park 1600-1750', p.26.
[216] WRO 549/8, *f*.23.
[217] PRO E 178/4728.
[218] *CSPD 1631-3*, p.114.

[219] National Trust (http://www.nationaltrust.org.uk/lodgepark /history.html).
[220] PRO E101/542/21. The length is about right for the Pady Course as plotted on Figure 32 (above, p.119).
[221] Rackham, 'Lodges', p.15; PRO E 101/542/22.

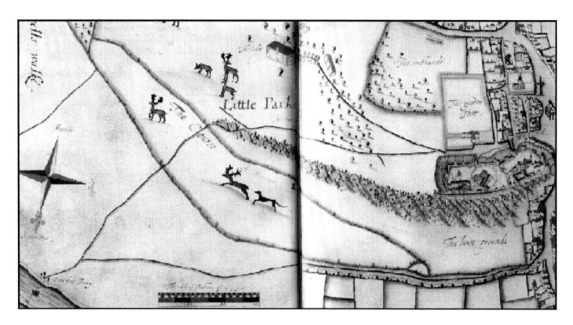

Figure 45. Detail of Norden's map of Windsor Little Park in *Survey of the Honour of Windsor* (1607), showing the deer course. Reproduced from J. Roberts, *Royal Landscape: The Gardens and Parks of Windsor* (London: Yale University Press, 1997), fig.130.

shape.[222] In any event the *c.*1640 map places the start of Clarendon's Pady Course opposite, and in full view of, the royal apartments just as at Windsor from which, in the words of John Stowe (*c.*1573), Elizabeth I would watch 'ye deare huntyd wt howndes...and yet not stirynge out of hir chambar'.[223]

It is tempting to assume, then, that the Pady Course predated the demise of the palace. Edward IV is known to have coursed deer at Windsor, whose course probably originated in the 1460s when the Little Park was enlarged.[224] Moreover current fieldwork suggests that many deer courses, previously considered early modern, are actually late medieval in origin.[225] Unfortunately no documentary evidence exists for the Clarendon example to suggest either a date of construction or a level of royal interest in the palace after the 1450s that might have merited its creation.

CONCLUSIONS

It is noteworthy that with the construction of the Pady Course and Standing the launds, and in particular the area around Hockamore directly opposite the palace, was again the main focus of deer-management and hunting in Clarendon Park, as it seems to have been under Henry III. Indeed one result of a rather less palace-based analysis of the 'built environment' than has been usual is that clear phases in the development of the park, in particular, have emerged. First, when the palace was embellished and

enlarged from the 1220s it seems probable that the park comprised the land to the north of the palace known later as the launds. Second, in the first half of the following century, the park was enlarged to perhaps the size it is today, and began to be studded with lodges, most notably the Lodge on the Laund. Third, its gatehouses were made impressive with battlements and other embellishments in the mid- to late-fifteenth century, and fourth (although rather more problematically in terms of dating) the park was remodelled, after the palace's removal as its hub, as an early modern hunting park complete with a deer course.

This study has shown that there was a new emphasis on the palace's immediate surroundings in the fourteenth century which coincided with a change in the seasonality of royal visits. Henry III spent only six of his 33 relatively long stays in June-September, whereas 53 of the 106 days spent at Clarendon by Edward I fell in July, August and September. As far as is known, Edward II made use of the palace only three times, the first being almost the whole of February and March 1317 through to mid-April. This visit may have been connected with the parliament Edward summoned to Clarendon in the same year, which may not, in the event, have taken place.[226] In 1320 Edward and his court sojourned for 9 days in early September, and returned in August 1326 for 19 days, on one of which occasions the king took '88 great bucks and 14 sorrels' in the park.[227] Edward III, too, preferred to stay in July and August, even into the 1370s.

---

[222] Picket Sanfoin is such a curious shape that it must have replaced something that previously existed on the ground, and that the crop sanfoin was introduced to Wiltshire in the late seventeenth century suggests the date of this occurrence. The field is even recognizable in the left of Stukeley's 1723 view (Fig.4).
[223] Roberts, *Royal Landscape*, p.138.
[224] Roberts, *Royal Landscape*, p.137.
[225] C.C. Taylor, pers. comm.

[226] James and Robinson, *Clarendon Palace*, p.35.
[227] PRO C 145/106/8/2. According to the document, this took place when Robert de Micheldever was warden, i.e. before February 1327, which is little help. However bucks and sorrels would not have been hunted between February and April, as stated in Chapter Two, so the episode could not have taken place in 1317.

Figure 46. Recorded expenditure on Clarendon Palace (discounting work on the lodges and park pale)

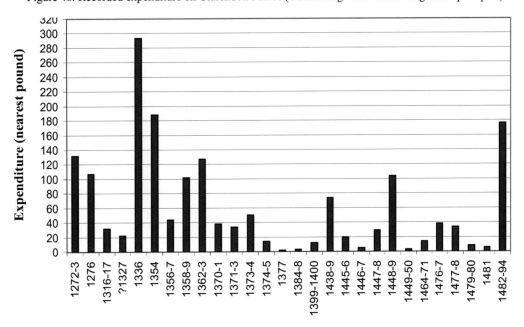

Analysis of the seasonality of royal visits has shown that a shift in hunting culture, most visible through the fourteenth century, was perhaps the primary factor in the development of the landscape and its buildings at this time (see also Chapter Two). Such a major change in attitude and site use deserves some exploration here. In some cases, the years before the Black Death were key in the creation of new parks and the enlargement of pre-existing ones. For example Bond has found for twelfth- to sixteenth-century Oxfordshire that 1300-49 is second only to 1250-99 in terms of first-documented references and emparking licences. It is also the only period other than 1100-49 for which references to the enlargement of pre-existing Oxfordshire parks exist — although admittedly only one park is in question in each case.[228] This may result from pressure on land and responses to encroachment at a period of high population. Other exogenous factors behind Clarendon Park's enlargement might include a desire to quarantine deer from the animal mortality accompanying the crop failures of 1315-21.[229] However it is more likely that shifts in the forest system are to blame.

Young has said that the years 1315-16 were key in regarding the status of the royal forest.[230] In three parliaments in 1316, Edward II was forced to concede nationwide perambulations based on those forced on his father in 1300-1. However he stipulated in the Easter session that all royal demesne woods in forest before Henry III's reign should remain so even if they had been disafforested under Edward I. Then in the parliament of August 1316, the king ordered the justices of the forest to arrange the driving of deer into the 'new' forest bounds

from disafforested areas. In the same period, he organised enquiries into the renting of wastes in order to pressurise tenants who had been using royal land since 1300.[231] This is the climate against which the imparkment should be measured. The demesne wood at Clarendon, probably in the south of today's (enlarged) park (see below, p. 121) almost certainly came into the first category, men were arrenting wastes in and around it from 1300, and what better way to ensure that deer stayed within a designated area than to construct a pale around the demesne wood in question? It seems clear that such royal imparkments as that uncovered in this study were performed to compensate for the decline of forest law. Moreover Edward III also had to accept the 1300 perambulations. Wiltshire was one of the counties hardest hit, with Chute Forest 'almost disafforested' by 1331, and Savernake shrinking from c.98 square miles to thirteen. Thus it is hardly surprising that the crown continued to place great emphasis on the park, which must have become one of the main hunting areas in the county — and certainly the most conveniently placed.

Figure 46 is compiled from the records of building works listed in the bibliography, and forms a useful addition to the analyses of calendared records undertaken in previous studies.[232] The graph shows that the palace was refurbished in the event of imminent royal visits, whether or not any occurred. It also reveals the great interest of Edward III, and the sizeable amounts that continued to be spent from 1482-94 despite a dearth of visits through the preceding decades and the century as a whole, not to mention the palace's abandonment very shortly afterwards. The chart also illustrates some of the connections discussed above (p. 57). It demonstrates

[228] Bond, 'Woodstock Park in the Middle Ages', p.23.
[229] Hinton, *Archaeology, Economy and Society*, p.173.
[230] Young, *The Royal forests of Medieval England*, p.143.

[231] Young, *The Royal forests of Medieval England*, p.144.
[232] For example James and Robinson, *Clarendon Palace*, and KACC I.

links between the palace and its setting, since peak years of expenditure correspond with significant building and remodelling projects in the park. The 1330s to the 1350s were the period in which the Lodge on the Laund was built, compartmentalised coppices set out, and ponds dug, while the mid-fifteenth century also saw ambitious work taking place in many of the lodges. In each case there was an amount of 'mirroring' of building materials, the Lodge on the Laund and the Great Hall of the palace each faced with Chilmark-type ashlar in 1344 and 1358, and the use of brick in the lodges and at the palace in the 1440s and 50s (see above, p. 78).

Figure 46 reveals also the link between the palace and the forest — particularly its administration — that has also been uncovered here. A major forest court sat in 1330, preceded by works in ?1327, another in 1338, preceded by works in 1336, another in 1355, others (forest inquests held 'at Clarendon') in 1360 and 1373, yet another in 1376, and so on. And if anything, such links have been found to be even more demonstrable in the case of repairs to the lodges.

In addition, analysis of the records of building works undertaken for this study has enhanced understanding of day-to-day administrative arrangements, for example the siting of the bowbearer's, deputy's and porter's lodgings. As stated above, Clarendon Palace did not grind to a halt when the king was not in residence. Yet royal visits continued to be a major impetus for building in the park, even after the palace's demise. Henry VIII's (at least proposed) visit of 1535 may have provided the impetus for the construction of the standing, especially since reused timbers in Queen Manor Farm have been dendrochronologically dated to 1537 and 1525-61, and mouldings in others there dated typologically to the 1530s onwards (see above, p. 80). Later, repairs to Queen Manor were begun just a few years before Elizabeth I's visit of 1574, and a survey was taken for its repair in 1603, the year when James I hunted in the park. Such evidence confirms the findings here that Queen Manor/The Lodge on the Laund, with the Haybarn were interconnected and important built components of the early modern hunting landscape at Clarendon.

Although it is regrettable that no definite construction date for the Pady Course and the Standing has been found, a detailed perusal of the documentary evidence for other of Clarendon's ancillary buildings, chiefly the lodges, has calibrated other information and thus made new contributions to our understanding. It cannot be coincidence that the dendrochronological dates of reused timbers have been found to correspond with the documentary evidence for major phases of building in the park. Most notably the section of reused roof in the present Queen Manor constructed of trees felled *c*.1330 (above, p. 71), alongside other reused materials such as brick, appears to confirm the hypothesis put forward here that the Lodge on the Laund became known as Queen Manor, and was situated near the site of the present building, eventually built in part from the materials resulting from its demolition.

To conclude, a focus away from phases of embellishment and repair at the palace towards the building and rebuilding of its immediate built environment has prompted new insights that range from the particular (the history of specific lodges) to the general (the seasonality of visits and attendant changes in the use of hunting landscapes). Thus '[looking] beyond the walls' has indeed helped to set the palace in the context of its immediate surroundings.[233] In the next chapter a yet wider perspective is aimed at by looking beyond the park pale to consider settlement in and around Clarendon Forest.

---

[233] Astill, 'Windsor', p.1.

Chapter Four: Settlement and Landscape

This section has two main aims; first to analyse Clarendon Forest's settlement pattern, and second to place the palace within the wider landscape and settlement context rather than treat it as an isolated structure. Methodology will include analysis of taxation records, and comparison with settlements outside Clarendon Forest including the shrunken villages around Whiteparish in Melchet studied by Taylor.[1]

That medieval high status complexes were themselves forms of settlement and simultaneously part of the wider settlement structure has recently been recognised in castle studies. Thus far the study of medieval palaces, only recently re-emergent, has had different concerns. It might be considered more apposite to compare Clarendon with manorial sites, but its scale, function and landscape setting puts it in the same bracket as a Windsor or Ludgershall. Moreover, although one would expect to find differences between castles and palaces, there are also similarities. Although Johnson has highlighted the folly of assigning to any one castle a primary function, it can be argued that many were built as hunting lodges from the outset, especially by the fourteenth century.[2]

Astill has shown that New Windsor was probably more disadvantaged than fortunate in its proximity to Windsor Castle,[3] and this begs a comparison with Clarendon. Both residences were set in deer parks and shared similar economies, and were attached to forests over whose inhabitants their officers exercised jurisdiction. Similarly, David Hinton has commented that 'at its worst, [Corfe Castle] could be a dangerous neighbour'.[4] Although he points out that the social and economic effect of this 'symbol of lordship' is infinitely more recoverable than what it meant emotionally, he concedes that:

> [Corfe's] great tower-keep... reared over Purbeck... Many Purbeck people would have seen it almost whenever they looked up, all would have passed under its shadow at some time or another.[5]

This is the language of castles, not palaces, which do not generally 'rear' over anything, much less possess looming shadows — at least in the historical and archaeological literature. However, a visitor to the palace site today will immediately see that Salisbury Cathedral, at least, is visible from it and the north western slopes of Clarendon Park certainly loom over northern Salisbury, Laverstock and the high road. Thus Hinton's comments are applicable, and are echoed here. Further, previous

references to thirteenth-century vistas over the 'ever growing cathedral...visible...to anyone [at Clarendon] who cared to look out to the west'[6] will be extended to suggest that the new city was *consciously* planned in reference to the palace.

NEW SARUM

Contrary to popular belief, Salisbury was *not* designed on what was, by the early thirteenth century, a greenfield site. By 1086 there were two Salisburys, one the king's borough on and around the hill now known as Old Sarum, and the other a manor or manors held by the bishop, confusingly known as 'Old Salisbury', or Salisburys (*veteres Sarisberias*) to contemporaries. In the south west corner of the bishop's meadows, vills and demesnes, Salisbury (New Sarum) would later rise.[7] Here there were mills, roads, drainage ditches and settlements, and the bishop evidently had a manor house on or near the site of the Cathedral Close by 1218 and perhaps earlier.[8] If this did not necessarily represent symbolic proximity to the palace, it would at least have facilitated ease of access via Milford (see Figure 47).

Most significantly in considering Salisbury's layout, two major roads, one running east-west and one north-south, already ran through the area later occupied by the city. The former, Winchester Street (now Milford Street) ran through Fisherton to the west, and, it has been suggested, through Clarendon Park to Winchester to the east.[9] If so, on the approach to Salisbury travellers would have most certainly passed under the palace's shadow. As Colt Hoare pointed out, the hollow ways leading to and from Milford bridge 'are plainly portions of an antient road'.[10] In any event, there is no reason to suppose that the park in the Middle Ages was a closed landscape in the way that private estates are today, and the palace was clearly meant to be seen from the north, its latrines projecting prominently over the scarp (see Figure 42) — 'a representation of the consumption of the household writ large'.[11] Even if the road through Clarendon Park was intended to bring guests to the palace only, visitors travelling from the Winchester (Roman) Road would have been led past (and beneath) the palace before

[1] Taylor, 'Whiteparish: A Study', pp.79-102.
[2] Johnson, *Behind the Castle Gate*, pp.1-18; For example Okehampton (Devon) and Thorne (South Yorkshire), built for the lords of Conisburgh (Creighton, *Castles and Landscapes*, p.188).
[3] Astill, 'Windsor', pp.5-10.
[4] Hinton, *Purbeck*, p. 101.
[5] Hinton, *Purbeck*, p.101.

[6] James and Robinson, *Clarendon Palace*, p.9.
[7] F. Hill, 'The Borough of Old Salisbury', in *VCH Wilt, VI* (Oxford: Oxford University Press, 1962), ed. Elizabeth Crittall, pp.51-67 (pp.51-2).
[8] Hill, 'The Borough of Old Salisbury', p.52.
[9] T. Slater, 'Planning Britain's Largest Medieval New Town: Ideology, Geometry, Metrology and Practicalities in Thirteenth-Century Salisbury', paper given at Leeds IMC, July 2002; M.K. Dale, 'The City of New Salisbury', in *VCH Wilts, VI* (Oxford: Oxford University Press, 1962), ed. Elizabeth Crittall, pp.69-194 (p.79).
[10] Colt Hoare and Nichols, *The Modern History of South Wiltshire*, p.112.
[11] Johnson, *Behind the Castle Gate*, p.43.

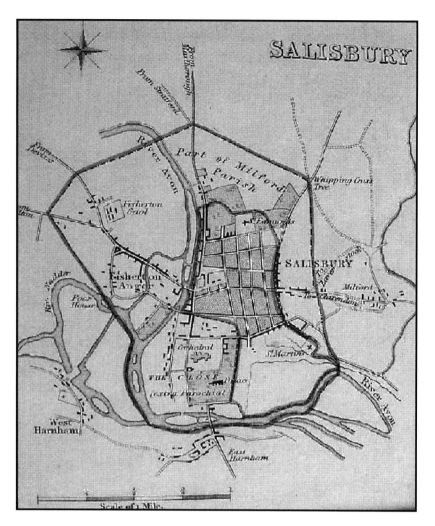

Figure 47. Dawson's map of Salisbury (1835), showing the road through Milford 'to Clarendon', sometime Winchester Street. Reproduced from Genmaps, *Old Maps of Wiltshire* (http://freepages.genealogy.rootsweb.com/~genmaps/genfiles/COU_Pages/ENG_pages/wil.htm).

Figure 48. View southwards from Figsbury Ring over the A30 and the Roman road towards Clarendon Park and Palace whose remains, since clearance, are visible with the naked eye (Spring 2002).

turning back on themselves and mounting the Upper Trench to reach the main gateway.[12]

It has been suggested that the 'road to Salisbury' through Clarendon Park was abandoned 'probably in the later Middle Ages' and the name Winchester Street transferred to the present road of that name.[13] There are several periods when this may have occurred. The first is when Henry III extended the palace from the late 1220s, the second is around 1317, when the park was enlarged and perhaps paled in its entirety for the first time, and the third is in the fifteenth century when new, battlemented gates were set in the outer park pale. Even so, if it did not 'rear', the palace would have loomed over at least part of the approach to Salisbury, for the ruins are today visible from Figsbury ring and a substantial section of the A30 (see Figure 48), from where it would have appeared as if commanding a pleasant valley.

Thus the palace may have been a considered element in the approach to Salisbury from Winchester and London. The city was laid out as accurately as possible, presumably by skilled masons. Many of these, notably Elias de Dereham, worked on the Close as well as the palace, and it is not implausible that they had a hand in the City's planning. The RCHME has noted similarities between the hall at Clarendon and that of the Bishop's Palace, begun in 1225 probably under de Dereham,[14] and at the very least, such men would have been sensitive to the palace's nearby presence.

The importance of the years 1226-7 in the establishment of the city has also been noted.[15] They are crucial to the earliest of the three phases of planning development in Salisbury — namely that in and around the Cathedral Close. Both the Franciscan Friary and St Nicholas' Hospital were founded in 1227. Each would benefit from royal patronage in the form of timber grants from the forest, while the latter would go on to hold rights within it, and both were established in the area topographically and symbolically closest to the palace as well as to the cathedral.

The same years are significant to the development of Clarendon and its landscape. From 1226, documentation of frenetic works at the palace survive, and in 1227 Salisbury was awarded its first royal charter,[16] not coincidentally the year in which Henry III finally declared his majority. This was when the king reconstituted Clarendon Forest, re-orienting it westwards towards Salisbury by severing its previous administrative links to the New Forest. Thus Clarendon Palace and the forest may have been influential in the planning of Salisbury. Visitors to the palace did not so much casually glance to the west because they 'cared to', but were probably expected and actively encouraged, to do so.

Salisbury: Social and Economic Relations
The idea that Salisbury prospered from its proximity to Clarendon Palace is rarely voiced. However it is not new. Marian Dale wrote in 1962:

[the city] benefited not only from being the seat of a bishopric, and in a good geographical position on the route between Southampton and Bristol, but also from its proximity to Clarendon Palace, which during the early days of the city's history attracted a constant influx of visitors.[17]

It is difficult to disentangle Clarendon's impact on Salisbury, especially in economic terms, due to the city's meteoric rise. Yet the palace was perhaps a factor in Salisbury's prosperity, as well as in the formation of its urban identity. Of course the city was under the sway of the bishop or more precisely, on a day-to-day basis, of the Dean and Chapter.[18] This would have bestowed an urban identity (which in a sense was imported from Old Sarum) whether or not the palace was close by. The bishop exercised full seigneurial powers over the citizens, and it is against the ecclesiastic authorities that conflict was often levelled. John Steane has even suggested that the wall around the cathedral close was erected to 'protect inmates from their immediate, often hostile, neighbours'.[19] Any commercial advantage that the citizens had came from the royal charter of 1227, and kings were often mediators.

There appears to have been little episcopal-urban hostility until 1302, when Salisbury's citizens refused Bishop Simon of Ghent's right of tallage — a sign of the self-confidence of the merchant community by this date. In March 1305, the mayor, citizens and community were summoned not to Clarendon to plead their case, but to Westminster where the council found for the bishop.[20] Nevertheless Edward I's arrival at Clarendon that year was unusual in that it was his only December visit to the palace, and it may have occurred in response to the crisis. Certainly in 1306 Salisbury's liberties were restored by royal charter suggesting that some kind of mediation had taken place. The result was an agreement incorporating 28 articles that sought to define the rights and privileges of both parties.[21] Other examples of royal mediation were less successful, including Richard II's attempt, in 1390, to head off trouble, again between the bishop and the citizens. Thomas Holland and the Earl of Salisbury were instructed to go to the church and city and take an oath from each side that they would not to break the peace. The king's worries that 'hurt and peril' might

[12] James and Gerrard, *Perspectives of Pleasure*, forthcoming.
[13] Dale, 'The City of New Salisbury', p.79.
[14] RCHME, *Salisbury: The Houses of The Close* (London: HMSO, 1993), pp.7, 60.
[15] Slater, Leeds IMC, 2002.
[16] Dale, 'The City of New Salisbury', p.94.
[17] Dale, 'The City of New Salisbury', p.124.
[18] See M. Thompson, *Medieval Bishops' Houses in England and Wales* (Aldershot: Ashgate Publishing, 1998), p.9.
[19] Steane, *The Archaeology of Power*, p.204.
[20] Dale, 'The City of New Salisbury', p.101, *CCR 1302-7*, p.242.
[21] See Dale, 'The City of New Salisbury', pp.101, 95.

arise from the 'great number of lieges…with no small temporal power' who would arrive with the Archbishop of Canterbury on his visitation suggests an element of self-interest behind the king's mediation,[22] and such potential unrest may have contributed to the paucity of royal visits to Clarendon at this time. Either way, in 1395 the bishop's rights were again confirmed by royal charter, Richard II's support of the bishop was resented (which may have been exacerbated by his 'invisibility' in the area), and Salisbury was among the first cities to declare for Henry IV.[23]

It is likely that conflict with the bishop has overshadowed that with the king's officers in the literature, and there was certainly friction with the forest administration through the fourteenth century (see also Chapter Five). Even without royal sanction, such men could be a nuisance, although that the palace was occupied relatively frequently by courtiers probably prevented abuses such as those in Purbeck in 1265 (admittedly during a period of nationwide unrest) when the constable of Corfe Castle and 'his following of strangers' pillaged the surrounding area.[24] Nevertheless, the Clarendon forester of fee Robert de Milford was charged with trespass in 1306 for cutting off with his sword the right hand of one Thomas Balle in Salisbury, by night and against the peace, and in 1305 it is recorded that 'William, a forester of Buckholt' stole 20 marks from various merchants in that forest, presumably returning from Salisbury to Winchester and London.[25]

However, if the documents are to be believed, the forest officers were more often on the receiving end of violence. This may suggest a degree of resentment concerning the proximity and reach of forest jurisdiction, evident in the case of William de Werdore, underkeeper of the manor and forest of Clarendon, who complained in 1327 of being 'violently assaulted and mistreated' by certain citizens on going to Salisbury to collect amercements for forest transgressions.[26] Similarly, Thomas Tychebourne, verderer of Melchet, alleged in 1355 that he had been attacked on his way to the city.[27] Since the purpose of Tychebourne's journey was to attend the forest eyre, an attempt to prevent him from discharging his duties is at least as likely as opportunistic robbery. Certainly the attempts of the foresters of Clarendon to collect cheminage were cited along with others in Wiltshire as against the tenor of the Forest Charter in an undated document.[28] However they do not seem to have prompted the level of protest aimed at the bailiff of Wilton who, it was complained in 1275, impeded the passage of merchants travelling to Salisbury, nor at the

earl of Gloucester's foresters of Cranborne Chase who, in the same year, allegedly took cheminage as far as the bridge of Ayleswade (later Harnham Bridge) on the king's highway into Salisbury, and used fence-month — which they seem to have interpreted as if a moveable feast — as an excuse to levy yet more charges.[29] The latter were more clearly regarded with animosity than Clarendon's foresters. There were complaints from Downton that they collected tolls from the bishop of Winchester's men taking carts of dry wood and timber from the New Forest to Salisbury market, and that they threatened crowds at Britford fair with violence. It was only when the chase passed into the hands of those more closely connected with the Crown, after the confiscation of the earl of Gloucester's lands, that the complaints subsided.[30]

Clarendon Forest and Salisbury seem also to have enjoyed a more harmonious relationship than did Groveley and Wilton, whose Guild Merchant frequently asserted their rights regarding cheminage in the forest courts.[31] By 1372, Wilton's citizens were refusing to turn up for swanimotes, although the Groveley Foresters claimed to have sent summons daily, and in 1374 it was finally ruled that they were not bound to attend any forest court.[32] The decade seems to have been one of widespread opposition to the forest system. Indeed the citizens of Salisbury rebelled against duties in Clarendon Park in the 1370s.[33] But although rebellion was in many ways part of the national scene, both the intransigence of the burgesses of Wilton and Salisbury's petition to the 1377 parliament may have been responses to what, more locally, was perceived as an unacceptable degree of royal interference.

By 1377, Salisbury ranked sixth among the provincial towns of England. The rights and privileges of its urban inhabitants were by now defined, and parliament decided that the forest officials had no authority beyond the park's bounds.[34] The eastern boundary of the forest, adjacent to

---

[22] CCR 1389-92, p.195.

[23] Dale, 'The City of New Salisbury', p.101; E.E. Dorling, A History of Salisbury (London: James Nisbet and Co., 1911), p.106.

[24] Hinton, Purbeck, p.101.

[25] Pugh, Feet of Fines, pp.150, 152, 156; R.B. Pugh, Gaol Delivery and Trailbaston 1275-1306 (Devizes, Wiltshire Record Society, 1978), p.105.

[26] CPR 1327-30, p.82.

[27] PRO E 32/267, m.13d.

[28] See Glossary. E.g. PRO C 47/12/2, m.9.

[29] Anon., Rotuli Hundredorum, II (London: Record Commission, 1818), p.267.

[30] E.H. Lane Poole, 'Cranborne Chase', The Victoria County History IV (Oxford: Oxford University Press, 1959), ed. E. Crittall, pp.458-60 (p.459).

[31] E.g. PRO C 260/84/15 (1355). For Wilton's decline in the thirteenth century, see M.K. James, 'The Borough of Wilton', The County History VI (Oxford: Oxford University Press, 1962), ed. E. Crittall, pp.1-50 (p.15).

[32] PRO E 32/318, m.22; Grant, VCH Wilts, p.432.

[33] 'Inspeximus at the request of the commonalty of Salisbury, of their petition to the king and council in the last Parliament, against certain of their number being burdened with certain offices in Clarendon Park, by warrant of the justices of the forest and of the endorsement thereupon, the officers and ministers of the forest having no authority beyond the bounds thereof' (CPR 1377–81, p.75).

[34] Steane, Archaeology of Medieval England and Wales, p.128; Grant, VCH Wilts, p.428; 'Inspeximus at the request of the commonalty of Salisbury, of their petition…to the king and council in the last Parliament, against certain of their number being burdened with certain offices in Clarendon Park, by warrant of the justices of the forest and of the endorsement thereupon, the officers and ministers of the forest having no authority beyond the bounds thereof' (CPR 1377–81, p.75).

Salisbury, came under much pressure at this time. Milford and Laverstock were by now disafforested, and two decades earlier the Manor of Britford had successfully claimed rights previously resting with forest officials (see above, p. 46). Indeed by Edward III's reign the forest system as a whole had gone into terminal decline. The jurisdiction of Clarendon's forest officers appears to have shrunk to encompass only the park, and the reduction of the forest and the petition of the burgesses is a clear sign that the balance of power and influence in the locality had shifted in the city's favour.

As to the effect of Salisbury on the forest, it is interesting to compare recent findings concerning the New Forest in Hampshire. Caroline Smith has drawn attention to the apparent failure of fourteenth-century New Forest officers to carry out royal orders concerning homicide inquests, suggesting that they were, in all likelihood, resentful of interference from central authorities.[35] Clarendon provides an interesting contrast. Those in charge of the 'more distinct [and] separate'[36] forest of which it had once been a part may have resented civil law impinging on their spheres of jurisdiction. But those at Clarendon appear instead to have been more than a little keen to enforce it. It was even claimed in 1338 that in Clarendon Forest, homicides and Crown Pleas belonged to the 'keepers' and verderers (see below, p. 134). Close proximity to a thriving city must have played a major part in the real or perceived blend of jurisdictions that gave Clarendon Forest its identity by the fourteenth century, as did the presence of the palace, thanks to which Clarendon's forest officers continued to receive the court in their midst regularly until the reign of Henry VI.

As indicated by the 1377 petition, much of the forest was run by men from Salisbury, and others held property in the forest itself. In the 1355 eyre, Wilton's citizens had complained that the town was 'ridden by the regarders as within the regard and the bounds of Groveley Forest'.[37] This would never have happened in Salisbury, not least because too many of the Clarendon foresters officers had interests there. Many verderers in particular were Salisbury men, and some acted also as underwood-vendors. Although the unpaid office of verderer was often considered a burden, it is a sign of its high standing that when in 1425 Walter Shirley witnessed a Salisbury will, he was listed as a Clarendon verderer, albeit after the city reeves.[38] In addition, from at least the 1350s, surveyors of the works at the palace and the park were generally canons of the Cathedral, and other Salisbury men also played a part. For example in 1362, the canons John de Upton and Martin Moulissh were joined in their endeavours as surveyors by John de Wilton, parson of St Thomas's' church in the city, as controller.[39] John

Chafyn of Salisbury fulfilled this duty in 1460,[40] and even after the demise of the palace, the forest's deputy warden in 1539-40 was John Goodale, gent, also bailiff of Salisbury.[41]

Thus in terms of the administrative and social landscape this *was* a symbiotic relationship. Those with administrative expertise and of high local standing were close at hand to act as forest officers and to fulfil other duties at the palace. In return, city institutions, including the Church, benefited from royal patronage. For example firewood was donated to the students of Salisbury in 1258 and to the treasurer ten years later, and one of the duties of the warden of Clarendon was to pay a reasonable tithe to the dean and chapter of Salisbury on 'the king's meadow' in the parish of St Martin south east of Salisbury.[42] But tithes had long been customarily given from Clarendon to the canons of Salisbury, as is evident from standard references in the late twelfth- and early thirteenth-century pipe rolls.[43] The origin of such donations seems to lie in the idea that forest amercements were contrary to natural justice, and in Angevin guilt for their rapacious exploitation of the forest. Thus charitable donations gave 'a respectable gloss' to the forest system.[44]

Salisbury townsfolk and authorities might also profit from subinfeudination. In 1370 the treasurer, Lord of the Manor of Pitton and Farley, owned a 'small grove' in Clarendon Forest (see Figure 49). His predecessors had probably occupied it from 1258 when the treasurer appears in an eyre roll as occupying a new purpresture of one acre in Pitton, or as early as 1244 when three parcels of assarted land in Farley were given up to him by Richard Archer, the King's Bowman.[45] By 1330 the treasurer held seven acres of 'old assart' in Pitton, ex the fee of Simon Cusyn (an agister in 1253-4, later amerced for wasting of his holding, Rodsley Wood), although classified at that date as disafforested by perambulation.[46] In addition, the commoner of the church of Salisbury took lay fees known as 'Lady's Chamber' (*Camera Domine*) from lands in Pitton and Farley for the use of the poor.[47] The warden and brethren of St Nicholas' Hospital in the city possessed temporalities at West Dean, for which they were evidently excused tax on account of poverty, and by 1330 they held 73 acres of old assart in Bentley Wood ex the fee of William Longespée.[48]

[35] Smith, 'The New Forest', pp.14-17.
[36] Smith, 'The New Forest', p.14.
[37] Grant, *VCH Wilts*, p.432.
[38] *CCR 1422-9*, p.206.
[39] *CCR 1361-4*, pp.177, 183.

[40] *CPR 1452-61*, p.607.
[41] PRO E 372/385 (*Wiltes*, m.1d.).
[42] *CCR 1256-9*, p.273; *CCR 1268-72*, p.10; *CCR 1247-1251*, p.313.
[43] For example f' *Willelmus de Neuill' r.c. de xxv li. de censu Noue Foreste. In thes. xvij li. et ix s. et ij. d. Et in decimis constitutis . canonicis Saresberie 1s. Et Hugoni de Neuill' lx s. et xd. ad custodiam domorum R. de Clarendon'. Et Willelmo Briewerre xl. s. in foresta de Bere de dono R.* (*Pipe R. 13 John, vol. 28*, p.179).
[44] Grant, *VCH Wilts*, p.392.
[45] M. Parsons, *The Little Manor of Pitton and Farley* (West Tytherley: Leonard Michael Parsons, 1995), pp.6-7.
[46] *CPR 1367-70*, p.458; PRO E 32/215 (*dorse*); PRO E 32/199, m.6; PRO E 32/198, m.8; PRO E 32/207, m.7.
[47] *CCR 1296-1302*, p.20.
[48] *CCR 1381-5*, p.231; PRO E 32/207, m.10.

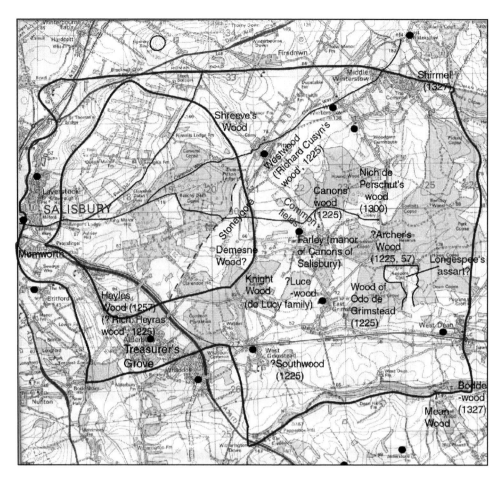

Figure 49. Selected woods and areas in Clarendon Forest, taken from medieval perambulations.
O. S. Map reproduced with kind permission of Ordnance Survey©, Crown copyright NC/03/22 21.
Adapted from R. Grant, 'Forests', in *Victoria County History Wiltshire IV*
(Oxford: Oxford University Press, 1959), ed. E. Crittall, pp.391-457 (p.454).

But was all this really as mutually-beneficial as it first appears? Tithes, and the gifts mentioned above, are characteristic of the relationship between royal forests and the church. Only rarely were gifts made to lay citizens, such as the ten oaks from Groveley promised to Robert de Lexington in 1238 in order to build his house in Salisbury.[49] It could be argued that the Crown was willing to capitalise on the administrative skills of the citizens (and of the collegiate church) while offering little in return. Certainly there were few opportunities to assart in Clarendon, in contrast to neighbouring forests (see below, pp. 93-96), and when transgressions of the vert occurred, the king and his officers were close enough to clamp down hard. For example when Robert Wycheford, canon of Salisbury, felled trees and underwood from a grove in West Grimstead *c*.1370 that had been 'sold' to him by Reginald Perot, it was soon made clear that the lumber belonged neither to Perot nor to himself, but to the king, to whom he had to answer in Chancery.[50] Indeed, the presence of rich ecclesiastics may have been considered an easy source of forest revenues. Distraints

were made against the Dean and Canons of Salisbury for the lawing of their dogs in 1250, and the chancellor of Salisbury, Ralph de Hegham, was amerced the huge sum of 40 marks in 1270 for poaching venison at Clarendon before being pardoned at the instance of Prince Edmund.[51]

The proximity of royal officers must sometimes have been irksome to the commercial community, for example two merchants were arrested in 1346, at the height of the Hundred Years' War, because they were natives of Picardy.[52] In the end, it is perhaps significant that it appears only to have been from the fifteenth century, when the forest system was in abeyance and royal visits to Clarendon few and far between, that Salisbury gained a council house, despite the fact that from the early fourteenth century the City had its own officers.[53] Nevertheless, compared to Wilton and to New Windsor, Salisbury enjoyed rather good relations with its forest neighbour.

[49] *CCR 1237-42*, p.19.
[50] *CPR 1370-4*, p.114.

[51] *CCR 1247-51*, pp.309, 376; *CPR 1266-72*, p.467.
[52] *CCR 1343-6*, p.678.
[53] Dale, 'The City of New Salisbury', pp.95-7.

SETTLEMENT PATTERN

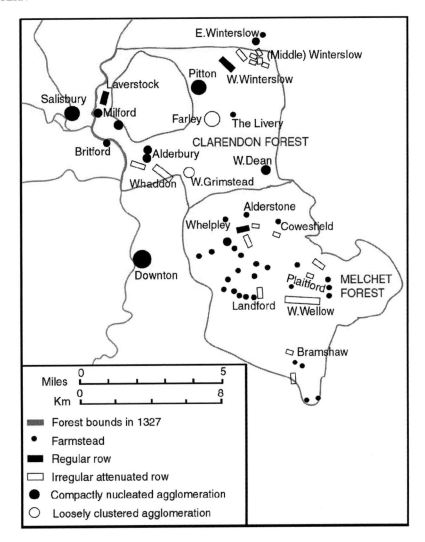

Figure 50. Settlement types in Clarendon and Melchet Forests.
Adapted from C. Lewis, 'Patterns and Processes in the Medieval Settlement of Wiltshire',
in *The Medieval Landscape of Wessex,* Oxbow Monograph 46
(Oxford: Oxbow Books, 1994), eds M. Aston and C. Lewis, pp.171-93, fig. 8.5.

Carenza Lewis has argued that the presence of forests is instrinsic to Wiltshire's overall settlement pattern,[54] and indeed much can be learned from the distribution of forest vills. At Groveley settlement pattern and forest bounds exhibit a striking correlation, partly due to its hilly terrain. But at Clarendon (and Melchet), settlements were established inside the forest. Most of those at Clarendon probably resulted from pre-Conquest assarting, although the pattern was sustained later, and it is likely that the vills continued to thrive because they were populated by those serving the palace and forest.

Clarendon's settlement typology (Figure 50), like that of most Wiltshire forests, is distinct from that of the chalklands where vills are usually set out in regular rows. It is as varied as its geological framework, comprising four compact nucleated agglomerations (parts of

Alderbury and Milford, Pitton and West Dean), two loosely clustered agglomerations (Farley and West Grimstead), two regular rows (Laverstock and West Winterslow), and three irregular attenuated rows (Middle Winterslow, part of Alderbury and Whaddon). Although the overarching pattern is dispersed, compared with Melchet Forest in particular there are noticeably few isolated farmsteads.

Can this pattern be explained? It is noteworthy that of the Clarendon 'semi-nucleated' villages two, Alderbury and Pitton, lay on the park's outskirts and were thus closest to the palace, and two were religious and seigneurial centres at least from the eleventh century — *i.e.* a probable Saxon Minster, then Ivychurch Priory at Alderbury, and Waleran's motte and bailey castle at West Dean. Thus a planned element may lie behind this group. But the paucity of isolated farmsteads is also indicative of control and in Wiltshire, aside from the eastern half of Cranborne

---

[54] See Lewis, 'Patterns and Processes', p.173.

Chase, only Chute Forest displays a similar dearth (apart from its north eastern extremity). It may be significant that, although Chute was drastically reduced in size in the 1330s,[55] each was a major royal landscape. Indeed, Ludgershall Castle played a similar role in Chute Forest to that of Clarendon Palace in Clarendon Forest, Chute even being eponymously named, like Clarendon Forest, for its focal residence during the thirteenth century.[56]

Most settlements in Clarendon and Melchet Forests are named either from topographical features or after forest officers, the latter especially in Melchet, suggesting post-Conquest foundations (e.g. Loveras, Spileman). [57] Although some at Clarendon must have originated through woodland clearance, place name evidence suggests that this took place much earlier than in northern Melchet, whose colonisation has been extensively discussed elsewhere (although it will be treated comparatively below). [58] This accords with Titow's observation that in anciently settled manors like those of Clarendon, the grubbing out of uncultivated wastes started early and reached its physical limits early. [59] Indeed toponymical evidence for the settlement cluster of Farley and the Grimsteads suggests early origins, as does the presence here of streams and fords for tracks. Stenton considered that Grimstead, first mentioned in Domesday, derived from 'grenehamstede' (the green homestead), probably deriving from the extensive, open pre-Roman arable lands along the stream. Farley, first mentioned in 1109 as 'fernlege', probably implies assarting northwards from this area, since '-ley' denotes a clearing, and 'fearn' bracken (although it has been suggested that the name may denote a lea that was 'far', in comparison to Pitton, from the palace).[60] Yet it should be noted that although settlements *around* Clarendon Forest contain the '-leah' element, for example Tytherley and Whelpley in Melchet, Farley is the only settlement inside it to do so, and –leah is quite a late Saxon component. In contrast, there are several examples inside Clarendon Park, including Ashley ('Asshelee', 1307-27, 'Asshelehull', 1362), Chisley ('Chisele', 1319, 'Cheselegh', 1343, 'Chissell Hill', 1650) and Netley,[61] suggesting that the area that became the park was already delineated by clearance by the mid- to late Saxon period, and separate from its more wooded surrounds.

There is a preponderance of compound placenames in and around Clarendon Forest — the Deans, Grimsteads, and Winterslows in the forest itself, and the Tytherleys, Winterbournes, and the Cowesfields (Melchet) on its

periphery. Clearly some were subsidiary settlements, demonstrating the fluidity of population given favourable economic conditions. Some may always have been relatively unimportant in the settlement hierarchy leading to their later desertion or shrinkage (e.g. Cowesfields Loveras and Spileman in Melchet) although the majority flourished, especially those in Clarendon Forest. Apart from the Cowesfields, most contain manorial or descriptive adjuncts, rather than being named for individual families, and they may indicate topographically the existence of earlier estates (above, pp. 5-7) which fragmented along 'fault lines' demarcating the lands of the smaller settlements within those estates.[62] The same can be said of East and West Dean, in Hampshire and Wiltshire (and Buckholt and Clarendon Forests) respectively (see Figure 12).

The compound placenames in and around Clarendon give evidence of estate breakdown and demographic mobility before Domesday. In addition, the Deans, Grimsteads and Winterslows are all within a mile of the later forest boundaries. They occupy unwooded terrain, at least today, indicating either that lack of woodland facilitated subsidiary settlement, or that they are the result of early clearance. Many of these features were shared by the Cowesfields and other shrunken and deserted settlements, all within two miles of the border between Clarendon and Melchet Forests. Yet these did not prosper into the post medieval period, and for this their later establishment may be a factor.

Richard Dennis has suggested that poor soil quality accounts for the high number of pre-Conquest thegns who continued to hold lands in Wessex forests in 1086,[63] so that perhaps those settlements in the hands of Normans in 1086 (West Winterslow, East Grimstead and West Dean) can be placed highest in Clarendon's settlement hierarchy (see above, p. 7). But it is more probable that the Conqueror had need of hunt servants with detailed local knowledge, and preferred to keep the Saxon administration intact. Indeed, it should be noted that those villages closest to what would later be Clarendon Park (Alderbury, Milford and Pitton) were all held by huntsmen and forest officials. In addition, the presence of harrier kennels and probably the king's mews (Alderbury and Pitton) reveal the specialisation in venery of Alderbury and Pitton in particular.[64]

One reason the settlements in Clarendon Forest thrived over the centuries was good communications. The study

[55] Grant, *VCH Wilts* p.425.

[56] Grant, *VCH Wilts*, p.424.

[57] Williamson, *Shaping Medieval Landscapes*, p.93.

[58] Taylor, 'Whiteparish: A Study', *passim*.

[59] J.Z. Titow, 'Land and Population on the Bishop of Winchester's Estates 1209-1350' (unpub. doctoral thesis, University of Cambridge, 1962), p.21.

[60] Parsons, *The Saxon Inheritance*, pp. 50-1, 42; M. Parsons, *An Unparticular Posterity: I* (New Milton: Leonard Michael Parsons, 2000), p.14.

[61] James and Gerrard, *Perspectives of Pleasure*, forthcoming.

[62] See Lewis, 'Patterns and Processes', p.187.

[63] R. Dennis, 'The Organisation of Wealth and Power in Domesday Hampshire' (unpub. doctoral thesis, Lincoln College, Oxford, 1992), p.313.

[64] Pitton, first mentioned in 1165, may derive from 'Putte's tun' (settlement or farm), and thus be Saxon or earlier in origin. Alternately it may derive from the Latin 'putta' (mousehawk), and thus betray the presence of mews from an early date (Parsons, *The Saxon Inheritance*, pp.44-5, 39). Parsons notes also a *c.*1140 reference to a member of the Turpin family of Pitton in connection with mews, surmising that Turpin was the king's falconer (Parsons, *Little Manor*, p.73).

area and its hinterland was well-served from an early date by roads, many of which centred on the palace. For example before the sewage works south of Petersfinger was constructed, the road that probably gave Britford its name could be traced running through its churchyard across the Avon towards Clarendon.[65] Further south, Downton's primary communication routes ran east-west before the building of the A338 as late as the nineteenth century. In particular, the ancient main route from Winchester to Downton and on to Wilton ran along the boundary between Clarendon and Melchet Forests on Dean Hill.[66] Another important route, the highway from Winchester to Old Sarum (the Roman road) served as the northern boundary of Clarendon Forest. Whether or not another 'public' route passed directly through Clarendon Park to Salisbury and beyond (see above), both forest and palace were within easy reach of through traffic.

Primary north-south routes also ran past Clarendon Forest. That on the east of the Avon provided access to Wilton and Old Sarum markets from Downton via Milford, and was originally the forest's western boundary. This route must be Saxon or earlier, since Barford, along its line, has been identified as a DMV of pre-Conquest origin.[67] The road forming the boundary between the forests of Clarendon and Buckholt was more remote, running from West Dean to the Roman Road through the once much larger Bentley Wood on the present Dean Road along the old county boundary. Like the route on the western bound of Groveley Forest in the early thirteenth century (see Figure 63), it may have originated as a drove road, connecting West Dean and the Winterslows.

Inside the forest itself, communications were extensive. Today Winterslow, renowned as one of the most extended villages in England, encompasses over 32 miles of footpaths.[68] Livery Road, running north from Grimstead to West Winterslow past The Livery (see Figure 50) was evidently in use in 1225, when it formed the eastern boundary of Clarendon Forest.[69] From the church at Winterslow, this road appears to have followed the present Clarendon Way along a track, along which the 1225 perambulators proceeded (see Figure 84), to emerge on the Roman road opposite Cobhill barrow. This was the likely site of the Winterslow gallows (or Waleran's Cross),[70] named in the perambulation which indicates the importance of the route, forming, as it did, part of a crossroads. West Winterslow was connected to Pitton by the drove (Salterway) running along Pitton Hill, today called Pitton Path, at the time of the perambulation of

1307.[71] This salter way ran eastwards along Dean Hill, then on to Danebury and beyond. It was probably used to bring salt to the palace from the New Forest,[72] and it is possible that the present Slateway, which enters the park through Pitton Gate, is derived from the name.

ASSARTING

As noted above (p. 92), –feld, -hurst and –ley elements in Clarendon Forest's placenames, indicating woodland with clearances, are rare. This is also the case in Purbeck (Dorset), where there was little opportunity for medieval assarting and the creation of new settlements. A contrast may be seen in the placenames of neighbouring Melchet (Whelpley, the Cowesfields).[73]

The (generally dispersed) settlement pattern in woodland is a product of its scope for colonisation, although the presence of royal forest might inhibit the clearances on which this depended. However, one should not interpret medieval forest laws as if they were intended to stop people doing things,[74] and fines for assarts, purprestures and wastes should be seen as permits rather than deterrents. Nevertheless, such data provides a useful source of contrast. Comparison between Clarendon and Melchet Forests will form a significant part of this analysis, and it will be shown that Clarendon was what Oliver Creighton has called a 'seigneurial green belt'.[75]

The support, or even ambivalence, of a lord towards assarting could result in changes in settlement pattern, since encroachment might either sustain the trend towards, or emphasise the existing pattern of, dispersed settlement.[76] On a purely practical level, agricultural development would have been inhibited by Clarendon's use as a hunting forest. In contrast very few deer are recorded as coming out of Melchet (above, Figure 17), indicating that it was exploited far less as a hunting reserve, probably the reason it was wasted more or less with impunity. The attitudes of tenants-in-chief in Melchet and Clarendon may have differed, but the king's interest was overarching, and royal ambivalence towards assarting in Melchet resulted in a very different settlement pattern.

There are problems in using documentary evidence when discussing settlements and assarts. Forest sources make it plain that many 'secondary' settlements existed by the thirteenth century. However few were separately taxed so that mother settlements or tithing centres might appear in Lay Subsidy records with inflated populations and dispersed settlement in colonised woodland may be

[65] Woodall, 'Britford Church and Parish', p.6.
[66] A.J. Gifford, 'An Archaeological Study of Routeway Development in Downton Parish' (unpub. paper, WRL, 1995), pp.6, 11.
[67] Gifford, 'Routeway Development in Downton Parish', pp.6-7.
[68] C. McKeown, 'Winterslow: Lions, Fires, Business and Fame, it all Happens in Winterslow', *Wiltshire Life*, February 1998, pp.60-62 (p.61); R.A. Titt, *A List of Places and Paths in Winterslow* (Middle Winterslow: R.A. Titt, 1991 [WRL]), p.1.
[69] See Parsons, *Pancet*, p.9.
[70] Parsons, *Pancet*, pp.9, 10.

[71] Parsons, *Pancet*, p.11; Titt, p.5.
[72] Parsons, *Pancet*, p.14.
[73] Hinton, *Purbeck*, p.93; Taylor, 'Whiteparish: A Study', *passim*.
[74] Rackham, *Illustrated History*, p.15.
[75] O. Creighton, 'Castles and Settlement Planning in Medieval England', paper given at *Castles and Hinterlands in Medieval Europe*, OUDCE conference, February 2001.
[76] Hunt, *Lordship and the Landscape*, p.139.

masked, a situation noted by Hare concerning Chippenham, and by Taylor concerning Abbotstone in Melchet.[77] There has even been disagreement about what medieval assarting was *for*. The consensus is that it occurred in response to demands for increased acreage of arable land. However, written sources are generally silent, and it has been suggested that assarts in West Yorkshire, at least, were in fact used for animal husbandry.[78] Again, this must have been historically, geographically, and locally specific, and it will be seen that the nature of assarting, and the status of its instigators, was very different in Clarendon and Melchet.

Finally, there is the vexed question of terminology. Assarts were defined in the twelfth century as 'clearings...that is, when any woods or thickets in a forest which are suitable for meadows and homesteads are cut down...and the land is ploughed up and brought into cultivation'. [79] Straightforward enough. However, purprestures — in theory unauthorised buildings, clearings, enclosures or excavations but often no more than unlicensed assarts — are very similar. Once reported, each was chiefly a means of collecting revenue, and frequently what was described as a purpresture in one eyre might appear as an assart in the next. The same can be said of waste. For example land held in Clarendon Forest by the Prior of Ivychurch, Robert de Micheldever and others was listed among arrentations of wastes in 1304 and what were clearly the same parcels of land, described as assarts, were 'inclosed in the park of Claryndon' in 1317.[80]

'Waste' is perhaps the most problematic of medieval terms denoting clearance, since it might mean no more than the cutting of wood beyond customary rights rather than wholesale destruction. However wasted woods were required to be enclosed in order to protect new shoots, their owners rendering fines for chartered rights over the land until growth was complete, and in this way wastes too were akin to assarts. Moreover, woodland might be purposefully wasted by lords as a precursor for assarting. This appears to have occurred in Bere, Chute, Clarendon, and Pamber Forests in 1301, when royal officials were ordered to sell timber for a modest price,[81] presumably because arrented assarts would bring in greater returns.

Thus assarting could serve the interests of lords, who had every reason to support the process. For example Titow has found that sales of wood were highest on the Bishop of Winchester's estates during periods of active assarting and colonisation, so that clearance was taken advantage of from time to time as a means of boosting manorial

profits. But it is usually difficult to ascertain whether assarting occurred following seigneurial instigation, or was a lordly response to an assarting 'movement' that was difficult to resist.[82] Here, too, lordship at Clarendon may be seen as pro-active in its restrictions, rather than reactive, as it was at Melchet. What is certain is that assarts, purprestures and wastes should be considered part of the same phenomenon, and this will be their treatment here although each category will be addressed independently in order to reflect subtle differences.

Figure 51. Clarendon Forest: assarts (recorded acreage. Compiled from forest eyre rolls).

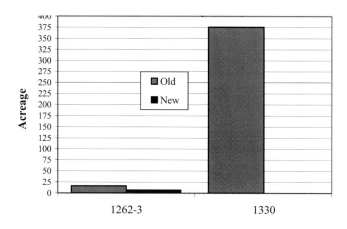

Figure 52. Melchet Forest: assarts (recorded acreage. Compiled from forest eyre rolls).

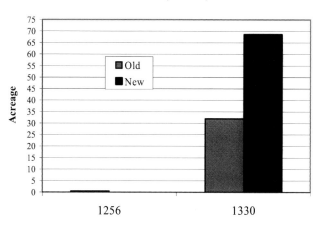

The contrast between Clarendon and Melchet can be seen in recorded acreage of assarts in the 1330 forest eyre (Figures 51 and 52). Although a larger area is listed for Clarendon, these are all 'old' assarts, in existence during the preceding eyre (in this case held in the previous century) and before, while 70 acres of *new* assarts are recorded for Melchet. Even in the 1262-3 eyre, around twice the amount of old as new assarts were noted, confirming that assarting and colonisation in Clarendon had stagnated before the mid thirteenth century, probably

[77] Hare, 'Agriculture and Rural Settlement', p.160; Taylor, 'Whiteparish: A Study', p.94

[78] M. Stinson, 'Assarting and Poverty in Early Fourteenth-Century Western Yorkshire', *Landscape History* 5 (1983), pp.53-67 (p.67).

[79] Grant, *Royal Forests*, p.43, quoting the *Dialogue of the Exchequer* (*c.*1176-9).

[80] PRO E 32/204, m.3; *CCR 1313-18*, p.507.

[81] Stamper, 'Pamber', p.47.

[82] Titow, p.64; Hunt, p.139.

a hundred years before it peaked in Melchet.[83] In contrast, only one acre of new assart had been recorded at Melchet in 1256 while 68.5 acres are noted in 1330. Thus, although assarts are mentioned in Clarendon Forest as early as 1090 and 1169,[84] no 'assarting movement' existed at Clarendon in the late thirteenth and early fourteenth centuries when it appears to have been at its height elsewhere. Unlike Melchet it was not affected by the countrywide rise in the number of acres assarted by the mid- fourteenth century, symptomatic of the tension between the forest laws and a demand for more arable land.[85]

The figures for purprestures are also revealing (Figure 53) especially since, in the sense of unlicensed assarts, they were often tacked onto official assarts as a means of bringing yet more land into cultivation.[86] As such, they might be tiny, and the fact that there were 295 acres in Melchet in 1330 and 345 acres in 1355 reveals an extremely dynamic demographic base and intensive exploitation of the land. Any thought that this might purely be the result of environmental and social upheaval in the wake of famine, agrarian crisis and plague must be ruled out by the figures for Clarendon Forest, which seems to have been as tightly controlled as ever. No purprestures appear to have been registered in 1269, and although acreage rose, there were hardly any more in 1330 than in 1226 and only 45 acres were recorded in 1355.

Figure 53. Purprestures recorded in Clarendon & Melchet Forests (Compiled from forest eyre rolls).

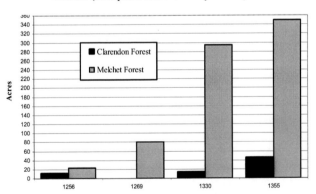

Purprestures in Clarendon were associated chiefly with the area around Pitton and Farley. Indeed there seems to have been extensive clearance before the perambulation of 1225, which features 'the head of a hedge surrounding the fields of Farley',[87] representing the vestiges of grubbed-out woodland between Houndwood and Bentley Wood. Such hedges were used in common to supply hazel for hurdle making, thorns for hedging and to provide shelter for crops and stock.[88]

In Melchet, most purprestures were listed as 'old'. However, there is a definite bias towards Landford and Wellow in the centre and south of that Forest, even between 1269 and 1300 when a flurry of new purprestures appear. Taylor maintains that the people of the parish of Whiteparish (Frustfield) had advanced into the forest more quickly, perhaps because the population was denser.[89] This is evidenced by the assarts themselves, in which Whelpley figures large. New assarts are recorded here in 1256 and 1270 (14½ acres); there is a total of 67 assarted acres (?old and new) in 1330, along with 6 at Whiteparish, while 68½ acres of new assarts are listed under Wellow.[90] Assarts at Clarendon, like purprestures, are most frequently listed for Pitton and Farley and it would seem from this evidence that they were the most vigorous of the Clarendon vills.

For the whole period, only two of Clarendon's purprestures are listed as 'new'. These were made, significantly, by the Treasurer of Salisbury Cathedral in 1256, and the forester John de Grimstead, who 'raised a fence about 80 perches long on a ditch, against the assize' in 1330.[91] Both were tenants-in-chief, and occupiers as well as perpetrators. Indeed in Clarendon Forest, the beneficiaries of assarting grants in general were mostly seigneurial or ecclesiastical, including high-ranking officials at the palace or the forest. For example Master David Carpenter, keeper of the king's houses of Clarendon had 5 acres of assarted land in Pitton in 1255.[92] In 1227, Richard le Archer had illegally enclosed with a ditch and a hedge some of Salisbury Cathedral's land near the holding in Farley granted him as serjeant and king's bowman.[93] Other notable names recorded in the 1330 eyre are Richard Sturmy, warden of Chute Forest, the de Milford, de Pitton and de Laverstock foresters, the Cusyns (holders of Rodsley Wood and sometime launderers and foresters), Robert de Micheldever, deputy warden, and the Priory of Ivychurch, which had assarted without license land in Pitton held of the gift of Robert de Stodlegh. In 1246, the assart was granted to them in Frank Almoin, and made quit of waste and regard.[94] A further 112 acres near the Priory was arrented to them in 1314 for 56s. a year, which they might bring into cultivation,[95] and this seems to have been the 'certain assart' held by Ivychurch imparked by Edward II three years later. Another seigneurial assarter was William Longespée Earl of Salisbury, lord of the Hundred of Alderbury and illegitimate son of Henry II. Longespée assarted 73 acres in Bentley Wood on which he probably intended to build a religious house, 'St Mary of the Bentlewood',

[83] Taylor, 'Whiteparish: A Study', p.91.

[84] Parsons, *Little Manor*, p.5.

[85] Young, *The Royal Forests of Medieval England*, pp.117, 121.

[86] Stinson, 'Assarting and Poverty', p.61.

[87] BM Stowe 798 *f.*9a.

[88] M. Parsons, *The Brittle Thread* (New Milton: Leonard Michael Parsons, 1997), p.27.

[89] Taylor, 'Whiteparish: A Study', p.90.

[90] PRO E 32/215; Taylor, 'Whiteparish: A Study', p.8; PRO E 32/207.

[91] PRO E 32/208, m.1.

[92] PRO E 32/207.

[93] Parsons, *Little Manor*, p.6. Ironically this is now nearly all woodland (*ibid.*).

[94] *CHR 1226-57*, p.304.

[95] *CFR 1307-19*, p.206; *CCR 1313-18*, p.507.

mentioned twice in his will. Instead his widow, Ela Countess of Salisbury, granted the land to the Hospital of St Nicholas, Salisbury, when she was sheriff of Wiltshire in 1227.[96]

What does analysis of wasted woods recorded in the forest eyre rolls tell us about clearance and colonisation in Clarendon and Melchet Forests? In both cases, acreage is not recorded and most waste is classified as 'old', thus it is unreliable for analytical purposes. Incidences of even new wastes recorded do not indicate when that waste took place, but rather when eyres were held or other legislation acted upon. Therefore the 'new' wastes belonging to the Prior of Ivychurch, Robert de Micheldever etc., later taken into Clarendon Park c.1317,[97] were a product of more rigorous prosecution of the forest system under Edward I. This said, apart from waste caused by John de Grimstead in Melchet Park 'new' wastes in Melchet, unlike those in Clarendon, do not seem to have featured in the inquisitions into arrentations of waste of 1299 and 1305.[98] This may indicate that woodland in Melchet was already depleted. Indeed, Lewis has noted with surprise the apparent lack of woodland in that forest as early as 1086, and it is noteworthy that when 46 acres of (probably) new waste *were* recorded for Melchet in 1355, much of it was furze, perhaps used for smelting.[99] Alternatively, royal officials simply did not *care* about waste in Melchet.

Unlike assarting and purprestures, prosecution of which lapsed with the demise of the forest eyre, the transgression of waste is more amenable to analysis over a long timescale. For Clarendon there is a distinct shift towards fines for wasting the coppices in the park by the second quarter of the fourteenth century, and those fined are invariably the better-off. Then, throughout the fifteenth and sixteenth centuries, as concern for timber stocks grew, waste assumed a more important role in legislation. For example the interrogatory issued in 1575-7 'on behalf of the queen's majesty...concerning woods and trees supposed to be...fallen in the forest of Pauncett', the court case following the inquest into spoil of wood in Wiltshire in 1596-7, and the warrant to stay process of 1604 resulting from its verdict.[100] Each is overwhelmingly indicative of a concern that people might try and make money out of wood belonging to the Crown. Attribution of blame for waste (in these cases to George Penruddock and the Clarendon foresters including the earl of Pembroke) had by now replaced the medieval concern to extract nominal rents and fines as a reliable and regular income — although in 1599 the

alleged perpetrators were fined the massive sum of £163 for the value of the spoils plus a penalty of £326.[101] Thus waste was now treated as 'wasteland' in the modern sense, as can be seen in some of the records of coppice sales, for example the 'Tenne acres in waste ground full of Connyes' recorded in Catsgrove coppice in 1594.[102]

In conclusion, although there were concentrations of communal clearance around Pitton and Farley, assarting in Clarendon Forest served on the whole to consolidate the position and income of those already holding land, in contrast to the more cooperative clearance associated with colonisation in Melchet. Only well off individuals or bodies could capitalise effectively on the favourable economic conditions of the twelfth and thirteenth centuries to create large assarts, and this may be a further reason why assarting at Clarendon, as opposed to Melchet, collapsed during the agrarian crisis of the early fourteenth century. Nevertheless, it can be assumed that piecemeal squatting, although generally obscured by the documents, occurred also at Clarendon.[103]

In thirteenth- and fourteenth-century Melchet, assarting was associated with relatively new settlement. Whiteparish had been established as Frustfield soon after 1086, and hamlets around Whelpley like Newton and Chadwell emerged sometime before 1350, probably in the reign of Henry III when a flourishing community is indicated by the foundation of Whelpley Chapel.[104] In Clarendon, however, opportunities for colonisation were practically non-existent. Assarting was associated with existing villages or with uncolonised woods in the hands of rich and influential families or organisations holding their land direct of the king or the Church, which may have served to restrict access on the part of villagers to woodland resources. Elsewhere, for example in the fourteenth-century Forest of Macclesfield, this might result in planned settlements under the aegis of the lords concerned.[105] But at Clarendon this was only possible in Melchet, for example the Cowesfields which were named for the Loveras and Spileman families. If Clarendon Park pale was a visible manifestation of the king's ability to restrict clearance and control resources, then so were the bounds of the forest — less apparent visually, but familiar to its inhabitants and neighbours.

[96] Atkinson, *The Manors and Hundred of Alderbury*, p.22; PRO E 32/207, m.10; Colt Hoare and Nichols, *The Modern History of South Wiltshire*, pp.126-7.
[97] See PRO E 32/204, m.3; PRO E 36/75, *CCR 1313-18*, p.507.
[98] PRO E 32/204; PRO E 36/75.
[99] Lewis, 'Patterns and Processes', p.176; *It(e)m Bruer[a] iux(ta) Brembulwode Ep'i ad q(ua)ntit' viginti acr' vast' p(ro) arfur' de novo set p(er) que(m) ignor'* (E 32/267, m.15).
[100] PRO E 134/18 & 19 Eliz/Mich I; PRO E 123/24 *ff*.198, 216, 334; PRO E 146/3/1.

[101] PRO E 124/3, *f*.95d.
[102] PRO E 101/140/14, m.1.
[103] Parsons cites a few dwellings established c.1245 where Hugh Lane met the communal pasture at Bourne Hill in Farley (Parsons, *Little Manor*, pp.5, 7).
[104] Taylor, 'Three Deserted Medieval Settlements', p.39-41.
[105] A.M. Tonkinson, *Macclesfield in the Later Fourteenth Century: Communities of Town and Forest* (Lancaster: Carnegie Publishing, 1999), pp.5-6.

MOATED SITES

An association of moated sites with royal forest, woodland and dispersed settlement has been noted throughout the country.[106] Thus, although scarce in Wessex and in Wiltshire in particular, their paucity in the Clarendon area is noteworthy in the light of the previous discussion. Accordingly, this section will address reasons for the lacuna in the light of the general consensus that moated sites should be read as status indicators.

Most excavated moated sites date to 1180-1320, and many excavated examples derive from the end of that timescale, at the height of the assarting phenomenon.[107] This was a time of widespread disafforestment in England generally. Assarting, then, was not the primary catalyst for the establishment of moated sites. Rather it was the removal of forest restrictions which facilitated that colonisation, and since Clarendon Forest was among the last in Wiltshire to remain in forest, moats will necessarily be scarce. Yet disafforestment is not the only factor in the provenance of such sites. Braydon and Chute Forests, for example, effectively disafforested by 1300, each display a lack of moats which may be attributed to extensive purlieu restrictions into the seventeenth century.[108] In Wombourne parish near Wolverhampton no moats are recorded despite firm evidence for woodland clearance from the twelfth century, and Purbeck in Dorset, disafforested early in the thirteenth century, contained no moated sites at all, partly because there was no room for new colonisation.[109]

Clearly there is more to moated sites than functional perspectives can explain. In the first place, behind disafforestment and seigneurial assarting are shifts in the nature and manifestation of lordship in the landscape. At Clarendon and elsewhere, this was a time generally of physical definition of the landscape which served to imprint yet more strongly the stamp of royal, and occasionally seigneurial, hands. But a forest or chase, although not usually bounded physically, is as much an indicator of strong lordship as a paled deerpark, as can be seen from the protracted court cases of the nineteenth century in connection with the franchise of Cranborne Chase.[110] Once disafforestment occurred, a vacuum existed that could be filled with more physical markers of lordship (which might include the construction of moats). But disafforestment had first to be accompanied by a withdrawal of royal interest.

Much writing on moated sites has concentrated on their distribution in the context of soil type and topography, and it is pointless to argue that the chalky subsoils at upper Clarendon would have sprung to mind as an ideal location for their construction. Yet there are relatively large pockets of suitable clayey soils. One such is the southern half of Bentley Wood, the site of seigneurial assarting on a scale best described as 'making a statement' — i.e. the Longespée's 40 acres, originally intended as the site of a grand religious foundation (see above, p. 95). Here the establishment of a moated site might be difficult, but certainly not impossible.

Not all authorities agree that moated sites reflect the 'growing assertiveness and sense of importance of the gentry'.[111] Platt sees them rather as manifestations of social unease in violent times, citing the exceptionally large number of homestead moats constructed and evidence of the elaboration and reinforcement of 'kindred fortifications', for example licences to crenellate.[112] But although the fourteenth and fifteenth centuries can be described as times of social upheaval, even by medieval standards, can the same really be said of the thirteenth century? The late thirteenth and early fourteenth centuries marked an upturn in building activity in any case.[113] Further, if the assarting peasantry of East Anglia and the west Midlands built moats because they were 'in need of...protection' — presumably due to fierce competition, land hunger and famine — can this argument really be applied to all areas in which moated sites were common?[114] In the case of seigneurial moats in particular, it is hard to see where architectural manifestations of 'the concern of the military classes with the problems of securing their own' end,[115] and those of social display and emulation begin. Nevertheless, the lack of moated sites around Clarendon might be linked with a sense of security attendant on a strong landlord (or even connected with the lack of a resident overlord), or with statements of invulnerability on the part of a royal landlord, well-understood by contemporaries.

It has been observed that low densities of moats generally occur where the lord of the manor was an ecclesiastical body,[116] and manors and holdings in Clarendon Forest were in the hands of ecclesiastical landlords as well as the Crown throughout the period studied. Salisbury Cathedral was visible to all as a symbol of ecclesiastical interests, just as the palace and park symbolised those of the Crown, should reminders be needed by forest-dwellers. In addition, seigneurial moated sites tend to be associated with tenants rather than overlords,[117] and at Clarendon, tenants-in-chief spent much of their lives performing duties in the forest and at the palace, as did

---

[106] Hunt, *Lordship and the Landscape*, p.98; C. Lewis, P. Mitchell-Fox and C. Dyer, *Village Hamlet and Field: Changing Medieval Settlements in Central England* (Macclesfield: Windgather Press, 2001), p.118.
[107] Lewis, Mitchell-Fox and Dyer, *Village Hamlet and Field*, p.114; Platt, *Medieval England*, p.111.
[108] C. Lewis, pers. comm.
[109] Hunt, *Lordship and the Landscape*, p.98; Hinton, *Purbeck*, p.93.
[110] See Wake Smart, *A Chronicle of Cranborne*, p.xviii.

[111] Hunt, *Lordship and the Landscape,* p.106.
[112] Platt, *Medieval England*, pp.113-4.
[113] Hunt, *Lordship and the Landscape,* p.106.
[114] Platt, *Medieval England*, p.111.
[115] Platt, *Medieval England*, p.111.
[116] Hunt, *Lordship and the Landscape*, p.106.
[117] Hunt, *Lordship and the Landscape*, p.104.

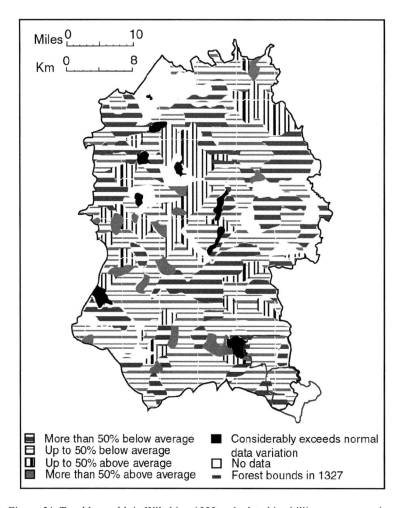

▦ More than 50% below average	■ Considerably exceeds normal
⊞ Up to 50% below average	data variation
⊡ Up to 50% above average	☐ No data
▨ More than 50% above average	▬ Forest bounds in 1327

Figure 54. Taxable wealth in Wiltshire, 1332, calculated in shillings per square km.
Bentley Wood, on the east of Clarendon Forest, is discernable. Adapted from C. Lewis,
'Patterns and Processes in the Medieval Settlement of Wiltshire', in *The Medieval Landscape of Wessex*,
Oxbow Monograph 46 (Oxford: Oxbow Books, 1994), eds M. Aston and C. Lewis, pp.171-93, fig. 8.8.

many of their social inferiors. As Hinton has pointed out, Corfe Castle, the only visible symbol of great lordship in medieval Purbeck, probably had the effect of restraining emulation,[118] and it is likely that of factors accounting for the dearth of moated sites in and around Clarendon, a local sense of what was appropriate was one of the most prominent.

EVIDENCE FROM TAXATION RECORDS

The problems of using records of taxation for demographic study have been well-rehearsed. As J.F. Hadwin puts it, 'the lay subsidy rolls rarely tell the whole truth and do not even lie consistently',[119] and no claim is

made that the figures used here are definitive either in terms of population or prosperity. However, much can be ascertained concerning settlement hierarchy when employing a comparative methodology, and although population estimates are notoriously problematic, patterns will emerge when a single location is analysed over time. Accordingly, attention will be given to recorded population and the relative diachronic prosperity of vills as well as to shrunken medieval settlements on the border of Clarendon and Melchet (Alderstone, Cowesfield Esturmy, More and Whelpley), in an attempt to analyse their failure.

The most meaningful taxation records for Wiltshire, as elsewhere, begin in the fourteenth century. The county rose from fourteen to fifth in rankings of taxable wealth per acre from 1334 to the early sixteenth century mostly due to the massive growth in the cloth industry especially in and around Salisbury. However, the picture is by no

---

[118] Hinton, *Purbeck*, p.102.
[119] J.F. Hadwin, 'The Medieval Lay Subsidies and Economic History', *Economic History Review* 36, no.2 (1983), pp.200-217 (p.201). See also Hare, 'Agriculture and Rural Settlement', pp.160, 165; Hinton, *Purbeck*, p.110; Lewis, 'Patterns and Processes', p.178; S.H. Rigby, 'Late Medieval Urban Prosperity: The Evidence of the Lay Subsidies' and A.R. Bridbury, 'Dr Rigby's Comments: A Reply', *Economic*

History Review 39 no.3, (1986), pp.411-16, 417-22; Taylor, 'Whiteparish: A Study', p.87.

Figure 55. Clarendon Forest: recorded populations, 1086

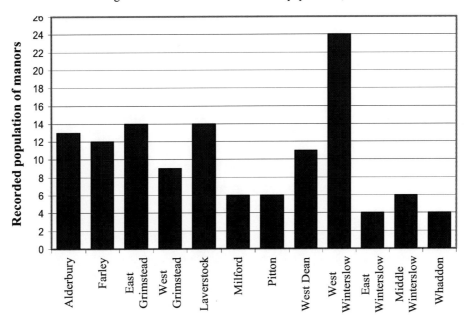

means uniform, and the overall impression is one of stagnation. It has been noted that the late fourteenth to early sixteenth centuries were a time not only of growing contrast between the 'chalk and cheese' areas of Wiltshire, but also of diversification within the regions.[120] Where did this leave the geologically and economically distinct forest areas, particularly Clarendon, and is there any discernible difference in relative prosperity before and after the demise of the palace?

In 1086 Wiltshire's most populous areas were those close to Warminster, around Salisbury in the Avon Valley and to the north of Salisbury Plain, while the forest areas on the east of the county were relatively sparsely populated.[121] Judging by information concerning assessed wealth in 1332 (Figure 54), the situation had changed little, presuming the most prosperous areas were those that produced the highest population. Here Clarendon, Chute Melchet and Savernake Forests form an enclave of their own. However, Clarendon and Melchet, adjacent to a highly populous area, may be anomalous in some respects. For example most of Chute Forest, coterminous with Clarendon Forest to its south (see Figure 7), was bordered on the west by the Plain itself, the higher slopes of which remained uncultivated between the Roman and post-medieval periods and which was far less populous than other areas of Wiltshire.[122]

Figure 55 shows settlements in Clarendon Forest mentioned in Domesday and their recorded populations.[123] Since relative analysis is aimed at, there seems little point in estimating 'true' population, although it is worth noting that multipliers of 4.5 or 5 might usefully be applied.[124] West Winterslow, with a recorded population of 24, was by far the most populous of the Clarendon vills in 1086, and although it would remain high in Clarendon's settlement hierarchy throughout the period studied, it may be speculated that this was due to its proximity to the Confessor's royal estate at Broughton, at the time more prominent than the hunting lodge which probably existed at Clarendon. Of the settlements closest to what would later become Clarendon Park, Pitton is comparatively small, with a recorded population of only six, Laverstock and Alderbury are relatively populous, at 14 and 13 inhabitants respectively, and Farley is close behind with 12 persons recorded.

By the time of the 1377 Poll Tax, the next reliable demographic indicator (Figures 56 and 57),[125] West Winterslow remained relatively populous, while Laverstock and East Grimstead do not seem to have increased in size at all. Neither does Milford, which can be assumed to have had an overall population of about 24 in 1086 if a multiplier of four is applied. The most striking change since 1086 is that Alderbury has become the most populous vill with 95 people over the age of 14 assessed, leaving Farley far behind. In addition, Pitton, which had risen to joint fifth place with West Grimstead, was now twice the size, in demographic terms, of Farley.

[120] Hare, 'Agriculture and Rural Settlement', pp.163-4; Lewis, 'Patterns and Processes', p.178.
[121] Lewis, 'Patterns and Processes', pp.177-8.
[122] D. McOmish et al., The Field Archaeology of the Salisbury Plain Training Area (Swindon: English Heritage, 2002), p.3.
[123] Compiled from Jones, Domesday for Wiltshire, pp.50-149.

[124] R. Smith, 'Human Resources', The Countryside of Medieval England (Oxford: Blackwell Publishers, 1988), eds G. Astill and A. Grant, pp.188-212 (p.190).
[125] PRO E 179/196/34; PRO E 179/196/35; PRO E 179/196/36; PRO E 179/196/37/1, 2.

Figure 56. Recorded taxpayers in Alderbury Hundred, 1377 (dark = in Clarendon Forest, light = outside forest)

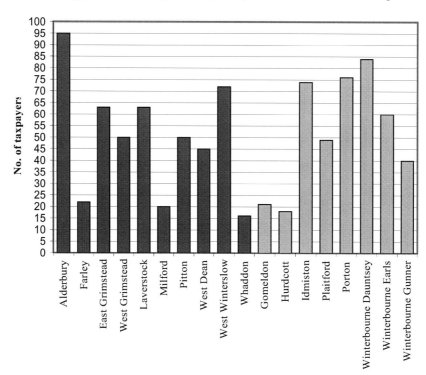

In Melchet all settlements represented in Domesday had increased quite dramatically by 1377 (particularly Whelpley, which had eleven recorded inhabitants in 1086), consistent with the colonisation discussed above. Of course, there are problems in interpretation, especially that of attempting to assign population figures to such small and dispersed settlements whose inhabitants were taxed at the nearest tithing-centre. The Cowesfield manors mentioned in 1086 were Cowesfields Esturmy and Spileman, with 13 inhabitants between them. Cowesfield Loveras had not yet existed, and other new settlements in existence on the cusp of the thirteenth and fourteenth centuries (Blackswell, Chadwell, Harestock — perhaps the site of harrier kennels — and Newtown) must be partially responsible for the general demographic increase.[126] The hamlet of More, in existence by 1086 but not directly mentioned in Domesday, lay within the tithing of Abbotstone and is thus illustrative of the problem.

It is timely here to consider background developments, since 'we are dealing not with a static society, but with one that was decimated by famine [and] wracked by...crises', particularly between 1086 and 1377.[127] Changes in the settlement hierarchy at Clarendon are noteworthy since there is little evidence to show a net gain in population in England as a whole at this time.[128] Set against the demographic and economic upturn in the twelfth and thirteenth centuries are the famines and murrains of 1315-22 followed by the Black Death. Thus

any general increase in population levels observed in 1377, compared to 1086, is likely to have resulted from re-colonisation, showing that the area presented opportunities to incomers.

Figure 57. 1377 Poll Tax: recorded taxpayers in Frustfield Hundred (melchet Forest)

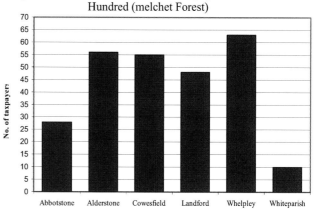

Edward III spent a month at Clarendon Palace in summer 1349, 'while the plague raged beyond the confines of his park'.[129] However, the effects of the Black Death were not uniform in Clarendon Forest. Details are sketchy but Ivychurch appears to have been badly hit to the extent that only one canon lived to tell the tale, although it has been suggested that they may 'simply have scattered'

[126] See Taylor, 'Whiteparish: A Study', pp.83, 88.
[127] Hadwin, 'Medieval Lay Subsidies', p.213.
[128] Smith, 'Human Resources', p.190.

[129] James and Gerrard, *Perspectives of Pleasure*, forthcoming.

Figure 58. 1378-9 Poll Tax: Taxpayers in and around Alderbury Hundred (black = inside the forest, grey = outside the forest)

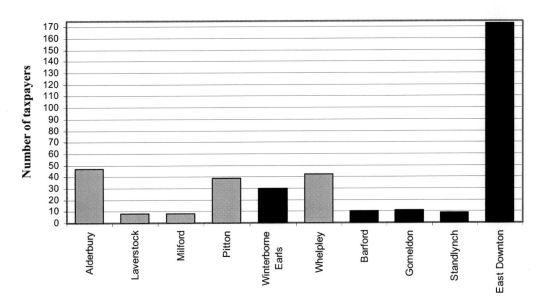

when the disease appeared in the Priory.[130] Most of the population of West Dean and East Grimstead perished, so that the latter's common arable went untilled in 1349, and only one ox team could be mustered at Dean in 1350.[131] Moreover, the rather better documented deaths of lords of the manor and others indicate that plague was not confined to these villages alone. The Heyras family of Alderbury appear to have been devastated, Richard having died by July 1349 and his juvenile heir William by October.[132] In West Grimstead, Alianora de Grimstead, who held the estate after her husband Adam's death in 1347, died in 1348 and her heir John in 1362, probably during the 'second pestilence'.[133] It may be that this second outbreak was the more violent at Clarendon, since at least five verderers perished.[134]

Yet there is little sign of shrinkage in the Clarendon villages in the mid-fourteenth century, and Taylor has shown that the Black Death did little to affect the fortunes of even the Melchet DMVs.[135] Only Cowesfield Loveras was seriously affected with all but three freeholders dead, although by 1361 there seems to have been substantial recovery.[136] This is likely to have been the case for most of the forest vills discussed here, and from the data preserved in taxation records, neither Clarendon nor

Melchet Forests seem to have suffered the emigration in evidence elsewhere in Wiltshire.[137]

Most pertinent here, between 1086 and 1377 the palace had assumed a significance in the local economy that is reflected in the growth of Alderbury and Pitton in particular. That of Alderbury probably reflects the need for locally-available building items, in this case most notably rooftiles, supplied and carted to the palace on a regular basis at least from the reign of Henry III. This is not to say that Alderbury's rooftile industry existed solely to serve Clarendon Palace, but its proximity can only have been fortuitous and it may even have been a primary catalyst in the industry's establishment. At least, the presence of rooftile in the fabric of the Clarendon floortile kiln,

constructed in 1244, hints at local production. By the mid fourteenth-century this very important industry dominated tile production through the entire county, and the records of the 1378-9 Poll Tax (Figure 58) reveal the presence in Alderbury of 17 tilers, a significant concentration compared to other Wiltshire villages where tilers, if any, numbered only one or two.[138] The village's clay deposits were to support a brickmaking industry from the early modern period that still sustained ten employees in 1925 and whose kiln continued to be fired twice-yearly in the 1960s.[139]

The pottery industry at Laverstock, where ten kilns have so far been excavated, probably also originated in order

---

[130] CPR 1348-50, p.260; J.F.D. Shrewsbury, A History of Bubonic Plague in the British Isles (Cambridge: Cambridge University Press, 1971), p.57.

[131] Shrewsbury, A History of Bubonic Plague, p.57; Parsons, Little Manor, pp.13-14, Sharps and Pollards, p.33.

[132] CFR 1347-56, pp.121, 169.

[133] CCR 1346-9, p.435; Atkinson, The Manors and Hundred of Alderbury, pp.55-6; Shrewsbury, A History of Bubonic Plague, p.126.

[134] Order to the sheriff of Wilts to cause verderers of the king's forests of Claryndon, Melchet, Gravele and Savernak to be elected instead of John Everard, Robert Gerberd, Thomas Tichebourne, Nicholas Lambard, Edmund Huse, John Daunvers and George de Weston, who are dead (CCR 1360-64, p.224).

[135] Taylor, 'Three Deserted Medieval Settlements', p.41; 'Whiteparish: A Study', p.94.

[136] Taylor, 'Whiteparish: A Study', p.92.

[137] See Hare, 'Agriculture and Rural Settlement', p.163.

[138] Hare, 'Roof-tile Industry', pp.88, 89-90. Chart compiled from PRO E 179/239/193/6; PRO E 179/239/193/11a.

[139] Alderbury and Whaddon Local History Research Group, Alderbury and Whaddon: A Millennium Mosaic of People, Places and Progress (Alderbury: Alderbury and Whaddon Local History Research Group, 2000), p.102.

to supply Clarendon Palace,[140] and can be assumed to have been partially responsible for the village's relatively high population in 1377. Although Musty tentatively ascribed to the kilns a date range of 1230-75, based on palaeomagnetic declination figures similar to those of the Clarendon floortile kiln (working 1237-52), he was able to do little more, in reality, than establish a sequence for the kilns excavated,[141] and Laverstock's population of around 70 in 1377 was high compared with many other Clarendon vills (admittedly, on a par with East Grimstead). Although no potter surnames are listed there in 1334, a John le Pottere was taxed in nearby Milford.[142] This may be the same John who possessed rights to brushwood above Laverstock in the park in 1318-23, in Ashley, Chesil and Catsgrove coppices, suggesting that kilns were still operational in the area at that date.[143] In addition, a William Cole of Laverstock, perhaps connected with the industry, was amerced in the 1330 forest eyre for several episodes of poaching in Ashley coppice, to which he seems to have had unfettered access.[144]

As for Pitton, there were no doubt similar opportunities to capitalise on demand from the palace. Into the 1920s, 'stone-pickers', usually women and old men, were paid to collect flints in and around the village, which were used to mend roads.[145] It may not be too fanciful to imagine them as the successors of medieval villagers performing the same task in order to provide flint infill for building works at Clarendon. Of all the Clarendon vills, Pitton was the primary draw to migrants in the mid-thirteenth century, at which time it supported twice as many villagers as its close neighbour Farley.[146] A classic forest settlement with a varied economy, it was once bounded to the south by dense oak-and-hazel woodland which made it ideal for production of the pales and rails that were in constant demand at Clarendon even after the palace's demise. In the last decades of the nineteenth century half the village was still employed in seasonal hurdle-making and turning, and wide hedges, all that remained of the oak-and-hazel woods after enclosure, were considered a valuable asset until recently.[147] The area was rich in other resources, such as nuts, demand for which at the palace is evident from the construction of a store for the king's nuts in the thirteenth century, from whence, presumably, the bailiff of Clarendon was to take the six quarts of nuts in his custody given by gift of the king to the Abbey of Amesbury in 1231. Indeed a farm called 'Nottes Place' existed at Pitton in the 1800s, which Colt Hoare suggested may have originated as a storehouse. It probably succeeded the tenement called 'Notes' first

mentioned as belonging to Adam and Agnes le Notere in 1340, and cited in *Inquisitions Post Mortem* through the fourteenth and fifteenth centuries.[148]

Winterslow's ability to support a relatively dense population also rested on economic diversification. Like Pitton it is within easy reach of both woodland and downland, and has seen perhaps even more trades prosper over the centuries, including sloe picking and even the hunting of truffles, which are especially suited to its chalky beech and oak woodlands.[149] It is even possible that there were vineyards at East Winterslow in the thirteenth century, when it was held by serjeanty of making the king's Claret, or perhaps earlier, when it was held by the Saxon thegn Earl Aubrey, the king's prebend (provisioner), under similar terms.[150] Either way, a link with the palace is evident, for in Edward III's reign John de Roches held the manor of Winterslow:

> *by the service that when the king should abide at Clarendon he should come to the palace...go into the butlery and draw out of any vessel he should find...at his choice, as much wine as should be needful for making a pitcher of claret...at the king's charge...*[151]

Surnames in the taxation records also hint at the importance of Clarendon Palace and Park in the local economy, including Colier and Carter in the 1327 and 1332 Lay Subsidy records for Alderbury.[152] Carter is a frequently-occurring local name, and another is recorded at Winterslow in 1332. It may be supposed that there were a number of charcoal makers, or colliers, associated with the palace and forest. References to the industry are few but a forest inquisition c.1330 shows that charcoal was made in winter in an allotted place in Melchet Forest, from wood pertaining to the de Grimstead foresters of fee.[153]

In Pitton in 1332, the surname Vyniter is also listed, perhaps connected with the supply of wine to the palace, and, as already mentioned, a Potter was resident in Milford in 1327 and 1332. Of course not all these people would have been solely connected with serving the palace — by this time Salisbury too was a magnet for craftsmen and tradesmen — and their names may not have directly reflected their occupations by the early fourteenth century. However, many local people were clearly involved in servicing the palace, as a glance at the records of building works alone attests. In the last week of September 1343 eleven of fifteen carpenters felling

[140] J. Musty *et al.,* 'The Medieval Pottery Kilns at Laverstock, near Salisbury, Wiltshire', *Archaeologia* 102 (1969), pp.83-150 (p.85).
[141] Musty, 'The Medieval Pottery Kilns at Laverstock', p.93.
[142] PRO E 179/196/8, m.25.
[143] Musty, 'The Medieval Pottery Kilns at Laverstock', p.83.
[144] PRO E 32/207, m.2d.
[145] R. Whitlock, 'Pitton: A South Wiltshire Village in the 1920s and 1930s', *Hatcher Review* 2, no. 13 (1982), pp.133-40 (p.16).
[146] Parsons, *Little Manor*, p.53.
[147] Whitlock, 'Pitton: A South Wiltshire Village', pp.135-6.

[148] *CCR 1231-4*, p.4; Colt Hoare and Nichols, *The Modern History of South Wiltshire*, pp.41-2.
[149] McKeown, 'Winterslow: Lions, Fires, Business and Fame', p.62.
[150] M. Parsons, *All the King's Men* (New Milton, Leonard Michael Parsons, 1994), pp.46-55.
[151] Colt Hoare and Nichols, *The Modern History of South Wiltshire*, p.47.
[152] PRO E 179/196/7, m.32; PRO E 179/196/8, m.25.
[153] *Et dicunt q(uo)d...quiddam carbonar' in Melchet q(ue) [em]al' emebant coippage de forestario de feodo ibid(e)m & inde faciunt carbone* (PRO E 32/215, m.2).

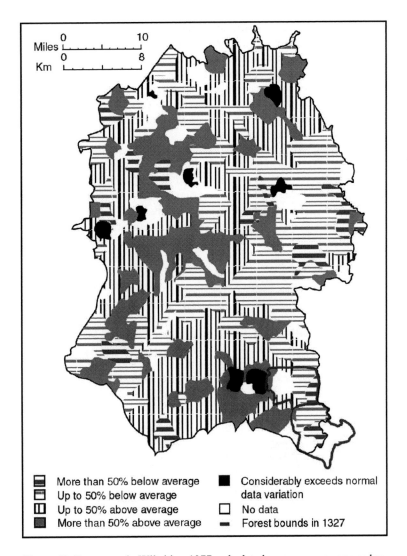

Figure 59. Taxpayers in Wiltshire, 1377, calculated as persons per square km.
Clarendon Park is immediately obvious. Adapted from C. Lewis,
'Patterns and Processes in the Medieval Settlement of Wiltshire', in
The Medieval Landscape of Wessex, Oxbow Monograph 46
(Oxford: Oxbow Books, 1994), eds M. Aston and C. Lewis, pp.171-93, fig. 8.9.

timber for the Lodge on the Laund came from Alderbury, one from Salisbury and another from Winterslow,[154] so that the palace, park and forest must have put significant sums into the local economy.

In 1327, there were 106 taxpayers in Clarendon Forest, a figure that had risen to 136 in 1332 suggesting relatively substantial growth over a short period.[155] But as Glasscock has said, 'the rolls of 1332 [and] 1327...tell us nothing of the total population nor should they be used to estimate it', and clearly different methods of assessment and collection must be taken into account.[156] Nevertheless, comparison with other studies, for example

Hinton's, which showed that taxpayers in the by now long-disafforested Purbeck actually decreased from 221 in 1327 to 214 in 1332, gives some context.[157]

Again at Clarendon, the most populous vills are prominent, with Alderbury, Laverstock and Pitton all increasing from 10-19, 12-16 and 11-16 taxpayers respectively. Moreover, of the surnames listed in the Clarendon villages in 1327 several occurred again in 1332, and some, such as Pipard, Archer and Fry had been among the eight jurors for Alderbury Hundred in the Hundred Rolls of 1254-55.[158] Many names recorded in 1332, for example Carter, Fox, Fry, King, Newman, Parsons, Prewett, White and Whitehorn were to remain in the area until the seventeenth century and later.[159] Such marked surname stability suggests that in common with

[154] PRO E 101/593/20, m.2.
[155] E 179/196/7, m.32; E 179/196/8, m.25. Cf. Hinton, *Purbeck,* p.107.
[156] R.E. Glasscock, ed., *The Lay Subsidy of 1334,* Records of Social and Economic History New Series 11 (London: Oxford University Press, 1975), p.xxiv. The twentieth of 1327 appears to have met with sometimes violent resistance, so that widespread evasion is probable (Jurkowski *et al., Lay Taxes,* p.37).

[157] Hinton, *Purbeck,* p.107.
[158] *Rotuli Hundredorum II,* p.240.
[159] Parsons, *Unparticular Posterity,* p.3.

many wooded areas Clarendon Forest was able to support not only a relatively fixed demographic base but also a substantial proportion of incomers. Again, the lack of a resident overlord, which would have fostered a certain independence, may have been a factor in the area's attractiveness particularly in the mid- to late fourteenth century. It can be no coincidence that both Pitton, which had no resident squire or parson for centuries, and Winterslow, the setting for Major Robert Poore's 'land court' of 1892, became centres of nonconformity in the nineteenth and twentieth centuries.[160]

The next tax to facilitate reasonably secure estimation of population is the Subsidy of 1524 (Figure 60),[161] 'perhaps the most effective general tax devised since 1377', which usefully occurred after Clarendon Palace went out of use.[162] At Clarendon, Dean was now uppermost in the settlement (or tithing-centre) hierarchy with 27 taxpayers recorded, although Winterslow remained close with 25. But the villages around Clarendon Park appear to have fallen behind, with Alderbury now smaller than Pitton and Farley, albeit taxed together. If Platt's methods of

Figure 60. 1524 Subsidy: taxpayers recorded in Clarendon Forest

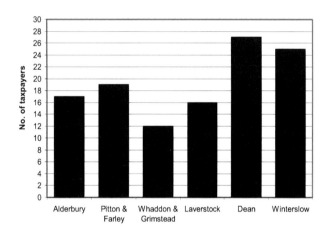

calculation for medieval Southampton may be applied to rural Wiltshire — and they are probably as good as any for this very rough estimation — the population of Alderbury had hardly risen since 1377 (around 100, allowing for younger children and evasion, compared with perhaps 124 in 1524).[163] In contrast, Winterslow and Dean had grown considerably, the latter threefold, which may indicate that the villages further away from the park were now more enticing to migrants. Certainly figures for 1524 show, in contrast to those of 1377, that

Clarendon and Melchet Forests contained the lowest number of taxpayers per square kilometre in the whole of Wiltshire (see Figures 57 and 59). Local processes, such as the demise of the palace in the intervening period, must have been in operation, since it has been estimated that the population level in England was little different in 1540 than in 1377.[164]

On a wider scale, taxation records suggest that urban wealth in England increased considerably between 1334 and 1527,[165] and rural-urban migration must have been significant. Migration to Salisbury from Clarendon and Melchet seems to have been common from at least the early fourteenth to the late sixteenth centuries. Indeed, it has been estimated that around half of those taxed in Salisbury in 1306 and 1334 were immigrants from within a ten-mile radius.[166] Several persons from Pitton, Farley and Whiteparish had contributed to the Tenth collected in the city in 1332, and in 1396 a number of affluent families connected to Clarendon Forest appeared among its three thousand taxpayers. Some, for example Thomas Farle, paid further substantial sums in aulnage, indicating their success in Salisbury's cloth trade.[167] Although archaeological evidence indicates a general fall in urban population through the fifteenth century, on the whole it was towns without a significant cloth trade that suffered,[168] and evidence from loans shows that by 1422 Salisbury ranked third among English towns, a position it was to hold for around a century.

The age of Salisbury's major prominence was beginning to pass in the early sixteenth century, but it must have remained attractive to migrants up to 1524 — and beyond, judging by complaints of overcrowding in the 1590s.[169] Negative influences on migration might include a series of good harvests around 1450, forcing down the price of grain in a locality where there was an insufficient number of consumers to produce a parallel demand. There was a consequent drop in agricultural employment opportunities, while fines and rents rose. Household necessities more than doubled in price, and food more than three times between 1500 and 1600. Nevertheless, as touched on above, most forest households lived by various skills and trades in addition to farming, which may have restrained migration.

Archaeological evidence points to increased rural prosperity in late medieval Wessex. For example many fifteenth and sixteenth century deposits reveal a marked rise in imported pottery compared with the preceding two hundred years.[170] Excavations at the shrunken medieval

[160] Whitlock, 'Pitton: A South Wiltshire Village', pp.137-8; McKeown, 'Winterslow: Lions, Fires, Business and Fame', p.61.
[161] Compiled from PRO E 179/197/162, PRO E 179/136/326.
[162] Nevertheless, between a third and a half of the population was exempted (C. Platt, 'Appendix 1c: Population and Social Stratification in Medieval Southampton', in C. Platt, *Medieval Southampton: The Port and Trading Community, A.D. 1000-1600* [London: Routledge and Kegan Paul, 1973], pp.262-266 [p.263]).
[163] Platt recommends a multiplier of 4 for the late medieval period ('Population and Social Stratification', p.263).

[164] Smith, 'Human Resources', pp.201, 191.
[165] Although see Rigby, 'Late Medieval Urban Prosperity'; Bridbury, 'Dr Rigby's Comments', and J.F. Hadwin, 'From Dissonance to Harmony on the Late Medieval Town', *Economic History Review* 39, no.3 (1986), pp.423-26, *passim*.
[166] Parsons, *Unparticular Posterity*, p.41.
[167] Parsons, *Sharps and Pollards*, p.36.
[168] Hinton, *Archaeology, Economy and Society*, p.194.
[169] Dale, 'The City of New Salisbury', p.129.
[170] Hinton, *Archaeology, Economy and Society*, p.206.

0 Miles 10   0 Km 8

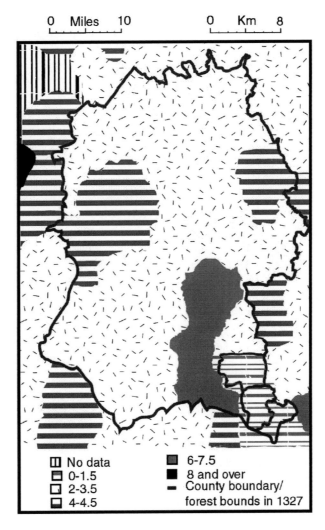

⊞ No data	▨ 6-7.5	
⊟ 0-1.5	■ 8 and over	
⊡ 2-3.5	▬ County boundary/	
⊡ 4-4.5	forest bounds in 1327	

Figure 61. Wiltshire 1524-5: taxpayers per square km.
Adapted from R. E. Glasscock, *The Lay Subsidy of 1334*, Records of Social and Economic History,
New Series 11 (London: Oxford University Press, 1975).

village at Hanging Langford, Groveley Forest (see Figure 61), revealed a settlement that throve at least as late as the fourteenth century. Finds indicated prosperity into the fifteenth century, including a higher proportion of fine glazed wares than might be expected for a rural site.[171] There are signs that the settlement benefited from passing trade, and it is likely that this was also the case at the Winterslows, spread along the Roman road which was the main road to Salisbury, accounting for their position in the settlement hierarchy into the sixteenth century at the expense of villages in the centre of the forest. Dean, which had also risen in the settlement hierarchy, was also well-served by roads, sited not only on the road along the Wiltshire/Hampshire (and Clarendon Forest) border from the Roman road, but also on the main road from

Winchester to Romsey, Downton and Wilton via Whiteparish.[172] In contrast, Alderbury and particularly Pitton may have seen a reduction in passing traffic after the palace went out of use, although recovery in Pitton and Farley seems to have been rapid.

Evidence for precise dating of desertion and shrinkage in the fifteenth to early seventeenth centuries is difficult to assess,[173] not least because of the vagaries of Tudor and Stuart Subsidy records, again based on tithings. All that can be done is to analyse those subsidies listing Alderbury Hundred which can be expected to include the most people (i.e. with the lowest tax thresholds). The next such is the subsidy of 1545 (Figure 62),[174] which assessed from 20s. in lands, but as high as £5-10 in goods. However, in common with all the later subsidies very few people are listed compared to that of 1523, and

---

[171] Wessex Archaeology, *Hanging Langford to Little Langford Pumping Main Renewal: Stage 1, Archaeological Monitoring of Hand-Excavated Test Pits*, Wessex Archaeology Report W596a (Trust for Wessex Archaeology, 1993), p.4; Wessex Archaeology, *Hanging Langford to Little Langford Pumping Main Renewal: Stage 2, Archaeological Excavation and Watching Brief*, Wessex Archaeology Report W596b (Trust for Wessex Archaeology, 1994), pp.3, 6, 13.

[172] See Gifford, 'Routeway Development in Downton Parish', p.6, Sleeve L.
[173] Taylor, 'Whiteparish: A Study', p.92.
[174] Compiled from PRO E 179/197/241 mm.2*d*, 5, 5*d*.

the thresholds are particularly low. Therefore their use as anything but a very rough demographic guide is problematic. They indicate rather proportions of relatively wealthy taxpayers in selected villages. But this may yet be a guide to the prosperity of those villages, and records of some taxes, for example those of 1545 and 1575, are valuable as indicators of social class.

Figure 62. Subsidy of 1545: taxpayers recorded for Clarendon Forest

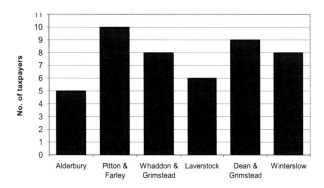

There is little doubt that the fifteenth and sixteenth centuries saw considerable economic change, including the breakdown of the manorial system, which almost certainly prompted greater freedom of movement resulting in a shakeup in the settlement pattern. For example Taylor has found that Whiteparish increasingly attracted migrants from its immediate surrounds, becoming the main focus of north Melchet probably by the mid-sixteenth century and resulting in the shrinkage of other settlements.[175] Whiteparish is not used exclusively as a tithing unit in taxation documents until the 1620s (see Figure 66, below), at around the same time that Whelpley's new manor house, dated 1627, was transferred to western Whiteparish.[176] However, its population is recorded as 10 in 1377, and it appears in both the benevolence of 1544-5 and the contribution of 1546-7, in each case with 7 contributors.[177] The contribution was a benevolence in all but name, and since benevolences were ostensibly levied for military purposes they fell outside the Exchequer's usual administration framework, so that established tithings were not necessarily used.[178] Thus, Whiteparish, with more voluntary taxpayers than Whelpley and the Cowesfields together, seems already to have been gaining the ascendant in 1544-5.

In addition, Figure 54 demonstrates, despite its deficiencies, that in 1377 the recorded populations of Alderstone (56), the Cowesfields (55) and Whelpley (63) compared well with Laverstock and East Grimstead (63)

and Pitton and West Grimstead (50) in Clarendon Forest. In fact they were larger than Farley (22), Milford (20) and Whaddon (16). However, in the case of Whelpley at least, the high figure merely reflects that it was the largest tithing in the parish.[179] As for the Cowesfields, only in the subsidy of 1547-8 and the reliefs of 1550-1 and 1552-3 is it possible to analyse each separately.[180] For the subsidy, only one taxpayer was registered in Cowesfield Spileman, paying 4d., while there were three each in Cowesfields Esturmy and Loveras, paying 8d. and £4 between them respectively. By the time of the reliefs, Cowesfield Loveras still contained three assessed taxpayers. Cowesfield Esturmy, later to be classed as a DMV, only contained one (John Hurst senior), as did Cowesfield Spileman (John Hurst junior), indicating that they had already shrunk to become the concern of a few households, probably from one family, by the mid-sixteenth century. Nevertheless, it must be significant that no Melchet DMV was included among the Poor Parishes of 1428.[181] All that can be said is that processes operating in the sixteenth and seventeenth centuries caused a relocation of population to Whiteparish from the hamlets of the extremely dispersed settlement pattern found in northern Melchet from the twelfth and thirteenth centuries.

'Deserted villages' are generally rare in woodland economies, but Groveley also has several. As well as the shrunken settlement at Hanging Langford, there are Baverstock, Fisherton de la Mere, Little Langford, North Burcombe and Ugford, and a DMV at Chilhampton (see Figure 63). It may be speculated that the shrunken and deserted settlements in both Melchet and Groveley owed something to disafforestment. Groveley was probably alienated by one of the later Tudors, and Melchet was inclosed in 1577 when the manor of Whiteparish, among others, surrendered its right to common pasture.[182] But in Clarendon Forest, disafforested 1577-1610,[183] a similar process did not occur. Lewis has noted the evidence for continued occupation of high status centres which transcended fluctuations in economic fortunes and provided a stabilising influence across the landscape, leading to continuity of settlement.[184] This may account for the lack of significant shrinkage around Clarendon even after the palace had gone out of use.

What demographic evidence can be gleaned from later taxation records (Figures 64-9) suggests that Pitton, which supported around twice the population of Farley throughout the period studied, remained significant in the settlement hierarchy through the sixteenth and

[175] Taylor, 'Whiteparish A Study', p.94.

[176] Taylor, 'Whiteparish A Study', pp.93-4.

[177] PRO E 179/197/230, m.5d; PRO E 179/197/245; M.W. Beresford, 'Poll Tax Payers of 1377', in Crittall, ed. (1959), pp.304-13 (p.308).

[178] Jurkowski *et al.*, *Lay Taxes*, p.xlviii. Whiteparish had never been used as a centre for collection of taxes, even under its pre-fourteenth-century name of Frustfield.

[179] Taylor, 'Three Deserted Medieval Settlements', p.40.

[180] PRO E 179/197/241, m.2d; PRO E 179/198/256a; PRO E 179/198/261aa.

[181] Whaddon, for example, was included. See M.W. Beresford, 'Poor Parishes of 1428', in *The Victoria County History IV* (Oxford: Oxford University Press, 1959), ed. E. Crittall, pp.314-5 (p.314).

[182] Grant, *VCH Wilts*, pp.431-2.

[183] Grant, *Royal Forests*, p.223.

[184] Lewis, 'Patterns and Processes', p.191.

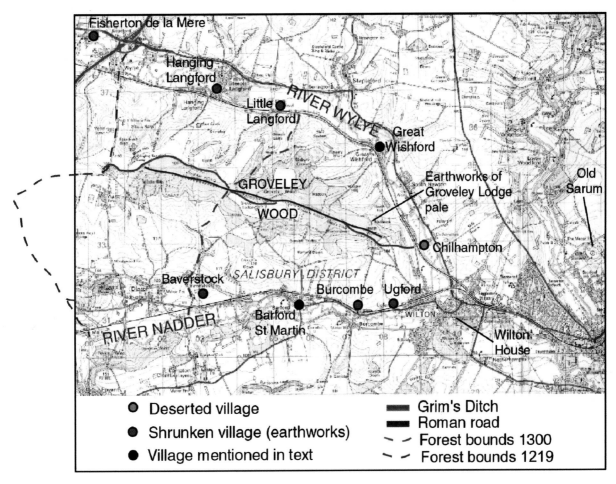

Figure 63. Shrunken and deserted villages in and around Groveley Forest, with other places mentioned. The forest was bounded to the north and south by the rivers Nadder and Wylye. Adapted from R. Grant, 'Forests', in *Victoria County History Wiltshire IV* (Oxford: Oxford University Press, 1959), ed. E. Crittall, pp. 391-457 (p. 457).
OS Map reproduced with kind permission of the Controller of Her Majesty's Stationary Office,
© Crown copyright NC/05/100041476.

seventeenth centuries despite the evidence of the subsidy of 1523-4.[185] Indeed from 1545, Pitton and Farley together contain the highest proportion of taxpayers, corresponding to a rise in proportional wealth in Alderbury Hundred generally in the late sixteenth century. The Subsidies of 1575 and 1593 (Figures 65 and 66), collected before and after disafforestation had begun, show a slight fall in numbers of taxpayers. However there are apparent shifts in the settlement hierarchy, perhaps because the relaxation of forest restrictions attracted better-off migrants to the area.

As shown in Figures 70 and 71,[186] Alderbury Hundred, always much richer than that of Frustfield (Melchet), rose

in the rankings of taxable wealth so that in 1550-1610 it overtook even Downton. In part, this is because the sinecures and tenure associated with the royal forest and park attracted speculators, providing opportunities for an affluent yeoman class whose opportunities increased especially with the Reformation, and who would fulfil duties in Clarendon Park. The properties of the thirteenth-century forester serjeants had remained roughly in their original units despite centuries of subinfeudination, for example the earliest deed of title in the Ilchester archives, dated 1462, corresponds with the old de Archer property at Farley. The de Pitton freehold, whose tenure was held by the Barons Zouche from the end of the fifteenth century, was later sold to the Evelyn family, and the medieval de Lucy properties in and around Farley went to the White family who owned much land in the Winterbournes.[187]

[185] Charts compiled from PRO E 179/198/275; PRO E 179/198/314, mm.4, 4d.; PRO E 179/199/370, mm.4d, 5, 6; PRO E 179/199/398, mm.2, 7d; PRO E 179/199/405, m.3; PRO E 179/239/207, m.2; PRO E 179/198/294, mm.33, 36.
[186] PRO E 179/196/12; PRO E 179/196/3; PRO E 179/196/4; PRO E 179/196/7; PRO E 179/196/8; PRO E 179/196/16; PRO E 179/196/20; PRO E 179/196/21; PRO E 179/196/23; PRO E 179/196/30; PRO E 179/196/50; PRO E 179/196/87; PRO E 179/136/326; PRO E 179/197/230; PRO E 179/197/245; PRO E 179/197/241; PRO E 179/198/266; PRO E 179/198/256a; PRO E 179/198/261a; PRO E

179/198/275; PRO E 179/198/284; PRO E 179/198/294; PRO E 179/198/297; PRO E 179/270/18; PRO E 179/198/314; PRO E 179/198/329; PRO E 179/199/370; PRO E 179/199/398; PRO E 179/199/405.
[187] Parsons, *Little Manor*, pp.15, 54-6.

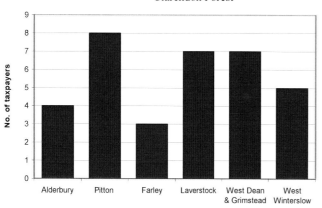

Figure 64. Subsidy of 1559: taxpayers recorded for Clarendon Forest

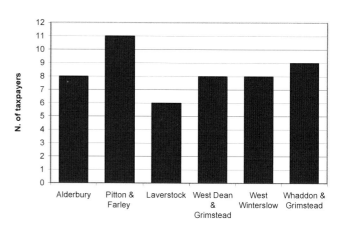

Figure 67. Subsidy of 1610: taxpayers recorded for Clarendon Forest

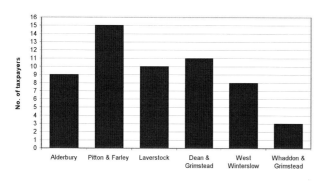

Figure 65. Subsidy of 1575: taxpayers recorded for Clarendon Forest

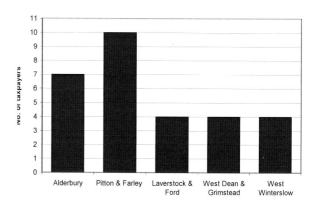

Figure 68. Subsidy of 1628: taxpayers recorded for Clarendon Forest

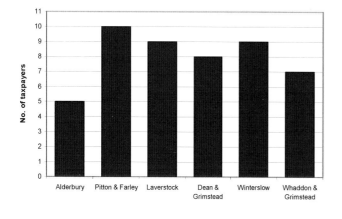

Figure 66. Subsidy of 1593: taxpayers recorded for Clarendon Forest

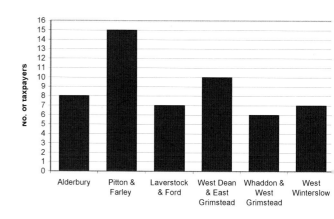

Figure 69. Subsidy of 1641: taxpayers recorded for Clarendon Forest

Figure 70. Taxes paid in Alderbury and Frustfield Hundreds

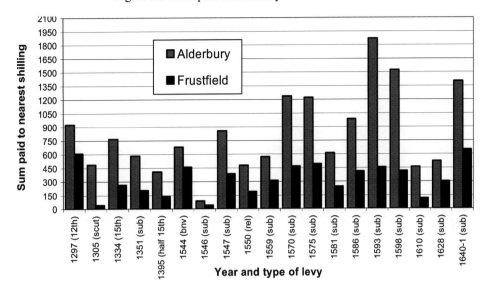

Figure 71. Taxes paid in Alderbury, Downton and Frustfield Hundreds

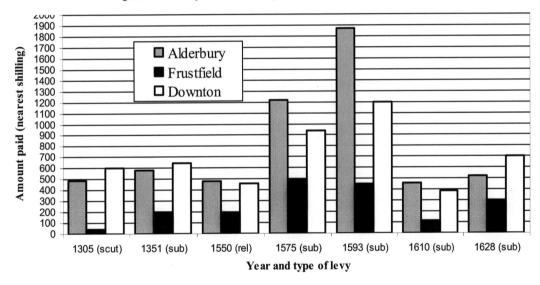

Others who worked in the park built prolifically not in the forest itself, but in the surrounding area. For example the Stockmans constructed Barford House, destroyed in 1815 but still discernible in an impressive avenue of trees running from Barford Farm to the Alderbury Road.[188] The epitome of this 'great rebuilding' in the area was the castle at Waleran's old holding of Longford, erected after 1574 by Sir Thomas Gorges who pulled down the manor house of the Cervingtons, lords of Longford for the previous 250 years, in order to build it. In addition, Edward Gorges may have been responsible for New House, two miles south west of Whiteparish and 'lately erected' in 1619, while Giles Eyre's house at Brickworth

was built c.1604 a mile to its north west.[189] Eyre's Folly on Pepperbox Hill, constructed c.1606, has been described as a 'digital gesture to the world...which doubled as a viewpoint for the ladies to watch the progress of hunting in comparative comfort'.[190]

Nevertheless, new buildings in Clarendon Forest were on the whole rather less grand than those on its outskirts, at least until it ceased to be a royal landscape after the Restoration,[191] and similar factors may have restricted their construction to those discussed above (pp. 97-98) in connection with moated sites. Certainly this period saw the culmination of centuries of royal ambivalence

[188] A.R. Woodford, *Notes on the History of Downton*, (unpublished, Wiltshire Library and Museum Service, RNF DOW 940), p.21. John Stockman was a Clarendon regarder c.1603-7 and keeper of the king's rabbits c.1609-10 (PRO E 101/542/21; PRO E 372/455 [*Item Wiltes*]).

[189] Woodall, 'Britford Church and Parish', p.5; Taylor, 'Whiteparish A Study', pp.95-6.
[190] S. Day, 'Pass the Pepperbox: A Walk Above Whiteparish', *Wiltshire Life* 2, no. 3 (1996), pp.26-9 (p.26).
[191] For example Farley Hospital and Church, built in 1681 by Sir Stephen Fox and traditionally ascribed to Wren.

towards Melchet Forest. The remaining deer were removed in 1610, and the forest was finally granted to Sir Lawrence Hyde in 1614.[192]

A probate inventory survives for West Grimstead that sheds light on the material possessions and wealth of Clarendon forest-dwellers in the early sixteenth century. John Fry the elder died in 1538 possessed of a messuage in West Grimstead with 100 acres of land, meadow and pasture, and around 100 marks worth of goods, including 'whole barley saches and hay', wheat in the field 'horses and gelding(es) to carte' and twelve plough oxen. He also possessed 24 cows and a bull, five heifers, five steers, 14 bullocks, fifteen yearling calves, four rams, 200 wethers, 60 ewes, and a boar and four sows. In addition, there were '40 logges' and a chimney, 'wood at the wood vyne' worth 20s., a valuation of £30 for 'wood that was sold at Knyght Wood', while his household goods included, not surprisingly 'all manner of trene vessell'. Subsidiary industries are also in evidence in that two 'tornes' (spinning-wheels) were listed, along with wool and yarn, and a pair of beam scales and weights.[193]

Fry, who was assessed for £40 in goods in the subsidy of 1524-5, the highest in his tithing, was evidently wealthy and of some local standing, since either he or his son John was collector of that subsidy for Alderbury Hundred.[194] But the archetype of the new social order in Clarendon itself were the Thistlethwaites of Winterslow. They first appear in local records in the subsidies of 1523 and 1524-5, when Alexander Thistlethwaite was assessed at £66 and 204s. (in goods) respectively.[195] Alexander, clearly a man of substance, bought the Manor and advowson of West Winterslow in 1530 around the same time that Giles Thistlethwaite, probably his brother, acquired that of Middle Winterslow.[196] The family's prominence in the local community is evidenced by the 1634 pew list of All Saints Church, in which Thistlethwaite men are shown occupying three of the four seats in the north front pew in the nave.[197] They are also found listed as foresters (1579-80) and regarders (1594, 1606, 1615), and by 1640 Edward Thistlethwaite was employed for a yearly fee by the earl of Pembroke to oversee the maintenance of woods and coppices in Clarendon Park.[198] Although not great builders, the Thistlethwaites were neither absent landlords nor inactive forest officers. This is clear from Alexander III's 1606 presentment, made with a fellow regarder, that underwood had been sold 'in [a] manner to make acomoditie and gaine to [the under-woodward] as we doo

verilie thinke',[199] and from Edward Thistlethwaite's many complaints that Edward Gandy had failed to maintain coppice hedges to a reasonable standard, recorded in an interrogatory of 1640.[200]

The forest, or to be more precise by this period the park, clearly remained an important element in the status and local standing of sixteenth- and seventeenth century gentry like the Thistlethwaites. It was also a significant factor in the resurgence of the immediate area after the manor of Ivychurch was leased by the Earl of Pembroke from c.1551. The Earls, wardens of the forest from 1551-1665 except for the years 1601-6, no doubt found Ivychurch a convenient base. However there is no evidence that they ever lived in the Jacobean mansion built by the second earl (1534-1601) on the site of the priory, of which only the remains of the walled garden, a large rectangular enclosure incorporating English bond brick with lozenge diapering in vitrified brick, is now visible at the north west corner of the priory ruins.[201] Little more is known about Ivychurch House, but it was clearly impressive, and it seems to have been a favourite of Mary Sidney, the wife of the second earl, whose brother, the poet Sir Philip Sidney, resided there as a guest for three years or so around 1580.[202] Mary is known to have been at Wilton in 1603 when her son entertained James I, and it is possible that she played a part in the king's visit to Clarendon Park in that year,[203] as she doubtless had during Elizabeth I's visit of 1574. But James had not stayed at Ivychurch, indicating that the mansion had gone out of favour with the death of the second earl in 1601. Instead he visited Winterslow, where he was perhaps entertained by the Thistleth-waites.[204]

Another resident of Ivychurch House was Sir George Penruddock sometime sheriff and MP for Wiltshire. He was probably the earl's sub-tenant c.1572-1581, since he was described as 'of Ivychurch' in 1572 and at his death in the latter year. From at least 1568 Penruddock was also 'lieutenant' (deputy warden) of Clarendon Park,[205] and his 'Ranger's Book', running from 1572-5, reveals the extent to which both he and the Pembrokes regarded the park as their personal hunting-ground, and how much of a focus it was for the local gentry. Aside from the many gifts of venison given by both parties to the mayor, the sheriff, the bishop of Salisbury and the dean of Winchester among others, Sir George and his brother killed a buck in the Out Woods sometime between November 1572-April 1573. Then, probably joined again

[192] Grant, *VCH Wilts*, p.431.
[193] PRO C 1/1428/82.
[194] PRO E 179/197/162; PRO E 179/136/326.
[195] C. Cohen, *So Great a Cloud: The Story of All Saints, Winterslow, Part One – The First Seven Centuries* (Winterslow: Winterslow Parochial Church Council, 1995), p.12; PRO E 179/197/162.
[196] Cohen, *So Great a Cloud*, p.12.
[197] Cohen, *So Great a Cloud*, Appendix 5.
[198] PRO E 372/425 (*Item Wiltes*); PRO E 101/140/14; PRO E 101/542/21; PRO E 178/4728.

[199] PRO E 101/140/14, m.5.
[200] PRO E 178/4728, part I, m.4d.
[201] Atkinson, *The Manors and Hundred of Alderbury*, p.71; DOE, *Lists of Buildings of Special Architectural or Historic Interest: Salisbury District*, 3 (London: Department of Environment, 1985), p.2.
[202] Atkinson, *The Manors and Hundred of Alderbury*, p.72.
[203] Atkinson, *The Manors and Hundred of Alderbury*, p.72. For the royal visit see PRO E 178/4728.
[204] PRO E 351/3239.
[205] Atkinson, *The Manors and Hundred of Alderbury*, p.72; PRO E 146/2/39; PRO E 101/140/11; PRO E 178/2417.

by his brother, he coursed and killed another two bucks in the park on 13 May 1573, followed by another buck and two sorrels over three days in July, on one of which he was joined in his coursing by a Mr Procter. Other gentry, too, took advantage of the game in and around the park, including 'Mr Thistelltwhaite and other gentillmen', who killed a sorell and a pricket in the Out Woods in Winter 1573.[206]

All this was insignificant, however, compared with the Pembrokes. On 8 May and 16 June 1572 the Earl killed a pricket, a buck and two sours, the latter two in the laund, returning on 8 July to kill three bucks. On 2 June 1573 he took two bucks, and another the next day which he killed at Bright's Lodge (Whitmarsh), followed on 6 June by another in the bailiwick of a forester known as 'Jockey'. The Pady Course and its associated pens appear to have seen some use later the same month, for the Earl killed two bucks 'owt of the p(ar)ockes' on 14 June, and three more 'in the p(ar)ockes' on the 23rd, after which he dispatched another in the Out Woods. On 15 June, he had killed another 'with coursinge', and on the 20th and 22nd he had seen off another two in Jockey's bailiwick. On the 25th, he was back to hunt and kill another buck in George Batter's bailiwick (either Shreeves Wood or more likely the Launds), and in August he killed three there and three more at Whitmarsh. He was still in the area in Autumn, for on 21 September he killed a buck which was sent to Downton, another two when hunting with 'H[ar]ille Jones' on 5 October, two more on the 19th and another, of which 'mathew of honniyton had one humb[l]es' on the 25th. Once the doe season began, the Earl returned to dispatch seven of them over the first three weeks in November.[207]

Although not as active as her husband, Lady Pembroke also hunted, personally killing a buck, a pricket and a fawn at Whitmarsh and two bucks in the parrocks in 1573.[208] Many deer were also killed *for* her, as well as for the earl and others, and there is a rare possibility to discern her networks of patronage from gifts of venison given. For example in 1573, Robert Bright killed a buck 'by my ladies gifte' to William Herbert which was sent to Mistress Estcourte; Edward Green, forester of Shergallgate, sent bucks on her behalf to Thomas Marshall, Miles Matthew and a Mr Earthe, and George Batter sent others to Mr Tucker, John Penruddock and Mr Proctor.[209] Such gifts show that the park was being managed much as it had been in medieval times, its venison a means to secure patronage and sustain largesse, and that its profile was raised at this time at more than a local level. Clarendon venison was sent to sheriffs, ecclesiastics and nobles, including Sir Henry Ashley and Lady Thynne, and seven does were sent to Ramsbury 'at my Lo. of leicesters being there',[210] while several

consignments went to London. Links with Salisbury clearly also remained strong, since recipients included the bishop, Misters Fulljames and Willford of Sarum, the sheriff, the mayor, the 'masters of the close', the canons of Sarum and the clerk.[211] Such social networks and patronage were still evident in 1638, when a William Calley (after decrying venison as fit only for those with a 'mechanic taste' — himself included!) wrote expressing the hope that the earl of Pembroke would 'bestow a warrant for a buck on me, out of Clarendon, Cramborne [Chase], or Groveley'.[212] At the same time, relaxation of royal control meant Clarendon's landscape was opened up to similar social strata. Antiquarians such as Leland and Camden began to note the park's history and raise it in the national consciousness, and by the 1670s Aubrey was describing Clarendon as 'that delicious parke (…accounted the best of England)'.[213]

Only the villages of Winterslow, Pitton and Farley are named as receiving gifts of venison in 1572-5.[214] This suggests a late sixteenth-century association, probably based on earlier custom, between Clarendon and the closest villages remaining in the forest, reflected in their relative prosperity when the park was remodelled as a pleasure ground for the 'new' local gentry. Such an affinity must have been shared by Alderbury, not least owing to the presence of Ivychurch House. But it does not seem to have encompassed Dean, Grimstead, Milford and Laverstock and Whaddon. Possible reasons might be that Dean and Grimstead never recovered enough from the Black Death to be economically attractive to the new landowning classes. In addition, from a purely cognitive perspective the two had always looked south to Melchet, especially East Grimstead whose manorial lords traditionally had charge of Melchet Park, so that the economy of the area may have suffered along with that of the north of that forest, reflected in the shrinkage of its settlements. Milford, composed of two manors, one royal, the other Episcopal, had also always been rather schizophrenic (and this must have been underscored by its rapid absorption into the suburbs of New Sarum). Its recorded population and assessments, unlike those of Laverstock, seem always to have been small, and by the sixteenth century had it long ceased to be part of the forest, or assessed as part of Alderbury Hundred.

Whaddon seems more definitely to have declined over the previous two centuries. By 1394 its church had been closed, and in 1536 Royal Commissioners noted the parochial use of Ivychurch Priory by Whaddon villagers.[215] Since it is likely that Whaddon was

[206] WRO 549/8, *ff.*12*d.*, 13*d.*, 16.
[207] WRO 549/8, *ff.* 7*d.*, 11, 12*d.*,13, 14, 14*d.*, 19, 19*d.*
[208] WRO 549/8, *ff.*12*d.*, 14, 17.
[209] WRO 549/8, *ff.*14-15*d.*
[210] WRO 549/8, *ff.*13, 17.

[211] WRO 549/8, *ff.*11, 12, 13, 14, 14*d.*, 20, 21.
[212] *CSPD 1637-8*, p.506: '"Venison! Bah!" You know who said it. I like it as well, for which my father upbraids me with a mechanic taste. You may see how continued breeding at home has metamorphosed nature, and made my palate degenerate' (*loc. cit*).
[213] James and Gerrard, *Perspectives of Pleasure*, forthcoming.
[214] WRO 549/8, *f.*13*d.*
[215] R.F. Atkinson, *Alderbury, an Ancient and Peculiar Parish: A Church History* (Alderbury: Richard F. Atkinson, 2nd edn 1992), pp.47-8.

established through clearance as a subsidiary settlement of Alderbury in the Anglo-Saxon period,[216] it has much in common with the subsidiary settlements in the north of Melchet, and it was affected by the same processes, — demographic growth, decline in the fourteenth century and reorganisation following the Reformation. Like the Melchet DMVs its shrinkage should not only be read as an indicator of adverse conditions in the late medieval and early modern periods but also placed in the context of earlier economic success.

This said, there was little change in Clarendon's settlement hierarchy during the first half of the seventeenth century. Pitton and Farley continued to contain the highest number of assessed taxpayers (see Figures 67-9) — in the subsidy of 1628 more than twice those listed for Laverstock, West Dean and Grimstead and West Winterslow.[217] But Alderbury seems never to have regained its earlier prominence, and indeed the few entries in its early seventeenth-century parish register suggest a small population base even allowing for inaccuracy of recording. For example in 1611 there were three baptisms, three marriages and twelve burials; in 1641 seven baptisms, six marriages and six burials.[218] Although economy must have played a significant part in Pitton and Farley's high assessment rates, it is possible that the opportunities that the park continued to present were also significant. With Ivychurch House, we come full-circle. Like the palace before it, it would have enjoyed superb views of Salisbury Cathedral, and was located in the more usual late medieval/Renaissance position on the edge, rather than at the centre, of a deerpark.

Throughout the period studied, Clarendon was very much a royal landscape, and as such had a profound effect on settlement. It affected settlement structure, in that there are fewer very small, dispersed settlements than in surrounding forests — echoed and produced by assarting restrictions — and it affected the settlement hierarchy, as can be seen, for example, in the stagnation of Alderbury after the palace went out of use. It also affected settlement form. In combination with geology, the palace and its landscape restrained emulation, for example in the erection of high status structures like moated sites and, later, elaborate early modern country houses. Thus, analysis of settlement has shown that Clarendon was a landscape of control, and this aspect of the forest and park will be further explored in the next chapter.

---

[216] Jpci.net: *Historical Wiltshire: Towns and Villages – a Brief History* (http://www.wiltshire-web.co.uk/ [searched 20 September 2002]).
[217] PRO E 179/199/398, m.2.
[218] Alderbury and Whaddon Local History Research Group, *Millennium Mosaic*, p.82.

Chapter Five: Closure, Contention and Control: Clarendon's Conceptual and Physical Boundaries

If landscapes are a reflection of the societies that made them, the creation of boundaries and subdivisions is a key issue, as demonstrated especially by Johnson in his work on closure.[1] Closure in physical terms is not in doubt at Clarendon, the park becoming the focus of the royal landscape in the fourteenth and fifteenth centuries, and therefore more exclusive and separate from the rest of the forest. The same process can be seen operating in the enclosure of private woods and the park's coppices in the late thirteenth and early fourteenth centuries, and in the calls for royal aid in constructing Salisbury's city fence in 1378,[2] a time, not coincidentally, when its burgesses sought independence by resisting customary duties in the forest and park. Such physical enclosure was both mirrored and given impetus by fourteenth-century legislation, for example the game law of 1390.[3]

Figure 72. The palace's excavator, Tancred Borenius, on the bank of Clarendon Park pale, 1930s. Reproduced from T. B. James and A. M. Robinson, *Clarendon Palace: The History and Archaeology of a Medieval Palace and Hunting Lodge near Salisbury, Wiltshire*, Society of Antiquaries Research Report 45 (London: Society of Antiquaries of London, 1988), pl. 10a.

Recent archaeologists and historians have tended to see past landscapes not so much possessing defined physical limits as having 'culturally meaningful boundaries and sectors within an otherwise continuous space'.[4] Indeed, boundaries can be conceptual as well as physical (or both). Austin has applied such an approach to the Forest of Dartmoor, concluding that the hidden agenda of forest law as far as the common person was concerned was the erosion of rights to justice and thus of the right to use space.[5] Although the Dartmoor commons showed little sign of 'humanised signification', the landscape was not bereft of social meaning or structure. Once peasants passed across the invisible boundary represented by sight lines, they would have found themselves more vulnerable 'when the king's forest reeves came over the horizon'.

Their responses to the landscape would have changed despite a lack of concrete boundaries.[6] So too at Clarendon.

Other, even less tangible boundaries existed. The historian S. H. Rigby has applied closure theory to medieval society in order to examine the ways in which access to authority and influence was limited to certain social groups, termed 'systacts'.[7] Such 'social closure' will be explored here, chiefly through discussion of customs and forest law operating in Clarendon Forest. In this way it will be possible to ascertain whether Clarendon was 'special' as a locality, as it has proved to be as a landscape (particularly when contrasted with Melchet). There will be a focus on gender; not for gratuitous reasons but because it is a useful tool for highlighting variations in social organisation from locality to locality. For example by focusing on the prevalence (or otherwise) of women clothworkers, Rigby has highlighted variations in the running of the medieval textile industry from town to town.[8]

The extent to which Clarendon Forest and Park were scenes of contention, negotiation and resistance will also be addressed here. The extortion practised by forest officers will be analysed, negotiated boundaries such as perambulations will be observed, poaching and parkbreak as forms of symbolic resistance will be considered and attention will be given to Clarendon Palace as a centre of local networks and the scene for negotiation with the Crown.

PHYSICAL BOUNDARIES

The Outer Park

Some physical boundaries have been remarkably persistent features in the landscape, and this is certainly true of Clarendon Park pale (Figure 73 and see above, p. 7). Whether or not the park 'was' the medieval deerpark through the whole of the period studied has already been touched on, and in this section evidence concerning the pale will be analysed in more detail in order to discern what the park and its boundary meant from 1200-1650.

Clarendon Park's creation (or remodelling) as a deerpark is a prime example of subdivision of the landscape. If medieval forests were 'landscapes of élite pleasure',[9] the construction of such boundaries made the concept

---

[1] See especially *Archaeology of Capitalism, op. cit.*
[2] *CPR 1377–81*, p.229.
[3] See Perry Marvin, 'Slaughter and Romance', *passim*.
[4] Darvill, Gerrard and Startin, 'Archaeology in the Landscape', p.15.
[5] Austin, 'Okehampton Park', p.72.
[6] Austin, 'Okehampton Park', pp.70-2.
[7] Rigby, *English Society, passim*, systacts being 'groups or categories of persons sharing a common endowment (or lack) of power by virtue of their roles' (*ibid.*, p.12).
[8] Rigby, *English Society*, pp.274-6.
[9] Short, 'Forests and Wood-Pasture', p.139.

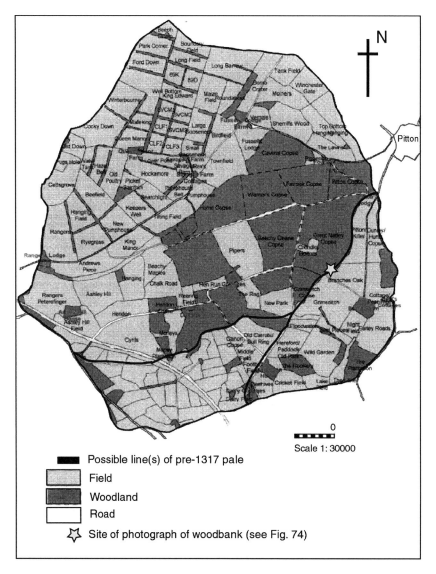

Figure 73. Clarendon Park: modern field names etc.
Map reproduced from Helen Barker and Jane Lickman,
'Clarendon Estate: Photographic Survey of Gates and Fences' (KAC, 1998).

concrete. Exactly when this happened at Clarendon is a matter for conjecture. No written evidence has been found before 1223, but this does not mean that a paled-in park did not exist earlier. Locals at least believed in 1225 that nearby Melchet Park, had been enclosed during the reign of Henry II, whose officials, they said, deliberately allowed deer to escape from it (see below, p. 129).[10]

The enlargement of the park under Edward II has been mentioned throughout this study. The imparkment itself is not in doubt, since a 1317 mandate to the exchequer states:

Order to cause the prior and convent of Ivychurch, Andrew de Grymstede, John de Grymstede, Philip Gogeon, Robert de Micheldevre, and Robert le Peleter to be discharged of the rent of certain assarts that they had

in the forest of Claryndon, as the king has caused the assarts to be taken into his hands and inclosed within his park of Claryndon.[11]

The assarts in question are those referred to in Chapter Four as having been arrented in 1304,[12] and most if not all were in the south of (what is now) the park. Ivychurch's 112 acres, adjacent to the priory, has already been mentioned (see above, p. 42).[13] Robert de Micheldever's assart was at Whitmarsh, and Robert le Poleter's was almost certainly the 'poletersclos' (*i.e.* Poleter's close) mentioned as in the wood between Pitton Gate and Whitmarsh *c.*1330.[14] Philip Gogeon's land was

---

[10] BM Stowe 798 *f.*9a.

[11] CCR 1313-18, p.507.
[12] PRO E 32/204, m.3.
[13] *Joh(an)nes de Crokesle...arrentavit...priori & convent(u)m monast(er)ij ederosi .Cxij. acr' de solo R'. iux(ta) monast(eriu)m ederosum in eadem foresta...*(PRO E 36/75).
[14] PRO E 32/204, m.3; PRO E 32/208. m.1.

at Rowaldesgrove, which was situated between the 'northern deerleap' and the Sleygate at Pitton according to the 1300 perambulation (see below, pp. 129-130).[15]

From modern maps, it seems possible that the area newly-imparked lay south east of a line running between Pitton Gate and Alderbury Lodge (see Figure 73). This line, which still forms the boundary between coppices and fields, has been walked from Pitton Gate to Grimsditch Plantation. Unfortunately little is to be seen on the ground — although the sizeable woodbank bank shown in Figure 74 is a possibility. Further, the alignment of fields in the south of the park in the 1713 map (see Figure 39), suggests the pre-1317 boundary may have run east-west between Pitton Lodge south of Long Coppice and Canon Coppice, perhaps placing Dog Kennel Farm and the site of the medieval dog kennels outside the park. Either way, it is now clear that the medieval deerpark's boundary was not static throughout the period studied.

Figure 74. Substantial woodbank bordering Branches Oak and Great Netley Copse, Spring 2002, (see Fig. 73), looking east.

Figure 75 shows expenditure on the park pale for which documentary evidence remains. It must be stressed that work within the timescales represented here was not necessarily continuous, and that repairs took place at other periods for which precise accounts are unavailable (here Figure 76, which details accounts specifying amounts of paling made, goes some way to filling the gaps). Nevertheless, Figure 75 reveals patterns. 1225-8 represents the period when the park was first paled — at least, there is no evidence that Clarendon possessed a paled-in deerpark before Henry III had an enclosure made in 1223.[16] It was repaired in 1252, following strong winds, and again in 1262-5. If it received attention under Edward I, this has gone unrecorded, and the neglect may

account for the shortage of deer there at this time (see Chapter Two).

Figure 75. Recorded Expenditure on Clarendon Park Pale

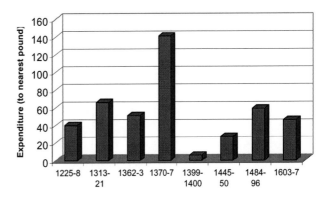

The period 1313-21 is that in which the park was enlarged under Edward II, and expenditure seems to have risen accordingly. Then from 1362, repairs followed the 'great wind' of that year, which felled the pale along with many buildings across southern England.[17] However, its rebuilding may also represent a response to the widespread parkbreak practised in previous decades (below). The subsequent campaigns, of 1370-7, again following strong winds,[18] involved the huge sum of nearly £140, which seems to indicate that the earlier repairs were ineffectual. Yet they had encompassed the entire park, from 'the king's highway above Penchet' to Milford Gate, from Milford Gate around the Launds to Winchester Gate, and from Winchester Gate to Pitton Gate, and it is more likely that the extensive reuse of old palings c.1362 exacerbated decay.[19] In addition, repairs to most of Clarendon's buildings were carried out on an ambitious scale in the early 1370s, and it is possible that the advisers of the by then senile Edward III, whose 1370 visit was the furthest he made outside London,[20] envisaged the palace as a retreat for his old age and attended to its setting accordingly.

Figure 76. Paling/pale boards made, 1313-1607

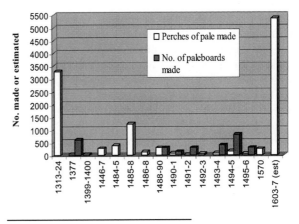

[15] PRO E 32/204, m.3; PRO C 260/136/31/2. The assarts may add up to c.214 acres, around 1/20 of the park's present 4,500a, although some figures may be duplicated. But the priory's assart is recorded in several of the above-mentioned documents as 112a.
[16] Rot. Litt. Claus I, p.541. See also PRO E 372/70, PRO E 372/72.

[17] CPR 1361-4, pp.177, 183; Jeremy Ashbee, pers.comm.
[18] See PRO E 101/542/12; PRO E 101/542/17.
[19] PRO E 101/460/2, mm.1-2.
[20] James and Robinson, Clarendon Palace, p.40.

Year	Document	Deerleap mentioned	Work done
1313-24	PRO SC 6 1050/5	-*Saltatorium* at Rodsley -Southern deerleap -Northern deerleap	-Repaired -Dug and repaired -Pale repaired from/to
1375	PRO E 101/542/17	'Le Sautour', east of 'Dedman'	Pale repaired from/to
1377	PRO E 101/499/1	'Great deerleap'	'Made' with fallen trees
1399-1400	PRO E 101/502/15	A new deerleap, 68 x 13ft.	Ditch dug, deerleap made with 24 oaks & covered in bitumen (*cum luto*)
1486-96	PRO E 101/460/16	-The great 'sawte' at Whitmarsh -The great southern deerleap -The little deerleap at Alderbury Shute End -Southernmost deerleap at Alderbury Shute -Deerleap called 'Grimstead's stile' -Deerleap called Ivychurch Stile, by Ivychurch gate -The 'Olde Sawte' -?Dolystyle -?Pitton Stile -?'Prior's Leapgate on Alderbury Hill'	-'Made' by carpenter -Pale repaired from/to -Pale repaired from/to -Pale repaired from/to -Pale repaired from/to -Repaired -Pale repaired from/to -Pale repaired from/to -Pale repaired from/to -Pale repaired from/to -Pale repaired from/to

Table 5: Mentions of deerleaps at Clarendon

The chart shows that, just as the bounds of the forest might be reasserted as a symbol of strong lordship on the accession of new monarchs (below, p. 127), so too the boundary around the park. Aside from the 1225-8 work, undertaken when Henry III gained his majority, this is most clearly seen in the later data. Attention was given to the pale following the Lancastrian *coup* in 1399-1400 (although little seems to have been outlayed) and £387.10s. was spent on the manor and pale together in the decade following the accession of Henry VI in 1422.[21] The main part of the work of 1445-50 shown on the chart was presaged by an order of 1447 to the clerk of works by Henry VI, which describes the 'Manor and Logges Within oure Parc of Claryndon and ye pale of ye same' as 'in greet ruyne for default of Reparac(i)on',[22] and reveals the way in which the park's resources were allocated for repairs.

Richard III almost certainly never visited the palace, but work was begun on the pale in 1483-4, and this was completed by Henry VII, who characteristically adorned it with castellated gatehouses.[23] On James I's accession in 1603, there was at least an intention to repair the pale again. However, the £46 indicated is actually an estimate for necessary repairs on the outer pale, the Great Rails and the parrocks together, which may never have been carried out. Nevertheless, new rails were made in the Laund in 1606, for which 106 oaks were felled, and a

further 50 oaks were used for repairs in 1615.[24] Charles I's accession marks the last of these royal 'statements'. In October 1625, six months after he ascended the throne, £331.16s.6d. was ordered to be paid to the woodward, John Essington, 'to be employed in repairing the lodges and pales of Clarendon Park',[25] and two years later 'a great many poor men' were still at work on it.[26]

The outlay on the park pale was considerably higher in 1313-21 than in 1225-8, which may betray the park's enlargement *c*.1317. Indeed the 3276 perches of pale made (see Figure 76) amounts to 16.42 km (10.2 miles) — roughly the circumference of the park today,[27] so that it is unfortunate that comparable figures do not exist for earlier periods. Another way to verify whether or not the whole of 'Clarendon Park' formed the deerpark at a given time would be to assess the number and location of deerleaps (see Figure 77). Three are shown on the map of *c*.1640 at Pope's Bottom (Whitmarsh), Hunt's Copse and Shute End (see Figure 9), but unfortunately detailed evidence for earlier periods is sketchy and confused (see Table 5). At least one *saltatorium* existed in 1267, and by *c*.1318 there appear to have been at least two, assuming that at Rodsley was the southern deerleap.[28]

---

[21] PRO E 101/460/7. The exact figure spent on the pale is not specified.
[22] PRO E 101/683/87.
[23] PRO E 101/460/16.

[24] PRO E 101/542/21, *ff*.1-3; PRO E 101/140/14, m.4; PRO E 178/4728/D.
[25] *CSPD 1625-6*, p.550.
[26] It seems Essington had withheld their payment, however (*CSPD 1625-49*, p.255).
[27] PRO SC 6/1050/5. As stated above, the 1603-7 estimate of 5360 perches (26.96 km, 16.75 miles) includes the fencing of the Great Rails, paddocks, etc. (PRO E 101/542/21, *ff*.1-3).
[28] *KACC* I, p.51; PRO SC 6/1050/5, m.1. Rodsley Wood, which survived as a field name in Pitton and Farley in the 1950s, was south-west of Pitton (Grant, *VCH Wilts*, p.427, n.27).

Figure 77. A deerleap in action. The devices were designed so that deer could leap into a park, but not out again. Reproduced from R. Prior, *Deer Watch: Watching Wild Deer in Britain* (Shrewsbury: Swan Hill Press, 1993), p.71.

Another leap may have been added in 1399-1400, when a 'new' deerleap 68 ft long and 13 ft wide (20.73 x 3.96m) was made, its erection described in detail (though not, alas, its location).[29] 24 oaks were felled for its construction, and 23 carpenters, two sawyers and 14 labourers worked on it for 411 person-days. Ten labourers excavated the ditch for six days, and four worked under the carpenters applying pitch or bitumen to the finished leap.[30] Later references to deerleaps are difficult to interpret, and there may still only have been three in 1486-96 despite the varied nomenclature in the accounts.[31] 'The great deerleap at Whitmarsh' and that at Alderbury Shute are clearly those of the *c.*1640 map, although there may also have been a series of smaller leaps (for example Grimstead's stile) and the 'Olde Sawte' may have been that mentioned in 1267.[32]

Figure 78, recorded person-days spent working on the park pale, confirms the emphasis on the park and its boundary in the reign of Edward III noted throughout this study, as does Figure 79, outlining numbers of timber trees, where specified, used in its construction. Most of the timber for the *c.*1362 repairs came from windfallen oaks in the park, and old paleboards and rails were also reused. In 1362, for example, 45 carpenters felled, split and trimmed oaks in the park and repaired the pale with boards and the resulting timber between 24 June and 1

August, while six carpenters shored it up and made wedges or pins (*cavill*) to strengthen it. At the same time, five men from 'various villages' dug and packed the pits into which the posts and shores would sit, loaded carts with timber and secured the boards with hammers, and 24 carts, each with four horses, went continually back and forth carrying timber.[33]

Figure 78. Recorded person-days spent on park pale

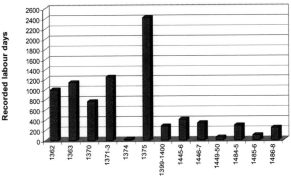

Oak was generally used for the posts and rails of the pale (see Figure 80). For example in 1371-3, obliquely-sawn (*ex transverso*) oaks from Clarendon Park formed the paleboards. However, in 1370, 32 obliquely-sawn Buckholt beeches were used alongside 207 Clarendon Park oaks for the posts and rails. This was relatively unusual, beech boards being more often used for fittings than for general purposes.[34] They presumably made the structure more durable, although in 1385 it was again

[29] PRO E 101/502/15, m.10.
[30] *ad re[m]iplend' dict' salt(at)ur' cu(m) luto* (PRO E 101/502/15, m.10).
[31] PRO E 101/460/16, *passim*.
[32] 'Stile' (from *stig*) may mean 'ascending path', however (M. Gelling and A. Cole, *The Landscape of Place-Names* (Stamford: Shaun Tyas, 2000), pp.66-7, 92-3.

[33] PRO E 101/460/2, mm.1-2.
[34] PRO E 101/542/12; PRO E 101/542/11; Salzman, *Building in England Down to 1540,* p.249.

'partly ruinous'.[35] Underwood from the park was also used, as in 1313-24, when 4a of underwood from Stoneygore was carried to the new pale at Milford Gate, alongside more from 'Candlestick Way', each of which is in the area probably enclosed *c*.1317. In the same period (1318-19), a hedge was erected around the launds, and brushwood (*ramalio*) planted into its ditch.[36]

Figure 79. Recorded timber trees used on park pale, 1370-1615

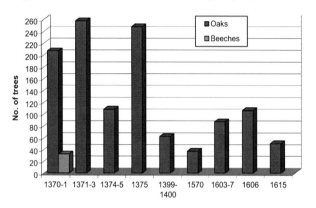

Figure 80. Deer leap and cleft oak paling fence at Wolseley Park, Staffs, in the 19th century. Cleft oak paling was strong, the timber being split along the grain rather than sawn. The long and short staves were intended to pose more problems to the deer than would a continuous panel. Reproduced from R. Prior, *Deer Watch* (Shrewsbury: Swan Hill Press, 1993), p.69.

Was the attention lavished on the park pale merely a symbolic gesture? After all, this one boundary enclosed an area which it endowed with economic, functional, social and symbolic meaning. As mentioned in Chapter Two, more deer were poached from the park than from Clarendon Forest in the 1340s and 50s. If the pale was intended primarily to keep poachers out, it clearly was not working, despite the fact that by the mid-fourteenth century the park seems to have been considerably

enlarged and better fenced — at least 1656 perches of pale (8.328 km, 5.17 miles) had been erected in March-May 1321 alone,[37] representing about a third of today's 16km circuit. Alternatively, in the park poachers were more likely to get caught.

Yet it is likely that the modern notion of such boundaries as devices intended primarily to keep people out is an over-simplification, as is a purely functional interpretation of medieval parks as 'larders for deer'. This view of deerparks negates their aesthetic and amenity qualities, and Clarendon Park was, after all, constructed in a forest presumably full of deer there for the taking. At the same time, the park pale as the demarcation of rarefied space is nothing if not a reflection in the landscape of medieval social relations, as is its division into defined coppices. As Rackham has said, 'compartmentation favours the owner of...trees [and]...implies strong landowners and weak commoners'.[38] This is perhaps rather obvious in a landscape owned by the king. But can we interpret the park as a mere display of rank and wealth in the landscape, bearing in mind that royalty would arguably have had less need of such self-promotion compared to other lords? Perhaps it is worth bearing in mind that it frequently received attention from new monarchs who had yet to make their mark. Indeed it seems to have originated in the lead-up to Henry III's coming of age, at the same time as the forest's administration was reconstituted and the palace was 'elevated to a state only marginally less magnificent than...Westminster'.[39]

The Inner Park
Since the ditch of the inner park is on the outside of its well-defined bank (see Figures 1 and 31), the purpose was clearly to keep animals out, and it has been suggested that this was the site of the demesne farm, set aside for agricultural purposes. As elsewhere, e.g. the castles of Fotheringhay (Northamptonshire) and Ludgershall, the inner park was clearly designed to embrace the palace site, and may have functioned as a pleasure park. The 'Little Park' at Fotheringhay was associated with an orchard, garden and pond,[40] all claimed by Borenius to have been represented on the 'medieval map' (see above, p. 63). Another possibility is that a species of deer other than that maintained in the wider park was kept here. At least where two parks were contemporaneous, they are likely to have had distinct functions. Other medieval 'double' deer parks have been cited as supreme examples of status in the landscape, displaying their owner's wealth and the capability to maintain specialised staff.[41] The deer at Clarendon seem almost exclusively to have been fallow (see Chapter Two), so that red deer are the obvious candidates. But although medieval belief held that red deer would kill fallow were they kept together, in reality

[35] *CPR 1381-5*, p.515.
[36] PRO SC 6/1050/5, m.1; *Et p(ro) fossat' p(re)d(i)c(t)is [im]plend' cum ramalio ne bestie planticiu(m) impo[s]it in eodem destruant crescenc'* (PRO SC 6/1050/5, m.5).

[37] PRO SC 6/1050/5, m.3.
[38] Rackham, *The Last Forest*, p.91.
[39] James and Robinson, *Clarendon Palace*, p.8.
[40] *KACC I*, pp.57-8; Creighton, *Castles and Landscapes*, p.190.
[41] J. Bond, pers. comm.

the species co-exist quite happily.[42] In addition, with the ditch on the outside there would be little to stop our hypothetical herd of red deer from escaping. In the end, little is known about the practicalities of medieval deer-management and still less about its associated features. For example a recently-excavated bank running for almost 1 km at Lyndhurst in the New Forest has defied interpretation, although it is probably related to Lyndhurst Deer Park which also contains 'some curious internal earthworks...thought to be associated with park purposes' (see Figure 82).[43]

Figure 81. The western end of the inner park pale, Spring 2002, looking south east. The external ditch is visible on the right.

Yet another hypothesis is that the area north of the inner park and the palace (*i.e.* the launds) was that which was actually thought of as 'Clarendon Park', at least in the thirteenth century, and this is possible given the topography of the area and the layout of tracks and field boundaries on the ground.[44] In this scenario, the ditch, rather than outside the 'inner park' pale, is actually on the *inside* of a bank around the launds. To test this theory requires archaeological investigation throughout the launds to locate possible associated ditches and banks.

In view of what has been uncovered in the course of this study concerning the enlargement of the park in the early fourteenth century, the above is within the realms of possibility. It is now known that the shape of what constituted 'Clarendon Park' was not static through the later medieval period. This might explain also the anomalous position of the palace, at the park's epicentre (see Figure 82). The usual position for a major residence associated with a medieval deerpark is on the park's periphery, or even outside it, while a central location is associated with the early modern period.[45] Medieval hunting lodges, however, *are* often found at the centre of parks. Either Clarendon Palace's position confirms its early establishment (typologically-speaking) as a 'hunting lodge', or it was not in the centre of the park to begin with, but only when the park was enlarged. Alternatively, when Henry III 'made' his park in the 1220s, the landscape was fashioned so that the newly-embellished palace lay in a conventional position on the periphery of *a* park (*i.e.* the inner park and/or the launds). Certainly in the thirteenth century the inner park was known as 'the king's park', and it might have been that ordered to be enclosed, as if for the first time, by Henry III at his majority in 1227.[46] It may also have been the park whose paling was replaced with a hedge in 1254.[47] Such a replacement of the *outer* park's paling, some 16km (10 miles) in circumference today, would be both unconventional and time consuming. In any case, this had been finished in 1252 and was to receive attention again ten years later.[48] Moreover, if the 1254 hedging indeed enclosed the inner park, the topographical detail given in the order — which cannot refer to the outer pale — makes a good deal more sense (see Figure 26):

> *To the sheriff of Wilts.* Contrabreve *to enclose the park of Clarendon with a hedge where paling was previously ordered [and] to remove 40 perches [c.200m] of paling from the top of the park to the bottom towards the laund...*[49]

Nevertheless, the *paling* of 'the park under [the king's] court' required attention, in tandem with building works at the palace, in 1265,[50] so that the written evidence is inconclusive. In contrast, an order of 1348 to repair the paling of 'the king's old park within [Clarendon] Park' seems to refer explicitly to the inner park.[51] This appears to have been followed up prior to 1358, when the new pale (*uno palesio*) was recorded as running 'from the warden's kitchen [probably on the west side of the palace] to Derngate,[52] thence to the East gate of the manor'. The pale as far as Derngate enclosed the king's stables and, as far as the east gate, the warden's garden.[53] If Derngate has been correctly identified, this suggests that by 1358 the inner pale contained ancillary buildings and gardens that would have merited protection from deer (see also above, Chapter Three).

[42] M. Small, pers. comm. Mr Small has charge of 260 fallow and 160 red deer existing together quite peaceably, in Charborough Park, Dorset, as well as similar herds at Savernake. He has never known any problem between the two species, who 'keep themselves to themselves'.
[43] A. Pasmore, 'The Lyndhurst Earthwork', *Hampshire Field Club and Archaeological Society Newsletter* 39 (Spring 2003), pp.viii-x (p.viii).
[44] I am indebted here to Paul Everson and David Stocker, who put some of my muddled thoughts into coherence.
[45] J.H. Bettey, *Estates and the English Countryside: Wealth, Rank and Ostentation in the Landscape* (London: Batsford, 1993), p.53.
[46] *To the sheriff of Wilts. Order to cause to be enclosed without delay what remains to be enclosed of the king's park at Clarendon, which he ordered to be enclosed* (*CLR 1226-40*, p.23).
[47] *CLR 1251-60*, p.180.
[48] *CCR 1251-3*, p.294; *CLR 1260-7*, p.76.
[49] *CLR 1251-60*, p.180.
[50] *CLR 1260-7*, p.191.
[51] *CCR 1346-9*, p.465.
[52] *KACC* I, p.57. See Figure 26, above, for the Derngate.
[53] PRO E 101/460/1.

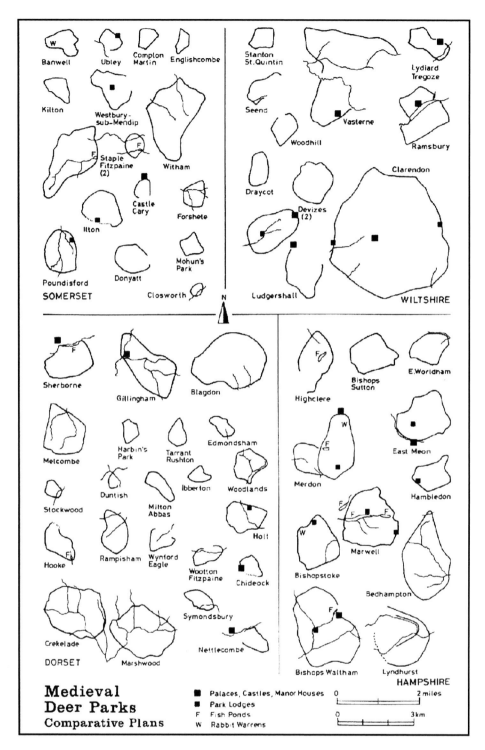

Figure 82. Comparative plans of medieval deerparks in Wessex showing the anomalous size of Clarendon Park. Reproduced from J. Bond, 'Forests, hases, Warrens and Parks in Medieval Wessex', in *The Medieval Landscape of Wessex,* Oxbow Monograph 46 (Oxford: Oxbow Books, 1994), eds M. Aston and C. Lewis, pp.115-58, fig. 6.10.

Yet the references to 'hedges' (hays) and 'pales' are ambiguous, and the terms may have been used interchangeably, although the choice of a hedge as the inner park's boundary is noteworthy as a contrast to the paled boundary of the outer park — a 'soft' border marking a kind of middle way between gardens of the palace above it and the wider park beyond. Even if the 'hedge' were a wattled affair, made from the 300 cartloads of hazel, maple, hawthorn and oak blown down by the wind in 1251 and used 'partly for enclosing the king's park',[54] this would have contrasted with the usual arrangement of cleft-oak palings.[55]

---

[54] *CCR 1251-3*, p.295.
[55] Bond, 'Forests, Chases, Warrens and Parks', p.140.

Alternatively, a reference of 1267 mentions a stone wall to be built around 'the houses and the 'King's Park'. This may simply refer to the enceinte of the palace precinct (Figure 83).[56] However the 'king's park' is specifically mentioned, and it is not without the bounds of possibility that the inner park was walled rather than fenced. Stone walls around parks were especially prestigious, and such a boundary, beneath the palace, would have been immediately impressive to the onlooker, perhaps hunting on the launds to the north or passing below on the road. Woodstock Park was entirely encircled with a stone wall about seven miles (c.11.3km) in circumference probably from as early as the thirteenth century, and there was special reference to the section facing the town.[57] The maintenance of the walls was a constant problem and focus of expenditure (thus also a potent signifier of lordship) in the medieval period and beyond — for example in 1616-17 they required filling 'where the pigeons had pecked them through by reason of the saltpeter therein'.[58] At Clarendon there was no immediately adjacent settlement (although the Slateway at Pitton, leading to one of the main entrances at Pitton Gate, would have run alongside any wall, and it would have looked impressive from the Roman road on the approach to Salisbury), and in an area not noted for its stone it would have been more practical to use abundant woodland resources. Nevertheless, it is certainly possible that for a time the inner park was partially of stone construction, like Bentley Park in Suffolk, walled only at the point where it came into view on approach.[59]

Figure 83. Section through the perimeter wall south of Clarendon Palace showing stone construction and ashlar dressing. Reproduced from T. B. James and A. M. Robinson, *Clarendon Palace: The History and Archaeology of a Medieval Palace and Hunting Lodge near Salisbury, Wiltshire*, Society of Antiquaries Research Report 45 (London: Society of Antiquaries of London, 1988), pl. 13b.

Location of the Demesne Wood

The demesne wood of Clarendon is mentioned often in the thirteenth century under various names, including the 'Wood of Clarendon' and the 'Wood of Penchet'. 'Penchet' (British in origin, meaning 'the end of the wood') is often interpreted, as it was from the late fifteenth century and later,[60] as nothing more than an alternative name for Clarendon, but a conceptual difference is revealed in 1255 when the 'agisters of the Forest of Clarendon' delivered money into the wardrobe at the palace 'for the Wood of Paunect',[61] so that it is likely that Penchet was more properly the name of the demesne wood.

Wherever the king's demesne wood was, it was probably well-enclosed, at least in the thirteenth century. In 1241, Robert de Ros, justice of the forest, was ordered to sell underwood in the king's demesne woods 'which are in defence' (see Glossary). He was also to 'make fixed metes and devises between the…demesne woods and…foreign woods adjoining, so that it may clearly appear which are the king's own and those of others'.[62]

Analysis of the documentary evidence suggests that, on balance, it is most likely that the demesne wood was located south of the park in the wood pasture area.[63] There are many references to foresters of fee having pastured animals there, and the prior of Ivychurch raised a piggery in it c.1330.[64] Indeed, the priory must have been close by, for c.1352, the prior of Ivychurch and a 'John Molindenar' of Panchet' were accused of receiving a poacher who had come, with his greyhounds, to take the king's beasts 'in the wood of Panchet'.[65] It seems also to have been close to Pitton, since c.1330, the village was ordered to answer for the price of a cart and four horses that William Saunders and Nicholas Golyas had used nightly to take wood from 'the king's demesne wood at Clarendon', suggesting a special responsibility.[66] Most tellingly, the perambulation of 1300 states:

> …and from derditch to roaldesgrove [above Pitton somewhere near the park boundary] and thence to the Sleygate [?Slateway] of Pitton, and thence descending by the three ditches to the corner of Rodsley [south of Pitton], and thence descending by the road [the Cock Road] between the wood of the lord king and [that of] Rodsley as far as langemanneswey, and thence through Rodsley…and therefrom descending to Stoneygore, and thence

[56] *KACC* I, p.57.
[57] Bond, 'Woodstock Park in the Middle Ages', pp.27-8. The park's wall today measures 14.5km in circumference (*ibid.*, p.28).
[58] PRO E 351/3251.
[59] J. Bond, pers. comm.

[60] Probably as a result of Henry VII's officials trawling through early documents to discover the procedure for their revived forest eyres, and the 'correct' bounds of the forest.
[61] *CCR 1254-6*, p.25.
[62] *CPR 1232-47*, p.247.
[63] The local historian Michael Parsons has concurred with this tentative interpretation, and with the possibility that the demesne wood was the wood of Penchet for which the forest was named.
[64] E.g. PRO C 260/89/32/B and PRO E 32/267, m.16; PRO E 32/215, m.1
[65] PRO E 32/267, m.5.
[66] PRO E 32/207, m.5.

ascending between the wood of John de Lucy [Lucewood]*...and thence by the road between the wood of the lord king and* [that of] *John de Grimstead to aynesgrovesende* [?Canon's Grove, Ivychurch]...[67]

This locates the 'wood of the lord king' firmly south of the park between Pitton and Alderbury.

Given its ostensible location, it seems likely that all or part of the demesne wood was taken into the park *c*.1317. Certainly a document of 1330 refers to an apparently recent time 'when the...demesne wood was outside the pale', and *c*.1369 it is fairly securely identified as at Stoneygore, in the same area and close to Pitton.[68] Thus it may have been the wood-pasture area in the south of the park identified as 'Sheer Wood' on the *c*.1640 map.

CONTEST AND RESISTANCE:
PARKBREAK AND POACHING AT CLARENDON

Locations
It has been shown in Chapter Two that more deer were recorded as poached from the park than the forest in the fourteenth century (see above, pp. 22-23). But were there preferred locations generally? An examination of the areas in the park and the forest from which deer were poached over the period covered by the forest documents (the timescale on Figures 15 and 16) reveals no clear preferred territories, although eleven incidences of poaching were recorded in and around Farley, an area of comparatively high population and attractive to incomers. Woodland is also well-represented. Two episodes are recorded for Westwood, two for Bentley Wood, a further two for Southwood, one in 'Heywood', one in the king's demesne wood, two in the foreign wood and three in Houndwood. Since the woodwards were often involved (see Glossary), one suspects that the royal foresters were asserting their jurisdiction over what was essentially private land. [69] Within the park the launds, not surprisingly, seem to have been favoured by poachers, with fifteen incidents reported between 1263 and 1328.

There is a discrepancy between deer recorded as poached in the eyre of 1330 and that of 1355 — around 40 as opposed to *c*.270 animals! This may be because the deer population was still recovering in 1330 after over-exploitation and the murrains and bad harvests of the first quarter of the century. There are historical reasons also. The Hampshire/Wiltshire and Northamptonshire/Buckinghamshire eyres of 1355 were the last to be held. By this time there was widespread opposition to the forest system and its courts, arguably leading to an increase in poaching as a 'complex social response to a privileged control...that lords enforced by lawfully abrogating hunting rights', [70] a control Clarendon in particular may have symbolised.

Incidences of Gang-Poaching
Poaching, of course, was endemic in royal forests, and the focus here will not be the actions of individuals, but of gangs. It is noteworthy that the concept of parkbreak, as in the formulaic term 'breaking the king's park', gains strength in the fourteenth century, in tandem with the increased focus on the immediate surroundings of royal castles and palaces, and on their boundaries as divides between public and private space. It comes also after the Black Death. For Clarendon, at least, the first episode thus termed comes in 1355, when 16 men with persons unknown, 'by force and arms [the formulaic *vi et armis*] broke the park of Clarendon and hunted deer there [with] cords, snares and other engines'.[71]

However the first sure mention of poaching at Clarendon involving a gang occurred, characteristically, at a time of national strife, in 1262 during the Barons' Wars, its wording suggesting this was not a list of men who had operated alone.[72] Richard and John of Pitton, David le Archer, Richard Cusyn senior, his son William, Robert le Clerc of Pitton, Adam Gaboel, William Bastard and William Harang (Hering) are described as entering the Forest of Clarendon by day and by night, killing and carrying off deer without licence, against the king's peace.[73] It is likely that times of widespread lawlessness were compounded at Clarendon by the paucity of royal visits to the palace (see Table 4 — none occurred between September 1260 and November 1267). And it can be no coincidence that many of the men named were either forest officials or (probably) their relatives,

---

[67] PRO C 260/136/31/2.

[68] *Dicunt tamen q(uo)d dum d(i)c(t)us d(o)m(ini)cus boscus fuit ext(ra) clausum et q(uo)d fere d'm' Regis tunc temp(or)is ingressum & egressum p(ro) voluntete eor(um) h(abe)re potuerunt Custodis manerij & foreste de Clarendon p(er)cip(er)e consueverunt co'i'b(us) an(i)m(al)is p(ro) herbagio d(i)c(t)i d(o)m(ini)ci bosci d'm' Regis* (PRO C 47/11/8/9);

It(e)m dic' q'd Henr' hayward carpent' de Ffarley s(er)viens Prioris de monkenfarle intravit d'm'cu boscu(m) d'm R' ap(u)d Stonygore & ib(ide)m cont(ra) ass(isa)m foreste p(ro)f'cint una' summag'[vigarum] p'c'.vj. d. & ill' duxit usq(ue)(Pitton) (PRO E 32/218, m.23).

[69] For example a stag was taken in Bentley in 1249 by Walter le Blunt, woodward of John de Grimstead; in 1327 another was poached there by Roger Harefoot, woodward to the Earl of Lincoln, and in Houndwood in *c*.1314, a buck 'slaughtered' by (*mactatos p(er)*) Ralph de Monte Hermer was removed by John de Fonton, woodward of John de Cromwell (PRO E 32/198, m.17*d*.; PRO E 32/207, mm.2, 3).

[70] Perry Marvin, 'Slaughter and Romance', p.225.

[71] PRO E 32/267, m.5*d*.

[72] In earlier examples it is impossible to tell whether men listed together as malefactors of the venison in the king's forest (e.g. PRO E 32/198, m.17*d*.) were or were not operating together.

[73] 'Whereas the King understood that Richard, son of master David of Pitton, John his brother, David le Archer, Richard Cosyn the elder, William his son, Robert le Clerc of Pitton, Adam Gaboel, William Bastard and William Harang, from night and by day enter into the kings forest of Clarendon, killing, taking and carrying off our wild beasts, without our license and against our wishes and against the king's peace, mandate to the sheriff of Wilts to take the aforesaid...and keep them in the king's prison until the king has ordered otherwise'. (*CCR 1261-4*, p.47).

including the Cusyn and Archer families.[74] Although no forester of fee was among them, it is certain that someone was turning a very blind eye.

The men named in the 1262 order, put together after the Barons' Wars, crop up again and again, not only the 1263 eyre, immediately after the episode, but also that of 1270, among them William Hering of Winterslow, Adam Gobel of Pitton and especially David le Archer, the king's serjeant bowbearer. Clearly a spell in prison had little effect, especially since le Archer, along with John, son of John de Grimstead (later a Franciscan friar), was among a gang of about 60 who entered the New Forest on 15 July 1270 'with bows and arrows, dogs and greyhounds, to harm the venison'. This was an altogether more intimidating gathering. The men stayed in the forest for several days, during which time they stole cheese from one of Beaulieu Abbey's granges, and descended on the house of one John de Brutesthon, taking and eating 'all the food they found there'.[75]

The New Forest, of course, was vast, sparsely populated and apparently laxly policed (at least in the fourteenth century) compared with Clarendon Forest, which may have lent it a certain attraction for such gatherings.[76] But while armed gangs appear to have been largely absent at Clarendon, poaching was frequent enough. Much of it occurred in the park, unlawful entry into which seems not to have been an issue in the early part of our period. For example in the 1270 eyre, Nicholas Longespée, canon of Salisbury (c.1218-97) and a number of his household (*familia sua*) were presented for taking game without warrant in 1263 'on the launds of Clarendon'. So also were Thomas de [B]aton, Walter de [?Merton] and a member of his household, Reginald and Richard Tayllard, John de Wyly, William Pastes, Nicholas de Thuddene and Richard Shayl of Pitton, who entered the forest in 1267 with bows, arrows, dogs and greyhounds and took a buck and a prickett (*Brokettu(m) dami*) on the launds without warrant.[77] Such gatherings would have reinforced communal identities, and indeed Birrell has described them as 'one manifestation of [the gentry's] normal social life'.[78]

There may be an important distinction here, however. The latter group, described as 'habitual malefactors', were clearly poachers, whereas taking deer without warrant was a formula describing the right of archbishops, bishops, earls or barons to take one or two beasts when traversing a forest, according to the 1217 Forest Charter.[79] Although Longespée did not become

bishop of Salisbury until 1292, he may have been exercising a perceived customary right at Clarendon as a relative of the king, or as a holder of office in the city.[80] Indeed he was pardoned in 1270 of his £40 fine at the instance of Robert Walerand and Philip Basset, canon of Salisbury and sometime justice.[81] Such confusing complexity is exacerbated by the fact that the pleas of the venison recorded in the eyre rolls list only trespasses from which the king might derive revenue, so that anyone expecting to discover quantitative information regarding poaching, especially by the peasantry, will be disappointed.[82]

Incidents of parkbreak did occur in Edward I's reign, but not so much at Clarendon as in the wider area. In 1283, unnamed persons 'broke the park of John, bishop of Winchester at Downton...hunted therein and carried away deer', and in 1290 several foresters of Cranborne Chase were accused of 'divers trespasses of venison...in the king's forests, the chaces of the earl [of Gloucester], and the parks of others'.[83] Even allowing for the absence at this time of evidence from forest courts, Clarendon seems to have been relatively peaceful. There is little evidence of forced entry, apart from an episode of 1304-5, when Richard de Farnhull of Hampshire, Richard de Sryvenham, Robert de Arundell and persons unknown came into the launds with their greyhounds to poach, after which they dispersed outside the bounds of the forest (perhaps actually the park) causing 'great destruction'.[84] This does seem to have been a time of general lawlessness in the forest. 'William, a forester of Buckholt' robbed passing merchants c.1305, and the following year a Robert le Frenshe, previously outlawed for trespassing in parks in Surrey, lurked in the forest robbing William le Ropere at Grimstead, and other 'men passing' at Shirmel (see Figure 49) and Buckholt.[85]

Incidences of gang-poaching often took place when the court was absent for long periods or the administration was elsewhere, as in the 1260s when the latter was at Old Sarum. The absences are rarely stated in the documents, although the 1270 eyre records that Robert and Thomas de Lucy frequently entered Clarendon Forest to hunt 'when Ralph Russell was at Salisbury Castle'; John Giffard, William Maltravers, Simon de Seresy, James de Lye, Ralph de Lymesye, Henry le Brut, John de Aqua and members of his household hunted there 'between the battles of Lewes [May 1264] and Evesham [August 1265]'; and in the 1330 eyre Gilbert de Botes, Nicholas

---

[74] Simon Cusyn was an agister, 1250-4 and also held Rodsley Wood (PRO E 32/198, mm.8, 18).

[75] Stagg, *New Forest Documents A.D. 1244-A.D.1334*, pp.98-9.

[76] Smith, 'The New Forest', *passim*.

[77] PRO E 32/200, m.6.

[78] Quoted in Tonkinson, *Macclesfield in the Later Fourteenth Century*, p.179, n.136.

[79] *Quicunque archiepiscopus, episcopus, comes vel baro transierit per forestam nostrum liceat ei capere unam vel duas bestias per visum forestarii si presens fuerit, sin autem faciat cornari ne videatur furtive*

hoc facire (G.J. Turner, ed., *Select Pleas of the Forest*, Selden Society 13 [London: Bernard Quaritch, 1901], p.xli). In 1224-5, the wording of the charter had been changed to 'archbishops, bishops, earls or barons *coming to us at our order*', in which case they were to make restitution to the king (Turner, p.xli, n.2).

[80] Nicholas's father, William Longespée, was an illegitimate son of Henry II, so that Nicholas was Henry III's cousin.

[81] *CCR 1268-72*, p.208.

[82] Turner, *Select Pleas of the Forest*, p.lxi.

[83] *CPR 1281-92*, p.102; *CCR 1288-96*, p.73.

[84] PRO E 32/207, m.3.

[85] Pugh, *Gaol Delivery*, pp.105, 163.

of Winton, vicar of Sarum and other (not surprisingly dead) malefactors were mentioned as having taken deer in the launds in 1297-8 'when [the king] was in Flanders'.[86] It is not clear whether such information was put forward as a factor behind the trespasses or as an *aide memoire*, but factor it was. For example in August 1307, a few months after Edward II's accession and a year after Edward I's departure for Scotland, Matthew de Fulflet, serf of the Prioress of Wilton, John, forester of William de Beauchamp (warden *c*.1308-13) and two others, took a full 30 fallow from Clarendon's launds.[87]

Edward II appears not to have visited Clarendon until 1317, ten years after his accession. Indeed a survey of 1315 listed dilapidations at the palace that would cost at least £1,830, and the pale was not repaired until sometime between 1313 and 1324.[88] Not surprisingly, there were signs of trouble at Clarendon and indeed elsewhere, and even the palace was affected. A commission of oyer and terminer was issued in April 1311 'touching the forcible entry of the king's manor of Clarendon by Robert de Micheldever and others, and the carrying away of timber, stones, iron, lead and other goods'.[89] This might not have been as bad as it sounded, Micheldever being deputy warden and thus having charge of the palace in any case, if it were not for similar disturbances taking place elsewhere. In August, Gilbert de Clare's Suffolk parks were broken by persons who 'hunted therein…and fished in his stews and fisheries', and in Dorset in the same year Queen Margaret's servants were assaulted and her millponds broken 'so that the water ran away and she lost the profits'.[90] This was a time of general fear of civil war,[91] although how far the Ordainer movement of 1310-11 can be blamed for such actions in the provinces is questionable. Yet it is revealing that large gangs of men including members of the household of the Earl of Lancaster, responsible for Gaveston's execution in 1312, are recorded as having entered Clarendon Forest with bows, arrows, dogs, cords and snares in February 1314.[92] Here poaching may have been used to make a political statement. The Earl would have been well aware of Clarendon's status even though Edward II had not yet graced the palace with his presence.

Also in 1314, a Peter de Perynton was in prison at Salisbury for 'receiving and buying the king's venison of

the forest of Claryndon', and a further two men were bailed from Salisbury Gaol over the following two years for venison trespasses there, one, caught poaching in the forest in 1313, known, rather incriminatingly, as 'John le Spicer of Salisbury'.[93] Perhaps not surprisingly, receivers of poached venison were often from Salisbury. There were Roger Turpich, Adam le Hore and Richard Hadyn *c*.1270; Richard de Forton in 1329, and a further seven men, including Richard le Frere, glover, *c*.1355, some of whom were fined as much as 100s.[94] In the same year another glover, John Prior of Downton, was recorded as receiving more than (*plusquam*) 30 deer pelts from the prior and canons of Ivychurch (of whom more later).[95] Then in 1372, Andrew de Dodmanstone and Thomas Forcer, foresters, were accused of killing 100 fallow deer over the previous four years and sending them to William [T]eynturer and 'other of their friends' in the City of Salisbury in exchange for bows, guns, hose, woollen and linen cloth, and 'other similar items'.[96]

Other receivers lived in the forest villages, and in 1329 a relatively sophisticated operation was uncovered after Robert le Bole, Richard Hering and John in le Hurne of Laverstock entered the wood of Ashley and took a doe by setting up a snare in a hawthorn. The head and guts, which they left at the scene, were found by John of Warwick, forester. Robert's house was searched according to the Forest Charter and ?venison delicacies (*[victu'] ferarum*) and bloodstained cloths were found. The foresters then investigated the house of John's mother Annora in le Hurne, where they found five heads of freshly-killed bucks and sorells which the poachers had hidden there.[97]

Occasionally the palace's Marshalsea prison was used for venison trespassers,[98] but they were more often detained at Salisbury. The distinction seems to be not whether they were caught red handed, but whether or not they were forest inhabitants. If they were not the sheriff was responsible for their incarceration, and they were sent to a prison from which they could only emerge on the king's order or that of the justice of the forest. Although foresters had no power in any case to attach any person outside the forest, the greater severity probably resulted from the fact that inhabitants might have good reason to be there in the first place.[99] But when forest inhabitants were caught in the act, things were different. For

[86] PRO E 32/200, m.6*d*. Ralph may have been related to John Russell, keeper of the manor *c*.1273 (*CFR 1272-1307*, p.10); PRO E 32/207, m.3*d*.

[87] PRO E 32/207, m.2*d*.

[88] James and Robinson, *Clarendon Palace*, pp.34-5; PRO SC 6/1050/5.

[89] *CPR 1307-13*, p.368. A Robert de Micheldever, forester of Clarendon, had been accused in 1306 of the murder of Maud Sweinn and for imprisoning falsely a man who later died (Pugh, *Gaol Delivery*, p.104). He was also deputy warden under John de Vienna (warden 1291-*c*.1308), forester of fee from *c*.1308-*c*.1313, and keeper of the manor of Clarendon in 1325 (PRO E 32/215, mm.1, 1*d*.; *CFR 1319-27*, p.355).

[90] *CPR 1307-13*, pp.173, 420.

[91] M. McKisack, *The Fourteenth Century: 1307-1399* (Oxford: Oxford University Press, 1959), p.18.

[92] PRO E 32/207, m.3.

[93] *CCR 1313-18*, pp.121, 179, 280; PRO E 32/207, m.3*d*. The deer le Spicer took ended up in the hands of the Earl of Gloucester (*ibid*).

[94] PRO E 32/200, m.6*d*; PRO E 32/207, m.2; PRO E 32/267, m.8.

[95] PRO 32/267, m.8.

[96] *It(e)m dic(unt) q(uo)d d(i)c(t)us Andr' & Thomas Fforcer p(er) iiij annos elaps(o) int(er)fec[era]vit C damos & damas infra balli(v)am de Claryndon p(er) di(ersi)s vices & ill' Will(elm)o [T]eynturer jun' & alijs amitis eor(um) de Civitato Nov(um) Sar(um) quor(um) no(m)i(n)a ignore(ant) [mi]seri[n]t & vend' p(ro) arc' Gonnes calig' pannis lanes & lines & hui(us)modi p(ro)ficius de ip(s)i(u)s h(ab)end'* (PRO E 32/318, m.22).

[97] PRO E 32/207, m.3.

[98] *CPR 1324-7*, p.311.

[99] Turner, *Select Pleas of the Forest*, pp.xxxiii-xxxiv.

example Geoffrey atte Purye, taken red handed in the park in December 1343, was delivered to the deputy warden Thomas de Lusteshull, who had him interred in Clarendon's prison, and in 1372 another deputy warden, Andrew de Dodmanstone was able to attach William Portchester in Farley, lead him to the palace and detain him (allegedly without cause) in the gaol.[100]

The prison at Clarendon seems not to have been perceived as worthy of constant repair, nor, consequently, does it appear to have been particularly secure. The survey of 1276 records that its wall had fallen down, although it was in use by 1292 since Edward I pardoned one of the de Pitton foresters held there after a forest trespass in that year. However in 1242 Richard le Reve, detained in the king's gaol at Sarum for a trespass committed in Clarendon Forest when Henry III was in Bordeaux, seems previously to have escaped from Clarendon's prison.[101] So too did William le Swopere and Stephen Davy c.1337 'recently taken…by the king's foresters', despite having been held in irons and stocks (*ferr(a) & cippis*).[102] This raises questions as to how secure the prison was intended to be, although c.1305 a man incarcerated by the deputy warden Robert de Micheldever for carrying wood through the forest apparently died 'by duress of prison' within three days.[103] Nevertheless, in 1359 Thomas de Radenore broke out of the prison where he had languished after killing a buck in Groveley Forest. This was not the first time de Radenore, a forester of Groveley, had enjoyed royal 'hospitality'. He had remained in prison at Clarendon, presumably for want of pledges, during the 1355 eyre in which he was indicted for various transgressions.[104]

By the mid fifteenth century the prison appears to have been renamed the Bolpit. It was repaired during works of 1449-50, when it was newly timbered. If this did not represent a major rebuild, this certainly occurred in 1471-2, when Thomas Troyes, the clerk of works, accounted for 'making a new prison…called le Bolpit for transgressors caught in the park of Claryngdon'.[105] This is significant in two ways. First, its purpose was not connected with policing the park as a privatised space *per se* through the thirteenth and fourteenth centuries, but was

rather part of the apparatus of wider forest jurisdiction, applying to residents of the forest rather than trespassers in general. Second, there is very little direct documentary evidence of poaching or other trespasses in the fifteenth century, and the necessity for a 'new' prison shows that it continued and had probably gone on in earnest through the Wars of the Roses, as it had in other periods of national strife. The gaol was repaired again in 1484-94, no doubt due to similar underlying causes.[106]

The reign of Edward III seems to have witnessed outbreaks of forest crime throughout — or at least the effort to stamp it out has left more traces in the records. The years around Edward II's deposition saw episodic raids on Clarendon Park, as in November 1326 when Nicholas de Estmust of Hampshire took a buck and a sorrel on the launds with his greyhounds, afterwards sequestering them in a ditch outside Winchester Gate. In the same month, a buck wounded by the swords (*gladios*) of six unknown men died in 'the marsh of Milford' where it was found by the forester Richard de Toulouse. There is no sign that it had been hidden so that the men could retrieve it later, and this sounds like an act of vandalism akin to those discussed as 'feud-poaching' by Perry Marvin, often involving the slaughter and 'desecration of the status-symbol' (venison).[107] It may be no coincidence that the following year orders went out to most sheriffs in southern England, including Wiltshire, to pursue the 'malefactors and disturbers of the peace, both horsemen and footmen', who assembled together daily in the county in order to 'commit divers evils'.[108] Yet Clarendon seems to have suffered little from such emblematic acts of vandalism, despite the (presumably) symbolic potential inherent in a major royal palace set in the biggest deerpark in the country.

But such destruction was widespread. In June 1339, when the king was absent in Flanders following the outbreak of the Hundred Years War in 1337, orders went out to all sheriffs:

> …*to cause proclamation to be made that no one, at his peril, shall hunt in the king's forests, parks or chaces or take…any beasts without the king's special licence…as the king has learned that the beasts in his forests, parks and free chaces are destroyed after his departure from the realm.*[109]

This emphasis on the royal hunting reserves and the animals inside them echoes the increased focus on the wider landscape in the fourteenth century — and in this reign in particular with its widespread construction of outlying lodges and lavish expenditure on park pales. In contrast, Henry III had worried, due to his absences

[100] PRO E 32/267, m.9.

[101] PRO C 47/3/48; James and Robinson, *Clarendon Palace*, p.34; 'Pardon to Richard le Reve, who was taken and is detained in the king's prison at Sarum for a trespass of the forest at Clarendon, for the said trespass and the escape which he afterwards made from the prison, and of any consequent outlawry' (*CPR 1232-47*, p.323).

[102] PRO E 32/267, mm.5d; *Et q(uo)d anno p(re)d(i)c(t)i Reg' E' decimo* [Jan 1336-7] *d(ict)us Will(el)m(u)s le Swop(er)e & Steph(an)us Davy p(re)d(i)c(t)us qui capti & detenti fueru(n)t p(ro) fforestar' d'm Reg' in p(ri)sona d'm Reg' de Claryngdon ferra & cippis custoditi ffreg(er)unt d(i)c(t)am p(ri)sonam nocte die d(o)m(ini)ce p(ro)x' post festu(m) s'c'i Ed(ward)i Confessoris anno p(re)d(i)c(t)o Reg' sup(ra)d(i)c(t)o & abinde evaserint* (PRO E 32/281, m.4).

[103] Pugh, *Gaol Delivery*, p.104. Both de Micheldever and Andrew de Dodmanstone, mentioned below, were accused of exceptional harshness in carrying out their duties.

[104] *CPR 1358-61*, p.258; PRO E 32/267, m.11d.

[105] PRO E 101/460/10, m.1; PRO E 101/460/14.

[106] PRO E 101/460/16.

[107] PRO E 32/207, m.2d.; Perry Marvin, pp.232, 236, 240-1.

[108] *CCR 1327-30*, p.204.

[109] *CCR 1339-41*, p.258.

during the Barons' Wars, that 'the *buildings*...of the lord king' were decaying (see below, p. 129).[110]

By the second half of the fourteenth century, this increased concept of private hunting areas, in tandem with modifications to the operation of the forest system, made novel measures necessary. For example in 1360, John de Beverley, the king's esquire, was granted free warren in the king's forests, chases, parks and warrens provided he carry 'a parti-coloured horn, to wit, of russet and black equally, which the king has given him as a sign of such hunting, to be returned to the king on failure of...heirs male'.[111] The symbolism of de Beverley's horn was echoed in the landscape. At Clarendon in the late fourteenth century the park was now a bounded space, its enclosure representing the difference between legitimate and illegitimate hunting. This is evident in the 1379 pardon of John Lane, the prior of Ivychurch's servant, and John Chelseye, a guest at the priory:

> *who when staying with the said prior chased a hare*
> *out of the king's park of Claryndon with two*
> *harriers of the prior, when, a priket leaping over the*
> *paling into the park, they killed the priket in the*
> *park, on which account the prior and canons fear*
> *that they may hereafter be questioned.*[112]

In earlier times, Lane and Chelseye would have been just as worried about killing prickets in Clarendon Forest.[113]

The involvement of the priory of Ivychurch in poaching is noteworthy, since it highlights the probable effects of the Black Death on such disorders. It has been mentioned (above, p. 100) that the priory appears to have been particularly badly hit, and that changes to the park's economy in the early fourteenth century had left it economically weakened. Before the 1350s, the prior and canons' 'crimes' included assarting without licence (1246), owing two years' pannage (1249), and acquiring land in mortmain (1334).[114] Although in the 1330 eyre the prior, Brother William de Canne, was named as a habitual receiver of venison,[115] it is from the 1350s that the canons are found participating in all manner of poaching activities and other trespasses. In 1352-3 Walter Frogmere *serviens* of the rector of Winterslow, John de Groundwell, Peter de Tarente, John de Salisbury and Robert Gowyn, 'fellow canons' (*concanonici*) of the priory, entered Clarendon Park with the greyhounds of the rector and Edward le Heyward and took the king's beasts, while the prior himself was accused of receiving John Wirschop, 'visiting the priory and Alderbury with

his greyhounds' in order to poach.[116] In the same year the prior and canons were caught supplying the glover John Prior with numerous deer pelts (see above, p. 124), and in 1356 they broke Joan de Grimstead's closes, houses and doors in West Grimstead, 'carried away her goods, and assaulted her men and servants at Alwardebury' and 'took away her bondmen in her service there, whereby she lost their service for a great time'.[117] Later, *c*.1360-1, Robert Sweyn and Peter atte Selos, canons, were caught poaching rabbits with nets outside the close of the priory (thus presumably in the park), and in 1369-70, four canons committed the heinous and almost unheard of (at Clarendon) crime of making a buckstall (*stabiliam*) in a certain field 'between the forest and [Treasurer's] grove' (See Figure 49), then driving the deer into it from the forest.[118]

Tonkinson has shown that Peak Forest became a scene of conflict and feuding from the 1350s,[119] and indeed the period after the Black Death was one of unrest, often manifested as lawlessness, generally. In 1356 three Clarendon foresters were assaulted at Alderbury by evildoers who afterwards broke the pale so that many of the king's deer escaped.[120] There was trouble with Salisbury also. In 1360 the king pardoned the commonalty of the city the 3,000 marks they had been fined for 'certain trespasses and contempts', although whether this had anything to do with the forest and park is not stated. Apparently also, the occasional robber still lurked in the forest, such as William Danyell, who committed many robberies with violence, including 'under Claryngdon Park', as did Henry Bailiff and an accomplice in 1374.[121]

Only a few snapshots of poaching remain from the fifteenth to the mid-seventeenth century, partly due to poor record keeping and the total collapse of the forest system, and partly because of the ascendancy of timber in the government's preoccupations. But it doubtless went on throughout, as the fifteenth-century refurbishing of the palace gaol testifies (above, p. 125). Poachers are recorded as coming into the park in the 1488 eyre, including seven listed together who may or may not have worked as a team, but they seem to have targeted rabbits rather than deer.[122] For the first time their status is recorded, and they are listed as husbandmen, labourers, tilers and yeomen. The gentry classes were still frequent

---

[110] Treharne and Sanders, p.217 (my italics).

[111] *CPR 1367-70*, p.181.

[112] *CPR 1377-81*, pp.427-8.

[113] The priory had, however, enjoyed free warren in their lands at Alderbury and Whaddon which were without the metes of the forest since 1341 (*CPR 1377-81*, p.58).

[114] *CHR 1226-57*, p.304; *CLR 1247-51*, p.269; *CPR 1334-8*, p.48.

[115] PRO E 32/207, m.3*d*.

[116] *qui visitati fuerint venir' as hoc' foreste ad P(ri)oratu(m) de Ivych(erch) & Alwardb(ur)y cu(m) lepor' ad capiend feras d'm' Reg' in bosco de Panchet* (PRO E 32/267, m.5).

[117] *CPR 1354-8*, p.386. The latter was presumably a consequence of their depleted numbers since the time of the plague.

[118] PRO E 32/279, m.1; PRO E 32/318, m.14.

[119] Tonkinson, *Macclesfield in the Later Fourteenth Century*, pp.140-3.

[120] *CPR 1354-8*, p.399.

[121] *CCR 1360-4*, p.48, *CPR 1374-7*, p.38; Cf. a similar case of oyer and terminer in Northamptonshire in 1341, in which the 'community of officials...both of the forest and elsewhere' were fined 4,000 marks 'for certain trespasses committed by them' (Grant, *Royal Forests*, p.167); *CPR 1374-7*, pp.37-9.

[122] PRO DL 39/2/20, m.15.

protagonists in the old forests, but now they had been used to taking deer for generations with little interference. Indeed when Henry VII sent his warrant of restraint to the warden of Chute in 1489 it seems to have occasioned some hilarity, being:

> red openly at a grete assemble of people at a Cristmas Dyn(ner) holden at George Munndy's house in the said forest...Hugh Mundy of Ludgarsale...said shortly & openly that for al that restraint [perforce] shuld mean they be in contempt of the king's writing.[123]

Some continued to use poaching as a means of resistance, however. For example in the reign of Henry VIII, Margaret York of Laverstock encouraged her servants to poach in the park and resist the keepers and even invited the local gentry to join her, because, she claimed, they had wrongly enclosed her land.[124] Immediately after the palace's demise, however, the impression is that of a landscape which was less a scene of contention as open to all takers. When 'parkbreak' is mentioned in the 1488 eyre, it is no longer a symbolic act of resistance, but (in both cases) the act of breaking down paleboards and making off with them for the perpetrators' own use.[125]

CONCEPTUAL BOUNDARIES

Medieval Perambulations

Nothing is more illustrative of the conceptual boundary than the medieval forest perambulation (see Figure 84), and since forest bounds waxed and waned according to political and economic pressures, they also represent the contested landscape writ large. Forest issues generally were prominent throughout the thirteenth and early fourteenth centuries. Magna Carta and Charter of the Forest were always reissued together and in popular complaints and demands for their confirmation, the latter was often mentioned first as if of greater importance.[126] The royal forests were also high among the Crown's priorities. One of Henry III's first acts on attaining majority in 1227 was to launch inquests into their extents, and within a year he had forced numerous revisions of their bounds.[127] In one such inquiry Clarendon Forest is as yet unnamed, described instead as 'the...bailiwick

which was Walter Walerand's'.[128] Thus the 1228 mandate concerning the king's 'new' forest of Clarendon is significant (see above, p. 59), being among the earliest evidence of Clarendon Forest as a concept in itself. In the late twelfth and early thirteenth centuries, when it was a northern bailiwick of the New Forest, pipe roll entries show clearly that Clarendon Forest was not thought of as an entity, at least by central administration, prior to Henry III's personal rule. Repairs to the 'King's houses' at Clarendon, the responsibility of the sheriff of Wiltshire, are listed under Wiltshire in the pipe rolls. The farm paid for them, however, appears under Hampshire with the returns from the New Forest, including those from Clarendon which is not delineated by name.[129]

Subsequent to the issue of the Forest Charter in 1217, royalists and former rebels had set out to define the boundaries inside which forest custom should run, and it is no coincidence that the Bishop of Salisbury was among the commissioners appointed to carry out the Wiltshire perambulations on its reissue in 1219.[130] A primary factor in the success (or otherwise) of new towns was choosing the right site,[131] and through its participation in defining the forest bounds the see would at least have been aware of where the most promising sites were in relation to forest restrictions. Although the testimony of local communities was used, most jurors were knights and presiding over the 1219 perambulations alongside the bishop of Salisbury and others was William Longespée, again hardly a disinterested party (see above, pp. 95-96). Such men were entrusted with the job of faithfully representing the extent of the king's forest.

It is hard to believe that other social strata would have welcomed disafforestment entirely. Those attached to royal demesnes could claim entitlement to fixed services and conditions, and were not compelled to perform the customary services of villeins.[132] They were free from tolls and customs, were not obliged to attend county courts, and could proceed by royal writ in property disputes. Thus, theoretically, they might bring a wider range of complaints against their overlords than those living under common law jurisdiction.[133] The effect that being put out of the forest might have is evidenced by Edward I's promise, after the 1305 ordinance of the forest, that any who wished to return to the forest would be received back as before. This had followed a rather petulant decree that if the king's beasts could not use the purlieus created, then the former forest inhabitants had

---

[123] PRO DL 39/3/32, m.2.

[124] James and Gerrard, *Clarendon: A Royal Landscape*, forthcoming.

[125] *Item p's' q(uo)d Ga[v]' Lyytt de Nova Sar(um) Gent' parcu' d(omi)ni Reg' de Claryngdon intran(vi)t & post' & palebo(r)dys de le Parkkepale fregit cepit & apportavit;*

Carolus Ringewode un(ius) fforestariu[s] p's' q(uo)d Rob(er)tus Martyn de Nova sar(um) labourer...parcu' d(o)m(ini) Regi(s) de Claryngdon intra(vit) & iiij⁰ᵣ palebordys de le parke pale de Claryngdon p(re)dict' fregit cepit & apportavit (PRO DL 39/2/20, mm.15, 16d.).

[126] F. Thompson, *The First Century of Magna Carta: Why it Persisted as a Document* (New York: Russell and Russell, 1967), p.89.

[127] R.C. Stacey, *Politics, Policy and Finance under Henry III 1216-1245* (Oxford: Oxford University Press, 1987), pp.8, 35.

[128] *Rex vicecomiti Wiltis' etc...Dicunt etiam quod ballia de [Groveley] est antiqua foresta sicut fuit perambulata, et tota ballia que fuit Walteri Walerand', in Wiltis' est antiqua foresta...(CCR 1227-31, pp.103-4).*

[129] E.g. in 1221-2 (PRO E 372/66, *rot.7*, m.1; *rot.15*, m.2).

[130] Stacey, *Politics, Policy and Finance Under Henry III*, p.7; Grant, *VCH Wilts*, p.399. For the 1218 order commanding nationwide perambulations, see *CPR 1216-25*, p.162.

[131] C. Dyer, 'The Economy and Society', in *The Oxford Illustrated History of Medieval England* (London: BCA, 1997), ed. N. Saul, p.153.

[132] D.A. Carpenter, 'English Peasants in Politics 1258-1267', *Past and Present* 136 (1992), pp.3-42 (pp.19, 25).

[133] Bennett, *Women in the Medieval English Countryside*, p.15.

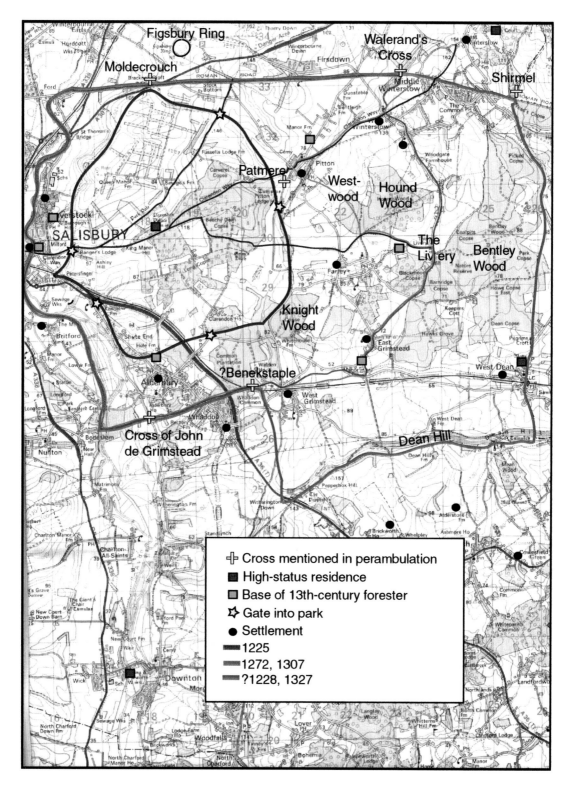

Figure 84. Mappable perambulations of Clarendon Forest. Adapted from R. Grant, 'Forests', in *VCH Wilts. IV*
(Oxford: Oxford University Press, 1959), ed. E. Crittall, pp.391-457 (p.454), with additions from
M. Parsons, *The Royal Forest of Pancet* (New Milton: Leonard Michael Parsons, 1995), ch.1.
OS Map reproduced with kind permission of the Controller of Her Majesty's Stationary Office,
© Crown copyright NC/05/100041476.

forfeited their right of common 'or any other easement' there.[134]

The knights and freeholders of Wiltshire paid £100 for confirmation of the 1219 perambulations. Yet they were revoked prior to the 1225 reissue of the Charters, causing resentment among local 'gentry' and magnates whose expectations had been raised. More perambulations followed, probably at Henry III's instigation, and that of 1225 at Clarendon disafforested all areas except royal demesne woods.[135] In Melchet, for example, only the park was to remain in forest, since the jurors swore that Henry II's officials had 'broken the park' deliberately, causing deer to escape and using the pretext to afforest a wide area. There may have been some truth in this, but perambulators undoubtedly took advantage of concessions during such times as Henry III's minority.[136] Moreover, given the interest of the community in assarting in thirteenth-century Melchet, the claim is dubious to say the least.

The perambulation of 1225 is reiterated in an eyre document of 1330. Like that of 1219 it demanded substantial reduction of the forest area, including those woods pertaining to subjects, i.e. Bentley Wood, Rodsley Wood, the wood attached to Winterbourne Dauntsey and the Wood of Odo de Grimstead (Hawk's Grove in West Dean) (see Figure 49). The deer, of course, continued to pertain to the king. However Westwood, pertaining to West Winterslow, was to remain in forest.[137] Thus in Figure 83, Houndwood, of which Westwood was a part, is inside the perambulation. Indeed it is revealing that it was not until 1272 that Houndwood, by then in private hands, was removed from the forest, reflecting a wider clamour for disafforestment as the century wore on. The 1330 restatement states, alongside a claim that crops might be enclosed without hindrance, that the foresters were forbidden to take security from forest offenders outside Clarendon Park.[138] The latter is in fact almost certainly a fourteenth-century interpretation, first because it would be highly irregular at such an early date, and second since the park is rarely mentioned in thirteenth-century documents.

A sudden change of policy on Henry III's majority in 1227 is evident at Clarendon. The 1225 perambulations were revoked, and those who made them probably threatened with amercement or imprisonment to acknowledge their 'errors'.[139] Henceforth, the forests were set to the king's understanding, according to new perambulations made in 1228. Henry's understanding clearly allowed for a 'new' forest established in the covert of the old, for it was in 1228 that the hereditary wardenship was abolished and Clarendon Forest's new administration established. Earlier in the same year the forest, again not graced with a name, was confirmed with Groveley as 'ancient', thus untouchable.[140]

By this time, the publication of Magna Carta and the Forest Charter had led to familiarity with their terms. They had been proclaimed by sheriffs, translated into French vernacular, and probably into English. Moreover, their 1225 confirmation in exchange for a grant of a fifteenth was seen as conferring added sanctity on disafforestments. The king's revocations caused such resentment that the matter was brought up in 1258 by the Barons, who complained in their petition that '...lands which are not within the metes of the forest, which by...the gift of [a fifteenth] to our lord king, were to be disafforested, he has reafforested of his own will'.[141]

Although it has been claimed that there was no breakdown in forest administration in the period of baronial reform and civil war,[142] men whose allegiance was not primarily to the king were appointed to office on royal estates. Indeed at Windsor in 1264, Nicholas Tonney was told curtly, on his refusal to serve under the incoming baronial custodian, that 'matters of this kind have nothing to do with a sergeant'.[143] Henry III's concern is evident in his 1261 complaint that 'the buildings ...and manors of the lord king and of his liberties are...falling into ruin for lack of repair'.[144] But at Clarendon, forest and palace officials do not seem to have had to choose between their allegiance and the smooth-running of their bailiwicks. Clearly Windsor, being a castle, was a much more strategic prize, but it will become apparent below that steps were taken to ensure that control was maintained over the forest and the protection of the king's interests there (see below, p. 134).

Under Edward I, opposition to the forest system intensified. There were further perambulations, and the king enforced forest law with a severity his father would not have recognised, often personally sitting in the forest courts.[145] The perambulation of 1272 placed most of Houndwood (then much bigger, as is evident from the perambulation traced in Figure 84) outside the forest. But that of 1300 declared that two woods in the king's hand without the bounds should remain in forest despite

---

[134] Stagg, *New Forest Documents A.D. 1244-A.D.1334*, p.13; Grant, *Royal Forests*, p.158.

[135] Grant, *VCH Wilts*, p.399.

[136] BM Stowe 798 *f*.9a; J.R. Maddicott, 'Magna Carta and the Local Community 1215-1259', *Past and Present* 102 (1984), pp.25-65 (p.39).

[137] PRO E 32/225, m.10; Grant, *VCH Wilts*, p.428.

[138] Grant, *VCH Wilts*, p.428. *Ita tamen q(uo)d om(ni)s ho(m)i(n)es infra has metas potuerunt bladum suu(m) claud[e]re & defendere sine cont(ra)dicc(i)one forestarior(um) Et q(uo)d nullus forestarius ex(tra) fossatum de Clarendon' vadimon[i]um cap(er)e potint* (PRO E 32/225, m.10).

[139] Grant, *VCH Wilts*, p.399.

[140] *CCR 1227-31*, pp.103-4; Grant, *Royal Forests*, p.68.

[141] Maddicott, 'Magna Carta and the Local Community', pp.30, 38-9; Stagg, *New Forest Documents A.D. 1244-A.D.1334*, p.10.

[142] Young, *The Royal Forests of Medieval England*, p.113.

[143] Carpenter, 'English Peasants', p.17.

[144] R.F. Treharne and I.J. Sanders, eds, *Documents of the Baronial Movement of Reform and Rebellion 1258-1267* (Oxford: Oxford University Press, 1973), pp.215, 217.

[145] Grant, *Royal Forests*, p.154.

their afforestation after 1154 — the touchstone for disafforestment according to the Forest Charter. These were 'Schireneswood' (Shreeves Wood), and 'Rowlesgof' pertaining to Winterbourne Earls and Dauntsey respectively.[146] The latter wood appears, like Shreeves Wood, to have lain on the park boundary, since in 1320-1 the pale was constructed from the northern deerleap as far as 'Rowaldesgrove'.[147] This is confirmed by the 1300 perambulation, which states:

> ...thence along the ditch as far as Cokyngdon [?Cockey Down], and thence along the ditch as far as holecombe wayeshened, and thence as far as wirdecnolle along the ditch, and from thence along the ditch as far as derditch, and from derditch to roaldesgrove, and thence as far as the Sleygate of Pitton.[148]

Most of the landmarks are unidentifiable, but Rowaldesgrove was clearly near both Pitton and the park boundary.

A declaration in 1300 stated that the bounds of Clarendon Forest had not changed since the reign of Henry III.[149] Yet the perambulation of that year covered virtually no more than the park. As Grant has said 'the declarations of the jurors [in 1300] reflected [their own] wishes and interests rather than the facts of recorded history'.[150] But this does beg the question as to why the park was perambulated — unless, of course it was not entirely circled by a pale at this time.

It is highly unlikely that Clarendon Forest had shrunk to encompass only the park in 1300, however. Instead the emphasis seems to have been on delineating parcels of the king's demesne rather than the bounds of the forest itself, since Westwood was also perambulated that year.[151] This mirrors the physical delineation of woods on the ground at this time. The process had always gone on, of course. In 1252 William Longespée the younger was granted permission to finish the enclosure of land to the 'North Est' of the king's meadow in Melchet Forest that his father had commenced, and in 1276 the 'clearings' (trenchia) were made in Clarendon Park.[152] But it speeded up around the turn of the fourteenth century, perhaps due to the same political pressures behind the more stringent perambulations. For example in 1303 Robert de Clifford, lord of West Winterslow, was given permission to make a 160ft trench (48.77m.) around his wood of Winterslow (Westwood) 'which is

within the metes of the forest of Clarendon as it appears by inquisition...that the only loss would be that the repair of the deer there would be diminished',[153] which as far as de Clifford was concerned was probably the point. In 1314, his successor John de Cromwell, was allowed to make a further trench 40ft-wide trench (12.19m.) around the same wood, and to fell and sell the trees growing in it.[154] There seems to have been a growing desire to mark out property in the forest if disafforestment *per se* was impossible.

The perambulations of 1272 and 1307 delineated smaller areas than those of either 1225, 1228, or (surprisingly) 1327. This may be because the 1327 perambulation records the whole area over which the royal writ ran. Indeed it has been suggested that it was intended as an *aide-memoire* for the incoming warden, Giles de Beauchamp, appointed by the new regime.[155] If so, it embodies the distinction between the forest's physical/economic bounds apparently represented by most other surviving perambulations, and its actual legal bounds. That is, it took no account of areas within the forest as a whole that had been removed from it by legislation, and is our surest guide to what was thought of as 'Clarendon Forest' by contemporaries.

The 1300 perambulations came about only due to threats of force by the magnates in parliament, and were revoked in an ordinance of 1306. However, they were eventually confirmed by Edward II in 1316, and the reduced bounds were finally accepted by the Crown on Edward III's accession.[156] Isabella and Mortimer also virtually repeated Edward I's ordinance of 1306, which largely concerned the curbing of extortion by forest officers, and fully implemented the Charter of the Forest, effectively for the first time. This was ratified by Edward III, who warned in 1330 that the perambulations of 1300 were strictly to be observed.[157] Indeed, in the margin of the forest eyre roll of 1330, assarts listed for Farley and Pitton are described in as 'outside the forest' (*extra foresta*), or 'now disafforested by perambulation' (*m(odo) deafforestant(ur) p(er) p(er)am(bu)li*).[158] So too is the sole assart listed for Alderbury, established by Richard Heyras 'without the king's demesne wood of Penchet'. For Winterslow the first of three assarts is arrented, the second 'outside the forest', and the third, held by John de Cromwell (Westwood), 'within the forest'.[159]

---

[146] Grant, *VCH Wilts*, p.428.

[147] PRO SC 6/1050/5, m.3.

[148] *...deinde p(er) fossatum usq(ue) Cokyngdon / Et de[in]de p(er) fossatu(m) usq(ue) holecombe wayeshened / et sic usq(ue) wirdecnolle p(er) fossatu(m) / Et sic p(er) fossatu(m) usq(ue) derdich' Et de derdich' usq(ue) roaldesgroue et sic usq(ue) la Sleyghete de puttone* (PRO C 260/136/31/2).

[149] Parsons, *Pancet*, p.3.

[150] Grant, *Royal Forests*, p.157.

[151] PRO E 32/225, m.11.

[152] *CCR 1272-9*, p.318; *CHR 1226-57*, p.392.

[153] *CPR 1301-7*, p.107.

[154] *CPR 1313-17*, p.95; PRO C 143/95/3a. The trenches around the wood remain visible today.

[155] Parsons, *Pancet*, p.4.

[156] *CPR 1313-17*, p.398; Grant, *VCH Wilts*, pp.399-400.

[157] Stagg, *New Forest Documents A.D.1244-A.D.1334*, pp.14, 35.

[158] PRO E 32/207, m.7.

[159] *Ex(tra) for(esta)*: *Ric(ard)us de heyras assartavit ibid(e)m de solo suo p(ro)p(ri)o ex(tra) d(o)m(ini)cu(m) boscu(m) d(o)m' Reg' de Panchet .vij. acras quas Ric(ard)us de Heyras modo tenet inbladat' Sem'l de t(ra)mes(io) iij.s. vj.d. Et q(uia) m(odo) deafforest' p(er) p(er)am(bu)li I(de)o decet(er)o no(n) imbl'* (PRO E 32/207, m.7); PRO E 32/207, m.7.

In Dean and Grimstead too, assarts had been placed out of the forest. They were held by Oliver de Ingham, Sybil de Sancto Martino and the de Grimsteads, indicating the social strata from which pressure had come. Indeed, in 1331 John de Grimstead was pardoned the large sum of £10 he had been fined for waste in his wood of Grimstead, 'then within the metes of Claryndon Forest, towards payment of his ransom of 100 marks when taken prisoner by the Scots at [Stirling]'.[160] William Longespée's old assart, now held by the Hospital of St Nicholas was also put outside the forest, along with the rest of Bentley Wood.[161] As for wastes of wood, old waste in Bentley Wood, Northwood, Southwood, Rodsley Wood, Alderbury, Farley and in Melchet Forest was discounted in the 1330 eyre 'because all the woods are now disafforested by perambulation'.

In Wiltshire as a whole, only the royal demesnes remained in forest by 1330.[162] For Clarendon in the 1355 eyre, pleas of the vert are restricted to Buckholt, Groveley and Clarendon Park (which suggests the demesne wood was by now enclosed within it), and the only new wastes listed are in Houndwood, committed by John de Cromwell and Edward Despenser. Whether old wastes were in forest or not is no longer mentioned, but woods in Alderbury were fined for, as was David le Archer's wood in Farley, Rodsley Wood, Westwood, and the woods of Anne le Despencer. The Prior of St John's wood remained in forest, however, along with the manor of Winterslow with Houndwood and Westwood. The manor of Britford was outside the forest, although this did not prevent Elizabeth de St Omer from having to claim her half of the River Avon in the eyre (see above, p. 45).[163]

The 1330 perambulations were the last to take place, revealing the shrunken prominence of forests as a political issue by this time. And although the extent of their boundaries waxed and waned according to political pressure, throughout the period studied conceptual acceptance of the forest as delineated in the ground in the 1327 example probably remained constant, and remained in the collective memory even longer. In 1829, Milford attempted to use its erstwhile forest status to its own advantage. A dispute concerning payment of church rates to St Martins, Salisbury, centred on whether or not Milford was extra-parochial. The village's inhabitants stated that it certainly was, being within the bounds of the late Forest of Clarendon. The jury of the assizes found, quite rightly, that part of Milford had indeed been inside the forest well into the fourteenth century. As a result,

the church rates were paid although Milford maintained its own poor until 1835.[164]

To stand on Dean Hill, the old boundary between Clarendon and Melchet Forests, and to look north and south reveals two distinctive landscapes which remain distinct from each other as well as from the surrounding countryside. There is little doubt that poachers and others would have 'found themselves...vulnerable' on entering these spaces, their responses to the landscape changing accordingly.[165] Indeed almost without exception forest bounds were made with reference to pre-existing features,[166] and thus the perambulations *make sense*. At Clarendon, the Roman road to the north was an obvious boundary, as was the rivers Bourne and Avon to the west. Such fixed boundaries prevented to an extent disafforestments like those possible on the east of the forest, for example of Bentley Wood, although paradoxically it was the western boundary that was nibbled away by demographic and seigneurial pressures, as the St Omer Britford claim shows.

In administrative terms the county boundary on the east of the forest is another obvious bound. However the amalgamation within the Clarendon forests of Buckholt over that border hints at a perhaps earlier association that overrode it, perhaps connected with Edward the Confessor's estate at West Tytherley. Indeed the fluidity of shire boundaries in this part of south east Wiltshire has been noted. It has been suggested that they may only recently have been established at the time of Domesday, and that their origin lay in the need to divide forest resources equitably.[167]

The siting of Walerand's motte on the county boundary reveals that the hub of the administrative forest of Clarendon had been oriented eastwards before New Sarum's institution. Strangely, the motte goes unmentioned in the perambulations, although it must have remained a prominent landmark. Those man-made features most often mentioned are crosses (see Figure 84). For example in 1327 'Moldecrouche' (today's Broken Cross) at Park Corner on the Roman road, which local legend holds to have the remains of a cross erected to St Thomas Becket. It is likely that another stood where the Roman road and the Hampshire boundary met at 'Shirmel' ('shir' – shire, 'mœl' – a Christian cross), also mentioned in 1327.[168] 'Walerand's Cross', listed in 1225 and 1307, probably stood on or near Cobb's Barrow.[169] It was almost certainly a gallows, since it occupied a prominent scarp overlooking a major communication route (the Roman road), was associated

[160] PRO E 32/207, m.10; *CPR 1330-4*, p.112.
[161] *Et q(uo)d Will(el)m(u)s de Longespeye dudu(m) comes Sar(um) d(i)c(t)um assartu(m) fier[i] fecit de solo suo p(ro)p'o d'n id(e)m solu' fuit ex(tra) forestam & Sim(i)l(ite)r d(i)c(tu)m solu' modo est ex(tra) forestam p(ro) p(er)ambul[i]. I(de)o d(i)c(t)us mag(iste)r hospital' p(re)d(i)c(t)i de nubl' eiusd(e)m assarti exon(er)et(ur) & d(i)c(t)um assartu(m) decetero no(n) imbladet(ur) nec in Regardo p(re)sentet(ur)* (PRO E 32/207, m.10d.).
[162] Bond, 'Forests, Chases, Warrens and Parks, p.125.
[163] PRO E 32/267, mm.12-12d, 13, 15, 18d; PRO E 146/3/11; PRO C 260/86.

[164] Colt Hoare and Nichols, *The Modern History of South Wiltshire*, p.110.
[165] Austin, 'Okehampton Park', p.70.
[166] Bond, 'Forests, Chases, Warrens and Parks', p.125.
[167] Pitt, 'Wiltshire Minster *Parochiae*', p.38.
[168] PRO E 32/225, m.6.; Gelling and Cole, *The Landscape of Place-Names*, pp., 240, 170.
[169] PRO E 32/225, m.10; BM Stowe798 *f.*9a; Parsons, *Pancet*, p.5.

with prehistoric earthworks, and lay on the Winterslow/Pitton and Farley parish boundary — common elements in Anglo-Saxon execution sites.[170] Another cross apparently stood at the round barrow by Pitton Gate ('Patmere'), referred to in the perambulation of 1225 and 1307.[171] In 1300 the cross of John de Grimstead is mentioned, which probably stood in Alderbury, and also 'Benekstaple' near one of Ivychurch Priory's crofts by Alderbury Common, which has been interpreted as 'Benedict's post/stone', named for one of the canons.[172]

It is noteworthy that some of these crosses were named for forest officers (Walerand and de Grimstead). Most were probably erected for the sole purpose of marking the boundary, and may have been instigated by the foresters in question. Although the perambulations do make use of rivers and woods, most boundary marks are man-made. Boundary ditches feature strongly, and even woods are described by the names of their recent or contemporary owners. Although it has been stressed here that forests are irrecoverable archaeologically, it should nevertheless be remembered that they possessed 'culturally meaningful boundaries and sectors',[173] not only understood but manipulated by contemporaries.

Religion and the Forest: Liminality in the Landscape
Poachers, usually accompanied by outlaws, are often mentioned in studies of forests. Although this reflects the nature of the extant administrative sources it is also a measure of our concerns, given the popularity of Robin Hood films through the twentieth century. What is rarely brought up, probably due to our secular mindset, is the forest as a religious or mystical place. Here Rackham and Astill are exceptions, drawing attention to the medieval hermitages in Hatfield and Windsor Forests respectively.[174] Rackham does not say whereabouts his hermits dwelt, but Astill describes the liminal situation of St Leonards Chapel and Hermitage, Windsor, noting that such establishments were often set up between cultivated and wooded areas, probably in order to reinforce the perception of hermits as mediators.[175]

Being so near to Salisbury and its cathedral may have made Clarendon Forest a particular focus for religious interests, as is evident in Table 8 (writs issued at Clarendon). In addition to the rights of Abbeys such as Wilton and Amesbury in the forest, the Augustinian friary of Ivychurch had privileged rights of pasturage, agistment, and assarted lands which it retained into the

fourteenth century, as discussed in Chapter Two.[176] In return for this, a grant was made in 1246 'for the soul of [Henry III's] mother, whose anniversary shall be celebrated yearly in the monastery'. In addition, the priory gained entry to its holdings in Whaddon through a grant of Edward II 'towards the sustenance of a canon to celebrate divine service daily in the monastery for the good estate of the king in life, for his soul after death, and for the souls of his progenitors and the faithful departed'.[177] Later, in 1423, the prior and convent where granted the church and chapel at Uphaven (Wilts.) provided they:

> celebrate a mass daily within their priory for the king and for Catherine his mother while alive, and for their souls after death, and for the souls of Henry V, Henry IV, Richard II, and other the king's...ancestors.
> Provided also that if the said prior and convent shall ever be lawfully put out of the said church...and chapel ...they shall recover their rights in the said park.[178]

Without such rights and concessions, religious establishments in forests could not have functioned. However the priory also received patronage from the forest's officers and landholders, and was an important spiritual centre for the community. Land was bequeathed by the foresters of fee in particular through the thirteenth century, and in 1333 Robert de Hungerford demised to it much property for a chaplain to celebrate divine service in Salisbury Cathedral for the souls of himself and his ancestors.[179]

Thus Ivychurch is a clear example of a reciprocal relationship with the forest and (especially) the palace, in whose chapels the canons said offices, and this is mirrored by its liminal setting immediately outside the park's southern boundary.[180] However, the priory may have originated as a chapel of a Saxon Minster at Alderbury, as an outlying oratory or retreat, so that it was originally liminal in relation not to Clarendon Park but to Alderbury. Certainly Alderbury church was associated

---

[170] A. Reynolds, *Later Anglo-Saxon England: Life and Landscape* (Stroud: Tempus Publishing, 1999), p.108.
[171] BM Stowe798 *f.*9a; Parsons, *Pancet*, p.11, 14.
[172] PRO C 260/136/31/2; Parsons, *Pancet*, p.34.
[173] Darvill, Gerrard and Startin, 'Archaeology in the Landscape', p.15.
[174] Rackham, *The Last Forest*, pp. 61-6; Astill, 'Windsor', pp.11-13.
[175] Astill, 'Windsor', p.11-13.

[176] See also *CHR 1257-1300*, p.159; *quinque carettas errantes singulis diebus ad ligna defendera ad predictum monasterium de* [Amesbury], *unam scilicet carrettam in bosco de* [Chute] *et unam in Groveley* [Graveling] *et unam in* [Winterslow] *que pertinent ad Bercamsted et unam in* [Bentley Wood - *Bentelwoda*] *quam predictum monasterium de* [Amesbury] *antiquitus habebat.*
[177] *CHR 1226-1257*, p.304; *CPR 1334-8*, p.48.
[178] *CPR 1422-9*, pp.106-7.
[179] For example in 1255 James de Pitton, forester of fee, granted them land in Pitton which they cultivated (*CPR 1247-58*, p.455). In the 1330s and 40s they were also demised land in Whaddon and Winterslow (*CPR 1334-8*, p.48; *CPR 1340-3*, p. 281); *CPR 1330-4*, p.434.
[180] E.g.: *Et i(n) elem(osina) cons(ue)t(udine). milit(ibus) de templ(is) .J. m. Et canonicis q(ui) ministrant' i(n) monasterio ed(er)oso in capella. de clarendon' .xxx. s. (et) v. d. Et p(ri)ori de monast(er)io ed(er)oso .xlv. s. (et) .vij. d....Et i(n) lib(er)at(ione) Capell[ano] de clarendon' .L.s. (PRO E 372/59, rot. 14, m.1).*

with it and with the chapels of Farley and Whadden in a grant of 1109-20.[181]

The question of liminality is significant. Clarendon Forest itself was liminal, lying on the county boundary, an area used for execution sites from prehistory.[182] Within the forest, the densely-wooded Bentley Wood, in the period studied more often out of the forest than in, and lying adjacent to the county boundary as well as on that between Clarendon and Buckholt Forests, was associated most often with religious interests, especially those least conventional. This was where William Longespée intended to establish his religious foundation, 'St Mary of the Bentlewood' (see above, p. 95). Moreover the land was afterwards given to the hospital of St Nicholas, Salisbury, in 1227, and medieval hospitals were commonly sited in liminal places.[183] Finally, in 1334 protection of one year was given to brother John of Warwick 'a hermit dwelling at [Bentley Wood] by Clarendon…and his men, seeking alms'.[184]

The association of hermits with woods and wilderness is well attested in medieval literature, and probably has classical antecedents.[185] For example the hero of *Sir Orfeo* (c.1300) heads off to the forest after abdicating his throne, becoming a hermit and existing by living off what he can gather in the peaceful woods, where wild animals are charmed by the sound of his harp:

In al the woode the soun gan shille,
That wilde beestes that ther beeth
For joy abouten him they teeth;
And alle the fowles that ther were
Come and sete on eech a brere
To here his harping afine...[186]

This aspect of forests was well-understood by contemporaries. Malory describes the meeting of Sir Galahad, Lancelot and Percival in a 'waste forest', before a 'hermitage where a recluse dwelled', and the discovery in woodland of hermit-saints by hunting parties is common in saints' legends, for example that of St Giles

in which an abbey is eventually built on the site of the saint's retreat.[187]

Rackham has gone so far as to say that 'no forest was really complete without a hermit',[188] and although John of Warwick seems to have been the only one that dwelt in Clarendon's woods, an anchorite was certainly associated with the forest for much of the thirteenth century. Her name seems to have been Nichola and she is first documented in 1222-3 and last mentioned in 1255. Her ankerhold was at Britford, whose church today bears evidence of a hagioscope or squint in the west wall of the south transept, revealing, perhaps, the presence of an anchorite cell.[189] Table 8, gifts given by the king at Clarendon, shows that the 'recluse of Britford' was one of the most frequent recipients of the king's largesse. Between 1222 and 1255, she received at least seventeen *robora* from the forest, and this is how she has found her way into the documentary record. The following is typical:

> *To the sheriff of Wilts.* Contrabreve *to fell two* [robora] *which the king has given to the anchoress of Brutford in the forest of Clarendon for fuel, and carry them to her anker-hold.*[190]

Little more is known of the recluse. But it is significant that she was at Britford, on the forest's western edge. Thus, like Bentley Wood, the village was liminal in relation to the forest. Indeed each was put outside it in the fourteenth century. It may also be significant that Britford lay on the river, considering the association of watery landscapes with female religious noted by Gilchrist.[191]

The presence of religious enclaves in forests could cause tensions, especially by the fourteenth century. In 1361 the abbot and convent of Grace Dieu complained that land around their chantry in the Forest of Dean ('Le Hermitorie') had all been assarted and their crops 'trodden down and consumed by the king's deer'. Its two monks could no longer be maintained, and they were compelled to leave and set up a chantry in the abbey.[192] Such events were less likely at Clarendon due to the king's control over the landscape (see Chapter Four). However, it will be remembered that the priory of

[181] Pitt, 'Wiltshire Minster *Parochiae*', p.28; *...ecclesiam de Alwarbiri cum omnibus appendiciis; in silvis, id est. Preostwde, et in terries, in pratis, in pascuis, scilicet, in Monasterium Hederosum* [Ivychurch], *et capellam de Fernlega, et capellam de Hwatdena...(ibid.,* p.27).
[182] A. Reynolds, pers. comm.
[183] Atkinson, *The Manors and Hundred of Alderbury*, p.22; Colt Hoare and Nichols, *The Modern History of South Wiltshire*, pp.126-7; Roberta Gilchrist, *Contemplation and Action: The Other Monasticism* (London: Leicester University Press, 1995), pp.38-48. See also Astill, 'Windsor', p.11.
[184] *CPR 1334-8*, p.5.
[185] This is discussed in greater detail in James and Gerrard, *Clarendon: A Royal Landscape*, forthcoming.
[186] B. Johnstone Flynn, 'The Power of Music Represented in Medieval Literature' (honours thesis, Department of Medieval Studies, Connecticut College) http://www.tiltedworld.com/brenda/msic/hangeheart.html

[187] H. Cooper, ed., *Sir Thomas Malory: Le Morte Darthur – the Winchester Manuscript* (Oxford: Oxford University Press, 1998), p.329; Rooney, *Hunting in Middle English Literature*, pp.118-21, drawing attention to the hunt as a primary symbol of worldliness used to represent the confrontation between the holy and the secular.
[188] Rackham, *The Last Forest*, p.61.
[189] *CCR 1242-7*, p.400; PRO E 352/33, m.8d; *CCR 1254-6*, p.87; Simon Roffey, pers. comm.
[190] *CLR 1240-1245*, pp.290-1.
[191] Gilchrist, *Gender and Material Culture*, p.66.
[192] *CPR 1361-4*, p.11. Perhaps such occurrences are a previously overlooked factor in the explosion of chantries in the interior landscapes of cathedrals and churches in the fourteenth century, leading to the consequent subdivision and 'privatisation' of such space (see Paul Binski, *Medieval Death: Ritual and Representation* (London: The British Museum Press, 1996), pp.116-20.

Ivychurch lost considerable revenues probably due to the enlargement of the park in 1317. Indeed in that year it was granted 100s. annually in compensation, 'in aid of finding a light burning for ever in the monastery', which Giles de Beauchamp later claimed he could not pay because the king had banned agistment in the park in order to gain more pasture for his deer.[193] In 1419, Henry V (1413-22) saw fit to bestow on the priory his own special protection after its property had been 'unduly withdrawn, detained and occupied...by divers of the king's lieges, in manifest contempt...of the king and...diminution of the divine services celebrated therein for [him] and his progenitors'.[194]

The presence of religious enclaves in the forest might thus result in tensions in the landscape. But their very presence shows that Clarendon Forest carried a multiplicity of meanings. It was not one entity — a bare container for myriad actions — but a series of overlapping conceptual landscapes, of which the administrative forest was another.

Forest Law

The purpose here is to discover what, if anything, made Clarendon Forest unique in terms of forest law. This is easier said than done, since custom and tenure are rarely touched on in studies of individual forests, which tend to be selective rather than holistic.[195] Indeed, François Duceppe-Lamarre has noted that in forest studies, historical approaches in particular 'possèdent souvent une vision réductrice'.[196] However, there are ways in which Clarendon Forest was 'different', centring on the effect of the palace and its relatively frequent royal visitors on the one hand and, particularly, on its close relationship with Salisbury and the shrievalty on the other.

The most significant claim for a unique jurisdiction operating in Clarendon Forest is that mentioned by Caroline Smith in her work on the fourteenth-century New Forest. Smith notes that whereas the New Forest keepers apparently failed to carry out royal orders concerning homicide inquests due to their resentment of interference from central authorities, Clarendon's foresters claimed in 1338 that homicides and crown pleas belonged to the keepers and verderers.[197] There is little sign of this in the thirteenth century, although two women

accused of robbery alongside Stephen le Forester, Richard his groom and John le Pynbyr' were 'acquitted before the King at Clarendon' c.1249,[198] and it is possible that such events led to an association of the palace not only with forest but also civil law.

In 1346 a murder case was recounted in an inquisition held at Salisbury which suggests that some kind of dual jurisdiction was customary by this time. Robbers had entered the 'king's precinct' of Clarendon and killed a man before dumping him in the ditch of Sharpegore. It was claimed that since the body was found not in any village, but in the king's demesne of Clarendon, the foresters should have charge of cognisance and execution of the perpetrators, as they did with all homicides and felonies.[199] In addition, when the Earl of March became warden of Clarendon Forest in 1355, he claimed 'infangthef' (see Glossary) and the 'right to make execution touching this in the park where of ancient time it hath been accustomed to be done'. Similarly, in 1272 the king had given Stephen de Eddeworth, then warden, 'a year, day and waste of lands, tenements, goods and chattels which were Peter de Tingrith's...if it should happen that he himself convicts Peter of that felony [he has committed]'.[200]

De Eddeworth, however, was also sheriff of Wiltshire, and it is possible that an overlap of the offices in the later thirteenth century was responsible for this blurring of civil and forest jurisdiction. In turn, the increased identification of one office with the other derives from measures taken around the time of the Barons' Wars which may have given Clarendon's forest administration the unique authority discussed here, and certainly fostered yet closer ties to the city of Salisbury.

Clarendon Forest and the Shrievalty

Robert Walerand had been made castellan of Salisbury Castle as one of the new custodians appointed to the royal castles under clause 24 of the Provisions of Oxford (June 1258), a year before becoming warden of Clarendon Forest.[201] A decision must have been made to grant him the wardenship *because* he was castellan, and to transfer

---

[193] *CPR 1313-17*, p.631; *CCR 1330-3*, p.7.

[194] *CIM 1399-1422*, p.350.

[195] E.g. G. Foard, 'Medieval Woodland, Agriculture and Industry in Rockingham Forest, Northamptonshire', *Medieval Archaeology* 45 (2001), pp.41-95; G.P. Maidment, 'An Analysis of Development and Change in the Settlement and Land Use of the Forests of Bere and Stanstead, Circa A.D. 400 to A.D. 1550, with Special Reference to the Village of Rowlands Castle and its Surrounding Area' (unpublished dissertation, Advanced Certificate in Local History, King Alfred's College, Winchester, 1992).

[196] F. Duceppe-Lamarre, 'L'Archéologie du paysage à la Conquete des milieux forestiers: ou l' objet paysage vu par l' archéologue de l' environnement', *Hypothèses 1998: Travaux de l' Ecole doctorale d'Histoire, Publications de la Sorbonne* 2 (1998), pp.85-93 (pp.87, 85).

[197] Smith, 'The New Forest', pp.12, 14-17.

[198] Stephen was outlawed and Richard and John were hanged in the presence of the king, perhaps also at Clarendon (Meekings, *Crown Pleas*, p.205).

[199] ...*quida(m) latron(e)s incogniti quenda(m) ho(m)i(n)em ignotu[m] infra p(re)cinctu(m) d(o)m(ini)ci d(o)m(ini) Regis de Claryngdon felonice int(er)fecerunt cui(us) nom' penit(us) ignora(n)t & ip'm de pannis & alijs bonis suis spoliaru(n)t & dep'darunt que mortuu' undu' in fossato de Sharpegrove...no(n) est infra aliquam villat' s' est de d(o)m(ini)co d'm Reg' de Claryngdon unde tam de corona ut de huiusmodi homicidijs & alijs felonijs & t(ra)nsgressionib(us) quibuscumq(ue) infra metas d(i)c(t)i d(o)m(ini)ci d(omi)ni Regis ibid(e)m illatis & p(er)petratis q(ua)m etiam de viridi & venac(i)o(n)e ad Custode & viridar' & alios ministros p(re)d'c'e foreste de Claryngdon & no(n) ad alique alii spectat cognicio & execution* (PRO E 32/281, m.4).

[200] *CPR 1354-8*, p.198; Grant, *VCH Wilts*, p.430; *CCR 1268-72*, p.565.

[201] Treharne and Sanders, *Documents of the Baronial Movement*, pp.81, 91, 103, 113; *CPR 1258-66*, p.28.

the centre of forest operations to Old Sarum by November 1259 — 'those to whom [Walerand] delegated the...*stewardships*' had gone also to the Castle.[202] Should civil war ensue, it would be foolhardy for the forest administration to remain centred in an unfortified palace, surrounded by forest inhabitants forbidden to bear arms.[203] Most importantly, combining the office of castellan and forest warden would ensure efficient utilisation of forest resources for provisions and fortifications. Henceforward, for a time, Clarendon, like many forests, was attached to the maintenance not of a palace but a castle. The administration remained there for around thirteen years, and there is evidence of continued co-operation and provisioning. The seven tuns of wine transferred to the castle from the palace in October 1261 almost certainly represent siege preparations, and indeed Salisbury briefly fell to the rebels the following June. When fighting again came dangerously close in 1264, Clarendon oaks were sent to the Castle for fortification, and underwood for the hearth along with 'anything [else] which is required'.[204]

In June 1266, it appears again to have been considered expedient to press into service the forest's resources under a warden/castellan. Robert of Glastonbury, previously custodian at Dover, was granted 'the Castle of Salisbury and the Forest of Clarendon'.[205] At this time renewal of war remained a real danger. The increasingly desperate rebels were active in neighbouring Hampshire in 1266, and the Earl of Gloucester's support for the disinherited in 1267 left Salisbury between his vast interests in the south west, and the centre of resistance in the south east.[206] In May 1267, six *robora* were ordered for Robert (referred to solely as castellan) for the Castle's provisioning 'without delay', and in July, the sheriff was ordered to attend urgently to its repair. In December 1267, when the threat of renewed war had passed, Robert surrendered the Castle, 'with armour and stock' to William de Dun, sheriff from November of that year.[207]

Grant considers only those appointed by letters patent to have been wardens of Clarendon,[208] but whether this was the understanding at the time is another matter. William de Dun, sheriff November 1267-May 1270,[209] seems to have seen things rather differently. Presumably he assumed a precedent had been set, and he came close to prosecution at the forest eyre for presuming to take the warden of Clarendon's estover for himself.[210] Yet Dun is referred to in June 1269, as 'lately custodian of the forest of Clarendon', indicating a degree of confusion. He may have been Robert of Glastonbury's deputy, but he seems to have presumed he was, *de jure*, warden — a view the justices did not share.

In the next warden, Stephen de Eddeworth (warden 1269-73) the crossover of jurisdictions is most evident. Although both he and de Dun were sheriffs of Wiltshire, and each (apparently) held the bailiwick of the warden of Clarendon, unlike William, Stephen is described explicitly as due the same customs as previous incumbents, as well as the obedience of the foresters.[211] He became sheriff in May 1270, and retained the wardenship until Henry III's death in 1272, when, as was customary, his tenure was terminated.[212] By this time, the forest's administration had been at Salisbury Castle for thirteen years, and a mix of jurisdictions thereafter is hardly surprising.

The close association between royal forests and castles has been well-rehearsed, most recently by Creighton.[213] Clarendon Forest was never attached explicitly to the castle at Old Sarum in the period studied, but it may have been earlier given the castle's location on what may have been the north-west fringes of the once-larger forest.[214] Indeed, it is likely that the palace usurped many of the castle's functions as a venue for forest courts, a prison for forest trespassers, and the major royal residence in the locality. Nevertheless in the case of Salisbury, forest resources during Henry III's reign seem to have gone chiefly to the Castle. The cathedral drew from a wider area.[215] In 1236 wood from the warden of Clarendon's bailiwick went to works at the Castle and its chapel, in

---

[202] (My italics) 'Since the king has entrusted to Robert Walerand both his castle at Salisbury, and custody of his houses and forest of Clarendon during his pleasure, and those to whom he had delegated the care of the said stewardship are staying in the aforesaid castle as the king allowed, the king gave permission to him that they should take a reasonable estover which the warden of Clarendon was accustomed to take in the aforesaid forest to burn at Clarendon by view of the foresters and verderers of the same forest...as long as he shall have custody of the aforesaid stewardships, just as the king's wardens of Clarendon were accustomed to take it in former times' (*CCR 1259-61*, p.13).

[203] Only foresters were allowed, under forest law, to carry weapons in the forest. In the 1242 Assize of Arms, those who dwelt in forests were explicitly excluded from an otherwise virtually universal obligation to bear arms (Carpenter, 'English Peasants', p.13).

[204] *CLR 1260-7*, p.69; Treharne and Sanders, *Documents of the Baronial Movement*, p.42; *De quercubus ad operaciones Castri Sarr'.- Mandatum est custodi foreste de Clarendon' quod habere faciat Radulfo Russel, constabulario castri Sar' decem quercus ad barreras, scalas et alia necessaria in predicto castro inde facienda, et xiij. carretatas de subbosco ad focum et alia quibus indiget in castro predicto* (*CCR 1261-4*, p.339).

[205] *CPR 1258-66*, p.603.

[206] Prestwich, *Edward I*, pp.56, 58.

[207] *CCR 1264-8*, pp.310, 419; *CPR 1266-72*, p.174 (and see Anon., *List of Sheriffs for England and Wales from Earliest Times to A.D. 1831:*

Compiled from Documents in the Public Record Office, Lists and Indexes Series 9 [New York: Kraus Reprint Corporation, 1963]).

[208] Grant, *VCH Wilts*, p.429.

[209] Anon., *List of Sheriffs*, p.152.

[210] *Rex justiciariis suis itinerantibus ad placita foreste in comitatu Wiltes' salutem. Cum dilectis et fidelis noster Willelmus de Dun, constabularis castri nostri Sar', ceperit buscam in foresta nostra de Clar'...ad comburendum in castro predicto...set ipsum inde quietum esse permittatis* (*CCR 1268-72*, p.172).

[211] *CPR 1266-72*, p.336. 'Grant to Stephen de Eddeworth of the manor and forest of Clarendon to keep during pleasure, so that he answer for the issues at the Exchequer. Grant also that he take of the said issues as much as other keepers have taken in the past. Mandate to William de Dun to deliver the manor and forest to him. Writ *de intendo* to the foresters and others'.

[212] Stephen was sheriff from May 1270-May 1272 (Anon., *List of Sheriffs*, p.152); *CPR 1266-72*, p.336.

[213] Creighton, *Castles and Landscapes*, pp.185-8.

[214] Cf. Creighton, *Castles and Landscapes*, p.187.

[215] For example one hundred oaks from the Forest of Dean in 1236 (*CCR 1234-7*, p.280).

1237 he was commanded to cause the bailiff of Salisbury to have twenty oaks for shingles for works there, and in 1241 the sheriff was to take wood from Clarendon and/or Groveley for the same.[216] But from Edward I's reign there is a decided drop in the provision of forest resources for the castle, by now was almost wholly given over to the shrievalty and rarely visited by the king. Occasionally the king's houses there were repaired, as in 1316 when the limekiln used was fired by 15 leafless Clarendon oaks, and in 1320, when 30 timber oaks from the forest were used. But the castle appears in later calendars chiefly as a jail, the final mention of repairs occurring in 1383.[217]

In 1339, Clarendon lumber had again been sent to Salisbury Castle in time of war 'because the king wishes the castle to be supplied, as his enemies propose to invade the realm', and the sheriff was ordered to pay costs to the warden, receive the underwood and deliver it to the castle.[218] But the kind of amalgamation that had taken place during the Barons' Wars did not occur. By now the Crown was endowed with unprecedented resources through systems of direct and indirect taxation.[219] Royal forests were no longer regarded as economically essential, and the forest officers stayed put in the palace. In contrast, during the more immediate dangers of Henry III's civil wars, when the forest was seen as one of the Crown's most important resources, the move to Old Sarum had helped to preserve Clarendon Forest's smooth-running.

The Social and Administrative Landscape

Forest Serjeanties
It is no coincidence that both the wood and cross of the forester of fee John de Grimstead (d.1288) feature in Clarendon Forest's medieval perambulations.[220] Because their office was hereditary and they lived in their loci of power, foresters of fee made a greater impression on local communities than did wardens, who were usually outsiders.

The services rendered by Clarendon's thirteenth- and early fourteenth-century tenants-in-chief reflected the presence of both forest and palace. For example it is recorded in 1249 that John of Forstbury held property by gift of William de Loveras, forester of fee for Buckholt (whose family kept wolfhound kennels at the Livery, Winterslow, and at Cowesfield for the lands they held in

chief there) for the service of hunting wolves.[221] William de Heyras' *inquisition post mortem* of 1257 records that he held land in Alderbury of the king by keeping a pack of harriers at the king's cost, and Stephen Turpin took seisin in 1327 of property held 'by service of a fourth part of a knight's fee and of making a drink of claret for the king at the king's expense when he come to Claryndon'.[222]

As for the foresters of fee, the de Grimsteads, of Norman descent, were granted their office and estates by subinfeudination from Waleran after the Conquest. They held the keepership of Melchet Park by service of 40s. fee farm yearly 'to be rendered by the hands of the bailiff of Clarendon'.[223] The de Laverstocks held a moiety of their land of the king in chief, in the village of the same name, for the service of keeping Clarendon Forest and the other half, which included Mumworth Mill, of the prior of Ivychurch. In Milford the de Milfords occupied a virgate of land of the king for the same service, and the most complicated serjeanty was held by the de Pittons, Clarendon's riding foresters. James de Pitton's *inquisition post mortem* of 1255 records that he held a virgate in Wiltshire of the king by service of 'keeping the forest by himself or another horseman and two foot serjeants at his own cost'. He performed these duties under (or alongside) the de Loveras foresters in Buckholt Forest, in which he also held land, rendering 20s. to 'the king's keeper of Clarendon'. By the mid-fourteenth century, the de Pittons also had charge of Clarendon Park, for which they had to find a forester.[224]

By the later fourteenth century, most of the above offices were sinecures, the services transmuted to peppercorn rents (see Table 6). Even the wardenship was subject to the same, William Beauchamp being granted the keeping of Clarendon Forest and Park after the death of Humphrey Duke of Gloucester in 1447, in tail male, at the rent of a pair of gilt spurs.[225]

The foresters of fee were effectively a 'closed' systact. But it will be seen below that such hereditary offices brought a measure of independence and access to authority from which women, for example, might otherwise have been excluded. Moreover, Turner has suggested that those living under the sway of hereditary foresters were less likely to suffer from the extortion practiced by appointed officers not entitled to the same customary perquisites.[226] Clarendon's medieval foresters of fee *were* indicted from time to time of a number of offences, but this usually occurred either when kings required extra income (as in the notoriously harsh eyres of Robert Passelewe and Geoffrey of Langley between

[216] *CCR 1234-7*, pp.280, 474; *CCR 1237-42*, p.367 (oaks for the roof of the castle's tower from Clarendon and underwood from either Clarendon or Groveley for its hearth).
[217] *CCR 1313–18*, p.357; *CCR 1318–23*, p.193; *CCR 1381-5*, p.340.
[218] *CCR 1339–41*, p.61.
[219] S. Walker, 'Civil War and Rebellion', in *An Illustrated History of Late Medieval England* (Manchester: Manchester University Press, 1996), ed. C. Given-Wilson, pp.229-47 (p.242).
[220] The *c.*1300 perambulation of Melchet was walked by Andrew de Grimstead (see Anon., 'The Perambulations of the Forests in Wiltshire', *WAM* 4 [1939], pp.197-8 [p.199]).

[221] Parsons, *Pancet*, p.81; *CCR 1242-7*, p.46.
[222] *CIPM Henry III, I*, p.101; *CFR 1327-37*, p.53.
[223] *CIPM Edward I, II*, p.416; Parsons, *Pancet*, p.81.
[224] *CIPM Henry III, I*, pp.47, 300, 88; *CCR 1343–6*, p.502.
[225] *CPR 1446-52*, p.55.
[226] Turner, *Select Pleas of the Forest*, p.xxi.

YEAR	HOLDER	ANCIENT HOLDING	SERVICE
1361	John de Tudworth	De Pitton serjeanty	6 barbed arrows per year
1390	Hugh Cheyne	De Milford serjeanty	4 barbed arrows per year
1401	Thomas Lynford (dep. warden)	Property in Laverstock	4 barbed arrows per year
1451	Richard Milborne	De Pitton serjeanty	5 barbed arrows per year

Table 6. Services owed by later foresters at Clarendon.*
* *CFR 1356-68*, p.181; *CFR 1445-52*, p.256; *CFR 1383-91*, p.325; *CCR 1399-1402*, p.440.

1244 and 1252),[227] in response to pressure from forest landholders, or at times of regime change when they might be discredited along with outgoing wardens. Moreover because they are traceable through a wide range of documents (unlike wardens, for example), there has tended to be an over-emphasis on the reported failings of foresters, with little consideration of possible reasons behind those failings.

Extortion
In 1383 a mandate was issued ordering a writ of *supercedas* to Philip Dauntsey, who had petitioned the king that:

> at the procurement of certain his enemies he is indicted for certain alleged trespasses in [Clarendon Park], and fears that he may be taken and imprisoned; as he is one of the collectors in Wiltesir of the moiety of a tenth and fifteenth last.[228]

Tax-collectors, not surprisingly, were among those local officers most vulnerable to retaliation, especially after the upheavals of the Black Death. [229] Resentment of customary obligations, often manifested as parkbreak and poaching, was endemic. Edward III's forest policy, which was harsh, met with widespread opposition, and many took advantage of royal absences from the country to make wholesale depredations on the deer in forests and parks.[230] Although a post in shire or forest administration might be an honour, certain posts, notably verderer, were unpaid so that officers often sought to reimburse themselves by other means. Indeed, as Ormrod has said, some members of 'gentry' society 'lived virtually double lives, fluctuating between thuggery and respectability'.[231] Equally, as Dauntsey's case shows, forest law might equally be used as a weapon against unpopular persons.

Perhaps the most disliked feature of the forest system was cheminage, partly because of the possibility of extortion on the part of foresters. Incidentally, allegations of its abuse can tell us much about the goods passing through particular bailiwicks. Sometime in the thirteenth century,

the knights of the Forest of Clarendon complained that the foresters took anything they could, including wheat and turves, to the detriment of the *patrie*,[232] and *c*.1330 it was alleged that they 'collected unwarranted cheminage (*indebite Chiminagium*) at 4d. per cart, that is for cartloads of victuals and tiles [presumably carried to and from Alderbury] and even for empty carts (*de car(uc)tis vacius*)'. In Groveley, unwarranted cheminage was also levied on empty carts, cartloads of victuals and, this time, stone, possibly passing from quarries at Tisbury to Salisbury and elsewhere. In addition, every foot-forester in the Clarendon forests had, since the last Forest Eyre, taken for themselves sheaves of corn, ewes, chickens (*collegerunt garbbas...agnos & gallere*) and other goods, against the tenor of the Charter of the Forests.[233]

In the 1355 Forest Eyre, the warden Giles de Beauchamp and his foresters were accused of taking cheminage on the king's highway (*strata*) to Winchester (presumably the Roman road), without the metes and bounds of Westwood, at this time outside the forest, and at ?Lucewood, Sharpegore and elsewhere. This time they levied charges on hay, tiles and wool (*lanarum*) from merchants' packhorses and their carts travelling towards towns, against the tenor of the Forest. [234] As for Groveley, in the 1330 eyre it was estimated that a total of 50 chickens had illegally been taken at Wishford and Bereford by only two foresters in the space of a few years, and it was claimed in 1372 that they went into Wilton and took cheminage from strangers who did not intend even to enter the forest.[235] Perhaps because of their relative isolation the Groveley foresters felt they had a free hand. But this does warrant the question of who was doing the accusing, and why certain officers felt they could behave in such a way while others did not.

A few Clarendon forest officials do stand out as worthy of note, perhaps the most infamous being Andrew de Dodmanstone *c*.1368-72. If his detractors are to be believed, Dodmanstone surpassed any other Clarendon

---

[227] See Stacey, *Politics, Policy and Finance Under Henry III*, p.251; Grant, *Royal Forests*, p.149.
[228] *CCR 1381-5*, p.417.
[229] W.M. Ormrod, *The Reign of Edward III: Crown and Political Society in England 1327-1377* (London: Guild Publishing, 1990), p.156.
[230] Grant, *Royal Forests*, p.167.
[231] Ormrod, *The Reign of Edward III*, pp.156-8 (quote at p.158).

[232] PRO C 47/12/2/9. The turves may have come from Whaddon Turbary on Whaddon common, although in the 1270s turf, bracken and underwood were brought to Salisbury and Wilton by road from the New Forest, presumably through Clarendon or Melchet (Grant, *VCH Wilts*, p.169).
[233] PRO E 32/207.
[234] PRO E 32/267, m.11.
[235] PRO E 32/215, m.1d; ...*colleger(u)nt chim' de div[er]sis ex[tra]neis non venientib(u)s infra forestam nec facien[s] aliq(ui)d cariag(iu)m un' chiminag(iu)m capi deb(er)et* (PRO E 32/218, m.22).

forest official in a spectacular career of bullying, extortion and fraud. Among other things, he allowed twelve paupers to act as stickers, taking 6d. yearly from each of them (when only aged paupers and mendicants should have had the right in exchange for 2 chickens annually); he pocketed the wages of Clarendon's eight foresters and two palicers which the sheriff had entrusted to him; he press-ganged workers of the *patrie* for three years running, led them to Clarendon and forced them to fell oaks ostensibly for deerbrowse, paying them nothing in return and afterwards selling leading the timber for a profit. He also took wood from the park pale and carried it off to Salisbury for his own use, 'wrongfully' imprisoned people (and their dogs) at the palace, and verbally abused others, including the woodward of Bentley Wood.[236]

Significantly, Dodmanstone was a deputy warden rather than a forester of fee, and he may have attracted opprobrium, or acted in the way he did because he was not strictly part of the community he policed. Another notable troublemaker was Robert de Micheldever (d.1327), who broke into the palace in 1311 (above, p. 124). Micheldever does not seem to have been the most sweet-natured of men — he was accused, among other things, of killing Maud Sweinn in Clarendon Forest. But it may be significant that he too rose from forester to become deputy, this time to John de Vienna (warden 1291-c.1308), then warden 1325-7.[237] Again, false imprisonment came high on the list of accusations against Micheldever,[238] and clearly the duty of deputies to throw poachers in the palace gaol did not endear them to forest communities.

The same could be said of Thomas de Bitterley, Giles de Beauchamp's deputy, who along with Beauchamp was accused of myriad offences in the 1330 forest eyre.[239] Deputies, in particular would have been dealt with the foresters on a day-to-day basis, actually carrying out the orders of largely absent wardens, and each might either be newcomers or strangers, or inexperienced in the office. One can imagine the possible effect on foresters of fee who were not only tenants-in-chief, but whose familiarity with the forest went back generations. Giles, however, seems to have been a hands-on warden, which ironically may have earned him the same type of opprobrium — after all it was the foresters that presented the charges at the eyre — and if the warden was out of royal favour, the crown might take accusers at their word. Giles, warden from 1327-30, was probably hauled over the coals in the 1330 eyre as a result of his instatement under Isabella and Mortimer, although he later regained the wardenship.[240]

The foresters of the thirteenth-century, when the palace was most frequently visited by the court, seem to have been less disposed to extortion and other trespasses. Those who forfeited their lands in the eyres of Robert Passelewe and Geoffrey de Langley can be discounted, for hardly a forester in the land emerged from them without accusation of wrongdoing, usually of a tenurial nature. Apart from that, the only evidence seems to be an accusation of nuisance by Robert de Mucegros that Robert de Laverstock and Richard de Meleford 'unjustly raided up a certain dike in [Milford]'.[241] Mucegros withdrew by licence, suggesting an out-of-court settlement, which was probably usual in such cases.

One more case should be considered; that of the forester of fee Robert de Milford (also Robert Osgodsby), who cut off the right hand of a citizen of Salisbury in the city.[242] This probably had little or nothing to do with his office. What is noteworthy is that among his pledges were Philip Goion, verderer, John de Nevill, agister and John Cusyn, whose family held various offices in the forest throughout the period studied.[243] Indeed there is much scope for a study of such social networks in the forest eyre rolls. To take just one family as an example, William de Harnham appears in the list of townships and verderers for the 1355 eyre. John de Harnham is present as a verderer or regarder, fined 2s.8d. for his fee, then as pledge for Walter Waleys, a poacher, and as juror assessing the lands of Richard de Tudworth, which had been taken into the King's hands. The petty misdemeanours of the family are also listed. John (by pledge of Oliver de Harnham) was himself fined £20 for coming into Clarendon Park and taking one buck and two does in 1346-7, four does and a fawn in 1350 and 1351, and had 'the most part' of the venison taken by Robert of Donyton in the forest of Groveley in 1352-3. In the section covering the pleas of the vert, even more Harnham misdemeanours are recorded, presumably facilitated by their office as underwood vendors. William took two oak saplings worth 9d. and other wood worth 2s. from Clarendon and was fined 20s.; John had 6 cartloads of green wood (*vigarum*) from the forester of Groveley and four ?apple trees (*p[om]er'*) from Clarendon Park, as well as having taken illegally cheminage and goods from forest malefactors.[244]

Such relationships must have involved negotiation and arbitration, and it is in the forest eyre rolls that we see the most strongly the forest officers acting as a community. Indeed it should not be forgotten, especially in a study such as this, that forest landscapes, both administrative

[236] PRO E 32/318, m.22.

[237] Pugh, *Gaol Delivery*, p.104; PRO E 32/214; *CFR 1319-27*, p.355; Grant, *VCH Wilts*, p.441.

[238] PRO E 32/215, m.1.

[239] E.g. PRO E 32/207, mm.6d. Like any other forest offender, Giles went to prison until he was bailed (PRO E 32/207, m.7).

[240] Although he would have had to resign his post on the death of the old king. Beauchamp was reinstated for life in December 1330, and held

the wardenship until 1354 (Grant, *VCH Wilts*, pp.441-2), in time for another round of accusations in the 1355 eyre. Indeed, he and Bitterley were again pardoned of several misdemeanours in 1354 and 1357 (*CPR 1354-8*, pp.95; 179, 180, 505).

[241] Clanchy, *Civil Pleas*, p.331.

[242] Pugh, *Gaol Delivery*, p.143.

[243] Pugh, *Gaol Delivery*, p.152. They were each fined ½ mark since Robert, presumably, had fled (*loc. cit.*).

[244] E 32/267, mm.10, 12d.

and physical, were full of people. Equally, the purpose of forest eyres was to make money, and trespasses like those of the Harnhams meant little once they had paid their fines. Men like de Micheldever and de Dodmanstone seem to have been the exceptions to the rule at Clarendon, and it may be postulated that comparatively frequent royal visits to the palace as well as the presence of hereditary foresters acting (on the whole) with the community, curbed serious malpractice.

The misdemeanours of sixteenth- and seventeenth-century foresters have been discussed in Chapter Two, and it is noteworthy — although not entirely unexpected — that at this time they concerned wood rather than deer. Indeed the 'stickers of Salisbury' almost entirely replaced poachers in the record (see above, p. 52), despite the high numbers of deer in the park in the early post-medieval period.

The amount of timber allegedly taken surreptitiously by appointed foresters in the sixteenth and seventeenth centuries (above, pp. 51-52) suggests that Turner may have had a point concerning hereditary foresters of fee. It has been said that at that time there was 'a gap in the lower levels of law enforcement' generally,[245] although it was actually the *structures* of power that had changed — the gentry were 'reinvented... in service mode' — so that the early modern foresters probably appear more lawless than they actually were.[246] Instead of the more localised forest courts there were the special commissions (PRO E 178) — Letters Patent authorising named individuals to carry out certain functions on the monarch's behalf. This was part of the Tudor Government's partnership with the county gentry, and it can be seen in the efficiency with which Alexander Thistlethwaite, for one, acted as a regarder.[247] It is likely that Tudor and Stuart legislation, under which regarders policed foresters in return for their income (see above, p. 51), had a divisive effect on communities of forest officers, as did the much larger fines involved, whereas medieval social ties were probably strengthened by systems of pledges and co-operation.

Nevertheless, despite the greater efficiency of the Tudor 'gentry commonwealth',[248] we are largely in the dark concerning the sixteenth- and seventeenth-century foresters' treatment of forest inhabitants. The extent to which their transgressions resulted from the new requirement to write everything down, or from increased distance from their overlords must also be open to question. But it must be significant that the forest officers now effectively policed themselves, ruling over a closed landscape (the park) bounded by banks, ditches and pale, with little regular outside interference.

Customs of Inheritance and Marriage

The intention here is to ascertain whether Clarendon was in any way 'special' in respect of custom, especially in relation to gender since Rackham cites the presence of independent women in forests as an indicator of non-peasant economies.[249] One such woman was Margaret Huse, carter, who fulfilled in person the duties of her late husband Philip during works in the park from 1492-5.[250] However, most of the evidence available, especially concerning tenure, relates to women of rather higher social standing.

The custom in Clarendon Forest in the early part of the period studied was, as elsewhere, inheritance in fee simple where in the absence of male heirs property was divided equally between daughters. Indeed the hereditary wardenship had come to an end in just such a way after the death *c.*1200 of Walter Walerand, one of whose three daughters was married to John of Monmouth,[251] although assisted in no small measure by the king, who eventually overrode the hereditary principle. It is likely that this had a great deal to do with the palace, *i.e.* the king wished to use the wardenship as an instrument of patronage, and thus to maintain tight control over Clarendon Forest.[252]

While tail male and uses were increasingly employed at Clarendon, as elsewhere, from the early fourteenth century, the custom of female inheritance — or at least inheritance through the female line — seems to have been sufficiently entrenched to encourage fee simple to continue. Sometimes the agency of the landholders, rather than of the Crown, can be observed, as in 1397 when Joan Stulard and Joan Syward, widow of a tenant-in-chief, demised land at Winterslow in fee simple without the king's license. Other measures also allowed the custom to prevail. For example Stephen Turpin inherited his lands and Claret-making serjeanty in 1327

---

[245] David Loades, *Power in Tudor England* (Basingstoke: Macmillan Press, 1997), p.31.

[246] Loades, *Power in Tudor England*, p.156.

[247] E.g. PRO E 101/140/14, m.5. See also above, p.196.

[248] Loades, *Power in Tudor England*, p.156.

[249] Rackham, *The Last Forest*, p.87. Rackham was discussing the period 1100-1460, the last century of which, of course, has been claimed as 'a golden age' for women, although this is a subject of some dispute (see Bennett, *Women in the Medieval English Countryside*, p.5).

[250] Margaret is found being paid 'for herself and her cart', carrying posts, rails and paleboards between Winchester Gate and Sleygate, and carting timber, lime, sand, tiles and water to Queen Manor (PRO E 101/460/16).

[251] *Joh(ann)es de Monemue q(ui) h[abui]t una(m) filiaru(m) Walt(er)i Walerand' cu(m) t(er)cia par(te) he(re)ditatis sue .xiij. m. (et) .iiij. s. (et) v. d. de v₃ feod' (et) dim[idiam] (et) .vj. p(ar)te J(us) . f. scil(ice)t de t(er)cia p(ar)te .xx. feodo(rum) q[?uod] ide(m) W[alterum - damaged] tenuit de .R(egis).*

Albreda de Bot'ell' alt(er)a filiar(um) .xiij. m. (et) .iiij. s. (et) v. d. de al(ter)ia t(er)cia p(ar)te p(re)d(i)c(t)or(um) feodor(um)

Will(elmu)s de Neouill' q(ui) h(abe)t t(er)tia(m) filia(m) .xiij. m. (et) .iiij. s. (et) v. d. de t(er)tia p(ar)te eor(un)d(em) feodor(um)...(PRO E 372/62, m.2);

'The lord king has granted to John of Monmouth the bailiwick of Clarendon with its appurtenances...to have until an inquiry is made, commissioned by the king himself, of that bailiwick which pertains by right to the bailiwick of the New Forest, which the same John holds by inheritance of his wife' (*CCR 1227-31*, p.79).

[252] Despite the presence of Ludgershall Castle, Chute Forest was treated differently, its wardenship remaining hereditary under the Esturmy family from 1083-1427, then the Seymours until 1675 (Bond, 'Forests, Chases, Warrens and Parks', p.124).

as son and heir of Matilda, wife of Nicholas de Perschut, who had held his property 'by courtesy of England of the inheritance of [Matilda]'.[253]

Courtesy of England, also known as English Law, allowed husbands to retain their deceased wives' property for life as long as they had had issue. If they had no surviving children, as was apparently the case with the Perschuts, it passed to the woman's own heirs. [254] Similarly Robert Osgodsby held land in Milford Richard in 1316 by English Law of the inheritance of his late wife Agnes, who had brought him the de Milford forestership of fee.[255] Thus in the thirteenth and fourteenth centuries the employment of borough English at Clarendon continued to facilitate inheritance in the female line.

Although women transmitted property, their husbands of course controlled it while they lived. Nevertheless, women might inherit and hold joint office. This seems particularly to have been the case concerning the Heyras and de Milford serjeanties, masters of the king's hounds and foresters of fee respectively. In 1250 Alicia de Heyras took over her late husband's property and post as master of the king's harriers. She remarried in 1253, when her new husband, John Spruet, assumed the surname Heyras, as did a 'Henry Heyras' who occupied the property in 1272.[256] Then in 1320, after Ralph de Heyras' death, his heir Christina took over the office with her husband, and nine years later their granddaughter and her husband in turn held joint seisin.[257]

In 1349, the Heyras property in Alderbury was taken into the king's hands due to the death not only of the heir but also his mother Eleanor, described as tenant-in-chief. Eleanor's mother Matilda (note not her mother *in law*), widow of Richard Heyras, held a third of the property in dower by knight service, and the remainder passed again to the female line. One heir was Eleanor's sister Joan, wife of William de Harnham, and the other Robert Pipard, son of her sister Agnes.[258] As to the de Milford property, in 1361 Joan, sister and heir of John de Tudworth, holder of the forestership, inherited. She was already married to Hugh Cheyny, and they were jointly enfeoffed. On being widowed in 1390, Joan inherited the 42½ acres of land and property in Milford Richard and Laverstock in her own right by doing fealty in person, receiving the issues of the bailiwick taken since Hugh's death.[259]

This said, it does not seem that Clarendon had a particularly distinctive tradition where land tenure was concerned, unlike, for example, Rockingham Forest, where the deceased's property was customarily divided between elder and younger sons.[260] As elsewhere the use, which might disinherit female heirs since feoffees had to dispose of land according to the foeffor's last will, was increasingly taken up as was fee tail, a device increasingly popular from the late thirteenth century whereby land might pass only to the grantee's direct heirs.[261] In addition such female inheritance, although doubtless owing much to the preferences of the families involved, can also be read in terms of seigneurial control. That specialised duties such as handling the royal hounds remained within the same, experienced families could only benefit the king.

At Groveley there was a similar, and perhaps even stronger tradition. In 1249 Matilda, daughter of Roger the Forester of Groveley 'who is in the king's gift' was married to William Quentin.[262] But they each held full seisin, and Matilda's 1283 *inquisition post mortem* confirms her as both forester of Groveley and tenant-in-chief. It reveals also that she had demised land to her daughter in free marriage. Like the custom of England, this was a provision whereby property, intended to pass only to the heirs of the woman's body, was granted on marriage. Most tellingly, although William Quentin seems not to have died until 1307, Matilda was described as the daughter, not the wife, of a forester.[263]

Women foresters were prominent at Groveley through the fourteenth and fifteenth centuries. The eyre roll of 1355 shows that Edith Peverell, widow of another William Quentin, was active in her office as forester of fee of the southern bailiwick.[264] At least, she actively pursued her customary rights, although like her male contemporaries she held by serjeanty of finding a man to fulfil her duties. Then in 1419 it was found that on the day of her death Elizabeth Stabbere — presumably widowed but not mentioned as such — had held in chief property in Great Wishford by service of keeping the 'le Northbaille, as Grimsditch divides' (see Figure 63), claiming throughout the year her rights as forester of housebote, haybote, firebote, fern (*fuegeriam*) and pasture. Elizabeth's heir

[253] *CPR 1396-9*, p.166; *CFR 1327-37*, p.53.

[254] Rigby, *English Society*, p.263.

[255] *CPR 1313-17*, p.470. Agnes' heir, Robert Cole, granted the reversion to Richard de Tudworth.

[256] Because of this, it has been suggested that new husbands of female heirs at Clarendon customarily took the family name. Although they may as well have done, since the surname refers to the office of master of the harrier pack its adoption in the thirteenth century is hardly surprising (Parsons, *All the King's Men*, p.32).

[257] Parsons, *All the King's Men*, pp.32-3.

[258] *CFR 1347-56*, p.169.

[259] *CFR 1356-68*, p.181; *CFR 1383- 91*, p.332; PRO E 372/207, *rot.*40.

[260] Bennett, *Women in the Medieval English Countryside*, pp.14-15.

[261] Rigby, *English Society*, p.265.

[262] Meekings, *Crown Pleas*, p.247; *Excerptae Rotulis Finium 1246-1272*, p.91.

[263] 'Maud, daughter of Roger Wodeward - Wilts. *Inq.* - Thursday after St Andrew, 12 Edward I. - Bereford. A messuage and two virgates of land held of the king in chief by keeping a moiety of the king's forest of Groveley, rendering 9s. yearly at the Exchequer by the hand of the sheriff of Wiltshire and to the smithy of the church of St Mary, Salisbury 12d. yearly; and one virgate of land excepting 9a. which she gave with her daughter in free marriage in the sixth year of King Edward, held of the prioress of Amesbury rendering 8s. yearly.' (*CIPM Vol. II: Edward I*, p.271); *CCR 1307-13*, p.502; G.J. Stampley, *Law and Abstraction in Twelfth, Thirteenth and Fourteenth-Century England: The Case of the Maritagium and the Gift in Tail* (http://www.whiterose.org/ginger/writing/swssa.html).

[264] PRO E 32/267, mm.7d., 11d.

was her sixteen-year-old sister Joan atte Nend, whose husband John Wylton was to do fealty, although again they were jointly enfoeffed.[265]

By 1421 John and Joan had died, Joan's heirs being her paternal aunts Edith and Agnes. Again, while their husbands took fealty the escheator was to 'cause [them] and their wives to have full seisin'. In 1434, Edith and her husband John Stone together were found to have held the office of forester of Groveley in Edith's right, and since they had died childless the forestership was taken into the king's hands.[266]

Perhaps not coincidentally, the forestership of Groveley's southern bailiwick, along with the manor of Barford St Martin, was granted by Edward IV to his sister Anne, Duchess of Exeter in 1461 (renewed 1467), the reversion granted in 1469 to his queen, Elizabeth Woodville.[267] There are similarities here with the de Milford holding at Clarendon, which possessed similar gendered associations in the thirteenth century (see below, p. 34).

As Bennett points out, only when seigneurial controls eased did property-holders eschew local customs and 'closely [follow] the common law in granting husbands extensive control over all conjugal properties', and it is probable that sustained seigneurial supervision of landholding worked to women's advantage, especially when the landlord was not only the king, but was largely absent.[268] This seems to have been the case at Clarendon, and certainly at Groveley, while royal interest continued. The custom in ancient demesnes was for both sexes of free blood to marry where they liked.[269] However, this seems not to have been the case at Clarendon, at least by the 1270s,[270] again suggesting strong royal control over the social landscape. For example in 1255 James de Pitton's widow Hawise's dower was assured on condition that she would not marry without the king's licence, for which agreement she was to provide security.[271] Yet Hawise's promise suggests that marriage without the king's licence *did* occur, or at least had occurred in the past.

In 1305 Agnes, daughter and heir of the forester of fee Richard de Milford, took seisin of her father's lands and serjeanty 'by service of keeping the...forest by one [foot-

forester]'.[272] Two months later an order was issued to the justice of the forest this side Trent not to molest or aggrieve Agnes for her marriage since it had been found by inquisition that the de Milford lands together with the marriage of the heirs had been granted to the late queen, Eleanor of Castile (d.1290). Apparently Agnes had 'satisfied William le Noble, who had her marriage by the grant of James Daubenay, to whom the queen had granted it, for her marriage'. This may indicate that Agnes had indeed married where she pleased, her husband being Robert Osgodsby (known as 'de Milford'), who held her property after her death in 1316 by English Law.[273]

Thus Agnes de Milford appears to have inherited the forestership in her own right, and may have had a degree of control over her own marriage. It is perhaps no coincidence that before the de Milford lands and forestership went to Eleanor of Castile, they had been granted in 1281 to Eleanor of Provence (d.1293), during the minority of Richard de Milford's heirs 'with the bailiwick of the said forestry',[274] and it is possible that the association with high-status women gave the de Milford women increased scope for agency.

Negotiation
Thus at Clarendon as elsewhere, quasi-hereditary positions such as foresterships of fee gave women scope for entry into public offices and access to influence, especially if they were widows. But what of those — men and women — lower down the social scale? In the types of sources available they are generally invisible. But the frequency or infrequency of royal visits must have been a factor in their relationship with their royal overlords, and in the light of other studies it is likely that where disputes arose people felt encouraged to approach the king in person when he was in residence. David Crook has found that the thirteenth-century inhabitants of the royal manors of Clipstone and Mansfield were emboldened by the idea that they were royal tenants, however low they might be in the social strata, and Bennett cites similar evidence for the manor of Brigstock in Rockingham Forest.[275] The downside, of course, is that because of the presence of the palace and frequent royal visits, there was little opportunity for the kind of initiatives in cutting back woodland noted elsewhere, even as close as Melchet.

Because of the king's position as supreme landlord at Clarendon, he was of course alluded to in the records of the eyre. Thus in a case of mort d'ancestor, the deforciant could not 'answer...without the King [who]...enfeoffed him of that land by his charter, which he proffers and which attests this'.[276] But the king is mentioned only on one other occasion in the cases

---

[265] PRO E 32/267, m.16; *CFR 1413-22*, pp.306-7. In contrast the South Bailey had devolved in tail male since at least 1397 (*CPR 1396-9*, p.122).

[266] *CFR 1413-22*, p.369; *CPR 1429-36*, p.343.

[267] *CPR 1461-7*, p.104; *CPR 1467-77*, pp.32, 137.

[268] Bennett, *Women in the Medieval English Countryside*, p.114.

[269] D. Crook, pers. comm.

[270] This is evident in the case of Agnes, daughter and heir of Adam Cook (warden c.1239-47). Land to the value of £10 had been bestowed on Adam, which he held by paying 6*d.* rent to the king at Clarendon Palace. Agnes married Robert Pipard, who died childless, whereupon Henry III 'granted the marriage of...Agnes to Henry de Candevre'. Agnes herself then died without issue, whereupon Edward I granted the property to de Candevre for life. Subsequently it reverted to the Crown as escheat (*CIPM Edward I, II*, p.167).

[271] *CCR 1254-6*, p.71.

[272] *CCR 1302-7*, p.270.

[273] *CCR 1302-7*, pp.285; *CPR 1313-17*, p.470.

[274] *CPR 1272-81*, p.425.

[275] D. Crook, pers. comm.; Bennett, *Women in the Medieval English Countryside*, p.15 and *passim*.

[276] Clanchy, *Civil Pleas*, p.88.

sampled, apart from standard references to forfeited land being taken into his hands, and one account of an acquittal before him 'at Clarendon'. Thus we must conclude that this particular evidence reveals no 'special relationship' with the monarch, any more than that of other forest areas.[277]

This said, that women often took themselves to court to plead their cases may suggest a more general level of expectation among Clarendon's forest-dwellers, built on their status as tenants of the Crown. In 1249 Joan, widow of the serjeant master of the hunt, Richard le Archer, pleaded against the forest warden, Henry le Dun, for a third of her husband's lands as dowry in the Wiltshire Eyre. On Richard's death, the lands had reverted to the king, as was customary, and were occupied by le Dun. Accompanying Joan were her son John and her daughter Hawise, also entitled to a third each, and they were successfully granted a chirograph to that effect. [278] Similarly, Avice and Petronilla, daughters of Jordan de Laverstock successfully petitioned in order to enfeoff their lands in Laverstock, Ford and Alderbury to William and Lucy Randolf in 1333. Most startlingly, in 1356 Joan, widow of John de Grimstead, successfully brought her case of oyer and terminer against the prior of Ivychurch after he and his canons had broken her closes and doors and assaulted her bondmen (above, p. 126).[279]

Clarendon Palace as a Centre of Social Networks

To what extent was the palace a forum for such negotiation? Table 7 is a breakdown of 146 orders concerning local business (the majority of writs issued there in any case) issued at Clarendon from 1204 to 1370 taken from the calendars of rolls.[280] Among other things, it is noteworthy that mandates concerning necessary repairs were issued while the court was in residence rather than before its arrival or after its departure. It is also particularly informative that the forest's resources were issued as gifts when the king visited, presumably after consultation with forest officers. Many such grants were probably given as a direct result of petitions made at the palace, as the appearance of so many local interests in Table 8, drawn from the same sample, indicates. Among the category 'others' is Maurice le Taylur of Laverstock, who was to receive an oak from the forest for repairs to his houses there in 1270, Raymond de Bovisville, granted another along with five cartloads of brushwood for the hedges of his close at Winterbourne in 1271, and the

forester Jordan of Laverstock, allocated two timber oaks, presumably also for building works, in 1280.[281]

Subject of order or mandate	*No. of orders*
Grants of trees and deer (mostly trees)	*64*
Payments into fiscal departments and to forest officers	*29*
Work on the king's houses of Clarendon	*25*
Organisation of the forest and park (e.g. grants of pasture)	*19*
Tenurial matters	*15*
Clearly identifiable reponses to petitions	*7*
Work on Salisbury Castle	*3*
Repairs to park	*3*
Notification of arrival of huntsmen (to Groveley)	*2*

Table 7: Breakdown of Sample of 146 orders issued at Clarendon Palace, 1204-1370.

Recipient of gift	No of gifts from sample
Abbess of Wilton	2
Hospital of St John, Salisbury	1
Treasurer of Salisbury	1
Priory of Ivychurch	2
Mottisfont	1
Friars Preacher, Wilton	4
Earl of Salisbury	1
Prioress of Amesbury	4
Hospital of St Nicholas, Salisbury	3
Hospital of St John, Wilton	2
Dean and Chapter, Salisbury (includes work at Cathedral)	4
Recluse of Britford	6
Friars Minor, Salisbury	4
Bishop of Salisbury	1
Wardens/ex-wardens of Clarendon Forest	3
Friars Preacher, Salisbury	2
Others	23

Table 8. Breakdown of 64 grants of the king's gift (mostly wood resources) given at Clarendon, 1204-1370.

Almost certainly the king or his officials were petitioned personally for the lumber granted. More generally, among other probable petitioners was Ralph de Hegham, chancellor of Salisbury, granted six *robora* in 1267 to compensate for those that Prince Edmund (b.1245) had

---

[277] Meekings, *Crown Pleas*, p.205; Cf. Bennett on Brigstock, *Women in the Medieval English Countryside*, p.15.
[278] Clanchy, *Civil Pleas*, p.66; Parsons, *Little Manor*, pp.9-10.
[279] *CPR 1330-4*, p.476; *CPR 1354-58*, p.386.
[280] The discrepancy between the number of orders sampled and the total number of orders in the table results from the fact that many mandates addressed more than one issue, and in some cases the categories chosen overlap.

[281] *CCR 1268-72*, pp.308, 446; *CCR 1279-88*, p.7.

taken from him, and Walter de Somery who left the palace in 1252 bearing a testification that his ear been cut off 'by some evildoer in the Forest of Clarendon', not because he had committed a felony.[282]

The categories in the tables are, however, arbitrary, and most of the orders probably originated by petition. Even the category entitled 'organisation of the forest and park' encompasses clear responses to requests for the king's grace. These include a 1267 grant to the Hospital of St Nicholas, Salisbury, that they might 'take their timber, brushwood and victuals through Clarendon Forest quit of cheminage', and (a rare glimpse into the interests of lower social strata) an order of 1252 to enclose the king's wood in Groveley so 'that the men of Barford and Wishford should not be inconvenienced by the emparking of their draught animals...When the aforesaid wood shall have regrown, [they] shall have their common rights there just as...before'.[283] Later the same year a similar writ was issued at Winchester, restating Barford and Wishford's common rights providing they kept out of the freshly-hewn coppices, suggesting the villagers felt they were still suffering from the oppression of the foresters and indicating further petitions on their behalf.[284] Other examples include the renewal of letters patent confirming a charter of Henry II to Ivychurch Priory concerning tithes from the forests of Berkshire, Dorset and Wiltshire,[285] and Reginald de Drumar's permission to keep sheep in the forest (see above, p. 43).

Further petitions are apparent in the tenure section of Table 7. It was at the palace in 1255 that Hawise de Pitton, petitioned the king, probably in person, for her 'reasonable dower' (above, p. 141), where Adam Cook was granted land in Fittleton for himself and his heirs in 1246 as he approached the end of his tenure of the forest wardenship, and where in 1258, Peter of Pitton and his wife Eular rendered two marks 'before the king at the palace' for a land-conveyance (*una ass[urantia]*).[286] Homage was also taken at the palace, as in 1256 when Jordan of Laverstock, William de Pitton and Richard de Milford each made fine in order to regain their bailiwicks, taken into the king's hands following the 1240s inquests of Robert Passelewe, in which they had each been accused of malpractice. Later, in 1270 the de Milford bailiwick was transferred to Reginald de Drumar, also at the palace.[287]

Writs issued at Clarendon tail off from the early fourteenth century, due to increasing bureaucratic centralisation. But evidently the palace continued to be a focus for the locality's business. For example Emma,

widow of Thomas Cheynduyt, successfully petitioned for the keeping of the manor of Barford St Martin, Groveley, by mainprise of the Prior of Ivychurch and others.[288] It was at the palace also that Stephen de Pulton was appointed parker in 1317 and where he was pardoned for a forest trespass nine years later, after which he was presumably released from the palace's Marshalsea prison in which he had been languishing.[289] In 1326 the keeper of the manor of Winterslow made oath 'in the king's presence' that he would not send any of the manor's issues, goods or chattels to his lord, John of Cromwell, out of favour for 'staying beyond the seas against the king's will'.[290] Other matters were more exceptional, including, via letters to all forest officers and other bailiffs, protection of one year given to the hermit Brother John of Warwick (see above, p. 133). By the 1350s, however, very few orders were issued at the palace, the last few occurring during Edward III's final visits c.1370.[291]

Figure 85. The annual Oak Apple Day celebration in Great Wishford, asserting the right to gather dry wood in Groveley Forest. Reproduced from B. Short, 'Forests and Wood-Pasture in Lowland England', in *The English Rural Landscape* (Oxford: Oxford University Press, 2000), ed. J. Thirsk, pp.122-49 (p.135).

It remains difficult to ascertain the interest of any but the highest social strata, apart, significantly, from the commoners of Groveley already mentioned (above, p. 143). And although gender has been employed here as a tool to elucidate both the nature of social closure at Clarendon and the extent to which its customs indicate its status as a defined locality, most of the women who appear in the documents, too, are of comparatively high social standing. In some ways this gives a skewed impression. Although widows were clearly dependent on the king for their future welfare, and his control over

[282] *CCR 1264-8*, p.411; *CPR 1247-58*, p.167.

[283] *CCR 1251-3*, p.122.

[284] *CCR 1251-3*, p.434.

[285] *CPR 1266-72*, p.399; *CCR 1256-9*, p.227.

[286] *Excerptae Rotulis Finium, 1246-72, p.280; CCR 1254-6*, p.71; *CHR 1226-57*, p.309.

[287] *Excerptae Rotulis Finium, 1246-72*, pp.234, 236; *CHR 1226-57*, p.455; *CCR 1268-72*, p.307.

[288] *CFR 1268-77*, p.90.

[289] *CPR 1313-17*, p.645; *CPR 1324-7*, p.311.

[290] *CFR 1319-27*, p.407.

[291] *CPR 1334-8*, p.5; A single documentary sealing at Clarendon in August 1371 is the last of Edward's reign (James and Robinson, *Clarendon Palace*, p.40).

women's marriages is evident, it is highly unlikely that royal interference would have been felt to such extents by unlanded women.

In many ways Clarendon was no different from any other locality. Broad shifts in inheritance terms were shared with medieval society in general. Tail male and the employment of uses gradually superceded fee simple, under the terms of which property and office might be divided equally between daughters in the absence of male heirs. But by the fifteenth century there seems to have been a difference in this respect between Clarendon and Groveley Forests, where women still acted as foresters of fee in their own right well into the fifteenth century. As Bennett has said, such women are 'aberrations to be explained, not norms to be used as examples',[292] and they may reflect the independent mindset evident at Groveley throughout the period studied. This is reflected in that forest's enshrined customs (themselves the result of protracted disputes with the earl of Pembroke in the sixteenth century) and its continued existence as a conceptualised landscape and locality to the present day (Figure 85).[293] Such independence is in sharp relief with Clarendon's self-identification with its royal landlords, with Salisbury, the shrievalty, and common law (compared with the New Forest) and was prompted perhaps by Groveley's isolation (compared with Clarendon and Melchet) from its overlord and from the centre of forest administration — each represented by Clarendon Palace.

By the sixteenth century, Clarendon was a royal landscape on the periphery rather than a thriving royal centre. It is notable in mapping the centres of the forest officers (see Figures 34 and 84) that from their early positions scattered throughout the wider forest they policed (especially if Walerand's motte and even Salisbury Castle are taken into account), there is a contraction by the fifteenth-century to the confines of the park, symbolised by the building of the lodges discussed in Chapter Three. This is partly the product of the decline of the forest system, the beginnings of which have been traced through the thirteenth- and fourteenth century perambulations. Indeed after the last perambulations of the 1330s attention shifted overwhelmingly to the park itself, with the building of lodges and other landscape modifications under Edward III. It is notable also that when Henry VII attempted to revive the forest system, attention was again given to outlying lodges, such as that at Groveley.[294] But this was short-lived and by the sixteenth century the park itself was subdivided into walks policed by the forest officers, or 'keepers'. These probably bore no relation to any

arrangement in the medieval period, when the park had come under the jurisdiction only of the de Pittons.[295]

Throughout the period studied the foresters left their mark in both the forest and park, not only on the social landscape through their policing and social networks, but also on the physical landscape, in the perambulations they rode and the boundary markers named for them. The landscape reflected the society that formed it in other ways also. The perambulations and forest eyres echo the 'nibbling away' of the forest's western boundary with the loss of Milford, Laverstock and Britford, and also of the woods inside it, almost certainly due in part to pressure from their owners. Conversely, through the medieval period at least, the boundaries of what was thought of as Clarendon Forest were remarkably static compared to other forests like Chute, despite fluctuations in the size of the 'economic' (or the 'political') forest through time.

Clarendon was an enclave, as were all forests. What made it different from other forests was the presence of the palace. This, and the proximity of Salisbury gave its administration perhaps unique characteristics. Indeed, the forest survived longer than most, largely due to the palace, although the capacity of its bureaucracy to adapt and thrive alongside other jurisdictions was also responsible for its survival. As Grant points out, when Charles II disparked the Park in 1664, he 'alienated the last remnant of the royal forests of Wiltshire'.[296]

In the end, Clarendon was a landscape of control. This is discernible in the social landscape also, especially in inheritance though the female line (which may also have given women access to influence they might not have enjoyed elsewhere). Forest offices were kept in the hand of specialised blood-families, and the king also had the last say where marriage was concerned. But a glance at the writs issued at Clarendon has revealed that if there was conflict there was also scope for negotiation, for which the palace, in the medieval period, was the backdrop.

---

[292] Bennett, p.3.
[293] See The Oak Apple Club of Wishford, *Sum of the Ancient Customs Belonging to Wishford and Barford* (Salisbury: The Salisbury Press, 1930 [WRL])
[294] PRO E 101/460/16.

[295] The de Pittons held in chief a messuage and 20a. of land in Pitton by service of finding a forester for the park (*CCR 1343–6*, p.502).
[296] Grant, *VCH Wilts*, p.401.

Chapter Six: Conclusion — an Actual, Conceptual and Documented Wiltshire Landscape Reconstructed

The main hypothesis of this study, that Clarendon Palace was a fulcrum in the actual and conceptual landscape, has been prominent throughout, whether the palace still functioned or in the vacuum produced by its demise. To an extent this was anticipated at the outset. A major royal residence embellished, from the 1220s, to a state 'only marginally less magnificent than that of the prime palace of the realm'[1] must have had some effect on its environs and the way they were perceived. What was not so expected is the extent to which the palace's 'lifecycle' was shaped by the more cyclical rhythms, administrative *and* ecological, of the forest. This has been elucidated by the focus on *interrelationships,* rather than concentrating on the palace and extrapolating 'outwards'. While it functioned, the palace and its setting were shaped and reshaped not only by royal visits (themselves determined by the breeding cycles of the king's deer), but also by the arrival of forest eyres and other courts.[2] In this way — and in its exploration of social and spatial relations with the city of Salisbury — the study has shed light on the 'relationship of Clarendon Palace to its medieval hinterland', a focus called for since the early 1990s.[3]

The study's main aims have also been achieved. First, the capacity of documentary methodologies to restore the wider conceptual landscape through time and space has been demonstrated. Detailed analysis of forest documents, alongside rather more well-trodden sources relating to the palace and (to a lesser extent) the park, has restored the archaeologically-elusive Clarendon Forest to its undoubted prominence in the medieval locality. Second, the documents have shed light on the management of the forest and park and the ways in which it changed over time. In particular, attention to early modern documents such as regarders' certificates has illuminated how the park was administered, and even thought of, in a period of Clarendon's history acknowledged to have been understudied,[4] and which has left comparatively little trace in the landscape compared to its medieval predecessor and later post-medieval successors.[5]

The decision to tackle a long chronology has been valuable, since it has shed light on wider issues, especially that of whether Clarendon was managed for

pleasure or for profit. It has highlighted fluctuations in the balance between the two, and has revealed Clarendon's place within more general economic trends. As outlined at the end of Chapter Two, the balance between pleasure and profit shifted according to the perceived economic and political needs of the time, and the whims of Clarendon's royal owners. But the profit principle, which came to the fore in periods when the palace was rarely visited by the court, was rarely long-lived, at least before the palace fell out of favour from the early fifteenth century. The park, by its very nature and great size, was essentially a landscape of élite pleasure almost certainly never intended primarily to be profitable in a monetary sense. Perhaps the question should be one of *exclusivity* versus profit, since it has been shown that the park was made more exclusive in reaction to the threatened loss of demesne lands in Clarendon Forest under Edward II, and to the actual loss of forest in Wiltshire in the following reign (above, p. 83).

The nature of the records — largely administrative/governmental throughout the period studied — has aided interpretation. The majority were compiled by officials unfamiliar with the landscape itself. However, the standardisation of information required by central authorities does nothing if not facilitate useful comparisons, for example of Clarendon and Melchet forests. In addition, because Clarendon was in royal hands for so long the documents produced facilitate the opportunity to study a long chronology, not least because, by their very central/administrative nature, their survival has been assured. The extended timescale studied here offers also the chance to observe, through changes in the type and content of written sources themselves, transformations in the social and cultural background that formed the context of their production — for example the hierarchical and formalised mandates for the taking of deer under Edward II and the relatively personal regarders' certificates of the sixteenth and seventeenth centuries. Each gives insight not only into the way the landscape was used, but also how it was perceived.

As the first study to analyse even calendared references to the park and forest systematically (rather than to the palace and its buildings) this project has broken new ground, pointed the way for future research, and enhanced previous knowledge of Clarendon Forest, Park and Palace from *c*.1200–*c*.1650. Apart from a brief period at the turn of the sixteenth and seventeenth centuries, the first 200 years of the study are undoubtedly the best-served in terms of written evidence. This is chiefly due to the detail in the calendars of rolls at this time (*i.e.* chancery and exchequer documents) and in the records of forest eyres up to 1355. Each has enabled this

---

[1] James and Robinson, *Clarendon Palace*, p.8.

[2] See above, pp. 26-29, 59-61, 83-84.

[3] Saunders, Review of James and Robinson, *Clarendon Palace*, p.156. The social and spatial relationships between Clarendon and Salisbury are yet other subjects acknowledged to have been under-explored in the past (James and Gerrard, *Clarendon: A Royal Landscape*, forthcoming).

[4] KACC I, p.62.

[5] The pattern of landuse seen today in Clarendon Park became fixed only around 1812 (James and Gerrard, *Clarendon: A Royal Landscape*, forthcoming), while overall, the park remains a relict medieval park landscape, most of whose buildings date from after the Restoration.

study to shed light on aspects of Clarendon's landscape that have hitherto been under-explored.

Knowledge of Clarendon in the thirteenth century has rested until now on analysis of the close and *liberate* rolls. But these have been used, in chief, to elucidate the phasing of the palace as excavated in the 1930s.[6] By introducing a landscape dimension, this study has introduced valuable new insights. Paradoxically, the approach has provided a more rounded picture of Clarendon Palace, facilitating greater awareness of its place in the wider locality by considering, for example, its effect on the layout of the city of Salisbury. The simultaneous involvement of master masons at the palace and the new city has more than once been noted.[7] However this study has added depth to such bald statements, noting the import of the years 1226-8 in the evolution of city, palace *and* forest. Indeed, an argument was advanced in Chapter Four for a major restructuring of the wider landscape in the 1220s involving the explicit identification of the palace — and the forest as a whole — with the new city, even to the extent that the forest was conceptually reoriented westwards by Henry III in 1228, a year after the city was granted its first charter (see above, pp. 85-87).

Clarendon Forest's thirteenth-century administration has also been well-rehearsed, most comprehensively by Grant in his VCH contribution.[8] But as Colvin has intimated (above, p. 29), the historian of a particular place enjoys the luxury of more detailed inspection of the sources. Most notably, in 'avoiding individual variation...and concentrating on...features...that were typical',[9] writers of more general works (such as Grant and Young) have taken little account of the forest's relationship to the palace. Thus this study is the first to note the decampment of Clarendon's higher forest officers to Salisbury Castle for a full thirteen years, due to the Barons' Wars (see above, p. 135). In considering the effect of the move on the forest's 'administrative landscape', the study has shown that the wardenship became closely identified with the shrievalty and thus became bound yet closer to the city of Salisbury, with concomitant effects on the nature of the forest's particular customs and its law (above, pp. 134-136).

Compared to its administration, Clarendon Forest's thirteenth- and fourteenth-century economy has not been so well-served by historians. An analysis of deer species recorded in the documents has never before been attempted, and although a preponderance of fallow might be expected in a classic medieval deerpark, the species' dominance throughout the entire period studied as indicated by the resulting data is striking (see Figure 15). The results go some way to answering vexed questions

concerning the landscape itself, such as the paucity of watering-holes in the park (see above, p. 29). Similarly, analysis of tree-species ordered in the thirteenth and fourteenth centuries, also hitherto unattempted, has revealed that a coppice-based economy may have operated at Clarendon much earlier than explicit references in the early fourteenth century indicate (see Figure 27 and cf. Figure 26). In addition, this study is the first to analyse thirteenth- and fourteenth century assarting as laid out in the forest eyre documents (PRO E 32/198-267), and its findings provide useful comparisons with Taylor's studies of northern Melchet, undertaken over thirty years ago (above, pp. 190-5).[10] Together with a study of settlement, results show that the palace had a profound effect on its forest locality, discernible in shifts in the settlement hierarchy both at its height and after its demise, and in the restriction of colonisation in the Clarendon Forest. In the end, this was a landscape of control.

Where the palace has been considered, it has been in fresh ways, for example the location of the quarters of its officers and of other ancillary buildings.[11] Moreover, a consideration of the *seasonality* of royal visits, in addition to the more usual analysis of their frequency and duration, has shown that the use of the landscape and of the palace itself was affected by cycles of regrowth and renewal, particularly after periods of overuse of forest resources. One example is a lack of summer visits by Edward III before 1333, by which time hedges and palings had been repaired and the deer population replenished (see above, p. 28). However, it has also been shown that forest resources were granted as gifts when the court was in residence, so that the palace's presence acted in turn on the forest, shaping the very cycles to which it in turn responded.

If the palace reached its zenith in the thirteenth century, the park did so a century later. Indeed this study has shown the fourteenth century to be key to understanding Clarendon's relict medieval landscape, a result that will prove useful in future archaeological and historical interpretations. The changes that took place at this time, and the park's subsequent prominence in the landscape, have been a feature throughout the study, and merit detailed discussion here. The imparkment occurred around 1317; in 1328 coppice-wood was ordered to be made in 'suitable places', followed in 1334 by a mandate to 'make new coppices in the park' and orders to enclose them with hedges in 1336.[12] Finally, ponds were dug and lodges built in the same reign.

Because documents concerning the forest and park have until now been neglected, the park's enlargement itself has hitherto escaped detection. Indeed, the discovery that

---

[6] E.g. James and Robinson, *Clarendon Palace, passim.*
[7] RCHME, *Salisbury: The Houses of The Close*, pp.7, 60; James and Robinson, *Clarendon Palace*, p.9.
[8] Grant, *VCH Wilts*, pp. 427-32.
[9] Young, *The Royal Forests of Medieval England*, p.viii.

[10] Taylor, 'Whiteparish: A Study', *passim*, 'Three Deserted Medieval Settlements', *passim*.
[11] See above, Chapter Three.
[12] *CCR 1327-30*, p.341; *CCR 1333-7*, pp.268-9; *CFR 1327-37*, p.475.

the amount of pale made between 1318 and 1324 constituted roughly the circumference of the park today suggests strongly that this was the first time the entire park as we know it was enclosed (see above, p. 116).[13] This might be considered a locally-specific finding, adding only to the history of a particular landscape and the manner in which it was created and sustained. Clearly, however, it fits into more general themes concerning fourteenth-century imparkment, and makes for interesting comparisons. For example Bond has found indications of medieval short term ploughing campaigns within Woodstock Park which may represent enlargement, and new areas were certainly inclosed there in the 1570s.[14] Such evidence is more than circumstantial. As Hunt puts it, decisions on the establishment of parkland represents a 'positive' or direct influence on the landscape. At the same time it provides a 'negative' or indirect influence on colonisation and settlement, which was effectively deflected elsewhere (in this case, as demonstrated in Chapter Four, towards Melchet).[15]

It is thought that so many royal parks were established in the thirteenth and early fourteenth centuries partly in compensation for a decline in areas under forest law,[16] and certainly, as discussed in Chapter Five, many manors, woods, assarts and lands at Clarendon were listed as 'now outside the forest' in the 1330 eyre. The enclosure may also represent a last great 'push' in land acquisition at a time of peak population growth, effectively deflecting elsewhere encroachments on the royal demesne. There are good grounds for arguing that deerparks contracted both in size and number from 1349, due to labour shortages and changed attitudes towards land-management resulting from disapproval of land kept exclusively (and extravagantly) for deer after the demographic disasters of the early fourteenth century were exacerbated by the Black Death.[17] Certainly more emphasis seems to have been placed on embellishment of the existing park from the 1340s, with the addition of lodges and vast expenditure on the park pale, rather than the acquisition of new land or equivalent modifications to customs such as agistment, which had occurred previously. Indeed a recurrent theme of this study has been the primacy of the park in the landscape in, and after, the reign of Edward III. This must, in part, reflect the preferences of certain kings, i.e. the extent of their personal involvement in hunting. For example Edward III spent prolifically on the hunt, averaging £80 yearly on dogs and huntsmen alone, compared to an annual £18 or less outlayed by both Henry IV and Richard II (neither of

whom visited Clarendon frequently, if at all — probably not coincidentally).[18]

Edward II, under whom the park was enlarged, is not remembered chiefly for his love of hunting. He is, however, supposed to have had what contemporaries considered an unseemly interest in hedging and ditching.[19] One wonders if this reputation owes something to the imparkments instigated by him at Clarendon and elsewhere, for example at Windsor whose park he extended by over a thousand acres.[20] So the extent of 'hedging and ditching' at Clarendon (and Windsor) cast this contemporary criticism in a new light, both in terms of intention and scale. At the very least, changes in the layout of orders to receive the king's huntsmen in Edward's reign reveal the emergence of a more formal, stylised approach to hunting. As touched on in Chapter Two, this may replicate a parallel formalisation and demarcation of hunting landscapes. There is little doubt that the park was becoming a more formalised and administratively-demarcated space at this time. For example the first known launderer was appointed in 1324 (see above, p. 37).

The trenches made by Edward I at Clarendon c.1276 are the antecedents of such demarcation. They may equate to deer-management, and to nascent changes in hunting culture itself, but they were also a source of lumber — in November 1276, the abbess of Wilton was granted 30 oaks 'from the...trenchiis that the king caused to be made'.[21] Similar trenches were excavated elsewhere and opinion is divided on their purpose. For example those dug in Woodstock Park from 1274 are interpreted as 'rides' by Bond.[22] Rackham, on the other hand, equates trenchia entirely with the statute of 1284 which laid down that underwood be kept back from roads in order to prevent highway robbery and murder.[23] This is possible given that the surviving Upper and Lower Trenches on the Clarendon Estate may, before 1317, have been outside the park proper. However in view of the lumber gained and of the early date, Edward I's policy of making the forests profitable appears to have been the prime motivation and, at least at Clarendon they should perhaps be interpreted as clearings. Thus they should be seen alongside the contemporary making of rentable wastes and the subsequent selling-off of resulting lumber at a time when Clarendon was managed more for profit than pleasure. Similarly when in 1303 Robert de Clifford was licensed to make a 'trench' around his wood in Clarendon Forest, he was also given permission to 'sell the wood

---

[13] PRO SC 6/1050/5.
[14] Bond, 'Woodstock Park in the Middle Ages', p.49; 'Woodstock Park in the Sixteenth and Seventeenth Centuries', in *Blenheim: Landscape for a Palace* (Stroud: Sutton Publishing, 1997), eds J. Bond and K. Tiller, pp.55-62 (pp.57-8).
[15] Hunt, *Lordship and the Landscape*, p.140.
[16] J. Bond, 'Deer Parks and Landscape Parks', paper given at *Parks in the Landscape*,
OUDCE conference, October 2000.
[17] Bond, 'Deer Parks and Landscape Parks'.

[18] Given-Wilson, *Royal Household*, p.61.
[19] It was said that the king himself enjoyed digging ditches 'and other unbecoming things' (*intendere circa fossata facienda et ad fodendum et eciam ad alia indecencia* [McKisack, *The Fourteenth Century*, p.95, n.3]).
[20] Astill, 'Windsor', p.11.
[21] *CCR 1272-9*, p.318.
[22] Bond, 'Woodstock Park in the Middle Ages', p.42.
[23] O.Rackham, *Trees and Woodland in the British Landscape* (London: J.M. Dent, 1981), p.112.

which he cuts down in making it'.[24] The fact that the c.1276 trenches facilitated a more open landscape that aided hunting may have been, at least at this time, merely a useful adjunct.

Yet it is the imparkment that represents probably the most significant episode in the phasing of the park's use. At first glance it represents a rapid change of policy away from a profit principle, in that around four years previously, in 1313, a commission was set in train to extend and arrent the king's wastes in several forests including Clarendon, and to 'levy all money in arrear from the tenants of other wastes in those forests before extended and arrented'.[25] There are several possible factors behind such a change of policy. First, there is the economic background, particularly the climatic disasters of 1315-22. In the closing years of the thirteenth century, Europe as a whole was already facing severe economic problems and by c.1300 the upper echelons of society had 'adopted a...stricter view of their fiscal rights'.[26] But the famine that began in the Spring of 1315, followed by one of the worst winters in the later Middle Ages, was more devastating than any in the previous millennium. This set the pattern for the following seven years, causing a crisis in crop yields followed by devastating murrain in food animals (presumably including venison). As such this 'ecological catastrophe caused by the weather' may have been responsible for the ongoing dearth of mast at Clarendon, and for the scarcity of pigs, which largely escaped the murrains only to end up being eaten instead.[27]

One definition of famine is a low level of supplies leading to disruption of social as well as economic life. Indeed the 1315-22 crisis saw an escalation in poaching and the commonplace exceeding of customary tithes of venison which led inevitably to an escalation of social tension between lords and their social inferiors.[28] As stated above, the more varied economy may have cushioned forest-dwellers somewhat. Nevertheless these were the conditions in which the Clarendon imparkment was carried out, exacerbated by the political backdrop of the royal forests, and not surprisingly the landscape was made more exclusive. The figures for Clarendon Forest show the converse of the general trend in royal forests for 'large increases in [numbers] of acres...assarted by the mid- fourteenth century...compared to a century earlier'.[29] Neither do there appear to have been any substantial meadows inside Clarendon Park, as there were at Woodstock, worked by tenants who owed services.[30] Clarendon Forest and Park appear more than most royal

landscapes to have been run with exclusivity and pleasure in mind rather than profit.

Young has said that the period 1315-16 was one of the most important concerning the state of the forests and the future of the forest system,[31] and it cannot be coincidence that this was when the imparkment took place. When the Ordainer earl of Lancaster (whose men, it will be recalled, ransacked Clarendon Forest in 1314[32]) seized power in the parliament of January 1316, Edward II was obliged to accept the reduced national perambulations of 1300. At Easter he made further concessions on condition that all demesne woods should remain in forest. That at Clarendon was almost certainly imparked sometime during the following year — perhaps the best way to safeguard a landscape that was linked more than most with the royal prerogative and self-identity. In a further parliament in August, the justices of the forest were ordered to arrange the driving of deer into agreed afforested areas,[33] shortly before deer were presumably driven from Clarendon Forest into the newly-enclosed and enlarged park.

Against this backdrop, royal imparkment can be seen as a reaction to the loss (or feared loss, in the case of Clarendon) of large areas of forest hitherto reserved exclusively as royal hunting-grounds. Such a reaction may be viewed alongside the 1313 arrentation commissions as symptomatic of the reassertion of royal rights to crown lands. They were similar, rather than rather than contradistinct, policies. However there is a third factor behind the park's early fourteenth-century enlargement — the shift in hunting culture posited throughout this study as observable in the change in seasonality of royal visits.

Hunting seems to have increased in magnitude among signifiers of courtliness and nobility in the fourteenth century. That this gained pace as the century wore on is evident in the survival rate of what might be termed hunting manuals. Most English examples, such as the *Boke of Huntyng* (c.1400) and *Master of the Game* (c.1406-13) are later. However they derive from previous works such as Gaston Phoebus's 1380s *Livre de Chasse*, itself based on yet earlier examples. Perhaps most significantly, the earliest English hunting treatise (and the second earliest European survival of the genre) is that of William Twiti, one of Edward II's huntsmen, probably dictated in 1327.[34] The trajectory of the culture of venery is evident in that Twiti's original account records only three variants of the hunting cry, whereas the c.1450

[24] *CPR 1301-07*, p.107.
[25] *CFR 1307-19*, pp.164, 183.
[26] W. C. Jordan, *Europe in the High Middle Ages* (London: Penguin Books, 2002), p.289.
[27] Jordan, *Europe in the High Middle Ages*, p.290.
[28] C. Dyer, *Standards of Living in the Later Middle Ages: Social Change in England c.1200-1520* (Cambridge: Cambridge University Press, 1989), p.265; Jordan, *Europe in the High Middle Ages*, p.294.
[29] Young, *The Royal Forests of Medieval England*, p.117.
[30] Bond, 'Woodstock Park in the Middle Ages', p.37.

[31] Young, *The Royal Forests of Medieval England*, p.143.
[32] PRO E 32/207, m.3 (see above, p. 124).
[33] Grant, *Royal Forests*, pp.159-62; Young, *The Royal Forests of Medieval England*, pp.143-4.
[34] See B. Danielsson, ed., *William Twiti: The Art of Hunting, 1327*, Cynegetica Anglica I; Stockholm Studies in English 37 (Stockholm: Almqvist and Wiksell International, 1977). The first is *De arte bersandi*, written before 1250 (Rooney, *Hunting in Middle English Literature*, p.8 (n.2).

edition contains sixteen, and both the 1405 *Master of the Game* and the 1486 version of the *Boke of Huntyng* describe a full 27.[35]

The observation that such works concentrate so much on such niceties that they are next to useless concerning the practicalities of the chase (at least to the modern reader) is well-rehearsed, although their attentiveness to hunting as a signifier of social status is testament to its role in shaping social and cultural boundaries in the later Middle Ages. Paradoxically, more can be gleaned regarding hunting methods from accounts in imaginative literature, which also flourished through the fourteenth century.[36] It is likely that the proliferation of popular literature among the nobility did much to increase the popularity of the chase — Chaucer, to take one (widely-disseminated) example, contains a plethora of references to hunting. As Cummins has said, huntsmen wrote, read, and listened to, imaginative literature and 'it is not outlandish to suppose that…an awareness of the literary may have strongly conditioned the delight of the practical'.[37]

Therefore it can be argued that hunting culture developed at a pace through the fourteenth century. In today's terms it became increasingly 'fashionable'. Regarding what has been suggested above in Chapters Two and Three, it may be significant that pictorial depictions of the hunt in the early fourteenth-century 'Queen Mary's Psalter' show a marked preference for stags or bucks as quarry, and that the artist's 'most favourite subject' was hunting on horseback (which would require a large hunting area preferably approaching the *c.*1800 ha. size of today's Clarendon Park).[38] Influences from imaginative literature would also have conditioned the way park landscapes were perceived. This may even have led to their predominance over more open hunting reserves, such as forests. As Alecks Pluskowski has explained:

> *Open hunting space could not be sculpted into a hunting paradise…[But] n the microcosm of enclosed space, such as a park, the owner had the opportunity to create…the illusion of being amid a limitless wilderness withi infinitely renewable sources of game; which would of course depend on the size of the park. This is further suggested by the idealised depiction of the park in romance context [and] hunting manuals.*[39]

As has been stated, Edward II is not remembered chiefly for his love of the chase. However, alone among medieval kings, direct evidence exists for his personal involvement in hunting at Clarendon (see above, p. 83) — although in view of Edward III's habitual Summer

visits we can presume that he was equally active. Even Clarendon's coppices would have contributed to this 'élite paradise'. Although decidedly run for profit, and, like all medieval woodland, managed, coppices are described in Gaston Phoebus's works as suitable for attracting a variety of prey, and they frequently formed the link between fields and dense woods in the illuminations of hunting treatises.[40] They too were an integral component in the hunting landscape. Therefore, changes in the use and management of the park in the early- to mid- fourteenth century reflected a cultural shift that was reinforced by the encroachment, perceived and actual, on more open hunting spaces such as Clarendon Forest.

Thus various influences came to bear on the park's enlargement — climatic, economic, political and cultural. However it is likely that the latter two were dominant, especially considering that Clarendon Park, and parks in general, gained precedence generally over forests (now waning, in any case, as a political issue) from this period on. Deterministic interpretations alone do not go far enough. Yet the economic conditions of the early fourteenth century must have precluded all except the very wealthy from following such a course. In Wessex, only a few of the bishop of Winchester's parks are known to have been enlarged in the same period as that at Clarendon.[41] Nevertheless, it must be remembered that were it not for the explicit reference of 1317 to assarts being 'taken into the king's park', even the imparkment at Clarendon would not have been uncovered.

The area newly-imparked *c.*1317 might even shed light on the ways in which medieval deer parks *worked*. Although the documents do not delineate precisely the area concerned, their close analysis during this study has revealed that it was almost certainly in the southern, wood-pasture area of the park (see p. 122). Three deerleaps were in place here by 1324, before which 'the king's deer had ingress and egress at their own volition',[42] so that it may have been envisaged as a holding area where deer from the forest were chosen for restocking the population held in the launds, an area mentioned separately from the wider park in forest documents until 1355, in records of building works up to 1492-3, and in the calendars as late as 1553 (although by this time 'the park and launds' was probably an entirely formulaic demarcation).[43] In this way an important aspect of the relationship between the park and the forest may have been elucidated through the findings of this study.

---

[35] Danielsson, *William Twiti*, p.14.

[36] See the extract from *Gawain and the Green Knight* reproduced above, p.56.

[37] Cummins, *The Hound and the Hawk*, p.9.

[38] Danielsson, *William Twiti*, pp.21, 24 (quote at p.24).

[39] Pluskowski, 'Power and Predation', p.8.

---

[40] Pluskowski, 'Power and Predation', p.3.

[41] Bond, 'Forests, Chases, Warrens and Parks', p.138.

[42] *Dicunt tamen q(uo)d d[um] d(i)c(t)us d(o)m(ini)cus boscus fuit ext(ra) clausum et q(uo)d fere d'm' Regis tunc temp(or)is ingressum & egressum p(ro) voluntate eor(um) h(abe)re potuerunt* (C 47/11/8/3, m.10).

[43] E.g. PRO E 32/267, m.6d., in which a deer is recorded as having been killed 'above the laund'; PRO E 101/460/16, where the water gully in the launds is repaired; *CPR 1547-53*, p.276, in the grant of the wardenship to William, earl of Pembroke.

The fifteenth century remains a shady period in Clarendon's history, chiefly because so few documents survive. However, it has been found that money was prolifically spent on the palace despite the paucity of royal visits (see Figure 46), and that attempts continued to be made to conserve the forest's resources (see above, p. 51). It was also suggested, through comparison with spatial arrangements at Windsor (see Figure 45), that the Pady Course may have been constructed when the palace was still in use. Here knowledge of the landscape was also significant in interpretation, for example in compiling the contour-map of the Paddy Course (Figure 37) which has calibrated previous interpretations of the *c*.1640 map that could not have been viable in places due to the steepness of the terrain.[44]

Fieldwork *per se* was not a primary focus of this study due to constraints of time and space, but it is the contention here that it is at best imprudent to write the history of a landscape without some practical experience of that landscape. For example it has been said that the site of the standing is 'wrong'; that it should be nearer the end of the deer course.[45] It is true that no visible evidence of the Standing remains on the ground where the *c*.1640 map indicates it stood (although an intriguing structure found by geophysics in 2002 is in roughly the right place and awaits interpretation[46]), but for this particular landscape it is an entirely appropriate position. Both the start — or at least where the deer would have surged over the brow of Hockamore hill — and the finish are visible (see Figure 37), and the sight as they were pursued towards the Standing would have been dramatic. Combined with documentary and cartographic evidence the field visits have also made it possible to predict archaeological sites, subsequently established by fieldwalking and geophysical survey, for example on the possible site of the Lodge on the Laund in Hockamore Field (see Figures 37, 39). Further surveys in Picket Sanfoin, where the start of the Pady Course and related structures may be discovered, are also hoped for, while the northern end of today's 'Tilting Field' has never yet even been fieldwalked, and may provide the key to understanding the medieval inner park.

The unidentified building in Hockamore Field on the *c*.1713 map (see above, p. 74) is among the new observations made during this study, and it is hoped that fieldwalking might shed light on its identity. Such locally-specific discoveries, inevitable in a study of a particular landscape, may appear only to raise (and hopefully answer) narrow questions in an antiquarian vein. Likewise James I's visit of 1603, which has not before been noted, is at first glance little more than a footnote in Clarendon's royal history.[47] Yet the king was clearly accompanied by a large crowd of local gentry and

dignitaries and others of lesser rank, including, for example, William Phillips the mayor of Wilton.[48] It is plain from the interrogatory that many of those present knew Clarendon well, underscoring the park's significance in county society at this time. Here the uncovering, during this study, of George Penruddock's ranger's book in the WRO is also significant, revealing the park as a nexus for social relations in the locality in the 1570s, relations that were cemented through hunting and gifts of deer (see above, pp. 110-111). Moreover it is apparent from the interrogatory that although (as far as we know) this was James I's only visit, he managed — in the course of one day — to influence profound changes in the landscape, just as his royal forbears had, by advising on the best seeds to plant in the park's coppices, and, especially, by ordering the destruction of its rabbit warrens.

Thus the documentary methodology employed here has uncovered new findings and suggested new avenues of research, although it has fully verified the observation that 'the true problem for historians is to succeed in expressing the complexity of reality'.[49] But the record's very abundance has allowed diverse 'realities' to be revealed — articulated here through the sections on economy, buildings, settlement and boundaries.

The study has shown the palace to have been the lynchpin in Clarendon's landscape, with profound effects on economy, buildings, settlement, and the creation and negotiation of physical, conceptual and social boundaries. Analysis of the seasonality of royal visits has enhanced our knowledge of royal perceptions regarding its function, chiefly in relation to hunting, and suggestions have been made concerning the effect of this on changes in the landscape over time. However, it was also a nexus for local patronage and negotiation, as revealed through analysis of orders issued while the court was in residence, and, of course, the centre of forest administration. Some evidence for this was demonstrated in Chapter Three, for example in repairs to the palace buildings and the park lodges before the arrival of forest courts.

As regards economy, discussed in Chapter Two, the palace's effect is most discernible with its demise. Little quantitative information exists to facilitate comparison with earlier periods, but the vast numbers of deer in the park from the 1480s to the 1650s and the fact that more than ever before appear to have been sent elsewhere for restocking, suggests that its function as a breeding-ground came to the fore after the palace went out of use. Royal disinterest over the following 150 years or so is evident in the non-payment of wages and (apparently) increased malpractice by the foresters in the late sixteenth and early seventeenth centuries. Concomitant effects on the landscape included destruction and waste in the coppices, and as early as the 1480s the pale was broken

---

44 See KACC II, fig.9.1.
45 C.C. Taylor, pers. comm.
46 Alex Turner, pers. comm.
47 See above, p. 39.

48 PRO E 178/4728/A.
49 Levy, 'On Microhistory', p.110.

up and removed by local citizens even as the palace fell into disrepair (and was on occasion purposely dismantled for use on the lodges).

By the time of the 1488 forest eyre little attention was accorded Clarendon's deer or its wood resources, contrasting with the contemporary eyre for the New Forest and suggesting that Clarendon's status and function as a royal forest had waned with the ongoing withdrawal of Crown interest from the mid- fifteenth century. The resulting seigneurial vacuum is discernible in the many claims to rights and perquisites in that eyre (which, in respect to Clarendon, appear to have been the prime concern), replicated, from the mid- sixteenth century, by the construction of gentry residences in and around the forest (see above, pp. 109). As mentioned above, this period at Clarendon has been understudied, and would repay future work which might link into studies concerning the development of 'county society', a subject it has not been possible to address here in any detail. Clarendon Forest might usefully be seen as both the locality (social territory) and the locale (the physical setting of that territory, created and known through common experiences and meanings) of its forest officers and inhabitants. As Coss has said, the tendency to 'look first to the county, to identify its "office–holders" and then study these as its "gentry"' needs revising. [50] Research in which it is possible to observe a distinct locality together with its locale might prove more insightful and more compatible with contemporary mindsets.

Certainly the inhabitants of Clarendon Forest would have had some concept of local solidarity. From the early thirteenth century Salisbury would have been part of the locality and an important element in the locale of the majority of its officers. Conversely, Clarendon Palace, Park and Forest were intimately bound up with the city, and should be regarded as key elements not only in its hinterland, but also (arguably) in the particular way it was planned. But Salisbury cannot entirely be read in terms of a 'town that throve at the [palace] gates'. [51] It was hardly typical among medieval towns in general, and would almost certainly have flourished anyway. Nevertheless, the palace's proximity must have been beneficial in its early years, and compared with other towns associated with royal houses and castles the two seem to have enjoyed a relatively harmonious relationship. Moreover, Salisbury seems to have been significant in the blend of factors giving Clarendon Forest its particular administrative characteristics, as discussed above and in Chapter Five, as well as in its social networks. Again, future work should be carried out in order to illuminate further the relationship, particularly on records held in Salisbury and at the cathedral.

Analysis of taxation records in Chapter Four has shown that of the Wiltshire Clarendon Forests only the Forest of Clarendon suffered no significant settlement shrinkage and desertion in the sixteenth century (above, pp. 225-6). This suggests that its erstwhile prominence as a royal enclave, its continued status as a royal forest and the presence of the park as a draw for labour and the benefits of local office stabilised it somewhat. Indeed it is in the discussion of settlement that the palace's influence on the wider landscape is most clear. Surnames like Colier, Carter and Potter recorded in lay subsidies highlight the significance of both palace and park in the local economy (above, p. 206), corroborated by the numbers of local workmen listed in building accounts. Moreover, Chapter Four has shown that what demographic indicators there are between 1086 and 1377 indicate a correlation between the palace's increased prominence and a rise in the fortunes of those villages closest to it, especially Alderbury and Pitton. In contrast, the Subsidy of 1524, collected after the palace had gone out of use, reveals that they had fallen behind, or had at least stagnated, compared with villages further away such as Winterslow and Dean. However later figures, drawn from taxes collected from 1545 to 1641, suggest a resurgence in those villages in the park's immediate hinterland, and in Alderbury Hundred as a whole, and it was argued that this was connected to the revival and remodelling of the park evidenced by the construction — or at least the increased use of — the Pady Course and the Standing.

In short, the demise of the palace had a destabilising effect on Clarendon Forest's settlement hierarchy — but only for a time. It should be remembered that this was still a royal landscape, and the park remained a very visible reminder of its absent royal landlords. Inside it, the Pady Course and standing, having evolved from medieval bow and stable hunting, functioned as signifiers of what the park's landscape was *for*. Status, and the old medieval hunting-codes so central to fourteenth- and fifteenth-century treatises, had become etched into the landscape. Indeed, Johnson has argued that in the post-Reformation landscape 'spaces...became problems... connections now had to be explicitly argued between things that before were...taken-for-granted'. [52]

Nevertheless, it is clear that to its sixteenth- and seventeenth-century royal owners the park was little more than a lumber-repository and a means of financial gain, and plans to modernise it do not seem entirely to have come to fruition. Reasons may be manifold. First must come the removal of royal interest, although the chicken-and-egg question of whether this would have revived had the palace been habitable will probably never be resolved. There were problems associated with the landscape itself, even today clearly a classic medieval park. A glance at improvements carried out at other royal houses shows clearly a contemporary focus on water features. For example work on the ponds in the park at Theobalds in

---

[50] Coss, *Lordship, Knighthood and Locality,* p.11.
[51] Astill, 'Windsor', p.5.
[52] Johnson, *Behind the Castle Gate,* p.135.

1625-6 included the 'making of divers bridges' and the planting of strawberries, primroses and violets around the palisade of the 'greate Island ponde'.[53] At Wilton House itself, the seat of the earls of Pembroke, Isaac de Caus was commissioned in 1632 to transform the gardens to include a variety of aesthetic water features stretching over 300 metres across the river Nadder,[54] and it may not be going too far to suggest that a lack of scope for such at Clarendon was one reason for its relative neglect. The only place where such landscaping was possible was at Whitmarsh, where (not coincidentally) the late seventeenth/early eighteenth century mansion now stands alongside its artificial lake (see Figure 72).

Paradoxically, the park might have been modernised more effectively had it gone out of royal hands earlier than it did. George Penruddock's ranger's book shows that it was used extensively by county society for hunting in the last quarter of the sixteenth century, and this alone must go some way to redressing the picture of complete neglect of the park in this period, noted by previous writers.[55] But the earl of Pembroke, as warden, did not enjoy an entirely free hand, as evidenced by his prosecution for woodspoils in 1589 and his being obliged to destroy the rabbit warrens on the command of James I (1603-25) *c*.1603 at great financial loss to himself.[56]

Although the forest indisputably shaped the day-to-day, year-on-year lifecycle of the palace, Clarendon Forest would not have been such a high-status concern, its wardens often notable political players (above, p. 19), had a major royal house not existed within it. Nor would it have survived for so long. In the 1330s, for example, Chute Forest, site of the by then out-of-favour Ludgershall Castle, was 'almost disafforested'.[57] The presence of the palace was also the primary factor underlying the vastly different attitudes displayed towards Clarendon and Melchet Forests. This is most discernible in the figures for assarts, purprestures and wastes recorded in thirteenth- and fourteenth-century forest eyres, which show Clarendon to have been a 'seigneurial green belt', while Melchet was left largely to its own devices. Clarendon was a landscape of control, particularly while the palace remained in use, evidenced by the lack of scope for assarting in the forest, the attendant paucity (compared to Melchet) of isolated farmsteads (see Figure 50), and in part by a lack of

moated sites and other symbols of lordship in the immediate area. Control is evident also in Clarendon's social topography. The wardenship ceased to be hereditary so that it might be regulated by the king, and inheritance through the female line may have functioned to keep relevant skills and posts connected with hunting in the hands of experienced blood-families.

The documentary methodology used in this study has been invaluable in illuminating trends over time. This is especially evident in Chapter Two which discusses economy. For this the function of Clarendon Forest and Park as royal pleasure grounds was responsible. The presence of the palace at their midst is key, since it ensured their survival for longer than most other forests in Wiltshire, making it possible to study their economy over a long timescale. In particular, Stamper's findings for Pamber Forest, that royal policy shifted from conservation to active exploitation around the mid-thirteenth century, were found to apply also to Clarendon. Yet there are important differences. Whereas Pamber's exploitation was followed by the release of Crown land for more extensive use by others, that at Clarendon preceded the acquisition of land for use by the Crown (the enlargement of the park *c*.1317), and a more jealous attitude to forest resources representing a swing back towards conservation. For example the loss of pannage-returns due to scarcity of fodder may have resulted from a lack of mature oaks, and seems to have prompted agistment restrictions in the park from 1327.[58]

Landscape conservation, and certainly landscape management, are not new. Although much early fourteenth-century 'conservation' at Clarendon seems to have been prompted by needs of the deer, similar concerns relating to depletion of timber-stocks are evident in the early fifteenth century and of course in the sixteenth and seventeenth century, when such matters were uppermost. Thus, the findings here link to current ecological concerns, and again there is scope for future analysis. As Thirsk points out, past parallels with our own preoccupations — 'the mood to start anew, in order to achieve a balanced ecological community' — exist and deserve attention, from St Benedict in the seventh century, through Thomas More in the sixteenth, and beyond.[59]

The application of techniques employed in current deer management has been invaluable to this project, chiefly the British Deer Society Cull Planning Maintenance Model, which can be used to calculate baseline populations from numbers of deer culled. Such methods

---

[53] PRO E 351/3259.

[54] Wilton House, *Wilton House: A Living History* (www.wiltonhouse.co.uk/pages/history/history.html).

[55] For example McWilliams, 'Clarendon Park 1600-1750', p.6.

[56] *And for that it also appeareth by the said order... that the aforesaid keep(er)s in Claringdon p(ar)ke are...Ministers in that behalf unto the righthonourable Henry nowe Earle Pembrock. It is therefore this daye ordered that proth shalbe awarded and goe forth joyntly aswell against the presaid righthon(our)able... Earl of Pembrock as against the said John Stalling and others the keep(er)s in Claringdon p(ar)ke aforesaid for the sev(er)all somes of money imposed upon the said keep(er)s by the aforesaid order...*(PRO E 123/24, f.334); PRO E 178/ 4728, part A.

[57] Ludgershall seems to have gone out of favour with the death of Henry III, after which it, like Gillingham Palace, was given over to queens consort (Ellis, ed. [2002], p.252); Grant, *VCH Wilts*, p.425.

[58] *D(e) annis RR E t(er)cij a conquestum j, ij, iij, iiij, v & vj n(ull)' p(ro) def(ec)tu' pesson et sim(i)l(ite)r eo q(uo)d d(omi)n(u)s Rex p(re)cepit p(ro) tempus p(re)d(i)c(tu)m n(u)ll(u)m agist(amentum) in eod(e)m fieri* E 32/ 207, m. 12). The Close Rolls have it that 'the king...prohibited the making of such agistments in the park in order to have more ample pasture for his deer *(ferarum)*' (*CCR 1330-3*, p.7).

[59] J. Thirsk, 'Introduction', in *The English Rural Landscape* (Oxford: Oxford University Press, 2000), ed. J. Thirsk, pp.9-24 (p.11).

might usefully be applied more widely in order to analyse past deerpark populations for which adequate quantitative evidence exists as a starting-point (which is unfortunately rarely the case here). Indeed, there is a growing acknowledgement that many skills have been lost since the medieval period regarding deer management, and archaeologists in particular are currently attempting to enter the mindset of medieval hunters and deer managers in order to comprehend more fully the evidence that remains. For example the group ARCH (East Sussex) have recently carried out experimental archaeology in butchering a doe carcass according to methods of 'unmaking' advocated by the *Boke of St Albans* (1486), since, as they point out, the process described is no longer that followed by modern butchers. [60] Similarly, attendance of the BDS Advanced Stalkers Course was a valuable adjunct to this project since it presented an opportunity to learn from those who live and work with deer on a day-to-day basis, rather than rely on the less than expert knowledge of academic writers. Whether or not the success of this strategy is evident here, it is heartening to report that other researchers have been inspired to follow the same course. [61]

Analysis of deer and tree-species in the documents also pointed up sharply differences in function between the group of forests administered by Clarendon's forest warden. In the thirteenth century (for which most evidence is available), Clarendon was the chief source of timber although its output consisted also of underwood from an early date, as did that of Groveley. In contrast, Melchet supplied almost exclusively oak, and Buckholt beeches (see Figures 26-8). As to deer, while Clarendon was stocked with fallow, Groveley was the main source of red and roe, Buckholt's output was negligible, and Melchet's practically non-existent (Figures 13-15, 17-18). The comparative strategy employed here might add significantly to our understanding of the forest system as a whole, particularly if similar studies are produced. In Wiltshire alone, Chippenham and Melksham Forests were also administered jointly and had been the sites of royal manors. [62] Did the arrangement merely result from earlier tenurial circumstances, [63] or, as the weight of evidence examined here suggests, were groups of forests managed purposely for their diversity?

The lack of work to date relating in detail royal houses and palaces to their landscape surroundings is regrettable, aside from Astill's and Roberts' respective works on

Windsor, and Bond and Tiller's on Blenheim/ Woodstock. [64] In particular the forest, palace and park of Gillingham, just over the border in Dorset, would have been ideal as a comparative case study, but little or nothing has been published on the palace, let alone its landscape context. Although some data concerning Gillingham was collated, to have produced from original sources enough material for meaningful comparisons would have amounted to a doctoral study in itself. Scholars of medieval palaces should follow the example set by castle studies, problematising their settings as Creighton and Johnson have done for castles. [65]

Wider comparisons are also possible, given the lead taken by French scholars. In particular, it was hoped at the outset to have compared Philip the Good's (1285-1314) 'manor' of La Feuillie, constructed *c*.1293. Like Clarendon, La Feuillie was known by contemporaries as 'the king's houses', possessed a deerpark (this time for red deer), and went out of use at the end of the fifteenth century. [66] But it was eventually decided, with regret, to leave continental comparisons for the future in order to do justice to the mass of documents that exist for Clarendon.

By concentrating largely on Clarendon itself, this study has enhanced current knowledge, placed the palace in its landscape context, and allowed broad statements to be made concerning changes over time and symbolism in the landscape — for example that the park pale as much as the forest boundary was reinforced by new monarchs and regimes (see above, p. 116). But above all, the documentary methodology has facilitated greater awareness of the relationship between the forest and the palace. Indeed, in the end the key word of the study is 'interrelationships'. As the Dialogue of the Exchequer put it *c*.1180:

> It is in the forests...that the king's chambers are, and their chief delights. For they come there, laying aside their cares...to hunt...It is there that they can put from them the anxious turmoil native to a court, and take a little breath in the free air of nature. And that is why forest offenders are punished only at the king's pleasure. [67]

It may be argued that the forest was the key element in the relationship, as the quote suggests. After all, without it Clarendon Palace might never have been established, and its rhythms — both administrative and ecological — formed and reformed the palace until the end of the fifteenth century. And it cannot be coincidence that the last gasp of the palace, represented by Henry VII's

---

[60] ARCH, *The Unmaking of a Deer* (http://www.arch-projects.org.uk/unmaking.htm [searched March 2003]).
[61] For example Stephen Mileson, presently working on a thesis entitled 'Landscape, Power and Politics: the Place of the Park in Later Medieval Aristocratic Society' at Keble College, Oxford.
[62] Grant, *VCH Wilts*, p.391.
[63] The bulk of the lands of Waleran, first warden of Clarendon and the New Forest, were in the Groveley area as well as Clarendon. Groveley does not seem to have come under the warden of Clarendon's purview until 1236, although it may have been added when Clarendon Forest's administration was reorganised in 1228 (Grant, *VCH Wilts*, p.393; Richardson, 'Clarendon: The Palace in the Forest', pp.39-40.

[64] Astill, 'Windsor'; Roberts, *Royal Landscape*; Bond and Tiller, *Blenheim: Landscape for a Palace*.
[65] Creighton *Castles and Landscapes*; Johnson, *Behind the Castle Gate*.
[66] Renoux, *Palais royaux et princiers*, pp.48-9.
[67] C. Johnson, ed. and trans., *The Course of the Exchequer by Richard son of Nigel, Treasurer of England and Bishop of London* (London: Thomas Nelson and Sons, 1950), p.60.

building works, occurred alongside that of the medieval forest system, in the shape of the 1480s forest eyres. Nevertheless, it was the palace that made the forest *special*, ensuring its longevity.

As an essentially medieval institution the royal forest is a key element defining the Middle Ages, and without individual projects such as this, called for by Young as long ago as 1979 and echoed by Stamper a few years later,[68] a complete picture of medieval Britain cannot be drawn. By considering Clarendon Forest alongside the park and the palace, this study has not only improved understanding of a particular landscape and locality, but has also contributed to wider questions and provided a springboard for future work. It is thus testament to the volume and diversity of available written sources, demonstrating their value in reconstructing past landscapes, both actual and conceptual.

---

[68] Young, *The Royal Forests of Medieval England*, p.viii; Stamper, 'Pamber', p.41.

Glossary of terms

All information, unless otherwise stated, has been taken from Cox, The Royal Forests of England; *Grant,* Royal Forests; *Young,* The Royal Forests of Medieval England; *and Rackham,* The Last Forest. *Capitals denote cross-references.*

AGISTERS - Knights who acted as unpaid forest officers. Like VERDERERS they were responsible to the king, to whom they took an oath, and not to the forest WARDEN. There were no perquisites attached to the office, from which people secured royal grants of exemption if they could.

At FOREST EYRES, agisters accounted for revenues, for example PANNAGE dues received since the previous eyre. Their chief duty was to supervise cattle and pigs in the forest and to tally them.

AGISTMENT – Properly means driving pigs into the woods between Michaelmas and Martinmas (7 October - 19 November). In practice, however, agistment began in September, at which time AGISTERS counted pigs as they entered the forest. It ended around 11 November, when PANNAGE dues were collected from the owners by the agisters (thus also known as 'the pannage season').

ASSARTS - Defined in the twelfth century as clearings made when woods or thickets in a forest suitable for meadows and homesteads are cut down, the roots torn up, and the land ploughed up and brought into cultivation.

REGARDERS had the right to seize any assarts which were made without warrant, and it was the Forest WARDEN's duty to seize them, together with any crop grown on them. But the crown turned assarts into a source of revenue, licenses to assart being granted in return for a fine and annual rent thereafter, and most were tacitly recognised by forest officials.

BAILIWICK - Ward of jurisdiction. See also WARDENS.

BLETRON – Sapling.

BUCKSTALL – Extended deer-traps of which nets form a component part. May also involve earth ramparts and wattlework.

CABLISH – Windfallen wood.

CHASES - Districts where the right of hunting deer belonged to a subject, often under the full measure of forest law.

CHEMINAGE – A fine for traversing a forest. Usually a toll on pack animals that was ostensibly levied to prevent overuse of forest roads, which might cause a nuisance to the deer.

CHIROGRAPH – A signed and sealed legal document to the effect that land or property had been granted. Also the last part of a fine of land, thus known as 'feet of fines'.

COMMON RIGHTS - Common rights did not belong to the public, or to local inhabitants in general, but to the occupiers of particular farms or houses. There might be categories of commoners within a forest with different rights.

COMPARTMENTALISATION – The practice of subdividing a forest or other wood-pasture in order to keep deer and livestock out of recently-felled areas lest they eat the young shoots.

CONEYGER – The medieval name for a rabbit (coney) warren. Not to be confused with rights of free WARREN.

DEER BROWSE – Extra feed cut for deer in winter whenever snow was on the ground for more than two or three days.

ESTOVER - A customary allowance of wood. Frequently a perquisite of forest officers.

FARM - Annual sum payable, either in rent, or by an official such as a sheriff.

FOREST – a) *legal forest*: region in which the king (or, more rarely until the late fifteenth century, another magnate) had the right to keep deer and to make forest laws. b) *physical forest*: common land in a legal forest on which the deer lived, not including the woods of subjects inside it. Nonetheless, although these might be privately owned and were supervised by WOODWARDS rather than royal FORESTERS, the deer within them continued to belong to the king. Hence the difference between the legal and physical forest is never clear-cut.

Medieval forests *did not denote woodland*. On the contrary they encompassed varied topology — that the entire county of Essex was forest is perhaps the supreme example.

FOREST EYRE - Many of the itinerant justices who sat at forest eyres were also common law judges, perhaps explaining the parallels between the two systems. They usually sat in the county town and heard pleas from all forests in that county. However if there were extensive forest areas in two or more counties, pleas were heard partly in each.

Those summoned to attend eyres were archbishops, bishops, abbots, priors, earls, barons, knights and all of lesser degree who held land in free tenure in the bounds of the king's forest in that county. Also four men and the reeve from every township in the forest, the FORESTERS and VERDERERS with their rolls of attachments, the REGARDERS with their rolls, and the AGISTERS with their accounts of agistment of the king's demesne woods in the forest.

Before eyres were held, a writ was issued from the Chancery ordering sheriffs to see that a REGARD was made, but the eyre's jurisdiction encompassed areas outside the forest if deer were killed there. Since they were the king's property, none might kill them wherever they were.

Barons and bishops had the right to have their cases referred to the central courts, specifically the court *coram rege*, as did household members and other civil servants.

FORESTERS OF FEE - Foresters of Fee performed duties similar to those of appointive foresters in the wards or subdivisions of a forest, but held their office by hereditary right. Their main duty was the safe keeping of vert and venison, and the forest rolls show them searching for, and apprehending offenders. They were also expected to help maintain the king's peace in times of civil disturbance. Sometimes they swore fealty to the WARDEN of the forest, to whom they usually paid a farm.

Foresters of fee were supposed to provide underforesters at their own expense, but in practice many took money from them for their appointments. They invariably had right of PANNAGE and pasture for themselves and their men. Some took also nuts gathered in the king's demesne woods.

HART – A red deer stag aged around five years (they live to be 17–20).

HAY – Either a hedge, a long net (for example for use in CONEYGERS), or a wood generally owned by the king set aside for the harvesting of timber.

HOUSEBOTE – The right to take wood from the forest in order to repair one's house. Housebote was often a perquisite of royal FORESTERS, along with heybote (to repair one's hedges) and firebote (for one's hearth).

IN DEFENCE – The exclusion of all grazing animals from a wood or coppice usually taken to mean that the wood was enclosed with a fence or hedge to keep them out.

INFANGTHEF – The right of manorial lords to judge local felons found with stolen goods and, if found guilty, to execute them.

LAUNDS/LAWNS – Relatively treeless areas of park or forest set aside for deer.

LAUNDER/LAUNDERER – The officer in charge of the launds in a park, who might have responsibility for rabbits as well as deer.

LAWING – According to the Charter of the Forest (1217) lawing involved cutting three claws from a dog's forefoot 'without the ball of the foot'. Its purpose was to prevent dogs from running after deer, but it soon became yet another means of financial exaction. Originally, under Henry II, lawing applied only to Mastiffs. By the thirteenth century, those whose dogs were found to be unlawed were amerced 3s, although like all forest amercements the sum rose in accordance with the trespasser's income

LOPPINGS – The crop from pollarding.

MURRAIN – The general word for an unidentified disease suffered by cattle, sheep and deer.

PANNAGE – Payment received by AGISTERS in return for setting pigs into wooded areas to forage for acorns (AGISTMENT).

PARKS - More definitely places of deer husbandry than were forests, hence their distribution more surely reflects woodland. Around thirty-five are mentioned in Domesday, although they were most prominent in the landscape around

1300. Their development was very costly, and the records of such show that the economic picture of the forests was not all profit.

Where parks abutted onto forests, deer may have been deliberately driven in. Their purpose may thus have been to hold stocks of deer that could be caught easily, their stocks replenished from time to time in this way.

PARK PALE – Hedge or fence surmounting a substantial bank around a deer park, often used today to describe the remaining bank and ditch. Ditches were dug on the inside, so that deer could get in (through breaks called *saltatoria*, or deerleaps), but not out again.

PARROCK – Probably the root of the word 'PARK' (AS *pearruc, pearroc, perh*), but difficult to pin down in the later medieval and early modern periods, when it seems to apply to a range of smaller enclosures. Defined by Webster's Dictionary as 'A croft, or small field; a paddock'.[1]

PRICKET – A yearling buck, before the antlers branch (the red deer equivalent is 'brocket'). See also HART, SORRELL, SORE.

PURLIEU – An area put outside the forest but to which certain restrictions still applied.

PURPRESTURES - Unauthorised buildings, enclosures, excavations, or any other man-made feature in the forest which ostensibly interfered with the movement of the deer, or was likely to frighten them away. In Eyres, they were closely allied to ASSARTS as a broad term, which might include enclosures.

REGARDERS had the right to throw down any purpresture erected without license. But in practice houses were rarely torn down, since purprestures were chiefly yet another means of raising money. The usual penalty was 12d.

THE REGARD/REGARDERS - Triennial inquiries into the state of the vert in a forest, ordered by writ of Chancery. Their primary object was to prevent the destruction of trees, bushes and other vegetation which gave food and shelter to the king's deer, although by the thirteenth century they were used to furnish central administration with a detailed record of sources of royal revenue. Where there were several forests in one county, a separate regard would be held for each, and offenders were punished in the FOREST EYRE.

The office of regarder was unpaid, and very unpopular among the knights of forest districts because it involved enforcing a system which forest dwellers found hateful. Regarders were expected to search out those who had unlawfully pastured animals in areas that were not common.

SORE/ SOWER– A fallow buck in his fourth year.

SORREL – A fallow buck in his third year (in his first year he is a fawn, in his second a PRICKET, in his fifth a 'bare buck', in his sixth a buck and in his seventh a 'great buck').

STICKERS – Name given in the Early Modern period to trespassers who entered PARKS such as that at Clarendon to purloin wood. It originally applied to those who were employed by others entitled to perquisites such as HOUSEBOTE, heybote and firebote, to gather fallen wood in forests or parks, or to those who had the customary right to do so, such as paupers.

SWANIMOTE/SWAINMOTE – Assembly of FORESTERS, VERDERERS and AGISTERS where arrangements were made for the AGISTMENT of the king's woods. The Charter of the Forest laid down that they should be held thrice yearly (on 15 September, when agistment commenced, 11 November at its close, and on 10 June to see that all animals were removed from the forest due to the supposed deer fawning season, or 'fence month'). From OE 'a meeting of swineherds'.

UNDERWOOD - Wood, whether growing or cut, consisting of coppice-poles, young suckers or pollard poles.

VERDERERS - Unpaid Knights of the locality elected to office in the county court, verderers shared with FORESTERS a general responsibility for the VERT and venison. They organised inquests with the foresters, whom they both supervised and assisted, and acted with them in FOREST EYRES. They also co-operated with foresters in supervising the exercise of customary rights, in making arrangements for the AGISTMENT of the king's demesne woods, and in carrying out various inquiries into the rights of the Crown and the perquisites of forest officials. The sheriff could seize

---

[1] ARTFL Project, *Webster Dictionary 1913* (http://machaut.uchicago.edu/cgi-bin/WEBSTER.sh?WORD=Parrock).

their lands if they failed in their duty, and if they neglected to present their rolls on the first day of a FOREST EYRE or the rolls were deficient, they were liable to amercement.

THE VERT - General term denoting trees and undergrowth. Pleas of the vert concerned offences of cutting wood in the forest of more than a certain value. The usual penalty for a vert offence itself was 12d, although rich and influential offenders paid more.

WARDEN - The head of administration of a single royal forest, or group of forests, termed his BAILIWICK. Hereditary wardenships had been the product of the Norman and Angevin kings' establishment of a part of local forest administration on a hereditary and territorial basis. By the thirteenth century, some were appointed by letters patent, usually to hold office during the king's pleasure. In exceptional cases and as a mark of royal favour, others held office for life. Members of the Royal family were provided for in this way, and Henry III and Edward I made provision also for a number of royal servants by appointing them to wardenships.

Wardens had staffs of foresters under them, assisted by VERDERERS, to uphold the forest law. They had to ensure that deer were supplied with sufficient food in times of scarcity, and see that they were not hunted by anyone without authority from the king or the chief justice of the forest. They had the right to arrest all poachers found within their bailiwicks, and to raise the hue and cry upon them. The sheriff could be called to assist, and to arrest those whose names the warden gave him.

WARREN – An area in which the king, or the holder of a charter of warren, had the exclusive right of hunting certain beasts other than the four beasts of the forest, including hares, foxes, wild cats and sometimes rabbits and game birds. This was termed 'free warren'.

If a warren were within a forest, it was subject to forest law and deer were thus preserved in it. Substantial fines were paid for charters of warren, and Henry III exploited this source of revenue by selling right of warren to any landowner who desired it. This was one of the complaints of the barons at the Parliament of Oxford (1258).

WASTE - The cutting of wood in a forest beyond limited customary rights. It was an offence looked into by the REGARD. Regarders had the right to seize any wood in which waste had been committed, and wasted woods had to be enclosed so that animals could not eat the new shoots and prevent new growth.

The owners of a wasted wood had to pay half a mark at FOREST EYRES until the woods grew back to their former state (enrolled as 'Old Wastes of Woods'). It was standard practice to collect a small fee from the owners for entering into the use of the waste, and an annual rent of two to four pence an acre depending on land-value. For these sums, a royal charter was issued confirming the right to use the land.

WOODWARD – All subjects who held demesne woods within a royal forest were bound to appoint sworn woodwards to keep the vert and venison within them. Thus they performed the same duties done elsewhere by royal FORESTERS.

Woodwards had to be presented to the justice of the forest on appointment, and at every subsequent FOREST EYRE, where they took an oath to perform their duties faithfully. If the justice of the forest found that a wood had no woodward, or that the woodward had not taken an oath, had neglected his duties, or committed a trespass in the forest, the wood in question would be seized for the king. However the owner usually regained entry on payment of a fine. Similarly, royal foresters, to whose authority woodwards were usually subject, could seize a wood if they discovered a trespass which had not been reported. They could then attach him to answer for his default.

Bibliography

PRIMARY SOURCES (MANUSCRIPT)

BRITISH LIBRARY, LONDON

Add. Ch. 26594, Charters (1364-7)
BM Stowe 79, Charters (seventeenth-century copy of 1225 perambulation)

PUBLIC RECORD OFFICE, KEW

Chancery Records
C 1/1428/82, Clerk's Office, Early Proceedings (1538)
C 47/3/48, Miscellanea (1276)
C 47/11/8/3, Miscellanea (1330-1)
C 47 11/8/9, Miscellanea (1330-1)
C 47/11/8/10, Miscellanea (1330-1)
C 47/12/2/9, Miscellanea: Forests (1278-9)
C 143/31, *Inquisitions ad Quod Damnum* (1273)
C 143/38/21, *Inquisitions ad Quod Damnum* (1301-2)
C 143/95/3, *Inquisitions ad Quod Damnum* (1313-14)
C 145/31, Miscellaneous Inquisitions (1273)
C 145/106/8, Miscellaneous Inquisitions (*temp.* Edward III)
C 260/84/15, Miscellanea (1355-6)
C 260/86/16, Miscellanea (1355-6)
C 260/89/32, Miscellanea (1355-6)
C 260/136/31, Miscellanea (1299-1300)

Duchy of Lancaster and Justice of the Forest South of Trent
DL 39/2/19, Forest Records (1486-7)
DL 39/2/20, Forest Records (1486-7)
DL 39/3/32, Forest Records (1480s)

Exchequer Records
Justice of the Forest: Records Formerly in Receipt of Exchequer
E 32/198 (1256-7)
E 32/199 (1262-3)
E 32/200 (1269-70)
E 32/204 (1303-13)
E 32/207 (1330)
E 32/208 (1330)
E 32/214 (1330-2)
E 32/215 (*temp.* Edward III)
E 32/225 (1330)
E 32/261 (1338)
E 32/267 (1355)
E 32/271 (1370-2)
E 32/272 (1373)
E 32/276 (1376)
E 32/279 (1360-1)
E 32/281 (1361-77)
E 32/318 (1361-77)
E 36/75 (1299-1305)

Accounts Various
E 101/140/4 (1363-7)
E 101/140/10 (1441-2)
E 101/140/11 (1567-73)
E 101/140/11 (1569-70)
E 101/140/12 (1590-1)
E 101/140/14 (1593-1620)
E 101/352/32 (1289)
E 101/459/27 (1317-19)
E 101/459/29 (1354)
E 101/459/30 (1356)
E 101/460/1 (1354-9)
E 101/473/2 (*temp.* Richard II)
E 101/499/1 (1377-81)
E 101/502/15 (*temp.* Henry IV)
E 101/519/22 (*temp.* Henry VIII)
E 101/536/12 (1583-4)
E 101/542/11 (1370-1)
E 101/542/12 (1374-6)
E 101/542/14 (1374-6)
E 101/542/17 (1375-6)
E 101/542/20 (1461-71)
E 101/542/21 (1603-7)

E 101/460/2 (1362-5)

E 101/460/7 (1422-32)

E 101/460/10 (1448-9)

E 101/460/11 (1461-72)

E 101/460/12 (1471-7)

E 101/460/14 (1477)

E 101/460/15 (1479-83)

E 101/460/16 (1482-97)

E 101/542/22 (1607-8)

E 101/593/9 (1321-2)

E 101/593/18 (1341-4)

E 101/593/20 (1341-4)

E 101/593/21 (1343-4)

E 101/595/41 (1610-12)

E 101/595/43 (1617-18)

E 101/683/87 (1446-7)

King's Remembrancer: Particulars of Account and other Records Relating to Lay and Clerical Taxation

E 179/136/326 (1524-5)

E 179/196/3 (1296-7)

E 179/196/4 (1299-1306)

E 179/196/7 (1327-8)

E 179/196/8 (1333-4)

E 179/196/12 (1281-2)

E 179/196/16 (1340-1)

E 179/196/20 (1344-5)

E 179/196/21 (1346-7)

E 179/196/23 (1346-7)

E 179/196/30 (1351-2)

E 179/196/34 (1377)

E 179/196/35 (1377)

E 179/196/36 (1377)

E 179/196/37/1 (1377)

E 179/196/37/2 (1377)

E 179/196/50 (1394-5)

E 179/196/87 (1427-8)

E 179/197/162 (1524-5)

E 179/197/230 (1544-5)

E 179/197/241 (1547-8)

E 179/197/245 (1546-7)

E 179/198/256a (1550-1)

E 179/198/261a (1551-2)

E 179/198/266 (1549-53)

E 179/198/275 (1559-60)

E 179/198/284 (1575-6)

E 179/198/294 (1575-6)

E 179/198/297 (1581-2)

E 179/198/314 (1593-4)

E 179/198/329 (1598-9)

E 179/199/398 (1628-9)

E 179/199/370 (1610-11)

E 179/199/398 (1628-9)

E 179/199/405 (1640-1)

E 179/239/193/6 (1378-9)

E 179/239/193/11 (1378-9)

E 179/239/207 (1641-2)

E 179/270/18 (1586-7)

Pipe Office

E 351/3239, Declared Accounts (1603-4)

E 351/3251, Declared Accounts (1616-17)

E 351/3254, Declared Accounts (1620-1)

E 351/3257, Declared Accounts (1623-4)

E 351/3259, Declared Accounts (1625-6)

E 351/3385, Declared Accounts (1614, 1621)

E 352/10, Chancellor's Rolls (1176-7)

E 352/12, Chancellor's Rolls (1178-9)

E 352/13, Chancellor's Rolls (1179-80)

E 352/33, Chancellor's Rolls (1222-3)

E 364/2, Foreign Accounts (1356-60)

E 364/57, Foreign Accounts (1421-2)

E 372/1, Pipe Rolls (1130)

E 372/22, Pipe Rolls (1175-6)

E 372/59, Pipe Rolls (1211-12)

E 372/62, Pipe Rolls (1217-18)

E 372/66, Pipe Rolls (1221-2)

E 372/67, Pipe Rolls (1222-3)

E 372/70, Pipe Rolls (1225-6)

E 372/71, Pipe Rolls (1226-7)

E 372/72, Pipe Rolls (1227-8)

E 372/204, Pipe Rolls (1357-8)

E 372/275, Pipe Rolls (1429)

E 372/304, Pipe Rolls (1458-9)

E 372/325, Pipe Rolls (1479-80)

E 372/345, Pipe Rolls (1499)

E 372/365, Pipe Rolls (1519-20)

E 372/385, Pipe Rolls (1539-40)

E 372/425, Pipe Rolls (1579-80)

E 372/455, Pipe Rolls (1609-10)

Miscellaneous Records
E 123/24, King's Remembrancer: Decrees and Orders (1596-1600)
E 123/29, King's Remembrancer: Decrees and Orders (1601-6)
E 124/3, King's Remembrancer: Decrees and Orders (1604-9)
E 134/18&19Eliz/Mich I, Special Depositions (1575-7)
E 134/22&23Eliz/Mich 2, Special Depositions (1579-81)
E 146/2/39, King's Remembrancer: Forest Proceedings (1568)
E 146/3/1, King's Remembrancer: Forest Proceedings (1604)
E 146/3/11, King's Remembrancer: Forest Proceedings (1355-6)
E 159/47, Queen's Remembrancer: Memoranda Roll (1272-3)
E 178/2348, Special Commissions (1591-2)
E 178/2400, Special Commissions (1566-7)
E 178/2417, Special Commissions (1579-80)
E 178/2446, Special Commissions (1596-7)
E 178/4728, Special Commissions (1612-13, 1615-16, 1640-1)
SC 6/1050/5, Ministers' and Receivers' Accounts (1318-24)
SC 6/1050/8, Ministers' and Receivers' Accounts (1344-6)
SC 6/1050/14, Ministers' and Receivers' Accounts (1414-15/ 1423-31)
SC 6/1050/17, Ministers' and Receivers' Accounts (1418-20)
SC 6/1050/18, Ministers' and Receivers' Accounts (1419-21)
SC 6/1050/19, Ministers' and Receivers' Accounts (1420-2)
SC 6/1050/22, Ministers' and Receivers' Accounts (1423-4)
SC6/Hen VIII/5885, Ministers' Accounts (1541-3)

Ministry of Works Records
WORK 14/1777, Clarendon Palace: Excavation of Remains (1942-60)

WILTSHIRE RECORD OFFICE, TROWBRIDGE

302/1 no. 1, Lease of Haybarn belonging to Queen Manor Lodge (1697)
549/8, George Penruddock's Ranger's Book (1572-5)
2478/2, Account of Timber Sales (1635)
Chapter/95/1, Tithes of Clarendon Park (1693)
Chapter/96, 'Survey and Valuation of the Tithes of the Manor of Clarendon in the County of Wilts: The Property of the Dean and Chapter of Sarum' (1802)

PRINTED PRIMARY SOURCES: CALENDARS OF ROLLS
(London and HMSO unless otherwise stated)

Calendars of Charter Rolls
Calendar of Charter Rolls, Henry III, 1: 1226-57 (1903)
Calendar of Charter Rolls, Henry III, Edward I, II: 1257-1300 (1905)

Calendars of Close Rolls
Calendar of Close Rolls, Henry III, 1: 1227-31 (1902)
Calendar of Close Rolls, Henry III, 2: 1231-4 (1905)
Calendar of Close Rolls, Henry III, 3: 1234-7 (1909)
Calendar of Close Rolls, Henry III, 4: 1237-42 (1911)
Calendar of Close Rolls, Henry III, 5: 1242-7 (1916)
Calendar of Close Rolls, Henry III, 6: 1247-51 (1922)
Calendar of Close Rolls, Henry III, 7: 1251-3 (1928)
Calendar of Close Rolls, Henry III, 9: 1254-6 (1931)
Calendar of Close Rolls, Henry III, 10: 1256-9 (1932)
Calendar of Close Rolls, Henry III, 11: 1259-61 (1934)
Calendar of Close Rolls, Henry III, 12: 1261-4 (1936)
Calendar of Close Rolls, Henry III, 13: 1264-8 (1937)
Calendar of Close Rolls, Henry III, 14: 1268-72 (1938)
Calendar of Close Rolls, Edward I, 1: 1272-9 (1900)

Calendar of Close Rolls, Edward I, 2: 1279-88 (1902)
Calendar of Close Rolls, Edward I, 3: 1288-96 (1904)
Calendar of Close Rolls, Edward III, 4: 1296-1302 (1906)
Calendar of Close Rolls, Edward III, 5: 1302-7 (1908)
Calendar of Close Rolls, Edward II, 1: 1307-13 (1892)
Calendar of Close Rolls, Edward II, 2: 1313–18 (1893)
Calendar of Close Rolls, Edward II, 3: 1318-23 (1895)
Calendar of Close Rolls, Edward III, 1: 1327–30 (1896)
Calendar of Close Rolls, Edward III, 2: 1330-3 (1898)
Calendar of Close Rolls, Edward III, 3: 1333-7 (1898)
Calendar of Close Rolls, Edward III, 4: 1337-9 (1900)
Calendar of Close Rolls, Edward III, 5: 1339-41 (1901)
Calendar of Close Rolls, Edward III, 7: 1343-6 (1905)
Calendar of Close Rolls, Edward III, 8: 1346-9 (1905)
Calendar of Close Rolls, Edward III, 10: 1354-60 (1908)
Calendar of Close Rolls, Edward III, 11: 1360-4 (1909)
Calendar of Close Rolls, Edward III, 12: 1364–8 (1910)
Calendar of Close Rolls, Edward III, 13: 1369-74 (1911)
Calendar of Close Rolls, Edward III, 14: 1374-7 (1913)
Calendar of Close Rolls, Richard II, 2: 1381-5 (1920)
Calendar of Close Rolls, Richard II, 3: 1385-9 (1921)
Calendar of Close Rolls, Henry IV, 1: 1399-1402 (1927)
Calendar of Close Rolls, Henry V, 1: 1413-19 (1929)
Calendar of Close Rolls, Henry VI, 1: 1422-9 (1933)
Calendar of Close Rolls, Henry VI, 3: 1435-41 (1937)
Calendar of Close Rolls, Edward IV, 1: 1461-8 (1949)
Calendar of Close Rolls, Edward IV, 2: 1468-76 (1953)
Calendar of Close Rolls, Edward IV-Edward V-Richard III: 1476-85 (1954)
Calendar of Close Roll, Henry VII, 1: 1485-1500 (1955)
Rotuli Litteram Clausarum in Turri Londinensi Asservati, I (Record Commission, 1831)

Calendars of Fine Rolls
Calendar of Fine Rolls, Edward I, 1: 1272-1307 (1911)
Calendar of Fine Rolls, Edward I, 2: 1307-19 (1911)
Calendar of Fine Rolls, Edward II, 2: 1319-27 (1912)
Calendar of Fine Rolls, Edward III, 4: 1327-37 (1913)
Calendar of Fine Rolls, Edward III, 5: 1337-47 (1915)
Calendar of Fine Rolls, Edward III, 6: 1347-56 (1921)
Calendar of Fine Rolls, Edward III, 7: 1356-68 (1923)
Calendar of Fine Rolls, Edward III, 8: 1368-77 (1924)
Calendar of Fine Rolls, Richard II, 10: 1383-91 (1929)
Calendar of Fine Rolls, Richard II, 11: 1391-9 (1929)
Calendar of Fine Rolls, Henry V, 14: 1413-22 (1934)
Calendar of Fine Rolls, Henry VI, 17: 1437-45 (1937)
Calendar of Fine Rolls,Henry VI, 18: 1445-52 (1939)
Calendar of Fine Rolls, Edward IV-Henry VI, 20: 1461-71 (1949)
Calendar of Fine Rolls, Henry VII, 22: 1485-1509 (1962)
Excerptae Rotulis Finium In Turri Londiniensi Asservatis, Henrico Tertio Rege A.D. 1216-1272: vol. II, 1246-1272
(London, Record Commission, 1836)

Calendars of Inquisitions
Calendar of Inquisitions Miscellaneous, Henry IV-Henry V: 1399-1422 (1968)
Calendar of Inquisitions Post Mortem and Other Analogous Documents, Henry III, 1: (1904)
Calendar of Inquisitions Post Mortem and Other Analogous Documents, Edward I, 2: Years 1-19 (1906)

Calendars of Liberate Rolls
Calendar of Liberate Rolls, Henry III, 1: 1226-40 (1917)
Calendar of Liberate Rolls, Henry III, 2: 1240-5 (1931)
Calendar of Liberate Rolls, Henry III, 3: 1247-51 (1937)
Calendar of Liberate Rolls, Henry III, 4: 1251-60 (1959)
Calendar of Liberate Rolls, Henry III, 5: 1260-7 (1961)
Calendar of Liberate Rolls, Henry III, 6: 1267-72 (1964)

Calendars of Patent Rolls
Calendar of Patent Rolls, Henry III, 1: 1216-25 (1901)
Calendar of Patent Rolls, Henry III, 2: 1225-32 (1903)
Calendar of Patent Rolls, Henry III, 3: 1232-47 (1906)
Calendar of Patent Rolls, Henry III, 4: 1247-58 (1908)
Calendar of Patent Rolls, Henry III, 5: 1258-66 (1910)
Calendar of Patent Rolls, Henry III, 6: 1266-72 (1913)
Calendar of Patent Rolls, Edward I, 1: 1272-81 (1901)
Calendar of Patent Rolls, Edward I, 2: 1281-92 (1893)
Calendar of Patent Rolls, Edward I, 3: 1292–1301 (1895)
Calendar of Patent Rolls, Edward I, 4: 1301-7 (1898)
Calendar of Patent Rolls, Edward II, 1: 1307-13 (1894)
Calendar of Patent Rolls, Edward II, 2: 1313-17 (1898)
Calendar of Patent Rolls, Edward II, 5: 1324-7 (1904)
Calendar of Patent Rolls, Edward III, 1: 1327-30 (1891)
Calendar of Patent Rolls, Edward III, 2: 1330-4 (1893)
Calendar of Patent Rolls, Edward III, 3: 1334-8 (1895)
Calendar of Patent Rolls, Edward III, 5: 1343-5 (1902)
Calendar of Patent Rolls, Edward III, 7: 1348-50 (1905)
Calendar of Patent Rolls, Edward III, 11: 1354-8 (1909)
Calendar of Patent Rolls, Edward III, 12: 1361-4 (1912)
Calendar of Patent Rolls, Edward III, 13: 1364-7 (1912)
Calendar of Patent Rolls, Edward III, 14: 1367-70 (1913)
Calendar of Patent Rolls, Edward III, 15: 1370-4 (1914)
Calendar of Patent Rolls, Edward III, 16: 1374-7 (1916)
Calendar of Patent Rolls, Richard II, 1: 1377–81 (1895)
Calendar of Patent Rolls, Richard II, 2: 1381-5 (1897)
Calendar of Patent Rolls, Richard II, 5: 1391-6 (1905)
Calendar of Patent Rolls, Richard II, 6: 1396-9 (1909)
Calendar of Patent Rolls, Henry IV, 3: 1405-8 (1907)
Calendar of Patent Rolls, Henry V, 2: 1416-22 (1911)
Calendar of Patent Rolls, Henry VI, 1: 1422-9 (1901)
Calendar of Patent Rolls, Henry VI, 2: 1429–36 (1907)
Calendar of Patent Rolls, Henry VI, 3: 1436-41 (1907)
Calendar of Patent Rolls, Henry VI, 5: 1446-52 (1909)
Calendar of Patent Rolls, Henry VI, 6: 1452-61 (1910)
Calendar of Patent Rolls, Edward IV: 1461-7 (1897)
Calendar of Patent Rolls, Edward IV-Henry VI: 1467-77 (1900)
Calendar of Patent Rolls, Edward IV-Edward V-Richard III: 1476-85 (1901)
Calendar of Patent Rolls, Henry VII, 2: 1494-1509 (1916)
Calendar of Patent Rolls, Edward VI, 1: 1547-48 (1924)

Calendars of State Papers
Calendar of State Papers, Domestic Series, Elizabeth I, 1591-1594 (Longmans, Green, Reader, and Dyer, 1867)
Calendar of State Papers, Domestic Series, Charles I, 1625-1626 (Longman, Brown, Green, Longmans, and Roberts, 1858)
Calendar of State Papers, Domestic Series, Charles I, 1625-1649 (HMSO, 1897)

Calendar of State Papers, Domestic Series, Charles I, 1631-1633 (Longman, Green Longman, Roberts and Green, 1862)

Calendar of State Papers, Domestic Series, Charles I, 1635 (Longman, Green Longman, Roberts and Green, 1865)

Calendar of State Papers, Domestic Series, Charles I, 1637-1638 (Longmans, Green and Co., 1869)

Calendar of State Papers, Domestic Series, 1649-1650 (Longmans and Co., 1875)

Letters and Papers Foreign and Domestic of the Reign of Henry VIII, vol. 9 (Longmans and Co., 1886)

PRINTED PRIMARY SOURCES, MISCELLANEOUS

Anon., *Nonarum Inquisitiones in Curia Scaccarii: Temp Edwardi III* (London: Record Commission, 1807)

Anon., *Rotuli Hundredorum II* (London: Record Commission, 1818)

Byerly, B. F., and Ridder, C., eds, *Records of the Wardrobe and Household, 1285-1286* (1977)

Byerly, B. F., and Ridder, C., eds, *Records of the Wardrobe and Household, 1286-1289* (1986)

Chatsworth Library (Origination of Maps), *Christopher Saxton's 16th Century Maps: The Counties of England and Wales* (Shrewsbury: Chatsworth Library, 1992)

Clanchy, M. T., ed., *Civil Pleas of the Wiltshire Eyre, 1249* (Devizes: Wiltshire Record Society, 1971)

Hunter, J., ed., *Magnus Rotulus Pipe 31 Henry I* (London: Record Commission, 1833)

Meekings, C. A. F., ed., *Crown Pleas of the Wiltshire Eyre, 1249* (Devizes: Wiltshire Archaeological and Natural History Society Records Branch, 1961) Pipe Roll Society, *The Great Roll of the Pipe for the Thirteenth Year of King John* [Pipe R. 13 John, 28] (Pipe Roll Society, 1953)

Pugh, R. B., ed., *Abstracts of Feet of Fines Relating to Wiltshire for the Reigns of Edward I and Edward II* (Devizes: Wiltshire Archaeological and Natural History Society, 1939)

Pugh, R. B., *Gaol Delivery and Trailbaston 1275-1306* (Devizes: Wiltshire Record Society, 1978)

Searle, E., ed. and trans., *The Chronicle of Battle Abbey* (Oxford: Clarendon Press, 1980)

Stagg, D. J. ed., *New Forest Documents A.D. 1244-A.D. 1334*, Hampshire Record Series 3 (Winchester: Hampshire County Council, 1979)

Stagg, D. J. ed., *A Calendar of New Forest Documents: The Fifteenth to Seventeenth Centuries*, Hampshire Record Series 5 (Winchester: Hampshire Record Office, 1983)

Turner, G. J., ed., *Select Pleas of the Forest*, Selden Society 13 (London: Bernard Quaritch, 1901)

SECONDARY SOURCES

Addyman, P., and Kightly, C., 'The Historical and Documentary Background' in *Ludgershall Castle: A Report on the Excavations by Peter Addyman 1964-1972*, Wiltshire Archaeological and Natural History Society Monograph Series 2 (Devizes: Wiltshire Archaeological and Natural History Society, 2000), ed. P. Ellis, pp.11-18

Alderbury and Whaddon Local History Research Group, *Alderbury and Whaddon: A Millennium Mosaic of People, Places and Progress* (Alderbury: Alderbury and Whaddon Local History Research Group, 2000)

Allen, R., 'The Pageant of History: A Reinterpretation of the 13th-Century Building at King John's House, Romsey, Hampshire', *Medieval Archaeology* 43 (1999), pp.74-114

Almond, R.,'Medieval Deer Hunting', *Deer* 9, no. 5 (1994), pp.315-18

Anon., *Itinerary of Edward III and his Household: Regnal Years 1-7* (Public Record Office)

Anon., *Itinerary of Henry III: 1215-1272* (Public Record Office)

Anon., *List of Sheriffs for England and Wales from Earliest Times to A.D. 1831: Compiled from Documents in the Public Record Office*, Lists and Indexes Series 9 (New York: Kraus Reprint Corporation, 1963)

Anon., 'The Perambulations of the Forests in Wiltshire', *Wiltshire Archaeological Magazine* 4 (1939), pp.197-8

Ashmore, W., and Knapp, A. B., eds, *Archaeologies of Landscape: Contemporary Perspectives* (Oxford: Blackwell Publishers, 1999)

Ashurst, J., and James, T. B., 'Stonework and Plasterwork' in T.B. James and A.M. Robinson, *Clarendon Palace: The History and Archaeology of a Medieval Palace and Hunting Lodge near Salisbury, Wiltshire*, Society of Antiquaries Research Report 45 (London: Society of Antiquaries of London, 1988), pp.234-58

Astill, G., 'Windsor in the Context of Medieval Berkshire', in *Windsor: Medieval Archaeology, Art and Architecture of the Thames Valley*, BAA Conference Transactions 25 (Leeds: Maney Publishing, 2002), eds L. Keen and E. Scarff, pp.1-14

Astill, G., and Grant, A., eds, *The Countryside of Medieval England* (Oxford: Blackwell Publishers, 1988)

Astill, G., and Grant, A., 'The Medieval Countryside: Approaches and Perceptions', in *The Countryside of Medieval England* (Oxford: Blackwell Publishers, 1988), eds G. Astill and A. Grant, pp.1-11

Aston, M., *Interpreting the Landscape: Landscape Archaeology and Local History* (London: Routledge, 1985)

Aston, M., and Lewis, C., eds, *The Medieval Landscape of Wessex,* Oxbow Monograph 46 (Oxford: Oxbow Books, 1994)

Atkinson, R. F., *Alderbury, an Ancient and Peculiar Parish: A Church History* (Alderbury: Richard F. Atkinson, 1992)

Atkinson, R. F., *The Manors and Hundred of Alderbury: Lords, Lands, and Livery* (Alderbury: Richard F. Atkinson, 1995)

Austin, D., 'The Castle and the Landscape: Annual Lecture to the Society for Landscape Studies, May 1984', *Landscape History* 6 (1984), pp.70-81

Austin, D., 'The Case Study: Okehampton Park', in *From the Baltic to the Black Sea: Studies in Medieval Archaeology,* One World Archaeology 18 (London: Routledge, 1997), eds D. Austin and L. Alcock, pp.54-77

Austin, D., 'The "Proper Study" of Medieval Archaeology', in *From the Baltic to the Black Sea: Studies in Medieval Archaeology,* One World Archaeology 18 (London: Routledge, 1997), eds D. Austin and L. Alcock, pp.9-42

Austin, D., and Alcock, Leslie, eds, *From the Baltic to the Black Sea: Studies in Medieval Archaeology,* One World Archaeology 18 (London: Routledge, 1997)

Bailey, M., 'The English Landscape', in *An Illustrated History of Late Medieval England* (Manchester: Manchester University Press, 1996), ed. C. Given-Wilson, pp.21-40

Baxter-Brown, M., *Richmond Park: the History of a Royal Deer Park* (London: Robert Hale, 1985)

Bellamy, J. G., *Criminal Law and Society in Late Medieval and Tudor England* (Gloucester: Sutton Publishing, 1984)

Bennett, J. M., *Women in the Medieval English Countryside: Gender and Household in Brigstock Before the Plague* (Oxford: Oxford University Press, 1989)

Bentley, M., *Modern Historiography: An Introduction* (London: Routledge, 1999)

Beresford, M. W., and Hurst, J. G., eds, *Deserted Medieval Villages,* (London: Lutterworth Press, 1971)

Beresford, M. W., 'Poll Tax Payers of 1377', in *The Victoria County History for Wiltshire, IV* (Oxford: Oxford University Press, 1959), ed. E. Crittall, pp.304-13

Beresford, M. W., 'Poor Parishes of 1428', in *The Victoria County History for Wiltshire, IV* (Oxford: Oxford University Press, 1959), ed. E. Crittall, pp.314-5

Bettey, J. H., *Estates and the English Countryside: Wealth, Rank and Ostentation in the Landscape* (London: Batsford, 1993)

Binski, P., *Medieval Death: Ritual and Representation* (London: The British Museum Press, 1996)

Birrell, J., 'Deer and Deer Farming in Medieval England', *Agricultural History Review* 40 (1992), pp.112-26

Blair, J., and Ramsay, N., eds, *English Medieval Industries: Craftsmen, Techniques, Products* (London: The Hambledon Press, 2001)

Bond, J., 'Forests, Chases, Warrens and Parks in Medieval Wessex', in *The Medieval Landscape of Wessex,* Oxbow Monograph 46 (Oxford: Oxbow Books, 1994), eds M. Aston and C. Lewis, pp.115-58

Bond, J., *Somerset Parks and Gardens: A Landscape History* (Tiverton: Somerset Books, 1998)

Bond, J., 'Woodstock Park in the Middle Ages', in *Blenheim: Landscape for a Palace* (Stroud: Sutton Publishing, 1997), eds J. Bond and K. Tiller, pp.22-54

Bond, J., 'Woodstock Park in the Sixteenth and Seventeenth Centuries', in *Blenheim: Landscape for a Palace* (Stroud: Sutton Publishing, 1997), eds J. Bond and K. Tiller, pp.55-66

Bond, J., and Tiller, K., *Blenheim: Landscape for a Palace* (Stroud: Sutton Publishing, 1997)

Bowden, M., ed., *Unravelling the Landscape: An Inquisitive Approach to Archaeology* (Stroud: Tempus Publishing, 1999)

Bridbury, A. R., 'Dr Rigby's Comments: A Reply', *Economic History Review* 39, no.3 (1986), pp.415-16

Brindle, S. and Kerr, B., *Windsor Revealed: New Light on the History of the Castle* (London: English Heritage, 1997)

Burke, P., ed., *New Perspectives on Historical Writing* (Cambridge: Polity Press, 1991)

Campbell, J., 'Some Aspects of the Natural History of Blenheim Palace', in *Blenheim: Landscape for a Palace* (Stroud: Sutton Publishing, 1997), eds J. Bond and K. Tiller, pp.157-67

Campbell, Mrs, and Gullick, B., 'Notes on the Flora of the Salisbury District', *Wiltshire Archaeological Magazine* 46, no. 157 (1934), pp.58-62

Carpenter, D. A., 'English Peasants in Politics 1258-1267', *Past and Present* 136 (1992), pp. 3-42

Chapman, D. and Chapman, N., *Fallow Deer,* (Powys: Coch-y-Bonddu Books, 1997)

Chase, E., *et al.,* eds, *Whiteparish: 100 Years of an English Village* (Salisbury: Whiteparish Historical and Environmental Association, 2000)

Clanchy, M. T., *From Memory to Written Record: England 1066-1307* (London: Edward Arnold, 1979)

Clifton-Bligh, J., and Griffith, D., *Lowland Deer Management: A Handbook for Land Managers* (Fordingbridge: British Deer Society, 2000)

Cohen, C., *So Great a Cloud: The Story of All Saints, Winterslow, Part 1 – the First Seven Centuries* (Winterslow: Winterslow Parochial Church Council, 1995)

Coles, C., *Gardens and Deer: A Guide to Damage Limitation* (Shrewsbury: Swan Hill Press, 1997)

Colvin, H. M., Review of T. B. James and A. M. Robinson, *Clarendon Palace, Medieval Archaeology* 34 (1990), pp.276-7

Colvin, H. M., ed., *The History of The King's Works: Volume 1 – The Middle Ages* (London: HMSO, 1963)

Colt Hoare, R., and Nichols, J. G., *The Modern History of South Wiltshire: Vol.5 Part 1, Containing the Hundred of Alderbury* (London: John Bowyer Nichols and Son, 1837)

Cooper, H., ed., *Sir Thomas Malory: Le Morte Darthur – the Winchester Manuscript* (Oxford: Oxford University Press, 1998)

Corcos, N., *The Affinities and Antecedents of Medieval Settlement: Topographical Perspectives from Three of the Somerset Hundreds*, British Archaeological Reports, British Series 337 (Oxford: Archaeopress, 2002)

Coss, P. R., *Lordship, Knighthood and Locality: A Study in English Society c.1180-c.1280* (Cambridge: Cambridge University Press, 1991)

Cossons, A., 'Roads', in *The Victoria County History for Wiltshire, VI* (Oxford: Oxford University Press, 1962), ed. E. Crittall, pp.254-71

Cox, J. C., *The Royal Forests of England* (London: Methuen, 1905)

Crawford, A., *Letters of the Queens of England 1100-1547* (Stroud, Alan Sutton Publishing, 1994)

Crawford, O. G. S., *Archaeology in the Field* (London: Phoenix House, 1960)

Creighton, O., *Castles and Landscapes* (London: Continuum, 2002)

Crittall, E., ed., *The Victoria County History for Wiltshire, IV* (Oxford: Oxford University Press, 1959)

Crittall, E., ed., *The Victoria County History for Wiltshire, VI* (Oxford: Oxford University Press, 1962)

Crook, D., 'The Later Eyres', *English Historical Review* 97 (1982), pp. 241-68

Crook, D., 'The Records of Forest Eyres in the Public Record Office, 1179 to 1670', *Journal of the Society of Archivists* 17 (1996), pp.183-93

Cummins, J., *The Hound and the Hawk: The Art of Medieval Hunting* (London: Weidenfeld and Nicholson, 1988)

Dale, M. K., 'The City of New Salisbury', in *The Victoria County History for Wiltshire, VI* (Oxford: Oxford University Press, 1962), ed. E. Crittall, pp.69-194

Danielsson, B., ed., *William Twiti: The Art of Hunting, 1327*, Cynegetica Anglica I, Stockholm Studies in English 37 (Stockholm: Almqvist and Wiksell International, 1977)

Day, S., 'Pass the Pepperbox: A Walk Above Whiteparish', *Wiltshire Life* 2, no. 3 (1996), pp.26-9

Denison, S., 'News: Medieval Enclosed Garden Found at Welsh Border Castle', *British Archaeology* 65 (June 2002), p.6

Department of Environment, *Lists of Buildings of Special Architectural or Historic Interest: Salisbury District*, 3 (London: Department of Environment, 1985)

Dorling, E. E., *A History of Salisbury* (London: James Nisbet and Co., 1911)

Duceppe-Lamarre, F., 'L'Archéologie du paysage à la Conquete des milieux forestiers: ou l'objet paysage vu par l' archéologue de l'environnement', *Hypothèses 1998: Travaux de l' Ecole doctorale d'Histoire, Publications de la Sorbonne* 2 (1998), pp.85-93

Duffy, P. J., 'Social and Spatial Order in the MacMahon Lordship of Airghialla in the Late Sixteenth Century', in *Gaelic Ireland c.1250-c.1650: Land, Lordship and Settlement* (Dublin: Four Courts Press, 2001), eds P. J. Duffy, D. Edwards, and E. Fitzpatrick, pp.115-37

Duffy, P. J., Edwards, D., and FitzPatrick, E., eds, *Gaelic Ireland c.1250-c.1650: Land, Lordship and Settlement* (Dublin: Four Courts Press, 2001)

Dunbar, J. G., *Scottish Royal Palaces: The Architecture of the Royal Residences During the Late Medieval and Early Modern Periods* (East Linton: Tuckwell Press, 1999)

Dyer, C., 'Documentary Evidence: Problems and Enquiries', in *The Countryside of Medieval England* (Oxford: Blackwell Publishers, 1988), eds G. Astill and A. Grant, pp.12-35

Dyer, C., *Standards of Living in the Later Middle Ages: Social Change in England c.1200-1520* (Cambridge: Cambridge University Press, 1989)

Dyer, C., 'The Economy and Society', in *The Oxford Illustrated History of Medieval England*, (London: BCA, 1997), ed. N. Saul, pp.137-73

Dyer, C., 'Trade, Urban Hinterlands and Market Integration 1300-1600: A Summing up' in *Trade, Urban Hinterlands and Market Integration c.1300-1600*, Centre for Metropolitan History Working Papers Series, 3 (London: Centre for Metropolitan History and The Institute of Historical Research, 2000), ed. J. A. Galloway, pp.103-9

Edwards, R., ed., *The Itinerary of King Richard III 1483-1485* (London: Alan Sutton Publishing and the Richard III Society, 1983)

Eiden, H., and Irsigler, F., 'Environs and Hinterland: Cologne and Nuremberg in the Later Middle Ages', in *Trade, Urban Hinterlands and Market Integration c.1300-1600*, Centre for Metropolitan History Working Papers Series, 3 (London: Centre for Metropolitan History and The Institute of Historical Research, 2000), ed. J. A. Galloway, pp.43-57

Ellis, P., ed., *Ludgershall Castle: A Report on the Excavations by Peter Addyman 1964-1972*, Wiltshire Archaeological and Natural History Society Monograph Series 2 (Devizes: Wiltshire Archaeological and Natural History Society, 2000)

Everitt, A., *Landscape and Community in England* (London: Hambledon Press, 1985)

Everson, P., Brown, G., and Stocker, D., 'The Castle Earthworks and Landscape Context' in *Ludgershall Castle: A Report on the Excavations by Peter Addyman 1964-1972*, Wiltshire Archaeological and Natural History Society Monograph Series 2 (Devizes: Wiltshire Archaeological and Natural History Society, 2000), ed. P. Ellis, pp.97-119

Eyton, R. W., *Court, Household & Itinerary of King Henry II Instancing also the Chief Agents and*

Adversaries of the King in his Government, Diplomacy, and Strategy (London: Taylor and Co., 1878)

Fagan, B. M., *In the Beginning: An Introduction to Archaeology* (New York: HarperCollins Publishers, 1991)

Farrel, W., *An Outline Itinerary of King Henry I* (Public Record Office: repr. by permission of Messrs Longmans, Green and Co. from *English Historical Review* 24, 1919)

Foard, G., 'Medieval Woodland, Agriculture and Industry in Rockingham Forest, Northamptonshire', *Medieval Archaeology* 45 (2001), pp.41-95

Fowler, P., 'Archaeology in a Matrix', in *Archaeological Resource Management in the UK: An Introduction* (Stroud: Sutton Publishing, 1993), eds J. Hunter and I. Ralston, pp.1-10

Fowler, P., *Landscape Plotted and Pieced: Landscape History and Local Archaeology in Fyfield and Overton, Wiltshire* (London: Society of Antiquaries, 2000)

Fowler, P., and Blackwell, I., *The Land of Lettice Sweetapple: An English Countryside Explored* (Stroud: Tempus Publishing, 1998)

Fraser, C. M., 'Prerogative and the Bishops of Durham, 1267-1376', *English Historical Review* 74 (1959), pp.467-76

Fry, S. P., *Castles of Britain and Ireland* (London; BCA, 1996)

Fumigalli, V., *Landscapes of Fear: Perceptions of Nature and the City in the Middle Ages* (Oxford: Polity Press, 1994)

Galloway, J. A., ed., *Trade, Urban Hinterlands and Market Integration c.1300-1600*, Centre for Metropolitan History Working Papers Series 3 (London: Centre for Metropolitan History and The Institute of Historical Research, 2000)

Gelling, M., and Cole, A., *The Landscape of Place-Names* (Stamford: Shaun Tyas, 2000)

Gerrard, C., *Medieval Archaeology: Understanding Traditions and Contemporary Approaches* (London: Routledge, 2003)

Gilchrist, R., *Contemplation and Action: The Other Monasticism* (London: Leicester University Press, 1995)

Gilchrist, R., *Gender and Material Culture: The Archaeology of Religious Women* (London: Routledge, 1994)

Given-Wilson, C., ed., *An Illustrated History of Late Medieval England* (Manchester: Manchester University Press, 1996)

Given-Wilson, C., *The Royal Household and the King's Affinity: Service, Politics and Finance in England 1360-1413* (London: Yale University Press, 1986)

Glasscock, R. E., ed., *The Lay Subsidy of 1334*, Records of Social and Economic History, New Series 11 (London: Oxford University Press, 1975)

Grant, R.,'Forests', in *The Victoria County History for Wiltshire, IV* (Oxford: Oxford University Press, 1959), ed. E. Crittall, pp.391-457

Grant, R., *The Royal Forests of England* (Stroud: Alan Sutton Publishing, 1991)

Grundy, G. B., 'The Ancient Woodland of Wiltshire', *Wiltshire Archaeological Magazine* 48 (1939), pp. 533-78

Gullick, B., 'South Wilts Plant Notes, 1933 to 1937', *Wiltshire Archaeological Magazine* 48 (1939), pp.82-6

Hadwin, J. F. 'From Dissonance to Harmony on the Late Medieval Town', *Economic History Review* 39, no.3 (1986), pp.423-26

Hadwin, J. F., 'The Medieval Lay Subsidies and Economic History', *Economic History Review* 36, no.2 (1983), pp.200-217

Hallam, E. M., *Itinerary of Edward II* (Public Record Office, unpub., undated)

Hammond, J. J., 'Clarendon Park', *Wiltshire Notes and Queries* 85 (1914), pp.1-7

Hanawalt, B. A., and Wallace, D., eds, *Medieval Crime and Social Control* (Minneapolis: University of Minnesota Press, 1998)

Hanson, M. W., ed., *Epping Forest through the Eyes of the Naturalist*, Essex Naturalist New Series 11 (Romford: Essex Field Club, 1992)

Hare, J. N., 'The Growth of the Roof-tile Industry in Later Medieval Wessex', *Medieval Archaeology* 35 (1991), pp.86-103

Hare, J. N., 'Agriculture and Rural Settlement in the Chalklands of Wiltshire and Hampshire from *c.*1200-*c.*1500', in *The Medieval Landscape of Wessex*, Oxbow Monograph 46 (Oxford: Oxbow Books, 1994), eds M. Aston and C. Lewis, pp.159-69

Harvey, P. D. A., 'The Documents of Landscape History: Snares and Delusions', *Landscape History* 13 (1991), pp.47-52

Hicks, M. A., 'Lawmakers and Lawbreakers', in *An Illustrated History of Late Medieval England* (Manchester: Manchester University Press, 1996), ed. C. Given-Wilson, pp.206-27

Higham, R. A., and Barker, Paul A., *Hen Domen, Montgomery* (Exeter: University of Exeter Press, 2000)

Hill, F., 'The Borough of Old Salisbury', in *The Victoria County History for Wiltshire, VI* (Oxford: Oxford University Press, 1962), ed. E. Crittall, pp.51-67

Hinton, D. A., 'A "Marginal Economy"? The Isle of Purbeck from the Norman Conquest to the Black Death', in *Purbeck Papers*, University of Southampton Department of Archaeology Monograph 4 (Oxford: Oxbow Books, 2002), ed. D. A. Hinton, pp.84-117

Hinton, D. A., *Archaeology, Economy and Society: England from the Fifth to the Fifteenth Century* (London: Seaby, 1990)

Hinton, D. A., '"Closing" and the Later Middle Ages', *Medieval Archaeology* 43 (1999), pp.172-82 Hinton, D. A., ed., *Purbeck Papers,* University of Southampton Department of Archaeology Monograph 4 (Oxford: Oxbow Books, 2002)

Hooke, D., ed., *Landscape: The Richest Historical Record*, Society for Landscape Studies Supplementary Series 1 (London: The Society for Landscape Studies, 2000)

Hoskins, W. G., *Local History in England*, 3rd edn (London: Longman, 1984)

Hunt, J., *Lordship and the Landscape: A Documentary and Archaeological Study of the Honour of Dudley c.1066-1322*, British Archaeological Reports, British Series 264 (Oxford: John and Erica Hedges, 1997)

Hunter, J., and Ralston, I., eds, *Archaeological Resource Management in the UK: An Introduction* (Stroud: Sutton Publishing, 1993)

Hunter, J., and Ralston, I., eds, *The Archaeology of Britain: An Introduction from the Upper Palaeolithic to the Industrial Revolution* (London: Routledge, 1999)

James, M. K., 'The Borough of Wilton', in *The Victoria County History for Wiltshire, VI* (Oxford: Oxford University Press, 1962), ed. E. Crittall, pp.1-50

James, T. B., *The Palaces of Medieval England: Royalty, Nobility, the Episcopate and their Residences from Edward the Confessor to Henry VIII* (London: Seaby, 1990)

James, T. B., and Gerrard, C., *Clarendon: A Royal Landscape* (forthcoming, Macclesfield: Windgather Press)

James, T. B., and Robinson, A. M., *Clarendon Palace: The History and Archaeology of a Medieval Palace and Hunting Lodge near Salisbury, Wiltshire*, Society of Antiquaries Research Report 45 (London: Society of Antiquaries of London, 1988)

Johnson, C., ed. and trans., *The Course of the Exchequer by Richard Son of Nigel, Treasurer of England and Bishop of London* (London: Thomas Nelson and Sons, 1950)

Johnson, M., *An Archaeology of Capitalism* (Oxford: Blackwell Publishers, 1996)

Johnson, M., *Archaeological Theory: An Introduction* (Oxford: Blackwell, 1999)

Johnson, M., *Behind the Castle Gate: From Medieval to Renaissance* (London: Routledge, 2002)

Johnson, M., *Housing Culture: Traditional Architecture in an English Landscape* (London: UCL Press, 1993)

Jones, W. H., *Domesday for Wiltshire* (London: Longman, Roberts and Green, 1865)

Jordan, W. C., *Europe in the High Middle Ages* (London: Penguin Books, 2002)

Jurkowski, M., *et al.*, *Lay Taxes in England and Wales 1188-1688*, Public Record Office Handbook 31 (Richmond: Public Record Office Publications, 1998)

Keen, L., and Scarff, E., eds, *Windsor: Medieval Archaeology, Art and Architecture of the Thames Valley*, BAA Conference Transactions 25 (Leeds: Maney Publishing, 2002)

Keevill, G. D., *Medieval Palaces: An Archaeology* (Stroud: Tempus Publishing, 2000)

Knapp, A. B., and Ashmore, W., 'Archaeological Landscapes: Constructed, Conceptualized, Ideational', in *Archaeologies of Landscape: Contemporary Perspectives* (Oxford: Blackwell Publishers, 1999), eds W. Ashmore and A. B. Knapp, pp.1-30

Lambert, D., *et al.*, *Researching a Garden's History: A Guide to Documentary and Published Sources* (Reigate: Landscape Design Trust, 1995)

Latham, R., and Matthews, W., *The Diary of Samuel Pepys*, vol. 5 (London: Bell and Hyman, 1971)

Latham, R. E., Revised Medieval Latin Word-List From British and Irish Sources (London: Oxford University Press, 1965)

Levy, G., 'On Microhistory', in *New Perspectives on Historical Writing* (Cambridge: Polity Press, 1991), ed. P. Burke, pp.93-113

Lewis, C., 'Patterns and Processes in the Medieval Settlement of Wiltshire', in *The Medieval Landscape of Wessex*, Oxbow Monograph 46 (Oxford: Oxbow Books, 1994), eds M. Aston and C. Lewis, pp.171-93

Lewis, C., Review of J. Hunt, *Lordship and the Landscape* (1997), *Medieval Archaeology* 43 (1999), pp.320-2

Lewis, C., Mitchell-Fox, Patrick, and Dyer, Christopher, *Village Hamlet and Field: Changing Medieval Settlements in Central England* (Macclesfield: Windgather Press, 2001)

Lewis, C., *Particular Places: An Introduction to English Local History* (London: The British Library, 1989)

Loades, D., *Power in Tudor England* (Basingstoke: Macmillan Press, 1997)

Lowenthal, D., 'Environmental History: From Genesis to Apocalypse', *History Today* 51, no. 4 (2001), pp.36-42

Macinnes, L., 'Archaeology as Land Use', in *Archaeological Resource Management in the UK: An Introduction* (Stroud: Sutton Publishing, 1993), eds J. Hunter and I. Ralston, pp.243-55

Maddicott, J. R., 'Magna Carta and the Local Community 1215-1259', *Past and Present* 102 (1984), pp.25-65

McKeown, C., 'Winterslow: Lions, Fires, Business and Fame, it all Happens in Winterslow', *Wiltshire Life*, February 1998, pp.60-2

McKisack, M., *The Fourteenth Century: 1307-1399* (Oxford: Oxford University Press, 1959)

McOmish, D., *et al.*, *The Field Archaeology of the Salisbury Plain Training Area* (Swindon: English Heritage, 2002)

Moore, N. J., 'Brick', in Blair, J., and Ramsay, N., eds, *English Medieval Industries: Craftsmen, Techniques, Products* (London: The Hambledon Press, 2001), eds J. Blair and N. Ramsay, pp.212-36

Moreland, J., *Archaeology and Text* (London: Duckworth, 2001)

Morris, C., ed., *The Journeys of Celia Fiennes* (London: The Cresset Press, 1947)

Musty, J., *et al.*,'The Medieval Pottery Kilns at Laverstock, near Salisbury, Wiltshire', *Archaeologia* 102 (1969), pp.83-150

Muir, R., The New Reading the Landscape: Fieldwork in Landscape History (Exeter: University of Exeter

Press, 2000)

Ormrod, W. M., *The Reign of Edward III: Crown and Political Society in England 1327-1377* (London: Guild Publishing, 1990)

Orser, C. E., and Fagan, B. M., *Historical Archaeology* (New York: HarperCollins College Publishers, 1995)

Parker Pearson, M., 'Visitors Welcome', in *Archaeological Resource Management in the UK: An Introduction* (Stroud: Sutton Publishing, 1993), eds J. Hunter and I. Ralston, pp.225-31

Parsons, M., *All the King's Men* (New Milton, Leonard Michael Parsons, 1994)

Parsons, M., *An Unparticular Posterity: I* (New Milton: Leonard Michael Parsons, 2000)

Parsons, M., *Sharps and Pollards* (New Milton: Leonard Michael Parsons, 1993)

Parsons, M., *The Brittle Thread* (New Milton: Leonard Michael Parsons, 1997)

Parsons, M., *The King's Sergeants* (New Milton: Leonard Michael Parsons, 1993)

Parsons, M., *The Little Manor of Pitton and Farley* (West Tytherley: Leonard Michael Parsons, 1995)

Parsons, M., *The Royal Forest of Pancet* (New Milton: Leonard Michael Parsons, 1995)

Parsons, M., *The Saxon Inheritance* (New Milton: Leonard Michael Parsons, 1990)

Pasmore, A., 'Landscape and Wilderness Quality in the Management of the New Forest 1800-2000', *The Hatcher Review* 5, no. 50 (2000), pp. 5-11

Pasmore, A., 'The Lyndhurst Earthwork', *Hampshire Field Club and Archaeological Society Newsletter* 39 (Spring 2003), pp.viii-x

Perlin, J., *A Forest Journey: The Role of Wood in the Development of Civilisation* (London: W. W. Norton, 1989)

Perry Marvin, W., 'Slaughter and Romance: Hunting Reserves in Late Medieval England', in *Medieval Crime and Social Control* (Minneapolis: University of Minnesota Press, 1998), eds B. A. Hanawalt and D. Wallace, pp.224-52

Platt, C., 'Appendix 1c: Population and Social Stratification in Medieval Southampton', in C. Platt, *Medieval Southampton: The Port and Trading Community, A.D. 1000-1600* (London: Routledge and Kegan Paul, 1973), pp.262-6

Platt, C., *Medieval Archaeology in England: A Guide to the Historical Sources*, Pinhorns Handbooks 5 (Isle of Wight: Pinhorns, 1969)

Platt, C., *Medieval England: A Social History and Archaeology from the Conquest to 1600 A.D.* (London: Routledge, 1978)

Platt, C., *Medieval Southampton: The Port and Trading Community, A.D. 1000-1600* (London: Routledge and Kegan Paul, 1973)

Poole, E. H. L., 'Cranbourne Chase', in *The Victoria County History for Wiltshire, IV* (Oxford: Oxford University Press, 1959), ed. E. Crittall, pp.458-60

Powell, E., 'Social Research and the Use of Medieval Criminal Records', *Michigan Law Review* 79 (1981), pp.967-78

Prestwich, M., *Edward I* (London: Yale University Press, 1997)

Prior, R., *Deer Watch: Watching Wild Deer in Britain* (Shrewsbury: Swan Hill Press, 1993)

Prior, R., *Trees and Deer: How to Cope with Deer in Forest, Field and Garden* (Shrewsbury: Swan Hill Press, 1994)

Rackham, O., Ancient Woodland: Its History, Vegetation and Use in England (London: Arnold, 1980)

Rackham, O., 'Lodges and Standings', in M. W. Hanson, ed., *Epping Forest through the Eyes of the Naturalist*, Essex Naturalist New Series 11 (Romford: Essex Field Club, 1992), pp.8-17

Rackham, O., *The Illustrated History of the Countryside* (London: BCA, 1994)

Rackham, O., *The Last Forest: The Story of Hatfield Forest*, 2nd edn (London: Dent, 1993)

Rackham, O., *Trees and Woodland in the British Landscape*, revised edn (London: Pheonix Press, 1990)

Renoux, A., ed., *Palais médiévaux (France-Belgique): 25 ans d'archéologie* (Maine: Université du Maine, 1994)

Renoux, A., ed., *Palais royaux et princiers au Moyen Age* (Maine: Université du Maine 1996)

Reynolds, A., *Later Anglo-Saxon England: Life and Landscape* (Stroud: Tempus Publishing, 1999)

Richardson, R. C., ed., *The Changing Face of Local History* (Aldershot: Ashgate Publishing, 2000)

Rigby, S. H., *English Society in the Later Middle Ages: Class, Status and Gender* (London: Macmillan Press, 1995)

Rigby, S. H., 'Late Medieval Urban Prosperity: The Evidence of the Lay Subsidies', *Economic History Review* 39, no.3 (1986), pp.411-14

Roberts, J., *Royal Landscape: The Gardens and Parks of Windsor* (London: Yale University Press, 1997)

Rogers, A., and Rowley, T., eds, *Landscapes and Documents* (London: National Council of Social Service Publications, 1974)

Rooney, A., *Hunting in Middle English Literature* (Cambridge: D. S. Brewer, 1993)

Royal Commission on Historic Monuments (England), *Ancient and Historic Monuments in the City of Salisbury 1* (London: HMSO, 1980)

Royal Commission on Historic Monuments (England), *Salisbury: The Houses of The Close* (London: HMSO, 1993)

Salford, E. W., ed., *Itinerary of Edward I* (Public Record Office, 1935)

Salzman, L. F., *Building in England Down to 1540: A Documentary History* (Oxford: Clarendon Press, 1997)

Samson, R., ed., *The Social Archaeology of Houses* (Edinburgh: Edinburgh University Press, 1990)

Saul, N., ed., *The Oxford Illustrated History of Medieval England* (London: BCA, 1997)

Saunders, P., Review of T. B. James and A. M. Robinson, *Clarendon Palace*, *Wiltshire Archaeological Magazine* 84 (1991), pp.155-7

Saunders, T., 'The Feudal Construction of Space: Power and Domination in the Nucleated Village', in *The Social Archaeology of Houses* (Edinburgh: Edinburgh University Press, 1990), ed. R. Samson, pp.181-96

Schama, S., *Landscape and Memory* (London: HarperCollins Publishers, 1995)

Schofield, J., *Medieval London Houses* (London: Yale University Press, 1994)

Short, B., 'Forests and Wood-Pasture in Lowland England', in *The English Rural Landscape* (Oxford: Oxford University Press, 2000), ed. J. Thirsk, pp.122-49

Shrewsbury, J. F. D., *A History of Bubonic Plague in the British Isles* (Cambridge: Cambridge University Press, 1971)

Schurer, K., 'The Future for Local History: Boom or Recession?', in *The Changing Face of Local History* (Aldershot: Ashgate Publishing, 2000), ed. R. C. Richardson, pp.179-93

Slater, T. R., 'Understanding the Landscape of Towns', in *Landscape: The Richest Historical Record*, Society for Landscape Studies Supplementary Series 1 (London: The Society for Landscape Studies, 2000), ed. D. Hooke, pp.97-108

Smith, R., 'Human Resources', in *The Countryside of Medieval England* (Oxford: Blackwell Publishers, 1988), eds G. Astill and A. Grant, pp.188-212

Stacey, R. C., *Politics, Policy and Finance Under Henry III 1216-1245* (Oxford: Oxford University Press, 1987)

Stamper, P. A., 'Landscapes of the Middle Ages: Rural Settlements and Manors', in *The Archaeology of Britain: An Introduction from the Upper Palaeolithic to the Industrial Revolution* (London: Routledge, 1999), eds J. Hunter and I. Ralston, pp.247-63

Stamper, P. A., Review of *Making English Landscapes: Changing Perspectives*, Bournemouth University School of Conservation Sciences Occasional Paper 3, Oxbow Monograph 93 (Oxford: Oxbow Books, 1998), *Medieval Archaeology* 42 (1998), pp.216-7

Stamper, P. A., 'The Medieval Forest of Pamber, Hampshire', *Landscape History* 5 (1983), pp.41-52

Stamper, P. A., 'Woods and Parks', in *The Countryside of Medieval England* (Oxford: Blackwell Publishers, 1988), eds G. Astill and A. Grant, pp.128-48

Steane, J. M., *The Archaeology of Medieval England and Wales* (London: Guild Publishing, 1984)

Steane, J. M., *The Archaeology of Power: England and Northern Europe A.D. 800-1600* (Stroud: Tempus Publishing, 2001)

Steane, J. M., *The Archaeology of The Medieval English Monarchy* (London: Batsford, 1993)

Stinson, M., 'Assarting and Poverty in Early Fourteenth-Century Western Yorkshire', *Landscape History* 5 (1983), pp.53-67

Stocker, D., and Stocker, M., 'Sacred Profanity: the Theology of Rabbit Breeding and the Symbolic Landscape of the Warren', *World Archaeology* 28 (1996), pp.265-72

Stoddart, S., 'Early Studies of Landscapes: Editorial Introduction', in *Landscapes from Antiquity*, Antiquity Papers 1 (Cambridge: Antiquity Publications, 2000), ed. S. Stoddart, pp.7-10

Stott, P., 'Jungles of the Mind: The Invention of the Tropical Rain Forest', *History Today* 51, no. 5 (2001), pp.38-44

Strong, R., *Lost Treasures of Britain: Five Centuries of Creation and Destruction* (London: Guild Publishing, 1990)

Sugarman, D., 'Writing "Law and Society" Histories', *Modern Law Review* 55 (1992), pp.292-308

Tabaczynski, S., 'The Relationship Between History and Archaeology: Elements of the Present Debate', *Medieval Archaeology* 37 (1993), pp.1-14

Taylor, C. C.,'The Plus Fours in the Wardrobe: A Personal View of Landscape History' in *Landscape: The Richest Historical Record*, Society for Landscape Studies Supplementary Series 1 (London: The Society for Landscape Studies, 2000), ed. D. Hooke, pp.157-62

Taylor, C. C.,'Three Deserted Medieval Settlements in Whiteparish', *Wiltshire Archaeological Magazine* 63 (1968), pp.39-53

Taylor, C. C., 'Total Archaeology or Studies in History of the Landscape', in *Landscapes and Documents* (London: National Council of Social Service Publications, 1974), eds A. Rogers and T. Rowley, pp.15-26

Taylor, C. C., 'Whiteparish: A Study of the Development of a Forest-Edge Parish', *Wiltshire Archaeological Magazine* 62 (1967), pp.79-102

Thirsk, J., 'Introduction', in *The English Rural Landscape* (Oxford: Oxford University Press, 2000), ed. J. Thirsk, pp.9-24

Thirsk, J., ed., *The English Rural Landscape* (Oxford: Oxford University Press, 2000)

Thompson, F., *The First Century of Magna Carta: Why it Persisted as a Document* (New York: Russell and Russell, 1967)

Thompson, M., *Medieval Bishops' Houses in England and Wales* (Aldershot: Ashgate Publishing, 1998)

Thurley, S., *The Royal Palaces of Tudor England: Architecture and Court Life 1460-1547* (Yale University Press: London, 1993)

Tiller, K., *English Local History: An Introduction* (Stroud: Alan Sutton Publishing, 1992)

Tilley, C., *A Phenomenology of Landscape: Places, Paths and Monuments* (Oxford: Berg Publishers, 1994)

Tonkinson, A. M., *Macclesfield in the Later Fourteenth Century: Communities of Town and Forest* (Lancaster: Carnegie Publishing, 1999)

Treharne, R. F., *Essays on Thirteenth-Century England* (London: Historical Association, 1971)

Treharne, R. F., and Sanders, I. J., eds, *Documents of the Baronial Movement of Reform and Rebellion 1258-1267* (Oxford: Oxford University Press, 1973)

Tyers, I., *Tree-Ring Analysis of Three Buildings from the Clarendon Estate, Wiltshire*, ARCUS

Dendrochronology Report 429 (Sheffield: ARCUS, 1999)

Wake Smart, T. W., *A Chronicle of Cranborne and the Cranborne Chase*, 2nd edn (Wimborne: The Dovecote Press, 1983)

Walker, S., 'Civil War and Rebellion', in *An Illustrated History of Late Medieval England* (Manchester: Manchester University Press, 1996), ed. C. Given-Wilson, pp.229-47

Wessex Archaeology, *Hanging Langford to Little Langford Pumping Main Renewal: Stage 1, Archaeological Monitoring of Hand-Excavated Test Pits*, Wessex Archaeology Report W596a (Trust for Wessex Archaeology, 1993)

Wessex Archaeology, *Hanging Langford to Little Langford Pumping Main Renewal: Stage 2, Archaeological Excavation and Watching Brief*, Wessex Archaeology Report W596b (Trust for Wessex Archaeology, 1994)

Whitlock, R., 'Pitton: A South Wiltshire Village in the 1920s and 1930s', *Hatcher Review* 2, no. 13 (1982), pp.133-40

Whyte, I., 'The Historical Geography of Britain from AD 1500: Landscape and Townscape', in *The Archaeology of Britain: An Introduction from the Upper Palaeolithic to the Industrial Revolution* (London: Routledge, 1999), eds J. Hunter and I. Ralston, pp.264-79

Williamson, T., *Shaping Medieval Landscapes: Settlement, Society, Environment* (Macclesfield: Windgather Press, 2003)

Wilson, C., 'The Royal Lodgings of Edward III at Windsor Castle: Form, Function, Representation', in *Windsor: Medieval Archaeology, Art and Architecture of the Thames Valley*, BAA Conference Transactions 25, (Leeds: Maney Publishing, 2002), eds L. Keen and E. Scarff, pp.15-94

Young, C. R., *The Royal Forests of Medieval England* (Leicester: Leicester University Press, 1979)

Unpublished Papers, Dissertations, Theses etc.

Clarendon Park Ecology Archive, courtesy of David Clements

Austin, D., 'Barnard Castle: There by Design', paper given at *Castles and Hinterlands in Medieval Europe*, University of Oxford Department for Continuing Education conference, February 2000

Austin, D., 'Understanding Settlement as Economy: The Narratives of the North Sea World in the Middle Ages', paper given at *The International Medieval Congress*, University of Leeds, July 2000

Barker, H., and Lickman, J., 'Clarendon Estate: Photographic Survey of Gates and Fences' (King Alfred's College, 1998)

Bond, J., 'Deer Parks and Landscape Parks', paper given at *Parks in the Landscape*, Oxford University Department for Continuing Education conference, October 2000

Creighton, O., 'Castles and Settlement Planning in Medieval England', paper given at *Castles and Hinterlands in Medieval Europe*, Oxford University Department for Continuing Education conference, February 2001

Darvill, T., Gerrard, C., and Startin, B., 'Archaeology in the Landscape: A Review', (unpub. draft typescript for *Landscape History, c.*1993)

Dennis, R., 'The Organisation of Wealth and Power in Domesday Hampshire' (unpub. doctoral thesis, Lincoln College, Oxford, 1992)

Gifford, A. J., 'An Archaeological Study of Routeway Development in Downton Parish' (unpub. paper, 1995, Wiltshire Reference Library,)

Henderson, P., 'Architecture in Parks', paper given at *Parks in the Landscape*, Oxford University Department for Continuing Education conference, October 2000

King Alfred's College Consultancy, *Clarendon Park, Salisbury, Wiltshire: Archaeology, History and Ecology–English Heritage Survey Grant for Presentation* I, English Heritage Project Number 1750 (Winchester, 1996)

King Alfred's College Consultancy, *Clarendon Park, Salisbury, Wiltshire: Archaeology, History and Ecology–English Heritage Survey Grant for Presentation* II, English Heritage Project Number 1750 (Winchester, 1996)

King Alfred's College Consultancy, *Clarendon Park, Salisbury, Wiltshire: Historic Landscape Management Plan* (Winchester, 1998)

Lavelle, R., 'Royal Estates in Anglo-Saxon Wessex' (unpub. doctoral thesis, King Alfred's College, Winchester, 2001)

Maidment, G. P., 'An Analysis of Development and Change in the Settlement and Land Use of the Forests of Bere and Stanstead, Circa A.D. 400 to A.D. 1550, with Special Reference to the Village of Rowlands Castle and its Surrounding Area' (unpub. dissertation, Advanced Certificate in Local History, King Alfred's College, Winchester, 1992)

McWilliams, J., 'Clarendon Park 1600-1750: From Medieval Deer Park to Post-Medieval Estate' (unpub. BA dissertation, King Alfred's College, Winchester, 1996)

Mileson, S., 'Landscape, Power and Politics: the Place of the Park in Later Medieval Aristocratic Society' (forthcoming doctoral thesis, Keble College, Oxford)

The Oak Apple Club of Wishford, *Sum of the Ancient Customs Belonging to Wishford and Barford* (Salisbury: The Salisbury Press, 1930 [unpub., Wiltshire Record Library])

Pickering, N., 'Habitat Monitoring and Protection Techniques', British Deer Society Advanced Stalker Course, November 2001

Pitt, J., 'Wiltshire Minster *Parochiae* and West Saxon Ecclesiastical Organisation' (unpub. doctoral thesis, King Alfred's College, Winchester, 1999)

Pluskowski, A., 'Power and Predation: Archaeological and Legal Evidence for Élite Hunting Space in Medieval Northern Europe' (unpub. paper given at *The International Medieval Congress,* University of Leeds, July 2003)

Richardson, N. A., 'A New Approach to the Study of Queens' Apartments in Medieval Palaces' (unpub. BA dissertation, King Alfred's College, Winchester, 1998)

Richardson, N. A., 'Clarendon: The Palace in the Forest - The Establishment, Operation and Control of Jurisdiction in the Reign of Henry III' (unpub. MA Dissertation, University of Southampton, 1999)

Smith, C., 'Medieval Legal Records as Sources for Modern Historians: Coroners and their Records in Hampshire and Wiltshire, 1327-1399' (unpub. doctoral thesis, University of Southampton, 1995)

Smith, C., 'The New Forest in the Fourteenth Century: A Jurisdictional Vacuum?' (unpub. paper given at *Recent Research in Fifteenth-Century History*, University of Southampton conference, September 1999)

Slater, T. R., 'Planning Britain's Largest Medieval New Town: Ideology, Geometry, Metrology and Practicalities in 13th-Century Salisbury', paper given at *The International Medieval Congress*, University of Leeds, July 2002

Titow, J. Z., 'Land and Population on the Bishop of Winchester's Estates 1209-1350' (unpub. doctoral thesis, University of Cambridge, 1962)

Titt, R. A., *A List of Places and Paths in Winterslow* (Middle Winterslow: R. A. Titt, 1991 [Wiltshire Reference Library])

Turle, R., 'Clarendon Standing Buildings: An Evaluation of Standing Building Values and Management at Clarendon Park, Wiltshire' (unpub. master's thesis, Oxford Brookes University School of Planning and Oxford University Department for Continuing Education, 1998)

Tys, D., 'Development of the Medieval Settlement Pattern and Landscape on the Coast of Flanders (900-1500): Integrated Historical Research and Archaeological Survey', paper given at the Leeds *International Medieval Congress*, July 2000

Woodall, T. J., 'Britford Church and Parish: Notes on Their History' (Wiltshire Reference Library [acquired 1943])

Woodford, A. R., *Notes on the History of Downton*, (unpub. paper, Wiltshire Reference Library)

ELECTRONIC SOURCES

ARCH, *The Unmaking of a Deer* (http://www.arch-projects.org.uk/unmaking.htm [searched March 2003])

ARTFL Project, *Webster Dictionary 1913* (http://machaut.uchicago.edu/cgi-bin/WEBSTER [searched May 2003])

Genmaps, *Old Maps of Wiltshire* (http://freepages.genealogy.rootsweb.com/~genmaps/genfiles/COU_Pages/ENG_pages/wil.htm [searched 5 May 2003])

Johnstone Flynn, B., *The Power of Music Represented in Medieval Literature* (honours thesis, Department of Medieval Studies, Connecticut College (http://www.tiltedworld.com/brenda/music/changeheart.html [searched April 2003])

Jpci.net, *Historical Wiltshire: Towns and Villages – a Brief History* (http://www.wiltshire-web.co.uk/ [searched September 2002])

Royal Commission on the Historic Monuments of England, *Thesaurus* (http://www.rchme.gov.uk/thesaurus/bm_types/P/98123.htm [searched November 2002])

Stampley, G. J., *Law and Abstraction in Twelfth, Thirteenth and Fourteenth-Century England: The Case of the Maritagium and the Gift in Tail* (http://www.whiterose.org/ginger/writing/swssa.html [searched March 2003])

The National Trust, *Lodge Park History* (http://www.nationaltrust.org.uk/lodgepark/history.html [searched April 2003])

Vince, A., *The Medieval Ceramic Industry of the Severn Valley* (http://www.postex.demon.co.uk/thesis [searched October 2002])

Wilton House, *Wilton House: A Living History* (http://www.wiltonhouse.co.uk/pages/history/history.html [searched April 2003])